INSIDER THREAT

Establishing a new framework for understanding insider risk by focusing on systems of organisation within large enterprises, including public, private, and not-for-profit sectors, this book analyses practices to better assess, prevent, detect, and respond to insider risk and protect assets and public good.

Analysing case studies from around the world, the book includes real-world insider threat scenarios to illustrate the outlined framework in the application, as well as to assist accountable entities within organisations to implement the changes required to embed the framework into normal business practices. Based on information, data, applied research, and empirical study undertaken over ten years, across a broad range of government departments and agencies in various countries, the framework presented provides a more accurate and systemic method for identifying insider risk, as well as enhanced and cost-effective approaches to investing in prevention, detection, and response controls and measuring the impact of controls on risk management and financial or other loss.

Insider Threat: A Systemic Approach will be of great interest to scholars and students studying white-collar crime, criminal law, public policy and criminology, transnational crime, national security, financial management, international business, and risk management.

Pierre Skorich has worked for over ten years across a broad range of Australian government departments and agencies, including the Department of Immigration and Border Protection, the Australian Federal Police, the Australian Transaction Reports and Analysis Centre (AUSTRAC, Australia's Financial Intelligence agency), the Department of Finance, the Department of Prime Minister and Cabinet, the Department of Climate Change and Energy Efficiency, Clean Energy Regulator, the Department of Agriculture, Water and the Environment, and the Attorney-General's Department. He also led the implementation team for the establishment of Australia's National Anti-Corruption Commission.

Matthew Manning is a future crime scholar. Currently, he is Head of the Department of Social and Behavioral Sciences at the City University of Hong Kong. He was previously a full professor of criminology at the Australian National University. He has worked in the fields of criminology and economics for two decades. His current ethical research focuses on how new technologies can be exploited to commit crime. Further, his empirical research evaluates strategies, frameworks, and models that can be employed by criminal justice actors to respond to these new and complex crimes.

Crime Science Series

Edited by: Richard Wortley
University College London

Crime science is a new way of thinking about and responding to the problem of crime in society. The distinctive nature of crime science is captured in the name.

First, crime science is about crime. Instead of the usual focus in criminology on the characteristics of the criminal offender, crime science is concerned with the characteristics of the criminal event. The analysis shifts from the distant causes of criminality – biological makeup, upbringing, social disadvantage and the like – to the near causes of crime. Crime scientists are interested in why, where, when and how particular crimes occur. They examine trends and patterns in crime in order to devise immediate and practical strategies to disrupt these patterns.

Second, crime science is about science. Many traditional responses to crime control are unsystematic, reactive, and populist, too often based on untested assumptions about what works. In contrast crime science advocates an evidence-based, problem-solving approach to crime control. Adopting the scientific method, crime scientists collect data on crime, generate hypotheses about observed crime trends, devise interventions to respond to crime problems, and test the adequacy of those interventions.

Crime science is utilitarian in its orientation and multidisciplinary in its foundations. Crime scientists actively engage with front-line criminal justice practitioners to reduce crime by making it more difficult for individuals to offend, and making it more likely that they will be detected if they do offend. To achieve these objectives, crime science draws on disciplines from both the social and physical sciences, including criminology, sociology, psychology, geography, economics, architecture, industrial design, epidemiology, computer science, mathematics, engineering, and biology.

INSIDER THREAT

A Systemic Approach

Pierre Skorich and Matthew Manning

Routledge
Taylor & Francis Group

LONDON AND NEW YORK

Designed cover image: gettyimages.ca/gremlin

First published 2025
by Routledge
4 Park Square, Milton Park, Abingdon, Oxon OX14 4RN

and by Routledge
605 Third Avenue, New York, NY 10158

Routledge is an imprint of the Taylor & Francis Group, an informa business

British Library Cataloguing-in-Publication Data
A catalogue record for this book is available from the British Library

ISBN: 978-0-367-51925-4 (hbk)
ISBN: 978-0-367-51921-6 (pbk)
ISBN: 978-1-003-05571-6 (ebk)

DOI: 10.4324/9781003055716

Typeset in Sabon
by Apex CoVantage, LLC

CONTENTS

FIGURES

TABLES

1

INTRODUCTION

The modern world, shaped by an interconnected and rapidly evolving digital landscape, has increased the vulnerability of large enterprises, including those in the public, private, and not-for-profit sectors. The risk to these enterprises, therefore, has similarly increased. Such risks potentially compromise their critical assets, sensitive information, reputation, and their ability to achieve their organisational objectives, whether they are commercial or public good objectives. Before we progress further, it is important to understand how we define the difference between vulnerability and risk. We define vulnerability as a weakness or gap in an enterprise's defences that could be exploited by a given threat. Risk is the uncertainty as to whether a particular vulnerability will be exploited, resulting in harm or damage to the enterprise's objectives.

While external digital threats (e.g. cyber-attacks, fraud) dominate media headlines, enterprises must also confront a significant risk that lies within: insider risk. We define "insider risk" as the likelihood of a particular enterprise being exploited by individuals within who have authorised access to sensitive information, systems, or resources. By "individuals within" we mean employees, contractors, or business partners who possess valuable knowledge, skills, and access privileges.

With such access comes the opportunity to misuse or abuse their privilege for personal gain or malicious intent. In addition, there is the potential for unintentional error that arises because of inadequacies in internal systems and processes. These errors themselves create vulnerabilities that can be exploited by other motivated actors to undermine the enterprise. Some studies have proposed that more than 50% of incidents were the

DOI: 10.4324/9781003055716-1

result of accidents and errors (The CERT Insider Threat Team, 2013). While a useful indicator of the unintentional threat, we take such quantified statistics with a grain of salt; deliberate insider activity is by its very nature concealed and is likely to be significantly under-detected and under-reported.

Managing insider risk is not a new concept. Most, if not all, enterprises recognise that they are vulnerable to threats from inside, and that risk is all present throughout their operations. Some insider incidents (either fraudulent or unintentional) are easily detected and dealt with while others are more insidious and may only be detected by chance or where an organisation actively understands its vulnerabilities and establishes the means and countermeasures to detect those incidents.

Many organisations rely on their employees as the first line of control to detect and tip off the enterprise in relation to mistakes and misconduct. While this does provide a means of detection, it is naturally biased towards those incidents which are easy to observe and in circumstances where individuals are comfortable to report their observations. Other incidents go undetected. This may be argued to be of greater concern, making it challenging to identify and mitigate effectively incidents in the future and thereby enabling ongoing harm to the enterprise and its objectives.

To address this complex challenge, organisations must adopt a proactive and comprehensive approach to managing insider risk. Reliance on traditional means of addressing insider risk in an increasingly digital high-velocity, high-volume world is simply no longer adequate.

In this book, we explore the key elements of managing insider risk and provide practical strategies and best practices to enhance organisational resilience against current and future insider threats. Our central contribution is the establishment of a new structured framework for understanding and assessing insider risk by focusing on systems of organisation. To achieve this, we take a systematised approach to exploring the elements that define insider risk, the motivations behind insider incidents, and the potential indicators to identify suspicious behaviour. The framework is designed to decompose those elements and systematically describe their interactions and effects on organisational risk.

By understanding the nature of insider risk and implementing a robust framework to detect, prevent, and respond to insider threats, organisations of any size can establish a vigorous security posture that protects their critical assets and safeguards their future. Here, we envisage a future where the focus is less on picking up the pieces from the intentional or unintentional actions of insiders who compromise critical assets, sensitive information, or reputation to one where the focus is on planning, prevention, and protection of the enterprise objectives.

Corruption and insider risk

Insider threat is not a recent phenomenon; there are countless examples of trusted insiders who have exploited their position to gain a personal benefit or to support a broader politically or ideologically motivated agenda and manipulate the organisations to which they belong. Whether the example is pocketing gold nuggets in gold mines in the 1800s or stealing corporate information in the world today, the motivation to exploit opportunity for personal gain within an enterprise context has remained relatively unchanged.

In contrast, in the same timescale, organisations have become vastly more complex in terms of their legal and corporate structures and the diversification of the activities they undertake. This complexity has vastly increased the surface area of threats that organisations are exposed to. Where a business previously might have been exposed to an insider stealing assets (gold nuggets in our example above), organisations today also have vast amounts of commercially sensitive information and intellectual property, along with complex domestic and international supply chains and automated systems of product and service delivery. With the general shift of first world economies moving away from manufacturing to service industries (Wilson, 2014), consumer and business decision-making have become assets in their own right, directing the allocation of value within complex economies. Where these decisions are manipulated for interests other than those of the enterprise, they distort the mission of the organisation and the achievement of its commercial or social/economic objectives. Similarly, with vast tracts of information stored and transmitted electronically both within and across organisations (Hong et al., 2018), or even more nebulously across the increasingly connected "Internet of things", there is a whole digital environment which is equally exposed to threat in ways that were not present even in the last half of the 20th century (Johnson et al., 2020).

In governments, the changes have been no less dramatic. As industry has transformed, government has had to respond by changing and increasing its regulatory interventions to protect economic and social value and the environment. Governments have equally grown the number of services, payment types, taxation bases, and activities they undertake in response to increasing citizen demand globally, and the greater availability of technology to automate processes and capture data. Governments' regulatory interventions impose costs on legitimate business in exchange for reducing the effects of an externality on other social, economic, or environmental interests (Lemaire, 2017). Equally regulatory interventions act to restrict the activities of criminal entities (Schell-Busey et al., 2016). This of course creates incentives to avoid or bypass regulatory controls, thereby reducing the cost on business or enabling ongoing criminal activity. It is not surprising, therefore, that government institutions are not immune to corruption and insider threat. The upshot is of course significant impacts on the public good that governments are designed to advance and protect.

In a global context, several high-profile incidents have demonstrated the fragility of insider threat mitigation mechanisms and the need to improve systems of management:

- A member of the CIA's Soviet/East European Division disclosing the identities of CIA and FBI human sources in exchange for payment (Cole & Ring, 2006), which reportedly resulted in the murders of several officials abroad.
- Highly organised drug smuggling operations involving border security officials in different jurisdictions globally; see, for example, *United States of America v Juan Martinez* and the Australian Commission for Law Enforcement Integrity's Operation Heritage Marca (Australian Commission for Law Enforcement Integrity, 2013).
- Corrupt conduct by biosecurity enabling business to bypass Australia's stringent quarantine arrangements (Australian Commission for Law Enforcement Integrity, 2017).
- Corruption across environmental regulators and various actors across timber supply chains in Brazil resulting in the deforestation of vast tracts of the Amazon rainforest (McCoy & do Lago, 2023).
- Collusion between a staff member of the Australian Bureau of Statistics and another person to commit insider trading of foreign derivatives utilising protected statistical information (Australian Securities and Investment Commission, 2015).
- Allegations a senior procurement official privately sold personal protective equipment while employed in the National Health Service in the midst of the 2020 coronavirus pandemic (Davies & Goodley, 2020).

These cases are illustrative of the vulnerabilities within government regulatory programmes and services, which enable their exploitation for personal gain or the gain of other malicious actors. They do not however illustrate the myriad additional harms of mistakes and errors in those same systems of activity for the public good.

While each of these cases was ultimately detected and, in most circumstances, defendants were prosecuted, the harm in each case had already been done, which posits an argument that more needs to be done to embed prevention mechanisms into the fabric of government and non-government organisations. As we'll outline in the chapters to come, a central proposition within this book is that a systemic risk-based approach will enable better mitigation of risk and thereby reduce the overall cost to society. While the current reactive approaches potentially allow the harm to occur with a focus on the prosecution of individual actors, we propose effort be placed on reducing the harm they cause in the first place.

Why should we care?

When considering the importance of controlling and mitigating insider threat and corruption, it is useful to look at its impacts through a range of lenses – institutional, governmental, and societal. At the institutional level, the relationship between insider threat and organisational loss is relatively straightforward. Evidence reveals that the median financial loss from fraud for the cases examined is USD130,000 with a total USD7 billion lost across inspected cases. Small business losses are almost twice as much per scheme, at USD200,000 per case (Association of Certified Fraud Examiners, 2018).

While the above ACFE report is a reliable source of information, the ACFE notes that the data to quantify losses to fraud and insider threat are imperfect and it is difficult to quantify real losses – direct, indirect, and intangible in nature. While we do not attempt to quantify these losses here either, actual cases of insider threat carry a range of indirect and intangible costs to organisations, including the costs of investigation, human resource costs (including for terminating employment and rehiring), and reputational costs and impact on the wellbeing of individual actors, respectively. The intangible costs here we posit are significant where, for publicised cases, the reputational impact not only affects the value of the business, but also negatively influences consumer confidence in respect of individual businesses and potentially across whole sectors of economies.

While it is easy to focus on financial losses as the major impact of insider threat at an institutional level, the impact on culture, motivation, and inspiration of its employees can be equally great and should not be underestimated. These in turn translate to new costs to the organisation in terms of reduced productivity and higher turn-over of staff, which can affect the viability of the enterprise in an ongoing manner. It is important to note that the financial and non-financial institutional impacts are felt across both public and private institutions.

When examined through a government lens, the effect of insider threat and corruption is distortion of the interventions that governments make to protect societies and economies. Our proposition here is that the role of government is to minimise the risk of market failure through regulation where such failures create harms to the overall economy, society, or the environment. Such acts of regulation in operation rely on the integrity of decision-making by public officials who arbitrate either by (1) restricting *undesirable* behaviour through education and physical or procedural restrictions, through building capability, or through civil or criminal enforcement or by (2) promoting desirable behaviour by creating market incentives through the injection of funding and resources (e.g. through the provision of grants and social security) or creating new market mechanisms, such as carbon pricing mechanisms. If decision-making is compromised by corruption, then the economic and social benefits can equally be compromised, particularly if corrupt conduct is systemic and ongoing (noting that in some circumstances even a single incident could cause substantial impact, for example the deliberate breaching of quarantine controls enabling a pandemic to occur).

In the Heritage–Marca case, for example, corrupt border officials compromised decisions around checking and clearance of luggage in the airport to allow illicit narcotics to enter Australia. Quite apart from the breaches to the regulatory controls, the importation of narcotics creates a host of flow-on impacts on the public good in terms health impacts, traffic accidents, social violence, and so forth (Attewell & McFadden, 2008), which were created through the actions of these officials. This is only one example, but when we consider the breadth of government activity, we can see that there are a substantial number of scenarios in which corrupt officials can create harm to individuals as well as broader social and economic objectives. We will explore further illustrative examples throughout the course of this book.

Lifting our focus to a broader economic and social level reveals that the impact of insider threat and corruption, when aggregated, creates significant costs and social impacts. Several studies have examined corruption as an economic issue for nations, notably *Corruption and Government* (Rose-Ackerman, 1999), which establish the impact of corruption, as a "use of privileged position to distort the efficiency of markets and the allocation of resources for solely personal gain . . . The overall conclusion is that nations . . . will be poorer overall if corruption levels are high" (Rose-Ackerman, 1999, p. 3).

In a chapter titled "Corruption and anti-corruption", Pearson (2001) also argues convincingly that corruption should be seen as an issue of not only economics but also human rights. Pearson contends that corruption not only directly contributes to violations of human rights (recognised through international covenants such as the *International Covenant on Civil and Political Rights* and the *International Covenant of Economic, Social and Cultural Rights*) but also plays a role in re-allocating resources away from social programmes, such as health and welfare, into high-capital infrastructure projects where corruption is more easily hidden. Further, there is also a direct impact on human rights outcomes, which results from corrupt decision-making, for example where corruption enables human trafficking or slavery.

While concepts and definitions of human rights may not be universally agreed upon, the touch point on the link between corruption and human rights may be used to illustrate the pervasiveness of the effects of corruption and insider threat on the issues that individuals and societies care about. At the international level, it is not just human rights which dominate the discourse between nations. There are also unilateral- and multilateral-level concerns regarding national and regional security which dominate international political and legal discourse. Nations invest in a range of measures to protect and preserve their interests on the global stage, including preserving their information assets through intelligence and counter-intelligence, protecting national infrastructure, entering multilateral defence covenants, and supplying aid, both financial and in terms of capability-building, to encourage regional stability and law and order. Taking just a few of these examples, we can conceive how corruption and insider threat has the potential to impact not just at the national or institutional level but more broadly on global order. The disclosure of sensitive intelligence shared under multilateral intelligence-sharing arrangements by a corrupt official not only affects short- and long-term national interests but may also undermine the integrity of agreements themselves and trust between nations, potentially impacting on trade, regional strategic interests, and allegiances between countries. For example, the corrupt diversion of aid funding anywhere along the aid supply chain could theoretically undermine regional security benefits or, worse, be diverted to support politically motivated entities to destabilise regional security measures.

The breadth of these examples demonstrates the importance of corruption and insider threat as an area of enquiry. However, the overall intention of this book is not to argue for the importance of the study into corruption and insider threat. Nor is it to focus on describing or analysing the macro-impacts of corruption and insider risk on companies, governments, and societies. Instead, we start with the premise that it is agreed that corruption and insider threats are real and genuine problems. Our focus, therefore, is on answering the practical questions about how organisations can, at an institutional level, develop mature systems, cultures, and practices to resist corruption and insider threat and importantly make well-informed decisions about how much to invest finite resources to control risk. In short, our priority is pragmatic rather than purely theoretical.

The case for a systemic organisational approach

Organisations are inherently complex, and with increasing scale the level of complexity increases exponentially. Diversified commercial and not-for-profit organisations might manage a host of different functions, including

- complex international supply chains;
- domestic manufacturing activities;
- asset leasing and sales;
- equity investment;
- welfare support programmes;

- health services; and
- marketing and advertising.

In government, they could be simultaneously handling

- registration and identity management services;
- social security payments;
- revenue raising;
- border control inspections;
- container examinations, law enforcement, and policing activities;
- environmental protection; and
- criminal intelligence analysis.

Dealing with insider threat in this environment requires a systemic response, something which is capable of dealing with this complexity without over-whelming the organisation with red tape and wasteful practices which hamper or undermine the value created by the enterprise.

Different approaches

There are several different schools of thought about the system to manage and mitigate insider threat and corruption. These have been described broadly as "interventionism", "managerialism", and "organisational integrity" approaches.

Interventionism describes a broadly reactive system which is focused on intervening after the commission of the corrupt or fraudulent activity, with an emphasis on enforcement and sanctions. The assumption is that any preventative effects will be because of a deterrent effect on actual or potential offenders. Under this model, the harm to the organisation and other broader interests has already been done, and in some circumstances is even allowed to continue in order to build a greater body of evidence for later prosecution of the malicious individual or entity.

In contrast, managerialism places its focus on prevention through business processes, systems, and rules imposed upon the discretions and actions of people within the organisation. It sees the problem of corruption and insider threat as a largely mechanical one and posits that prevention is better than cure. The chief criticism levelled against this approach is a tendency to neglect the relationship between human nature and the mechanical organisational system (Larmour & Wolanin, 2001, p. xviii).

Finally, the organisational integrity approach focuses primarily on the development of corruption-resistant organisations through the development of resilient cultures, norms, and values. Its main proposition, which has indeed been demonstrated through empirical study (e.g. Larmour &

Wolanin, 2001), is that values can guide behaviour even in circumstances where other personal benefits or interests might be at stake (e.g. financial benefits). A challenge under this approach can be creating and reinforcing the legitimacy of the cultural integrity norms. This is particularly the case in large, complex and/or geographically dispersed organisations, where local norms and cultures may come to dominate desired whole-of-enterprise codes of behaviour.

While these separate definitions of modes of intervention are useful from a descriptive perspective, the limit on these schools of thought is that they tend to see these approaches as discrete and focus on looking for which approach is more effective than others in isolation. In contrast, our view is that these different models should be seen as part of an integrated system which is capable of dealing with the human, process, and behavioural aspects of the insider threat and corruption environment. Rather than seen as discrete, they should be seen as a toolkit, and the main challenge, therefore, is to make informed decisions about which tools are most effective and cost effective to use in different organisational and environmental contexts. Additionally, while aspects of managerialism appear to be derided in literature concerning insider threat prevention, there does not seem to have been a genuine attempt to describe, in more than rudimentary terms, what a robust managerial system would look like. This is precisely what we attempt to do in this book.

Managerialism, more broadly defined than the definition outlined above, can describe the overall system of organisation rather than be restricted to describing the anti-corruption or insider risk management mechanisms. Under a broader definition, the understanding and design of systems of organisation has been steadily evolving in both industry and government. The advent of information and communication technology, and such disciplines as enterprise architecture, data modelling, and system theory, has driven advances in the way that organisations define and design themselves to achieve their objectives with greater efficiency and effectiveness. These schools of enquiry have also increasingly incorporated behavioural approaches emanating from organisational psychology, effectively providing a point of integration between the human nature aspects of the organisational integrity approach and mechanical process aspects of managerialism.

Managerialism, then, can be used to describe a system which integrates processes, ICT systems, the cultures and values of the organisational integrity approach, and the enforcement mechanisms favoured under the interventionist model. Managerialism under this definition can effectively subsume the other two approaches, guided through organisational systems for decision-making and investment of finite enterprise resources. In our view organisational integrity and interventionist approaches require a managerialist approach to direct those resources into the highest areas of risk. As we outline in later chapters, cultural intermediations, and interventions to investigate and prosecute incidents of insider threat, should be seen as part of a system of countermeasures rather than being viewed as separate systems to other forms of enterprise control. It is also worth noting that rules-dominated organisational approaches, which tend to dominate the discourse on "managerialism", have given way to automation, where rules are embedded seamlessly into business practice, reducing the relevance of academic discourse regarding the inability to rely on compliance with rules and business processes. This is not to say that automated processes cannot be circumvented, but merely that this change in organisational approach should shift the discussion on insider threat – but in much of the literature this transition has been too slow.

What we do in this book is describe how a more integrated managerial system can work and provide substantial benefits to organisations in terms of reducing risks and losses to insider risk.

Towards an integrated approach

"It is tempting, if the only tool you have is a hammer, to treat everything as if it were a nail" (Maslow, 1996, p. 15). The same statement can hold true for approaches to protecting organisations from insider threat. Under an interventionist approach, for example the preferred tool is investigation and prosecution and all insider risk incidents are to be resolved using these tools, irrespective of the fact that preventable loss has already occurred. Under an organisational integrity approach, cultural intermediation is the preferred tool and all risk is managed through these interventions.

If instead, we accept that we need different tools for different circumstances, then we also need a way of identifying which one to use to solve a particular problem. When the insider "problem" exists within a broader and often complex organisation, then the toolkit needs to be designed to match this complexity.

It is also important that we can keep a line of sight to the outcomes or objectives of an integrated approach. Managing insider risk cannot just be a frivolous exercise for interest's sake but should be result in measurably better outcomes than a system which does not protect itself from threat. As such, we describe four outcomes (Figure 1.1) that should be achieved through a more systemic approach to managing threat:

- A *greater alignment and consistency* of approach across the organisation. This means the process is more connected, senior decision-makers have greater control over the level of investment of finite resources and level of acceptable risk, risks to the organisation are more effectively managed, and loopholes are reduced. We contrast this with systems where risk is managed in an ad hoc way in response to detected incidents rather than through the identification of the risk. Equally this objective can be contrasted with systems where risk is managed through structural lines of management control, resulting in localised rather than enterprise approaches to managing risk resulting in inconsistency, inefficiency, and misalignment of resources to risk.

- The practice should be *more efficient*, with information on risk captured once and then reused. Resources for risk mitigation should also be more efficiently deployed across the organisation, with greater opportunities for re-use rather than over-reliance on local risk mitigations resulting in duplication. The baseline we use for considering efficiency is within managerial insider threat systems, which are siloed and delegated to lines of business. This results in duplication of effort, for example each organisational function being required to conduct its own assessment of risk and creating its own countermeasures against those risks. As above, we contrast this with approaches that focus on structural managerial control rather than a system of enterprise control, which results in the inefficiencies outlined above.
- The approaches to mitigating risk should be *more effective* – if we better understand the risks, we can measure the effectiveness of mitigation strategies and ensure that there is clear accountability for risks and risk control mechanisms. This results in more effective controls, rather than relying on uninformed decision-making, which, as we'll explore in later chapters, is dominated by heuristic mechanisms which reduce the quality of decision-making in response to complex problems such as systemic insider risk.
- Finally, because the risk environment is not static, mechanisms to ensure *continuous improvement and evolution* in the threat control environment are needed. This includes monitoring, future-facing intelligence, and evaluation and improvement mechanisms embedded within the system. We contrast this with systems of management which either respond to incidents as they occur rather than generating foresight to future risk or do not reconsider risk in response to the changing environment. In particular, an effective insider risk management system must recognise the relationship between the insider risk environment and the drivers for risk derived from the external context in which an organisation operates and the objectives it aims to achieve. We will explore this further as we understand the linkages between the organisation's assets at risk and how they otherwise contribute to the achievement of its objectives.

We have also developed a set of principles or factors (Figure 1.1) which serve as a point of reference to describe and measure the performance of the system. Investment in controlling or mitigating insider risk should be informed and evidence based, avoiding knee-jerk, inefficient, or ad hoc

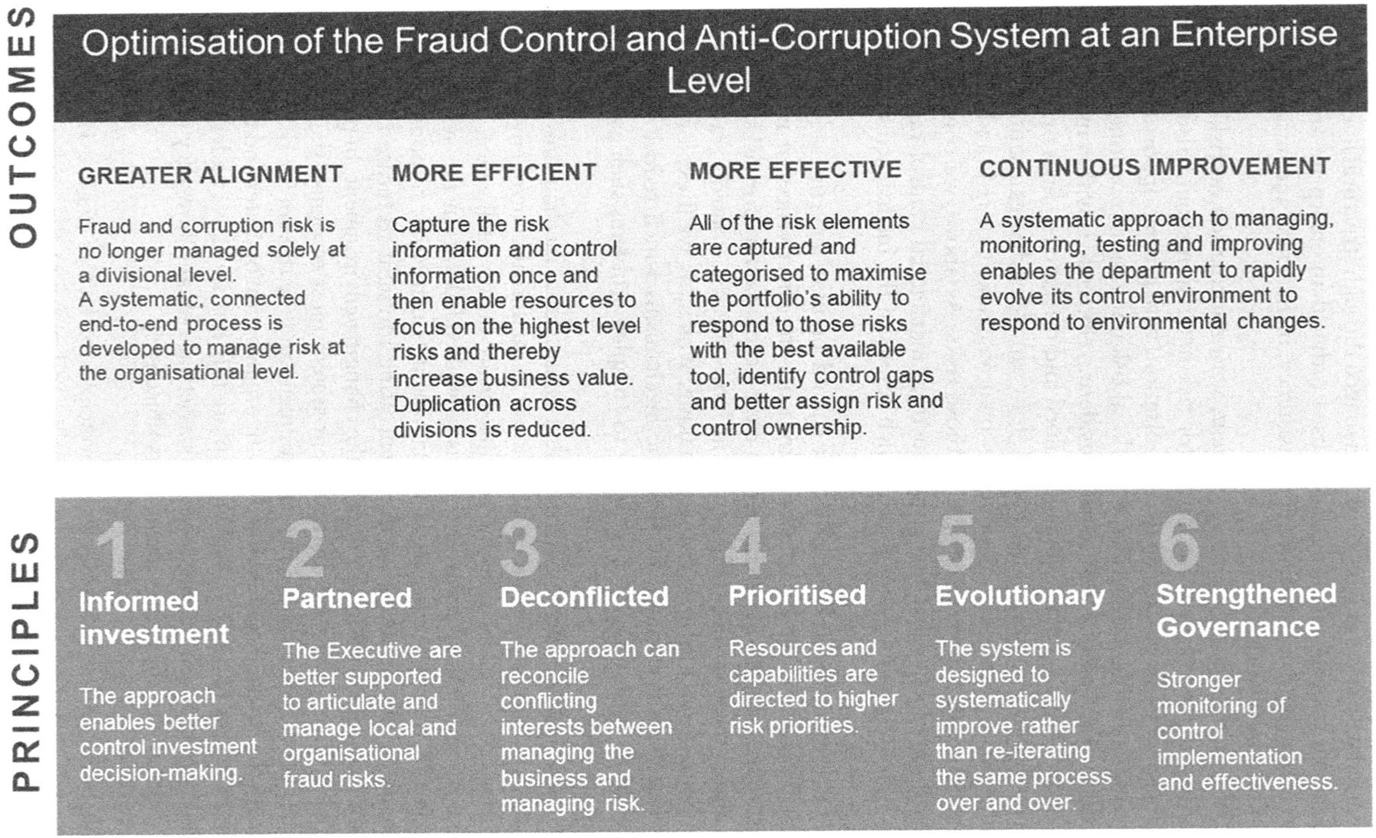

Optimisation of the Fraud Control and Anti-Corruption System at an Enterprise Level

OUTCOMES

GREATER ALIGNMENT	MORE EFFICIENT	MORE EFFECTIVE	CONTINUOUS IMPROVEMENT
Fraud and corruption risk is no longer managed solely at a divisional level. A systematic, connected end-to-end process is developed to manage risk at the organisational level.	Capture the risk information and control information once and then enable resources to focus on the highest level risks and thereby increase business value. Duplication across divisions is reduced.	All of the risk elements are captured and categorised to maximise the portfolio's ability to respond to those risks with the best available tool, identify control gaps and better assign risk and control ownership.	A systematic approach to managing, monitoring, testing and improving enables the department to rapidly evolve its control environment to respond to environmental changes.

PRINCIPLES

1 Informed investment	2 Partnered	3 Deconflicted	4 Prioritised	5 Evolutionary	6 Strengthened Governance
The approach enables better control investment decision-making.	The Executive are better supported to articulate and manage local and organisational fraud risks.	The approach can reconcile conflicting interests between managing the business and managing risk.	Resources and capabilities are directed to higher risk priorities.	The system is designed to systematically improve rather than re-iterating the same process over and over.	Stronger monitoring of control implementation and effectiveness.

FIGURE 1.1 Outcomes and Objectives of an Optimised Inside Risk Management System

investment. The system should involve a coordinated defined partnership and clear accountability between different functions in the organisation, rather than pure delegation of responsibility, siloing of responsibility, and duplication of function across the organisation. In our final chapter, we will set out the system of organisation which enables our approach to function effectively considering the different roles and interests that exist within the enterprise system.

There should be a clear way of de-conflicting the objectives of protecting the organisation from insider threat versus broader business objectives which may come into conflict. The system needs to help decision-makers to prioritise the allocation of finite resources to the activities where they will make the greatest impact or generate the biggest return. The system should have mechanisms which enable it to evolve rather than remain static while the nature of risks continues to change around it. The system should be governed in an ongoing way, thereby ensuring there is ongoing decision-making about the optimal investment and continuing accountability for the health of the system through time.

The above principles provide us with a point of reference for designing a new approach to dealing with insider risk. These will become transparent throughout, demonstrating how our framework can improve the management of threats to the organisation. Importantly, the framework outlined in this book has been applied in several government organisations, resulting in improved understanding and more coordinated approaches to managing their respective insider risk profiles.

Drawing on the opportunities of a digital age

New digital technologies and the connectedness of the digital age have no doubt provided new vectors for insider risk; however, they also provide us with new ways of understanding the threat environment and embedding detection within business practice. A systemic approach to managing insider risk (or any form of complex risk) is now possible because of the advances in ways to model, capture, and analyse the data and information about complex problems, thereby building knowledge about those problems.

Bridging the information–knowledge divide

There is a twofold challenge to understanding the insider threat environment in an organisation. The first is the ability to convert the individual knowledge of specialist fraud and corruption functions and officers into institutional knowledge rather than residing in the heads of individuals. The second is the ability to convert the vast and complex information and data about insider threats into knowledge which can be acted upon quickly to make decisions about how and where to intervene in an organisation to mitigate risk effectively.

Traditionally, these have been achieved through repositories of documents, in particular risk assessment tables which are held within organisations and periodically refreshed (sometimes as infrequently as biannually). More recently, there have been attempts to take a more structured approach, with risk management systems emerging to better capture and display risk information. This change has been a positive one, enabling easier reference to risk information and a greater ability to keep information refreshed and provide prompt action in response to changes. However, there are even greater opportunities to capitalise on new technologies, which are now more capable of structuring and relating complex information and providing flexibility in reporting and visualising data. Enterprise architecture software provides the means of capturing the complexities of an organisation's design in terms of organisational capability, process, roles, assets, ICT applications, data, and infrastructure. As we'll see in later chapters these elements are critical to a systemic and enterprise understanding of insider risk.

The above technological advancements should be used to improve our ability to describe risk and to pinpoint where the greatest risks reside, make informed investment decisions, understand our current investment profile, judge what impact insider threat mitigation is having on managing risk and in relation to competing business objectives, and maintain pace in a changing environment. The key to achieving these benefits is to have a structured approach to collecting and categorising the data about insider threats for quick interpretation. Our framework provides such a conceptual data structure for insider threat, linking them to other domains of enterprise architecture such as function, capability, roles, and structure.

Chapter 11 sets out the how to structure a "smart" register of risks, effectively providing a data model which can handle the complexity of organisations and of insider threats that they face. The aim is to provide meaningful information and actionable knowledge to decision-makers across the organisation, including executives, local managers, and employees and centralised insider threat management functions.

Limitation of traditional methods

When considered by reference to the principles we have outlined above, it is our view that the methods that have been traditionally used have been ill-equipped to handle insider threat at this level of complexity for a variety of reasons, which we set out in the sections below.

Understanding the threat

Insider threat mechanisms are based upon an assessment of risk, generally comprised of an assessment of likelihood of the threat occurring versus its consequence. Flowing from this assessment comes a decision about what to do about the risk. The main weakness in this approach is a tendency to rely on the subjective assessment of likelihood and consequence, rather than applying a more reliable objective model to determine the probability of an insider being able to exploit a weakness. To understand how this might work, we explore one of the examples mentioned in Box 1.1.

BOX 1.1   CASE STUDY EXAMPLE

Operation Heritage/Marca:
   The corrupt conduct observed in Operation Heritage–Marca involves long-term collusion between a small number of Customs and Border Protection officers at Sydney International Airport. So far as can be ascertained, these officers commenced unauthorised importations of steroids in 2007, an enterprise which expanded in the intervening years to include more officers and the importation of the precursor drug pseudoephedrine. The evidence gathered over more than two years of investigation reveals a concerning picture. Some officers used their inside knowledge to defeat surveillance and interdiction systems. This knowledge included information about law enforcement techniques and systemic vulnerabilities. They had privileged access to the secure border environment, and access to law enforcement databases. By working together, they exploited weaknesses in the supervision system at Sydney International Airport to manipulate rosters and job placements, thereby increasing their capacity to facilitate larger importations of drugs. They used their official positions and made use of friendships and other connections that they had developed at Sydney International Airport to gather information, and to cover their tracks.
   Australian Commission for Law Enforcement Integrity, 2013, p. 5.

The Commissioner for Law Enforcement Integrity notes in his report that the Australian Customs and Border Protection Service did not have a good appreciation of the systemic risks of this kind of exploitation of its systems and processes. Given the relative sophistication of this corrupt activity, it is unlikely that a traditional risk assessment would have deemed it very likely to occur, even though all the systemic weaknesses were certainly in place (as evidenced by the fact that it did occur). These included predictable shift patterns, access to CCTV control locations, central points of marshalling and coordination through border-screening processes, and a lack of oversight of the screening activities themselves (Australian Commission for Law Enforcement Integrity, 2013). All of these contributed to the likelihood of exploitation, but a traditional risk assessment would not have comprehensively taken them into account when assessing the risk – nor did it.

Equally the fact is, without a framework for understanding risk at a detailed and nuanced level, these assessments of risk are inherently influenced by heuristic thought patterns and mental shortcuts, which ease the cognitive load of understanding a complex problem. The most prevalent heuristic in risk assessment is the availability heuristic: A mental shortcut that occurs when people make judgements about the probability of events by the ease with which examples come to mind (Tversky & Kahneman, 1973). In an insider threat context, likelihood tends to be assessed based upon previously detected or well-known cases rather than understanding the organisational features or risk drivers which have given rise to them. This in turn means that previously observed cases potentially become more likely than they truly are, while undetected instances of insider threat, which may be more insidious and damaging, remain perceived as unlikely to occur.

In the above example, the relative sophistication and complexity of the corrupt behaviour and the fact that it evolved over the course of several years make it unlikely that a person conducting or participating in a risk assessment would have it in front of their mind. What is more likely is that following the public exposure of this case of corruption, extreme focus would be put on the parts of the Customs Service where this case occurred, whilst ignoring risks in other parts of the business, again based upon the availability heuristic. With this in mind, we must ask ourselves whether any of the effort on these kinds of risk assessment is worth the investment if they are evidently not an accurate predictor of threat. What's the value or return on investment?

Another important dimension is understanding the threat across complex organisations and being capable of making informed assessments of the relativity of risk across different business activities. Threats and risks are not evenly distributed across enterprise functions and assets. For example, the improper grant of a licence has a higher impact on a licensing organisation than on the theft of pencils. So how are we to differentiate between the risks at an organisational level, especially when we can't accurately determine the likelihood or consequence of risks as they relate to the organisation overall?

The ability to compare relative risk is critical to making informed decisions on where to invest in mitigating them and where they should be accepted because the return on investment for treating the risk doesn't stack up. Equally, as we've outlined above, the external environment and context in which organisations deliver value are ever changing. If the assessment of risk is based only upon previous events or incidents and a subjective assessment, then how is an organisation to understand threats when the environment changes or it enters new business activities, partnerships, or ventures?

In our view the heuristic and biased basis for decision-making around insider threat is, at least in part, attributable to the fact that current information and technology systems, which are used to support organisations to manage insider risk. do not provide the level of sophistication to capture an accurate representation of the risk drivers or their impact on organisational objectives. We will suggest in our final chapter an information/data meta-model, which is intended to form the basis for an enhanced risk management information system.

Focussing on perpetrators

Much of the literature on fraud, corruption, and insider risk focuses on identifying the "profile of a perpetrator" (Association of Certified Fraud Examiners, 2018, p. 33). The assumption here is that there are sufficient similarities between fraudsters and corrupt actors for them to be identified early and to bring their activities to an early end or ideally to prevent them entirely. However, when we look more closely at these "profiles" we generally find that they are incredibly generic: for example, employees of the organisation who are (1) male; (2) at a median age of 45; and (3) in the accounting or sales departments (Association of Certified Fraud Examiners, 2018, pp. 33–51). Clearly, these profiles do not provide a compelling basis for identifying a malicious insider within an enterprise.

Research by the Association of Certified Fraud Examiners (2018) also identifies that there are a series of behavioural indicators which are correlated with insider fraud and corruption, including financial difficulties, living beyond means, unusually close relationships with vendors, and an unwillingness to share duties. While these indicators may be suggestive of potential insider threat, it is our contention that they are still too general to enable organisations to pinpoint insider threat – the reason is simply this: people do not follow sufficiently systematic patterns for us to be able to accurately differentiate between fraudsters and other workers who behave or have the same characteristics for entirely different reasons. The upshot is that using these profiles as part of a program of detection is costly and produces substantial levels of false positives, both of which increase based on the size and scale of the organisation.

In contrast, the framework which we introduce focuses instead on business processes and systems to assess risk and build detection mechanisms. By definition, processes are repeatable and consistent and, therefore, provide a more reliable way of differentiating between valid behaviours and those which are indicative of exploitation of process. We will go into this in considerable detail in Chapter 2.

Another aspect of the excessive focus on perpetrators concerns the way that organisations think about preventing insider threats. Many of these interventions focus on influencing potential perpetrators' *motivations* for corrupt or fraudulent behaviour rather than by influencing their *opportunity* to commit them. Without discounting these measures entirely, they rely on the deterrence theory, which envisions people as rational maximisers of self-interest, responsive to the personal costs and benefits of their choices yet indifferent to the moral legitimacy of those choices (Paternoster, 2018). There are several issues with this approach. Most notably the reliability of deterrence depends substantially on the certainty of detection (Nagin & Pogarsky, 2001). This means that unless the ability of the organisation to accurately identify and act against exploitation exists, deterrence is likely ineffective at preventing insider threat. As we will further explore, there are better ways of designing detection mechanisms, which are a necessary complement to any attempt at deterrence.

Another issue to consider is that deterrence theory posits that people are indifferent to the moral legitimacy of their actions. However, evidence shows that people are strongly influenced by the moral correctness and legitimacy of rules (Tyler, 2006). As we've discussed above, this is the foundation of the organisational integrity approach to managing insider risk. The influence of these moral frameworks on behaviour, in our view, justifies investment not only in purely deterrent or physical controls on behaviour but also in the building of a moral or cultural framework for the organisation which promotes legitimate behaviour and builds individual loyalty and through these mechanisms is an important means of mitigating insider threat. We will further explore the aspects of culture building as an insider threat mitigation strategy in Chapter 10.

Poor or lacking governance

Organisational control is typically exerted from the top, with ultimate accountability for organisational decision-making residing both legally and practically with peak authorities, such as boards, chief executive officers, or other accountable authorities. In essence, the governance of the organisation is about having decision-making and control mechanisms for the investment of finite resource effort into creating or protecting organisational value. The resource effort for mitigating insider threat should be no different, in that it requires genuine investment of resources and provides differing risk returns depending on the types of investments selected.

Based on our observation, in practice, senior governance bodies do not tend to consider insider threat mitigation as a core component of their business strategies or investments and consequently the management and mitigation of insider threat tends to be delegated to dedicated fraud control functions or managed purely at a line of business level. This approach often adds a layer of cost and burden to lines of business without well-informed and balanced decision-making about investment in mitigation. This tends to result in ad hoc, inconsistent, and generally sub-optimal approaches to managing insider threat, with under-investment in some areas and over-control relative to risk in others. The lack of centralised decision-making over fraud investment often also leads to lost opportunities for efficiency that can be harvested through consistent and reusable mitigation mechanisms, which can be rolled out across business across the entire organisation level.

As outlined above, organisations are vastly complex organisms – the reason for the lack of governance we observe does not stem generally from neglect, but instead from the challenges of making informed decisions which account for this level of complexity. In Chapter 11, we will outline how our framework can contribute to better informed and more nuanced decision-making by providing better data and information to decision-makers supported by centralised decision-making assurance.

Over-reliance on tip-offs

ACFE's research shows that approximately 40% of fraud detections occur through tip offs, primarily from employees (Association of Certified Fraud Examiners, 2018). While this certainly demonstrates the value of tip-offs as a detection mechanism, we contend that there are several weaknesses when compared with more sophisticated detection mechanisms, such as audit log monitoring and business data analysis.

Tip-offs are clearly effective when dealing with highly visible and simple observable business activities, for example procurement of goods and services, where a range of people are involved and there are mechanisms to provide outcomes to unsuccessful vendors. On the other hand, for more complex or concealed business activities, such as ICT development activities, with a limited number of skilled personnel, the likelihood of detection through tip-off decreases significantly. It is likely that the fraud and corruption activities which organisations are detecting represent the most visible and easiest to detect via tip-offs from co-workers, and this has created a confirmation bias indicating that tip-offs are one of the most effective detection mechanisms.

In 2018, monitoring and analysis accounted for significant reductions in fraud losses and duration in organisations which had implemented them, but these mechanisms were under-utilised to combat insider threat (Association of Certified Fraud Examiners, 2018). We contend that this provides at least a partial basis of evidence that tip-offs should not be relied upon as the only or primary mechanism of detection, but instead that new opportunities in business intelligence and data analysis be explored to provide better mechanisms for systemic, reliable, and repeatable detection. In Chapter 7, we will outline in considerable detail the different types of controls including a broader range of available controls to detect insider risk events.

Conclusion

Bearing in mind the weaknesses we have outlined above, it is our conclusion that the mechanisms that have been traditionally used to manage and mitigate insider threat are not fit for purpose. They tend to focus on the wrong drivers for insider threat, don't invest adequately in mitigation, often under- or overestimate the impact of potential incidents, and do not provide a systemic way of categorising the threats to increasingly complex organisations, thereby enabling better decision-making in a resource constrained environment.

However, given the costs to organisations individually and to our economies and societies, insider risk is not an issue that we can simply ignore. Instead, we need a better way of managing it. It is with this conviction that we present a new framework for managing insider threat, internal fraud, and corruption, which we contend bridges the gaps in existing models and can provide organisations with a more effective and efficient means of controlling the losses, both financial and non-financial, from insider threats.

The previous sections have highlighted opportunities to improve the management of insider threat by taking a more systemic approach. With this in mind we will outline a new framework for managing insider threat, which will be developed in increasing depth throughout the course of this book, with reference to real-world examples drawn from experiences across the globe.

The four building blocks

The Fraud Control and Anti-Corruption Framework is built upon four building blocks which describe the overall management system to treat insider threats (see Figure 1.2)

Culture and commitment

We begin at the bottom of the pyramid in Figure 1.2 – *Culture and commitment*. An organisational culture which is resistant to internal fraud and corruption is vital to ensure that staff who are targeted for corruption are resilient to such advances and further that people who witness fraudulent or corrupt activity have the confidence to report what they've seen and the assurance that the organisation will act appropriately on their concerns.

As famously quipped by management consultant and writer Peter Drucker "culture eats strategy for breakfast", while Drucker doesn't contend that strategy isn't important, he points out the importance of culture in guiding and normalising both desirable and undesirable behaviour. As such, the building of a culture resilient to insider threat should not be seen as something which should be left to evolve unguided but should instead be actively pursued through leadership and the setting of the appropriate "tone from the top".

Culture plays an enormously important part in creating a commitment to the shared organisational endeavour and a tendency to protect that

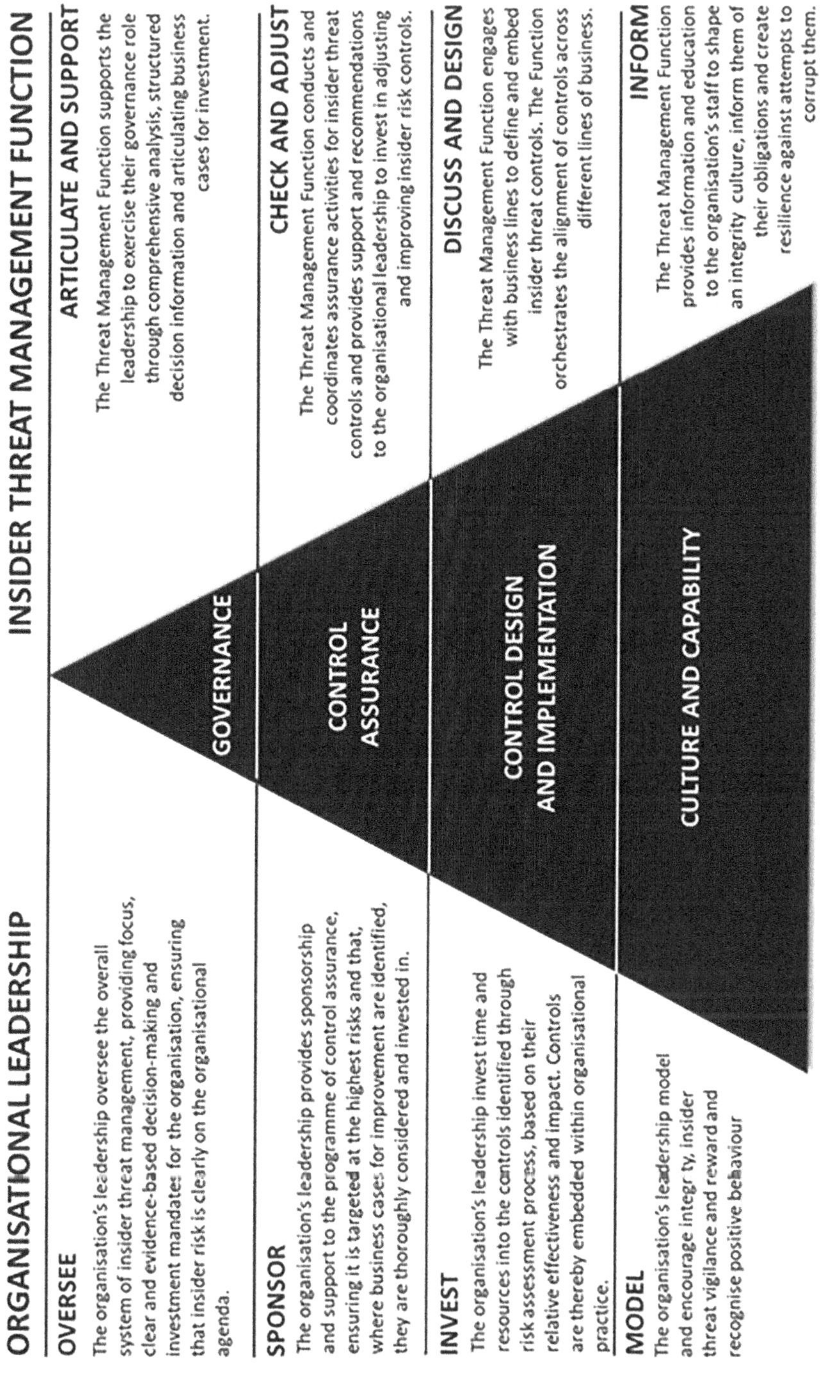

ORGANISATIONAL LEADERSHIP

INSIDER THREAT MANAGEMENT FUNCTION

ARTICULATE AND SUPPORT

The Threat Management Function supports the leadership to exercise their governance role through comprehensive analysis, structured decision information and articulating business cases for investment.

CHECK AND ADJUST

The Threat Management Function conducts and coordinates assurance activities for insider threat controls and provides support and recommendations to the organisational leadership to invest in adjusting and improving insider risk controls.

DISCUSS AND DESIGN

The Threat Management Function engages with business lines to define and embed insider threat controls. The Function orchestrates the alignment of controls across different lines of business.

INFORM

The The Threat Management Function provides information and education to the organisation's staff to shape an integrity culture, inform them of their obligations and create resilience against attempts to corrupt them.

OVERSEE

The organisation's leadership oversee the overall system of insider threat management, providing focus, clear and evidence-based decision-making and investment mandates for the organisation, ensuring that insider risk is clearly on the organisational agenda.

SPONSOR

The organisation's leadership provides sponsorship and support to the programme of control assurance, ensuring it is targeted at the highest risks and that, where business cases for improvement are identified, they are thoroughly considered and invested in.

INVEST

The organisation's leadership invest time and resources into the controls identified through risk assessment process, based on their relative effectiveness and impact. Controls are thereby embedded within organisational practice.

MODEL

The organisation's leadership model and encourage integr ty, insider threat vigilance and reward and recognise positive behaviour

GOVERNANCE

CONTROL ASSURANCE

CONTROL DESIGN AND IMPLEMENTATION

CULTURE AND CAPABILITY

FIGURE 1.2 Inside: Threat Management Model

endeavour from threats, which is vital to reducing the motivation for exploiting the organisation but also for promoting reporting of suspected or actual instances of fraud and corruption. To take an active and thoughtful approach to building and changing culture, we need to understand the elements of culture and be able to identify instances of good and bad cultures at both local and organisational levels.

Complementing culture are knowledge and awareness. Both knowledge and awareness provide individuals with an understanding of their obligations within the organisation and the tools and techniques to address ethical dilemmas which can manifest through their roles in the organisation or through conflicts of interest which emerge at the confluence between their roles in the organisation and their private lives. Building on research into culture change (Johnson & Scholes, 1999, p. 74), we will explore how to diagnose, identify, and develop a fit-for-purpose culture to manage insider threat in a variety of organisational contexts. We will also propose some new methods for using data to inform more targeted awareness and education programs based upon the most prevalent insider threats to a particular line of business.

Internal fraud and corruption controls

The second level up in Figure 1.2 is *Control Design and Implementation*. Controls against internal fraud and corruption form the central component of the framework. They provide the physical line of defence which prevent, detect, and respond to suspected or actual incidents of insider risk within the organisation. They must be embedded within business processes to operate effectively and be fit for purpose to manage the threat to a line of business. Chapters 2 through 7 will set out our approach to understanding and categorising risk and designing improved fraud and corruption controls into business activities.

We need first to categorically understand the assets the organisation uses to create value. These are the subjects of insider threats. We identify three forms of asset:

1 Discretionary decisions: Organisations are hives of decision-making. It is these decisions which are the greatest creators of value across supply chains, driving strategy and the execution of business activities. Whether it is decisions about how to invest, whether to grant a service or right, or how to dispose of an asset, these decisions can all be subject to exploitation or undue influence. Equally, inadvertent error may plague these decisions, creating risk and impact to organisations.

2 Information: Information is increasingly understood as a key organisational commodity, whether it is information about an organisation's products or operations or external information regarding clients and markets.

This information is of value to both the organisation and to other interested parties who could exploit or damage it for personal benefit.
3 Physical and intangible assets: The physical assets of an organisation can evidently be subject to theft, damage, or manipulation. It is vital that we have a way of classifying these assets and their value in financial terms, but more importantly, in terms of their contribution to the objectives of the organisation, and therefore the impact when they are compromised.

We anchor our understanding of risk around these assets to provide a clear line of sight between the assets that create the most value to the organisation and those which are at greatest threat. In Chapter 3, we expand on the classification of organisational assets to better assess risk.

Designing effective controls equally relies on a well-developed understanding of the risks to specific business activities. The framework will outline a new approach to breaking down fraud and corruption risks to understand the mechanisms or drivers for those risks and thereby to define effective controls which act on those mechanisms. Our focus is not just on understanding the risk itself but more specifically what is it about how a particular business activity is undertaken that drives risk to the organisation's assets and how specifically those drivers can be mitigated to protect the organisation's assets. The outcome of this enquiry is a high-quality dataset at an organisational level that allows organisational leaders to determine the areas of greatest risk, make informed decisions about managing those risks, provide the basis to test controls, and ensure they effectively mitigate insider threats.

Chapter 11 sets out how to leverage this enhanced dataset to create new forms of business intelligence which can inform strategic decision-making but also can be used to develop detection mechanisms for fraud and corruption risks within business. We also provide examples of new visualisations of the data which can be used in different decision contexts to promote understanding of what the data tells the organisation about threats.

Control assurance

With a clear understanding of the business control environment (what controls are in place and what risks they manage), it is crucial to ensure that these controls are working in practice and, if necessary, adjust them to meet changing demands. This assurance is critical to ensure the continuous improvement of existing controls and minimising sunk investment in ineffective controls.

Another important aspect of control assurance is enabling organisational leadership to better understand the impact of controls on other organisational priorities, such as productivity or occupational well-being. This is important in that risk controls, while they protect value, do not contribute directly to value production and quite often impact on the cost and efficiency of value production. Therefore, it is critical to know whether the return on investment for controls is positive or negative (i.e. is the value protected greater than the value foregone.)

Chapters 8 and 9 set out how to draw on the risk data to develop a methodology for testing controls with line of sight to risks, as well as prioritising the programme of assessment and aligning with other organisational assurance mechanisms such as quality management and internal audit.

Governance

The Fraud Control and Anti-Corruption Framework represents a management system for dealing with fraud and corruption risk. As outlined above, this system requires investment and balancing against the other priorities of the organisation, both in terms of investment priorities and in terms of the relative priority of mitigating a fraud risk against other priorities, such as streamlining and simplifying processes for clients and staff, which might be impacted by the insider risk countermeasures. The management of these investments requires a properly supported governance mechanism, which is well informed and capable of making evidence-based decisions to manage fraud and corruption in the context of the organisation's other business priorities. This requires a structured approach to developing and providing decision evidence, building business cases for implementation, managing the investment portfolio and budget for insider threat control, consuming, and overseeing the implementation of insider threat controls within lines of business.

Chapter 11 sets out mechanisms to use enhanced data to inform better decision-making and ties together the different components of a governance structure to drive investment in insider threat mechanisms throughout the organisation. We also set out proposed institutional arrangements which are enacted through a strategic partnership between the organisational executive, individual lines of business, and centralised insider threat mitigation functions. Such an arrangement, we propose, provides stewardship for the overall system of mitigation and supports the organisation through assurance.

In closing this chapter, we reiterate that insider threat has the potential to seriously damage an organisation's ability to perform its mission, divert funds and resources available for delivering products and services to the public, and undermine confidence and trust. In the chapters that follow, we delve deeper into this issue to develop a complete and formalised model of insider risk. The model we develop standardises the language regarding risk drivers, sets out the interaction between those drivers, and draws relationships between the drivers for insider risk and the controls that act as countermeasures against each of the drivers.

Our goal is to move beyond the limitations of existing practices, providing a systemic and structured approach to investing resources as efficiently and effectively as possible. To be truly successful in mitigating insider risk, organisations need to identify and direct resources to where they are needed most. But in saying this, we recognise that the risk control mechanisms we propose may impact other business objectives. Thus, controlling insider risk needs to be balanced against those competing objectives.

In this book you will find we regularly refer and draw upon routine activity theory (Cohen & Felson, 1979). We note the importance of the "Capable Guardian" to manage risk and attempt to define a system of typologies of "guardians" that play different roles within the insider risk management system, and as a collective, maximise the protection of organisations against insider risk.

Finally, it is our view that the model we provide is a more complete and systematic approach to identifying and managing insider risk. The model we develop here is not based on just our opinions. Rather, the model has come about because of years of work and practice in different contexts including Australian policing, financial regulation, and immigration and border protection. It is also underpinned by theory and empirical evidence. We ask the reader to remember that model development is not a static process. Rather, it is dynamic, where it continually evolves as we embed and test it in a range of contexts over time. In particular, there are substantial opportunities to develop the data models and technology systems to support the framework in ways we can only touch upon in a written body of work. With further implementation, testing, and refinement we hope that the model will be capable of enhancing organisations' ability to manage risk in a more effective and efficient manner while protecting the interests and the ultimate goals of the organisation.

References

Association of Certified Fraud Examiners. (2018). *Report to the nations: Global study on occupational fraud and abuse.* https://www.acfe.com/report-to-the-nations/2018/

Attewell, R., & McFadden, M. (2008). Measuring the benefits of drug law enforcement: The development of the Australian Federal Police drug harm index. *Bulletin on Narcotics, LX*, 45–57.

Australian Commission for Law Enforcement Integrity. (2013). *Operation heritage (final report) – a joint investigation of alleged corrupt conduct among officers of the Australian Customs and Border Protection Service at Sydney International Airport.*

Australian Commission for Law Enforcement Integrity. (2017). *Operation Karoola – an investigation into potential conflicts of interest of a biosecurity officer.*

Australian Securities and Investment Commission. (2015). *15–058MR two men sentenced in Australia's largest insider trading case.* https://asic.gov.au/about-asic/news-centre/find-a-media-release/2015-releases/15-058mr-two-men-sentenced-in-australia-s-largest-insider-trading-case/

The CERT Insider Threat Team. (2013). *Unintentional insider threats: A foundational study.* Software Engineering Institute CMU/SEI-2013-TN-022.

Cohen, L., & Felson, M. (1979). Social change and crime rate trends: A routine activity approach. *American Sociological Review, 44*(4), 588–608.

Cole, E., & Ring, S. (2006). *Insider threat: Protecting the enterprise from sabotage, spying, and theft.* Syngress.

Davies, H., & Goodley, S. (2020, May). Revealed: NHS procurement official privately selling PPE amid Covid-19 outbreak. *The Guardian.*

Hong, S., Park, S., Park, L., Jeon, M., & Chang, H. (2018, May). An analysis of security systems for electronic information for establishing secure internet of things environments: Focusing on research trends in the security field in South Korea. *Future Generation Computer Systems, 82,* 769–782.

Johnson, G., & Scholes, K. (1999). *Exploring corporate strategy* (5th ed.). Prentice Hall.

Johnson, S., Blythe, J., Manning, M., & Wong, G. (2020). Exploring the impact of security labelling schemes and consumers' stated preferences and their willingness to pay for domestic IoT devices: A discrete choice experiment. *PLoS One.* https://doi.org/10.1371/journal.pone.0227800

Larmour, P., & Wolanin, N. (2001). *Corruption and anti-corruption.* Asia Pacific Press.

Lemaire, D. (2017). The stick: Regulation as a tool of government. In *Carrots, sticks and sermons* (pp. 59–76). Routledge.

Maslow, A. H. (1996). *The psychology of science: A reconnaissance.* Maurice Bassett Publishing.

McCoy, T., & do Lago, C. (2023, July). Amazon undone. *Washington Post.* (Original work published 2022)

Nagin, D. S., & Pogarsky, G. (2001). Integrating celerity, impulsivity, and extralegal sanction threats into a model of general deterrence: Theory and evidence. *Criminology, 39*(4), 865–892.

Paternoster, R. (2018). Perceptual deterrence theory. In D. Nagin, F. Cullen, & C. Lero Jonson (Eds.), *Deterrence, choice, and crime* (Vol. 23, pp. 91–116). Routledge.

Pearson, Z. (2001). An international human rights approach to corruption. In P. Larmour & N. Wolanin (Eds.), *Corruption and anti-corruption* (pp. 30–61). Asia Pacific Press.

Rose-Ackerman, S. (1999). *Corruption and government: Causes, consequences, and reform.* Cambridge University Press.

Schell-Busey, N., Simpson, S., Rorie, M., & Alper, M. (2016). What works? A systematic review of corporate crime deterrence. *Criminology and Public Policy, 15*(2), 387–416.

Tversky, A., & Kahneman, D. (1973). Availability: A heuristic for judging frequency and probability. *Cognitive Psychology, 5,* 207–232.

Tyler, T. R. (2006). *Why people obey the law.* Princeton University Press.

Wilson, R. (2014, September 3). Watch the U.S. transition from a manufacturing economy to a service economy, in one gif. *The Washington Post.* https://www.washingtonpost.com/blogs/govbeat/wp/2014/09/03/watch-the-u-s-transition-from-a-manufacturing-economy-to-a-service-economy-in-one-gif/?noredirect=on&utm_term=.44a6d4664863

2
ASSESSING RISK TO TARGET INVESTMENT

Introduction

All organisations, across every facet of the public, private and not-for-profit sectors, have finite resources to manage their operations and deliver value. Such constraints mean that organisations face trade-offs and opportunity costs. There is a subtle but important difference that needs to be acknowledged here. Firstly, the term "trade-off" is used to describe the course of action given up to perform the preferred course of action while "opportunity cost" is the cost of opting one course of action and forgoing another. Secondly, a trade-off refers to all the other alternatives which are foregone to achieve the goal. Conversely, the opportunity cost is the expected return on the potential or actual investment other than the existing one. Finally, a trade-off represents what is relinquished to get what is wanted. Opportunity cost, however, represents the amount expected if the resources are put to the next-highest-valued alternative (Manning et al., 2016). These trade-offs or opportunity costs, therefore, mean that decisions to invest resources to mitigate insider risk should ideally involve a highly targeted approach to understanding where these risks occur. Thinking and acting strategically arguably results in the optimisation of outcomes (Gelles, 2016). In reality, organisations tend to spread resources thinly on mainstream generalised mitigation activities, or invest heavily in mitigation following highly publicised cases (such as in Australia where corruption was uncovered in Sydney Airport through the Australian Commission for Law Enforcement Integrity's Operation Heritage). This arguably compromises their ability to invest in more effective mitigation strategies or to take a more graduated approach to investing in high-risk areas.

DOI: 10.4324/9781003055716-2

This chapter explores how insider risk can be better assessed and understood, utilising a detailed framework that focuses on the assets at risk, the opportunities for abuse, motivational factors, and understanding of the potential corrupting entities. The intent of this detailed assessment is to provide a nuanced approach to targeting resources where they are needed most. It also provides the basis for identifying the most appropriate risk control tool to deal with a particular insider risk type.

Risk management in context

The concept of risk has evolved over the past century, with references in management literature in the 1920s but not formally recognised as a practice until the 1950s (Dionne, 2013). From its earliest conception, the prevailing model of risk has been focused on hazards, losses, and the mitigation of harms and hazards. More recently the science and practice of risk management has been codified into newer models which define risk quite differently as "the effect of uncertainty on objectives" (Association of Certified Fraud Examiners, 2022).

The reason that this definition of risk is important when understanding and addressing crime and in particular insider risk is that (i) by focusing on "objectives" of the organisation at any scale, be it a company, a government institution, the whole of government, or even the whole of the international community, we focus on those insider threats which really matter, those which impact most on the value created by the organisation – rather than on distractions which can waste precious time and investment yielding little benefit; (ii) the concept of "uncertainty" focuses analysis of insider threat away from narrow concepts, such as trying to understand "the profile of a fraudster" or looking simply at insider threat typologies (e.g. embezzlement), and instead stresses that the presence of an insider threat in a particular set of circumstances is "uncertain". The usefulness of this concept is that it stresses "relativity in risk" rather than "absolute risk". Id est, while it is uncertain that insider threat will emerge in identical circumstances, the likelihood can be higher and equally the consequence can similarly be higher in certain circumstances.

The concepts of risk management are so critical to understanding the remaining substance of this book that without wanting to replicate the international standard, it is necessary to set out the critical steps in the cycle and how they operate in a general sense, as we set out below. The remaining chapters describe how a generalised risk framework needs to be adapted to fully understand and address insider threat.

Risk management process

Much of this book provides a framework for analysing and assessing insider threats in context, providing a structure to better identify and classify how threats are likely to eventuate, and assessing which threats are most likely to impact on the organisation's overall goals and objectives. Below we provide an outline of the seven steps in the general risk management lifecycle (also see Figure 2.1). While this general lifecycle of risk management needs to be explained as part of our context setting, in reality our model represents a tailoring of this general lifecycle to the understanding of insider risk.

Establishing the context

We begin by setting out the context in which insider risk emerges (Figure 2.1). This step is critical in ensuring that measures to address such risk align with the strategic and operational objectives of the entity in which they emerge. The importance of context setting is that the insider threats of most consequence to the organisation are those with the potential to most affect the achievement of the organisation's goals and objectives. By way of example:

- *If the organisation is a commercial entity* – this context is likely to mean that those threats which are of greatest consequence are those that are

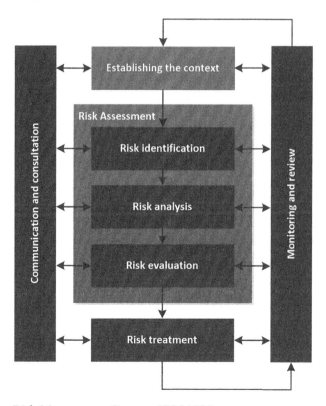

FIGURE 2.1   Risk Management Process: ISO31000

likely to impact its ongoing profitability and brand reputation. If the profit base is focused on particular market segments, insider threats that are most likely to affect reputation, trust, or engagement with those sectors will be more consequential to the company's overall profitability. On a relative scale, therefore, these are the threats the company should invest most in treating.

- *If the organisation is a government regulator* (e.g. regulating and enforcing legislation and regulation to reduce pollution) – then threats associated with the most likely or more harmful polluters/pollutants would be most crucial to achieving its anti-pollution objectives.
- Similarly, *if the organisation is a border control agency* then its objective is to protect its national economy, society, and environment from the harms associated with illicit goods and to promote orderly migration. As such, those threats which are likely to have the greatest impact on those economic, social, and environmental goals, such as the effects of illicit drug importation and use, will be of greatest consequence to its strategic goals.
- *In a military organisation* the goal, roughly speaking, is to protect the assets and infrastructure of the nation against foreign threats by matching and exceeding foreign military capability while adhering to the rules and norms governing the international order. Insider threats that threaten superior capability, for example illicit sale of material, designs or strategic, operational, and tactical information, which are of greatest importance to maintaining that capability, will be of greatest importance and therefore the focus of investment to guard against insider threat.

In addition to establishing the overall objective of the organisation to protect that objective, it is critical to also establish questions regarding internal and external context and how that objective is realised. For example:

- *Internal context*: What are the internal functions of the organisation and how do they contribute to achieving the objective? Which functions are most critical and which are less important? What assets are used and created? What are the key processes that create value?
- *External context*: Who are the key partners and how do they contribute to the achievement of the objective? Who are the competitors and in what sectors or markets do they compete?

This stage is important as it acknowledges that without a clear definition of the objective, it is difficult to comprehensively identify and assess what constraints or impediments could prevent that objective from being fulfilled. In Box 2.1, we propose questions that need answering in order to establish context.

BOX 2.1   KEY QUESTIONS OF ESTABLISHING THE CONTEXT

Key questions: Establishing the context

- What are the organisation's objectives and what does success look like?
- How do its functions contribute to the objective, and which are most critical?
- Who are the organisation's key partners or markets? How do they contribute to success?
- Who are the key competitors or adversaries?
- Is this something that we can handle on our own, or will we need help from someone else?

Risk identification

Building from the established context in which risk management is being undertaken, risk identification (Figure 2.1) seeks to determine what events, constraints, or factors could potentially affect the fulfilment of the organisation's goals and objectives. We will not dwell on this element of the risk management process, as in effect this is the stage in which an organisation would identify insider threat as a risk to its overall objectives, in parallel to a suite of other potential risks, such as workplace health and safety risks, and financial risks.

The important factor in this stage of the risk management process is that the organisation acknowledges insider threats as a risk to its achievement of its objectives.

A failure to recognise insider threat at this stage of a risk management lifecycle inevitably means that there will be minimal to no investment in managing the risk, often until the risk has been realised. As we set out in Chapter 1 (following from Box 1.1), organisations need to be conscious of the availability heuristic when identifying risk. Complex insider risks by their very nature will not be "easy to recall" thereby potentially meaning they will not be considered likely to occur. In Box 2.2, we suggest questions that need answering regarding risk identification.

BOX 2.2   KEY QUESTIONS OF RISK IDENTIFICATION

Key questions: Risk identification

- Does the organisation recognise insider threat as a key risk to its objectives?
- Does the organisation value the analysis and management of this risk? In short, does it take it seriously?

- Has the organisation previously been affected by insider threat or had near misses?
- Does its board, executive, and managers at all levels recognise the potential for insider threat to affect the achievement of its objectives?

These are threshold questions that will determine the organisation's success in managing insider threat.

Risk analysis

The risk analysis stage (Figure 2.1) of the risk management process involves the comprehensive and detailed assessment of the risk. From an insider threat perspective, it involves developing a deep understanding of the different typologies of insider threat the organisation is subject to, setting out the potential relationships between the cause and effect.

Here, it is necessary to recognise the relative likelihood/probability and quantifying or qualifying the consequences/impacts on organisational objectives. The primary objective of risk analysis is to develop the best possible understanding of the identified risks, which in turn will inform the control and treatment actions that manage these risks and determine the relative priority of investing in mitigating insider threats within different areas of the business (Aven, 2015).

The risk analysis stage is the point in the risk management process where an indicative risk rating is attributed to the risk. Risk ratings are designed to provide a mechanism through which the organisation can make relativistic decisions in relation to the management of risks by determining whether insider threat events have a low, medium, high, or extreme impact on the objectives of the organisation. Risk ratings are determined through an analysis of the likelihood and impact of the identified risks, which are then used to determine and rate the severity of the risk overall.

The final component of the risk analysis stage is to identify what controls are already in place and determine how effective they are in reducing the likelihood or impact of insider threat events should they occur. This analysis of existing controls and their effectiveness assists in informing the prioritisation of treatment actions and identifies whether additional controls are required. In Box 2.3, we now suggest questions that need answering regarding risk analysis. Again, our model provides the basis for detailed risk analysis.

BOX 2.3   KEY QUESTIONS OF RISK ANALYSIS

Key questions: Risk analysis

- How likely is it that the insider threat will be realised and how much impact on objectives is this likely to create? Chapters 3 through 6 provide a framework for answering these questions.
- Are current controls effective at managing the potential risk/threat? Chapters 7 to 9 provide a structured approach to making this appraisal.

Risk evaluation

The risk evaluation stage (Figure 2.1) of the risk management process is focused on determining whether the risk is above or below the level which the organisation is willing to accept or tolerate. Determining the tolerability of the risk event assists in making informed decisions on which risks need to be treated and with what level of relative priority. Decisions as to whether a risk is acceptable or unacceptable are informed by the likelihood and the severity of its impact, both of which are established in the risk analysis stages of the process.

While risk analysis might indicate that an insider threat is high or low, risk evaluation determines which insider threats should be treated first. In Box 2.4, we suggest questions that need answering regarding risk evaluation.

BOX 2.4   SUGGESTED QUESTIONS OF RISK EVALUATION

Suggested questions: Risk evaluation

- Is the level of insider threat acceptable or unacceptable considering its impact on the organisation's objectives?
- Are there already controls in place? Is it feasible to do anything further?
- Will the treatment of the insider threat create more benefit than harm to the organisation? We will expand on this question in Chapters 7 and 9.

Risk treatment

Treatment (Figure 2.1) is the action taken where it has been determined that the insider threat is beyond what is tolerable to the organisation. Risk treatment is a cyclical process where individual risk treatments (or combinations of treatments) are assessed to determine if they are adequate to bring the residual risk levels to a tolerable or appropriate level. If not, then new risk treatments are generated and assessed until a satisfactory level of residual risk is achieved.

Importantly, risk treatments must involve a specific action that reduces the likelihood and/or impact of the risk. While monitoring the risk is an important component of the risk management process, the management of the risk must involve controls and treatments that have measurable effects on the risk. Examples of strategies to manage and treat risk can include the following:

- Avoiding the insider threat entirely by not undertaking a high insider threat business activity
- Sharing the risk with other parties
- Accepting and retaining the risk through informed decision-making
- Changing the likelihood and/or impact of the risk by modifying the controls in place

Additionally, treatments need to be proportionate to the insider threats that are being managed and negative impacts of those controls on business objectives and activities need to be mitigated or limited. In our framework, we provide a structured and standardised set of controls which can apply across organisations, including assessments of what factors will make those controls effective and what impact on business they are likely to have. We will go into considerably more detail on risk treatment and controls in Chapters 7 and 9. In Box 2.5, provide suggested questions that need answering regarding risk treatment.

BOX 2.5 SUGGESTED QUESTIONS OF RISK TREATMENT

Suggested questions: Risk treatment

- What additional actions can be taken to prevent, detect, or respond to the insider threat?
- What level of cost, time, and effort is required in order to treat the risk? Is it proportional to the level of risk?
- Who is responsible for treatments and when will they implement them?
- What level of treatment is required to get the risk down to an acceptable level?
- What are the negative impacts of the proposed treatment?

Monitoring and reviewing risk

Organisations continue to change their focus, objectives, and business functions over time and hence the management of insider threat in this ever-changing environment needs to be equally dynamic and evolving. As a result, insider threat monitoring and review (Figure 2.1) is integral to successful risk management and should be a pre-planned and deliberate part of the process.

Key objectives of risk monitoring and review include the following:

- Detecting changes in the internal and external environment, including evolving entity objectives and strategies and changes in the capability and intent of corrupting influences outside the organisation
- Identifying new or emerging threats and risks which may result from changes in business objectives or the external environment
- Ensuring the continued effectiveness and relevance of controls and the implementation of treatment programs
- Obtaining further information to improve the understanding and management of already identified risks
- Analysing and learning lessons from events, including near-misses, successes, and failures

The monitoring and review of risks, controls, and treatments should be time based, event based, or both. Importantly, the frequency of the review process should be commensurate with the significance of the risk and the rate at which the organisation and its operating environment is changing. In Chapter 9, we deal with monitoring of controls through assurance and in Chapter 11, we explore practices for reviewing risk using our model to enhance the ability to integrate insider risk management with organisational change.

Communication and consultation

Communication and consultation (Figure 2.1) are an essential attribute of good risk management and therefore are important at each step of the risk management process. Communicating risk information with stakeholders maintains confidence and trust and develops a common understanding of the entity's risks. Good risk communication should

- encourage stakeholder engagement and accountability;
- maximise the information obtained to reduce uncertainty;
- meet the reporting and assurance needs of stakeholders;
- ensure that relevant expertise is drawn upon to inform each step of the process; and
- inform other entity processes such as corporate planning and resource allocation.

Where the risk is complex or involves many stakeholders, the development of a communications plan may assist the management of the risk. The purpose of a communications plan is to ensure that the right information is communicated to the right people at the right time. Ideally, it should include information on the chosen approach for the management of the risk, the identification of risk, and control owners and the status of controls and treatments.

Similarly, establishing a model that attributes actions and descriptions against stakeholders based on whether they need to be responsible for, accountable for, consulted on, or informed of the management of the risk may assist in managing communication in a formal, coordinated manner. In Box 2.6, we provide suggested questions that need answering regarding risk communication and consultation.

BOX 2.6   SUGGESTED QUESTIONS OF COMMUNICATION AND CONSULTATION

Suggested questions: Communication and consultation

- Who have, or should, I talk to about this risk?
- Which stakeholders are responsible for, or have an interest in, the management of the risk?
- How regularly should we meet or discuss the management of the risk?
- What needs to be documented and how visible should it be to the organisation?

Risk management and type I and type II errors in insider threat

While the practice and standards around risk management have evolved substantially with the development of national and international standards, it is our view that there remains a deficit in its application to analyse, understand, and control insider threat including internal fraud and corruption.

It is possible to abide by the standard set out above and fall victim to several traps that can undermine the effectiveness of an organisation's insider risk management approach. At the very highest level we could categorise these traps as systemic examples of *type I* (i.e. false positive) and *type II* (i.e. false negative) error. The upshot of false positives is the excessive level of resourcing required to achieve an acceptable level of protection for the organisation. On the other hand, false negatives equate to effectively untreated risk for the organisation.

Some type I examples

Fraudster/insider profiling

Globally, there have been a range of attempts at profiling the typical fraudster or insider to provide a typology for organisations to focus their risk assessments on. For example, the global accounting firm KPMG (2023) published findings indicating that a typical fraudster is

- "between the ages of 36 and 55 (69% of fraudsters investigated);
- predominantly male (79%), with the proportion of women on the rise at 17 percent, up from 13 percent in 2010;
- *a threat from within* (65% are employed by the company);
- holds an executive or director level position (35%);
- employed in the organisation for at least six years (38%);
- described as autocratic (18%) and are three times as likely to be regarded as friendly as not;
- esteemed, describing themselves as well respected in their organisation;
- likely to have colluded with others (62% of frauds, down just slightly from70 % in the 2013 survey); and
- motivated by personal gain (60%), greed (36%) and the sense of "because I can" (27%)".

While these statistics provide an interesting overview of the findings of the demographics of investigated fraud incidents, they don't consider the null hypothesis. That is, they may represent the broader workforce composition of the organisation, or at least organisations that are subject to higher levels of insider threat, such as financial institutions; or are more active in investigating it.

Other profiling models (see for example Butler et al., 2021) focus on the evolution of personality traits in malicious insiders. Examples of such traits include aggrandised views of their own capability and achievements, sense of entitlement, and seeking immediate gratification and satisfaction, with these behaviours evolving into more destructive behaviours such as refusing to take responsibility for their actions, workplace complacency, and rebelliousness, which can all be indicators of malicious insider activity.

While these profiles can be useful indicators of potential motivation (which we'll touch on in Chapter 6), when used in a risk context they can generate significant false positives that need to be sifted through to apply resources to treating the right risks. For example, surveilling all employees between the ages of 36 and 55 who hold an executive position is likely to be a very resource-intensive activity, which is unlikely to be cost efficient, though it may detect some malicious activity and prevent losses. Worse, this kind of activity could have exactly the opposite effect by disgruntling employees who resent the lack of trust afforded by their organisation.

These profiles are simply too generalised to be able to proportionately target risk management resources towards the risks that matter. Furthermore, people are not "systemic" by nature, an event that may make one person behave maliciously towards their organisation, may not produce the same behaviour in another person with similar mannerisms and characteristics.

Some type II examples

Failure to differentiate between inherent risk and detected risk

Insider threat, by its nature, is concealed and insidious within organisations, and not something which is done out in the open given the potential consequences to the employee. Organisations need to invest in trying to find where it occurs, to address the risk and monitor the effectiveness of the measures it puts in place. For example, if an organisation puts in place a range of controls on financial management processes to identify unauthorised transactions, then naturally we would expect that the organisation will detect more unauthorised transactions than other forms of insider threat, such as information leaks or corrupt decision-making.

As set out in Chapter 1, availability bias deals with the tendency for frequency or probability judgements to be made on the basis of the ease with which instances or occurrences can be brought to mind (Demuth, 1997). In the context of insider threat there is, therefore, a tendency to rate highly the likelihood of insider threat events that have been previously observed, while rating as less likely events that have yet to be observed.

The obvious issue with this heuristic is that insider threat events that have been observed previously have somehow been detected earlier, whether by luck or by design. In general, however, there will be strong incentives for fraudsters and corrupt officers to conceal their activities from the organisation. Therefore, an insider threat event may never be detected in the absence of some investment in detecting it in the first place. Organisations can conflate risk events that have been detected with areas of highest risk, and therefore continue to invest in controls on these risks while ignoring other threats and risks that may be going undetected.

Adding to the above, the Association of Certified Fraud Examiners (2022) reports that around 40% of identified internal fraud and corruption was detected by internal tip-offs by employees, equating to nearly three times as many cases as the next detection method. This illustrates that tip-offs remain a strong mechanism for detecting malicious insider activity; however, we could also posit that it may be a control that is over-relied upon and is subject to some weaknesses.

Bystander effect, which has been extensively studied in a range of different contexts, shows that diffusion of responsibility can and does occur (Keppeler et al., 2015). The bystander effect is also more pronounced (i.e. individuals less likely to intervene) when they believe the intervention role is held by a higher authority (e.g. police, security, or in the case of insider risk managers or specialised risk management functions) (Ajzen, 2005). Such effect, therefore, reduces the likelihood of individuals, within those contexts, from intervening in incidents or emergencies to which they bear witness. In an insider threat context, this bystander effect can act to reduce the likelihood that a perceived or actual malicious or inadvertent insider activity will be reported to the organisation.

Group conformity

Another area of extensive study, including within a criminology context, concerns the building of group cohesion and normalisation of group behaviours. This effect can reduce the likelihood of tip-offs or whistleblowing, particularly in certain kinds of organisations with strong group dynamics such as policing organisations (e.g. the so-called blue wall of silence) (Park & Blenkinsopp, 2009; Richardson et al., 2012). This research notes that one's attitude towards a particular behaviour is a function of behavioural beliefs and perceived outcome evaluation. In other words, if the individual believes that little will come from a tip-off, they are less likely to do it. Further, several empirical studies have identified an association between subjective norms and a person's intention to undertake whistleblowing (see for example Bagustianto & Nurkholis, 2017; Lee et al., 2021; Trongmateerut & Sweeney, 2013). Subjective norms in this context are defined as a person's perception of accessible referents such as family, friends, and co-workers who display or not display certain behaviours. The subjective norm is a function of normative belief and represents the motivation to comply or not comply. The normative belief is an individual's belief of whether others will agree or disagree on certain behaviours. The motivation to comply thus forms a social pressure to display or not display the behaviour.

Confirmation bias

Confirmation bias favours pre-existing beliefs or attitudes and can impact on tip-offs in several ways:

- If individuals believe the organisation, their division, or unit is at low risk of insider threat, then observed behaviour to the contrary will likely be dismissed or ignored;

- If a malicious actor is well liked within the organisation, again any behaviour indicating malicious activity is likely to be dismissed in favour of explanations that preserve that person's likeability (Plous, 1993).

Reliance on observation

Given tip-offs rely on a second person observing the malicious or inadvertent behaviour of a perpetrator, those behaviours must be readily observable. As a result, detection by tip-off is likely to be more effective at identifying types of behaviour while more concealed behaviours are less readily detected. If tip-offs are used as the main means of detecting insider threat events and these events are considered to be the most prevalent in a risk assessment process, then that risk assessment will be biased through the inherent biases and deficiencies of that control. All insider threats that are not readily detectable may therefore erroneously be treated as low likelihood resulting in a false negative: type II error.

Weaknesses in traditional assessment models

Risk assessment practice

Assessing the event

Traditional risk assessment models tend to focus on the assessment of the likelihood of a particular risk event occurring and, following ISO3100 (International Organization for Standardization, 2018) processes, make determinations of the likelihood and the consequences of the risk event occurring. This, in turn, provides the inputs to decide whether the risk is worth treating or not and what controls are appropriate to treat the risk if required. Figure 2.2 represents what such a risk assessment looks like and is probably very familiar, as it is the standard format for assessing a range of different risk types, all the way from strategic risk to operational risks like workplace health and safety and security.

Focusing on individual risk events will generally create a proliferation of events that become unwieldy for an organisation to manage systemically. This long list of different event types generally fails to consider the factors that are systemically driving the risk event. For example, in an insider threat context, there are a range of consistent motivators (as we'll expand upon in Chapter 6). If we focus on each different event separately, then we fail to look at how to intervene systemically on the key motivators – for

Risk	Cause	Likelihood	Consequence	Rating	Current Controls	Treatment	Post Treatment Rating
Credit Card Fraud	Access to credit card	possible	Medium	Moderate	Card reconciliation Credit Card Training	Credit Card usage checks	Low
Unauthorised access to information	Password leaks Failure to secure documents	possible	Medium	Moderate	Access Control Safes Security Checks	Quarterly Security Sweep	Low
Embezzlement	Financial approval powers	possible	High	High	Financial Checks	Integrity Training	Low
Industrial espionage							

FIGURE 2.2   Fraud Risk Assessment Spread Sheet Example

example, through education, setting broad cultural expectations and equipping staff to recognise behaviours that signal potential problems.

This brings us to the crux of the issue: in order to manage a risk organisations need to focus on predictors of risk (or causal factors), rather than the risk itself. The factors, which we outline in this work, operate systemically across all different risk event typologies and should therefore be identified and addressed systemically to manage risk. This contrasts with managing each risk and as an individual event, thereby spreading limited resources more thinly across risks or worse failing to manage key risks.

Risk data structure

Another aspect regarding weaknesses in traditional assessment models is the structure of the information and data collected and assembled through risk assessments. Using the first row in Figure 2.2, if we consider each element of the risk to be a different "data object" (Fowler, 2003) (using some rough definitions):

- Fraud is a wide variety of deceptive behaviours to receive an unfair or illegal gain.
- Credit card is a means by which value can be held or transferred and is the object on which the fraud is conducted.
- Control is a systemic action that reduces the likelihood or impact.
- Treatment is a control that has yet to be implemented.
- Reconciliation is a process to ensure two sets of records are in accordance with one another (often two accounts/sides of the financial ledger).

(p. 116)

As depicted in Figure 2.2, the different data objects/concepts are muddled together in this structure and do not follow logical relationships with one another. As a result, conducting detailed analysis on this set of data to determine the highest areas of risk and where investment should be directed would be challenging or can only be done at a very high level according to the subjective assessments of likelihood and consequence.

There are also some gaps in the data that we can readily identify:

- Who is the actor that can or is likely to perpetrate the fraud?
- Where is it likely to occur?
- How could it be done?

These are key questions to manage the risk and do not consistently appear in the assessment of risk. In Chapter 11, we go into considerable detail about the modelling of the risk against these different data objects.

From a traditional model to a structured model

As discussed above, while risk management is central to managing insider threat, insider threat is a complex risk; it occurs across organisational contexts and is generated through a multifaceted set of factors. Addressing this risk, therefore, requires a model that can account for its complexities and help organisations to make sense of where their greatest vulnerabilities occur and what interventions are available to them to manage the risk at the lowest possible financial and organisational cost.

Establishing the context

Breaking down the business

Insider threat occurs within an organisational context, including the purpose, value chains, functions, and structures of the organisation. To truly understand potential threats to the organisation it is critical to deconstruct the organisation and the means by which it delivers its objectives, outcomes, and value including customer value. Such decomposition is critical as it provides a complete view of the business assets (such as financial assets and information) and processes that are subject to threat by insiders.

There are several ways to disaggregate the organisation into its component parts to establish the context in which the insider threat arises, and there is no need to be fully prescriptive about how this mapping is done. Frameworks such as the Business Architecture Body of Knowledge (BIZBOK®) (Business Architecture Guild, 2022) and The Open Group Architecture Framework (The Open Group, 2006) provide guidance on how to undertake this decomposition.

For our purposes, there are a few key elements that fall under either internal or external context. These elements assist in establishing the setting in which insider threat arises within the organisation (see Figure 2.3):

- *Value streams or services:* detailing the value chains from a client perspective and/or services offered to clients. For government agencies, these "services" need to be seen in the broader regulatory context in which they exist. For example, granting a license might be seen as a service to a client, but in its broader context is there to ensure that only qualified actors can participate in an activity (such as driving).

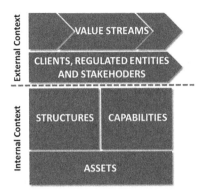

FIGURE 2.3   Disaggregation of Organisational Architecture to Establish Context for Insider Threat Risk

- *Capabilities:* In an organisational context, we'll define capabilities as the capacity and intent to achieve and sustain a desired effect or output to meet one or more strategic objectives. Capability is generated through combining fundamental inputs, such as people and skills, processes and procedures, information and data, infrastructure, and technology. Capabilities are distinct from organisational structures and functions, and are structurally agnostic, describing what the organisation must be capable of doing rather than where or how a specific instance of the capability is executed.
- *Structures:* setting out how the organisation is structured in terms of management, leadership, function, and mapping of structure to the capabilities as set out above.
- *Assets:* assets are inputs to organisational capability, but as we'll set out below and in the next chapter, they have a particular importance – they are the targets of insider threat.

A worked example

For our example, let's create an imaginary migration and border control agency with responsibilities akin to those of the Department of Homeland Security in the United States. For our example, we do not decompose every aspect of the organisation, such as its enabling and corporate capabilities and functions. However, when assessing insider risk the whole organisation needs to be modelled to enable investment in risk control to be appropriately allocated to the highest areas of threat.

Value step 1: Deciding to visit

As set out at Figure 2.4, the client value stream for this organisation commences with a person deciding that they want to visit the relevant country for some purpose, which could be

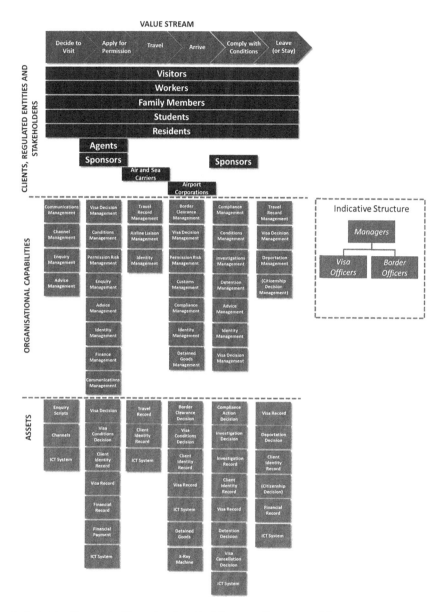

FIGURE 2.4   Example Organisation Architecture Decomposition

- as a tourist/visitor;
- to work;
- to reconnect with family who may be living there;
- to study in a local university; or
- to take up residence in the country.

The person may be supported in their decision by advertising and communications, indicating that the country is a great place to visit/study/work and are supported if they make enquiries in this regard. This, therefore, necessitates our organisation having the capability to communicate with the public and to receive and respond to enquiries and provide advice. The assets that would be used to do this might include the relevant communication channels supported by scripts to manage enquiries.

Value step 2: Requesting permission

Once the individual has decided that they wish to travel to the country, under the rules they must apply for the correct visa, which gives them permission to visit, work, study, reconnect, or reside permanently. The visa also applies policy conditions they must meet to be approved. For example, barring them from working if they are only visiting or specifying a certain level of skill in the local language if they are coming to work.

Notably, they may choose to have an agent act on their behalf to apply for the relevant visa and will pay them for providing this service. Additionally, some workers may require a sponsor to sponsor their application and confirm that they will have steady employment upon arrival.

Our exemplar organisation will, therefore, require capabilities to receive, manage, and decide upon the application, to confirm the applicant's identity, to assess applicable risks associated with the application and the applicant (e.g. the risk that they have criminal intent), to apply and record the relevant conditions, and to accept and process payments for the application. The assets involved are the visa decision itself, the client's identity record that will be created, accessed, and updated, and financial systems and records of payment.

Value step 3: Travel

Once the person has received permission to enter the country, they will travel to the country, which could be undertaken by themselves or could involve an air, sea, or road carrier to bring them to the destination. In our example, our agency retains a record of the journey taken to arrive in country, including stopovers, which assists it to make determinations of the risk presented by the person once they arrive at the destination. For example have they passed through a country affected by a disease epidemic?

In order to acquire this information, the agency liaises with air and sea carriers and updates movement records for the person, and creates risk assessment profiles. The assets called upon here are the client's identity and travel record, and the relevant information and communication technology systems where these records are stored.

Value step 4: Arrival

Once the person has arrived in the country, their visa will be examined to ensure they have the correct permission and risk profiles. This may mean additional interventions are enacted. One example could be screening them for drugs or other contraband (which if detected would be detained and stored). Once this is complete, a decision is made by the immigration officer on whether to clear them for entry into the country. If they are not cleared, they may be turned around or detained. In our example these activities may take place in an air or sea port, necessitating cooperation with the airport corporation or seaport authority.

Value step 5: Comply with conditions

Once the person is in the country, they must comply with the conditions applied on their visa. These conditions may be generalised, such as not engaging in criminal activities, or specific ones applied to their visa, such as refraining from working if they are on a student visa. The agency undertakes compliance campaigns to remind visa holders of their obligations and may launch investigations into suspect non-compliance. If a person is found to have not complied with their visa conditions, their visa permission may be cancelled and they may be detained.

To manage these activities, the organisation must have capabilities to undertake compliance activities, including campaigns, to undertake investigations, to detain people and their possessions, and to make decisions to cancel visas. The assets involved at this stage include decisions to launch an investigation, to cancel the visa, to detain the person and would involve accessing the client identity and visa decision records.

Value step 6: Leave (or stay)

In the final value step, either the person voluntarily leaves the country once their stay is complete or if they have failed to comply with the relevant conditions or have committed criminal acts they may be deported from the country. *Alternatively, the person may decide to stay and apply for citizenship, but this would involve describing a whole new value stream and domain of our imaginary organisation.*

In all but the last scenario above (italicised), the agency will require the capability to update the visa record to show that the person has departed or will need to be able to affect the deportation of the person back to their country of origin. The assets involved here include the deportation decision, the client record, and the visa record.

Application to other organisations and scenarios

While we have described a particular kind of organisation, the component parts that make up our imaginary organisation will apply to any real-world organisation, in both commercial and government sectors.

Briefly, for example:

- A financial institution would have a value stream around mortgage finance, which might start with a person deciding to purchase a home and end with the final discharge of the loan. This would involve capabilities around the grant of the mortgage, the management and reconciliation of repayments, and the discharge. Assets would be the finances themselves, the deed title, the account, and so forth.
- An environmental regulator would have a value stream around land-use applications, which might start with deciding to use natural land for a purpose such as farming or commerce. This would involve capabilities to conduct environmental impact assessments and make decisions on compliance or non-compliance.
- Even policing organisations have value streams around preserving social cohesion and minimising economic and social harm. These value streams require capabilities to communicate, investigate, arrest, and develop briefs of prosecution.

Assessing the risk: focusing on drivers of risk

As touched on above, assessing risk events individually can create unwieldy information that can arguably make it more challenging for organisations to target and intervene on the right risks. Frameworks such as the Cumulative Act Effect (or Swiss cheese) model (Reason, 1990) demonstrate that the realisation of a risk is generally through the interrelationship and "lining up" of a cumulative set of causal factors. So, for example, in aircraft safety, the focus should not be on air crashes as the risk. But, instead, a focus on the causal factors that result in air crashes, such as instrument failures, pilot error, and weather events, must be invested into how to avoid or mitigate these causal factors.

Insider threat risk drivers

In an insider threat context, we have identified a key set of drivers which are consistently involved in creating insider threats and can result in the realisation of risk of fraud, corruption, or other harm to the organisation. Within the organisational context of value streams, capabilities, structures, and assets, there are six established drivers (see Figure 2.5):

1 **A role/perpetrator**: roles within the organisation empower people to make certain decisions and access assets, including physical and information assets.

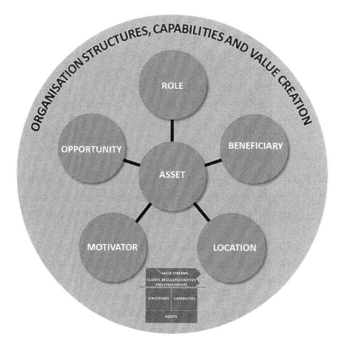

FIGURE 2.5   Systemic Drivers of Insider Risk

2 **Assets**: Organisational assets include the following:

  a Discretionary decisions assets: these decisions form the basis of the value the organisation delivers, for example the decision to grant or remove a permission, to arrest or not arrest.

  b Information assets: which are created, accessed, modified, or eliminated in the course of business.

  c Physical assets: including equipment and financial assets.

3 **A beneficiary**: The beneficiary of the insider activity may be the perpetrator themselves but may also be an external actor. For example in many corruption scenarios an insider is groomed or induced to commit a malicious act (Liebling et al., 2011).

4 **Opportunity factors**: A core element of our model articulates, in a systemic and consistent way, the factors that provide an opportunity to the perpetrator to commit the insider activity, whether deliberately or inadvertently. We will go into much more detail in Chapter 4. In brief, opportunities are created as a result of the way that decision processes are undertaken or assets are handled within the organisation.

5 **Motivating factors**: For deliberate and malicious acts there are factors that motivate insiders to act against their organisation and for their own benefit. These factors create pressure on them, induce them to act, and help

them to rationalise the reason that they have chosen to act maliciously. We go into this in more detail in Chapter 6.

6 **Locations**: The location where a decision is made or an asset stored can be a relevant risk factor, particularly for large organisations, which may have distributed locations that undertake their processes using local arrangements. As a result, different locations may have different levels of exposure to insider threat.

Risk, control, and investment

To close this chapter, let's briefly touch on the relationship between the assessment of risk and the investment of resources to control and manage insider threat. This is another area we will explore in more depth in subsequent chapters.

As we have outlined above, risk assessment allows us to identify the causal processes or factors which increase the likelihood and consequences of a malicious or inadvertent act. If we take a systemic approach, we can make sense of where those risks will occur relative to the organisational context. To manage the risk that we have now identified, we must implement treatments and controls that will mitigate either the likelihood or the consequence of the risk. These controls require resources to fulfil. Therefore, in a world of limited resources, it is important that the investment in controls is targeted at the highest areas of risk and the most effective and efficient controls so that each dollar is expended to achieve the maximum impact in terms of reduction of insider threat.

Back to our example . . .

We will expand upon this in later chapters, but let's go back to our imaginary organisation(s) to illustrate. Imagine that criminal entities are more likely to target a particular type of visa to facilitate drug importation, whereas fraud by students who don't meet the qualifications for study in a country would target short-stay student visas. Arguably, given the higher social impact of drug importation, managing insider risk in working visas is of higher value than managing the same risk in the student visa class: because the social impact of unqualified students drawing on education resources is arguably lower. Equally, let's imagine the causative opportunity factors are roughly equal, therefore, resulting in an equivalent likelihood that the different classes of decision will be targeted, albeit by different actors. In this case if we could not treat both risks, it would be logical to preferentially invest in the one that prevents corruption for the purposes of facilitating the drug trade. Here, the potential losses are vastly different and, therefore, the return on investment calculus influences our policy decision. We will continue this exploration in the following chapter.

Chapter key points

- A risk-based approach enables an organisation to identify and target where to intervene to manage risk.
- The approach to assessing risk needs to be structured and systemic; otherwise it can be affected by biases and errors which affect its accuracy and utility.
- To establish the context in which insider threat occurs, it is critical to decompose the organisation and its mechanisms for delivering value.

References

Ajzen, I. (2005). *Attitudes, personality, behaviour* (2nd ed.). Open University Press.

Association of Certified Fraud Examiners. (2022). *Occupational fraud 2022: A report to the nations*. https://legacy.acfe.com/report-to-the-nations/2022/

Aven, T. (2015). *Risk analysis*. Wiley.

Bagustianto, R., & Nurkholis, N. (2017). Factors affecting the interest of civil servants (Pns) to carry out whistle-blowing actions (studies on PNS BPK RI). *Equity, Journal of Economics and Finance, 19*(2), 276.

Business Architecture Guild. (2022). *A guide to the business architecture body of knowledge (BIZBOK® Guide)*. https://www.businessarchitectureguild.org/page/002

Butler, L. C., Graham, A., Fisher, B. S., Henson, B., & Reyns, B. W. (2021). Examining the effect of perceived responsibility on online bystander intervention, target hardening, and inaction. *Journal of Interpersonal Violence*. https://doi.org/10.1177/08862605211055088

Demuth, S. (1997). Understanding the "loner": Delinquency and the peer, family, and school relations of adolescents with no close friendships. *Youth & Society, 35*(3), 366–392.

Dionne, G. (2013). Risk management: History, definition and critique. *Risk Management and Insurance Review, 147*(1), 147–166.

Fowler, M. (2003). *Patterns of enterprise application architecture*. Addison Wesley.

Gelles, M. (2016). *Insider threat: Prevention, detection, mitigation and deterrence*. Butterworth-Heinemann.

International Organization for Standardization. (2018). *Risk management*. ISO.

Keppeler, V. E., Sluder, R. D., & Alpert, G. P. (2015). Breeding deviant conformity: The ideology and culture of police. In R. Dunham & G. P. Alpert (Eds.), *Critical issues in policing: Contrmporary readings* (7th ed.). Waveland Press, Inc.

KPMG. (2023). *Globsl profiles of the fraudster: Technology enables and weak controls fuel the fraud*. https://kpmg.com/be/en/home/insights/2016/05/global-profiles-of-the-fraudster.html

Lee, H., Kang, M. M., & Kim, S. Y. (2021). A psychological process of bureaucratic whistleblowing: Applying the theory of planned behavior. *The American Review of Public Administration, 51*(5), 374–392.

Liebling, A., Price, D., & Shefer, G. (2011). *The prison officer*. Willan.

Manning, M., Johnson, S., Tilley, N., Wong, G., & Vorsina, M. (2016). *Economic analysis and efficiency in policing, criminal justice and crime reduction: What works?* Palgrave.

The Open Group. (2006). *Welcome to TOGAF: The open group architecture framework*. https://pubs.opengroup.org/architecture/togaf8-doc/arch/

Park, H., & Blenkinsopp, J. (2009). Whistleblowing as planned behavior – a survey of South Korean police officer. *Journal of Bussiness Ethics, 85*(4), 545–556.

Plous, S. (1993). *The psychology of judgment and decision making*. McGraw-Hill.

Reason, J. (1990). The contribution of latent human failures to the breakdown of complex systems. *Philosophical Transactions of the Royal Society of London, 327*(1241), 475–484.

Richardson, B. K., Wang, Z., & Hall, C. A. (2012). Blowing the whistle againts Greek hazing: The theory of reasoned action as a framework for reporting intentions. *Communication Studies, 6*(2), 172–193.

Trongmateerut, P., & Sweeney, J. T. (2013). The influence of subjective norms on whistle-blowing: A cross-cultural investigation. *Journal of Business Ethics, 112*, 437–451.

3

ORGANISATIONAL ASSETS AT THE CENTRE

Introduction

Insider risk is often explored in general terms, with a focus on the perpetrator of the corrupt or fraudulent act. For example, the Association of Certified Fraud Examiners in its Report to the Nations (2018) provides a generalised profile for fraud perpetrators. We argue, instead, that such profiles are too generic to provide significant value when mitigating insider threat. Organisations, instead, need to focus on understanding and categorising their organisational assets to better understand where and when insider risk will present itself and where it will create the greatest harm.

In this chapter we propose three forms of organisational assets, which are the subject of insider risk: (i) administrative decisions; (ii) information; and (iii) physical and intangible assets. We also propose ways of systemically classifying these assets to enable organisations to better understand which targets are of greatest value to an organisation. In the context of border control and financial institutions, the complexity of the services and products of these institutions often means that getting a holistic view of the environment is challenging. But this also means that a greater opportunity exists to implement a systematic approach to contextualise and understand the factors that impact upon these institutions.

Why are assets important?

As we touched on in Chapter 2, assets are an input or means by which organisations deliver the value they produce, whether in a commercial sense to a client or customer or in a government context to the broader public and the nation.

DOI: 10.4324/9781003055716-3

The problem from an insider threat perspective is that these same assets can create alternative forms of value to insiders themselves or to external entities, such as value to criminal endeavours or market competitors. Financial and physical assets will also have inherent value on the market and could be used or resold at a profit. In addition to being illegitimately used to create value for other actors, these assets can also be used by insiders to undermine and weaken the organisation's achievement of its own purpose. For example, these assets could enable polluters to contravene environmental legislation, providing competitors with access to critical intellectual property or sabotaging critical infrastructure.

Another reason that assets are crucial to analysing and protecting organisations from insider threat is that, unlike people/perpetrators, an organisation's assets can be consistently and repeatedly classified in terms of their value to the organisation's mission and their potential value to internal and external actors.

It would be extremely difficult if not impossible, and very likely a negative return on investment, to protect all the organisation's assets. As such, there needs to be a risk-based methodology for determining the importance of the asset to the organisational mission and determining its level of exposure to threat (Gelles, 2016).

Core asset types

There are three types of assets which contribute to an organisation's overall objectives, value streams, and capabilities (as set out in Chapter 2) and which are subject to insider threat:

- *Discretionary decisions* that determine how, when, and whether to provide products, benefits, detriments, and services to stakeholders.
- *Information:* The body of knowledge the organisation holds about its operations, strategies, clients, stakeholders, and intellectual property.
- *Physical, intangible, and financial assets:* The physical, intangible, and financial assets that enable the organisation to deliver its value.

Decisions in context

Decision-making is at the heart of organisation, enabling the employees/agents of the organisation to pursue the goals of the organisation as a whole and solve problems that impact on its goals (Witzel & Warner, 2015). In many circumstances, decision-making is optimised through rules and processes that create consistency in decisions (Monahan, 2000) while retaining the necessary discretion to fit decisions to specific circumstances.

Decisions in a government regulatory setting

Governments regulate to intervene in private markets to produce policy outcomes which might not otherwise occur (Orbach, 2012) and mitigate risks to economies, protect social order and the environment, and minimise harms to all, which may eventuate if the market were left unfettered (Sparrow, 2011). Broad global and domestic market forces (such as globalisation, middle class economic growth, climate change, global infrastructure development) combine with the interests of market actors to create strategic risks which create effects at national and international levels. The role of the organisation according to Sparrow (2012) is to

> identify harms, risks, dangers, or threats of one kind or another, and then either eliminate them, reduce their frequency, mitigate their effects, prevent them, or suppress them, and, by so doing, provide citizens higher levels of safety and security.
>
> *(p. 345)*

Governments, therefore, create legislative obligations or incentives for market actors to modify market behaviours and mitigate risk. They often establish regulatory agencies that are granted with the powers to restrict access to the market and to ensure the conditions of participation in the market are adhered to or to distribute those incentives according to the policy rules established by government. Compliance with the rules of the market is achieved by regulators through the application of a set of graduated preventative, detective, and responsive risk controls which are underpinned by decisions delegated by law or enshrined in internal policy. The lifecycle of government intervention in market to solve strategic, economic, social, and environmental risk is depicted in Figure 3.1.

Example 1: Prudential regulators mitigate the risk of economic and social harm which may arise from the failure of financial markets to manage financial risk arising from loans, insurance, and retirement plans/pensions/ superannuation. They do this by licensing businesses to operate (effectively providing or denying or permission outlining conditions to enter the market) and setting and enforcing requirements on how they govern and manage prudential risk to ensure they can make good on financial promises made to their beneficiaries. Licences exist to mitigate potential risks such as the Global Financial Crisis of 2007–2008.

Notable decisions:

- Grant or annulment of license
- Application of fine or other detriment for non-compliance

Example 2: Carbon energy market regulators mitigate the dual risks of excess carbon in the atmosphere while balancing the economic cost and shocks of transitioning fundamental energy markets to new technology. They do this through a range of mechanisms, but in market-based systems, it is by creating a price signal for pollution, requiring reporting on emissions production

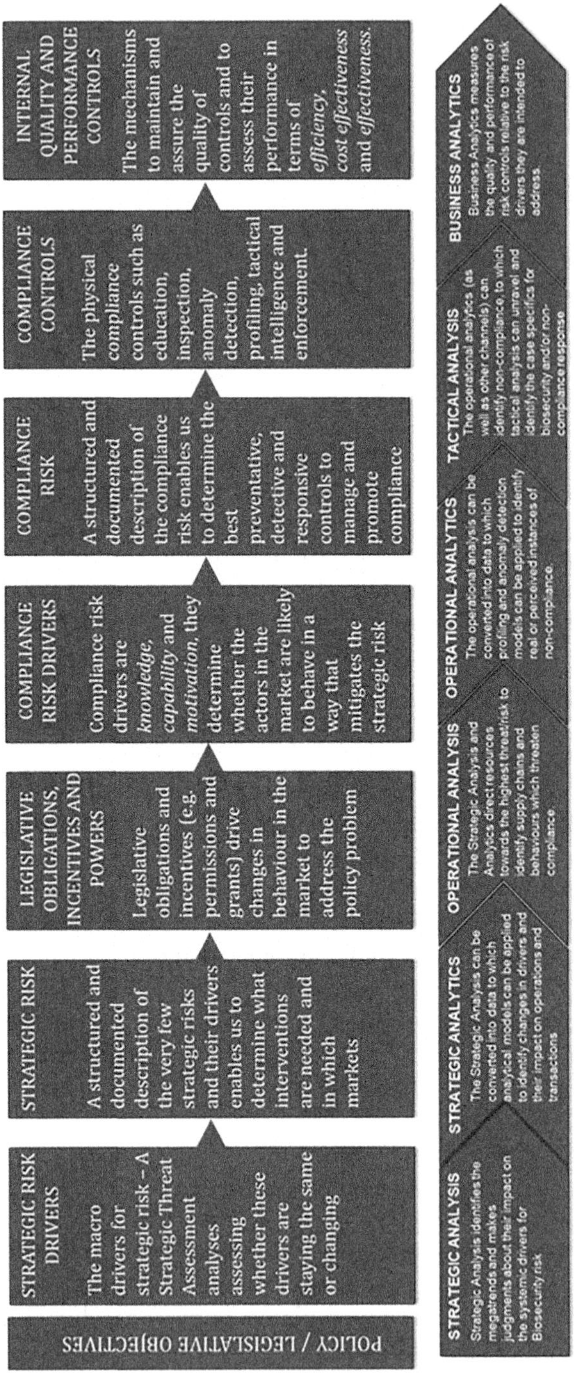

POLICY / LEGISLATIVE OBJECTIVES

STRATEGIC RISK DRIVERS

The macro drivers for strategic risk – A Strategic Threat Assessment analyses assessing whether these drivers are staying the same or changing

STRATEGIC RISK

A structured and documented description of the very few strategic risks and their drivers enables us to determine what interventions are needed and in which markets

LEGISLATIVE OBLIGATIONS, INCENTIVES AND POWERS

Legislative obligations and incentives (e.g. permissions and grants) drive changes in behaviour in the market to address the policy problem

COMPLIANCE RISK DRIVERS

Compliance risk drivers are *knowledge, capability* and *motivation*, they determine whether the actors in the market are likely to behave in a way that mitigates the strategic risk

COMPLIANCE RISK

A structured and documented description of the compliance risk enables us to determine the best preventative, detective and responsive controls to manage and promote compliance

COMPLIANCE CONTROLS

The physical compliance controls such as education, inspection, anomaly detection, profiling, tactical intelligence and enforcement.

INTERNAL QUALITY AND PERFORMANCE CONTROLS

The mechanisms to maintain and assure the quality of controls and to assess their performance in terms of *efficiency, cost effectiveness* and *effectiveness*.

STRATEGIC ANALYSIS

Strategic Analysis identifies the megatrends and makes judgments about their impact on the systemic drivers for Biosecurity risk

STRATEGIC ANALYTICS

The Strategic Analysis can be converted into data to which analytical models can be applied to identify changes in drivers and their impact on operations and transactions

OPERATIONAL ANALYSIS

The Strategic Analysis and Analytics direct resources towards the highest threat/risk to identify supply chains and behaviours which threaten compliance

OPERATIONAL ANALYTICS

The operational analysis can be converted into data to which profiling and anomaly detection models can be applied to identify real or perceived instances of non-compliance

TACTICAL ANALYSIS

The operational analytics (as well as other channels) can identify non-compliance, to which tactical analysis can unravel and identify the case specifics for biosecurity and/or non-compliance response

BUSINESS ANALYTICS

Business Analytics measures the quality and performance of risk controls relative to the risk drivers they are intended to address.

FIGURE 3.1   Public Sector Value System

and abatement, maintaining the trade platform for carbon-equivalent units/ instruments, and licensing participants to engage in the market.

Notable decisions:

- Grant or annulment of access to carbon market platform
- Rescind carbon equivalent unit
- Application of fine for incorrect reporting of emissions

Example 3: Border agencies mitigate the economic, social, and environmental risks which might arise in movement of people, animals, and goods across the border were uncontrolled. They regulate the permissions to enter the country, including visas and important licensing, detect and deter illicit and illegal products from crossing the border, and apply tariffs which protect domestic pricing for goods produced locally. They may also administer anti-dumping legislation, equally to protect domestic pricing and competition.

Notable decisions:

- Grant or cancellation of visa or import permit
- Grant or refusal of entry for people, goods, or animals
- Detain goods, persons, or animals
- Destroy illicit goods
- Deport person
- Refer to law enforcement for criminal investigation

Regulated markets are, therefore, inherently contested environments, with natural market forces incentivising non-compliant behaviour which can create a competitive advantage, by potentially reducing the regulatory cost on business and/or time to market. The decisions a regulator makes in respect of entry to the market, and in respect of compliance with market conditions, are therefore very valuable to market participants, including in many circumstances criminal entities. There are strong incentives to bypass regulatory controls, and if it is challenging to bypass controls externally then entities may shift and displace their tactics towards influencing the decision-makers who exercise those controls within regulatory organisations (Rowe et al., 2013) (Figure 3.2).

Depending on the breadth and size of the regulatory organisation, these decisions are likely to be delegated to operational levels within the organisation, with internal policy frameworks governing the evidentiary requirements and processes and recording practices for decisions. Aspects of the decision-making framework may also be enshrined in the enacting legislation or general principles of administrative law.

TACTICAL DISPLACEMENT

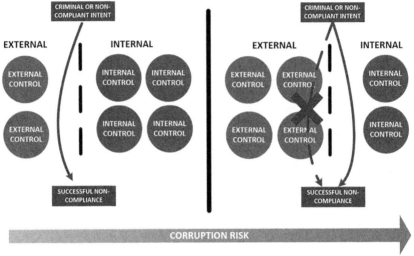

FIGURE 3.2 Tactical Displacement: Insider Threat

Given the mission of these organisations is to mitigate market risks, to manage the insider threat to its objectives, it must first define which of its decision assets is most critical to achieving the objects of its regulatory framework.

Decisions in a commercial setting

Decision-making is no less of a critical organisational asset for commercial entities as it enables organisations to define and execute commercial strategies, provide products and services to clients for profit, purchase inputs to production or services, manage debt, and retain solvency. Decisions are subject to several key elements, including the commercial activity undertaken, issues regarding commercial compliance, and enabling decisions.

Commercial activities

In a commercial setting, the decision-making context ranges from simple agreements to providing products and services to clients or establishing supply arrangements for stock and production inputs. In other more complex commercial organisations which may have, multifarious investment decisions, complex supply chain agreements, and may provide services in the context of high uncertainty and possible losses, decisions are underpinned by organisational risk management frameworks designed to protect the organisation from loss. For example, the decision to provide a loan, whether secured or unsecured, carries a level of risk for both the client and the lender. As such, financial risk frameworks underpin these decisions, which are nonetheless delegated to officers to make in accordance with those frameworks. These decision frameworks consider different uncertain factors including future market conditions, the clients future earning potential and regulatory provisions. Organisational incentives such as sign-up bonuses can incentivise officers to take ever more risky loan decisions to boost their own sales and earning potential.

We will not attempt to classify the wide variety of commercial decisions However, the above example illustrates that decision assets are no less at threat within commercial organisations than in government ones. Therefore, to adopt a systemic approach to managing insider threat it is equally important for commercial organisations to stocktake the key decisions which they make in order to further their commercial objectives.

Commercial compliance

In addition to decisions which are at threat in the course of normal business, regulatory frameworks are established to treat market risk to economies, social order, and the environment. The provision of commercial goods and services is, therefore, constrained by rules imposed through legislation and potential sanctions to organisations that contravene those regulations deliberately or inadvertently. The flipside of regulatory decision-making is the decisions by entities to provide or restrict services in accordance with those regulations. From an insider threat perspective, the threat arises where the organisation's intent to comply does not align with incentives and controls over its workforce. Therefore, individuals may decide to contravene compliant decision-making for their own profit motives. Following are three examples to illustrate this point.

Mitigation of money laundering and terrorism financing

To reduce the incidence of money laundering and terrorism financing, legislation is established that requires financial institutions to "Know Your Customer" (KYC) – essentially an obligation for the institution to confirm the identity of their clients. For commercial entities, the ownership of those entities requires the reporting of suspicious transactions to regulators to mitigate the risk that financial platforms are used as a means of laundering the profits of criminal activity. Financial institutions are not only bound by KYC obligations but a series of other international standards that aim to protect a country's financial system. The Financial Action Task Force (FATF) provide a set of recommendations, articulating the international standard, for countries to follow to bolster their anti-money laundering and counter terrorism financing strategies (Financial Action Task Force, 2019). These strategies can be disaggregated into 7 areas that now make up a series of 40 recommendations: (i) AML/CTF policies and coordination; (ii) ML and confiscation; (iii) terrorist financing and financing of proliferation; (iv) preventive measures; (v) transparency and beneficial ownership of legal persons and arrangements; (vi) powers and responsibilities of competent authorities and other institutional measures; and (vii) international cooperation (Manning et al., 2020). KYC processes falls under category (v) and are undertaken by financial services employees in accordance with their own internal policies. Theoretically, it would be possible for those employees to dishonestly grant KYC and expose the entity to the threat of prosecution for non-compliance with KYC requirements.

Prudential regulation

Prudential regulations prohibit loan providers from granting loan products to clients who are unlikely to be capable of repaying them, to protect both the client and the financial institution from excessive financial risk. It would however be possible for the loan officer to contravene these rules and grant a person access to a loan to benefit their sales target and win a signing bonus. The seriousness of this potential risk is highlighted by the extent to which the sub-prime mortgage crisis precipitated the ensuing Global Financial Crisis of 2007–2008 (Iannuzzi & Berardi, 2010; McKibbin & Stoeckel, 2009).

Customs brokers

Customs brokerages are responsible for facilitating trade and customs compliance on behalf of importers in accordance with import conditions and national tariff arrangements. An individual broker within a broader brokerage organisation could be tempted to facilitate the import of illicit goods and avoid cargo inspections or tariff duties by misdeclaring goods. For example, a United States customs broker was indicted for fraud in relation to the declaration of duty-free goods and funnelling funds to his own account (United States Attorney-General's Office Central District of California, 2023); in a separate case two customs brokers allegedly facilitated the importation of methamphetamine through their expertise of the customs systems (Herald Sun, 2019).

Enabling decisions

The final class of decisions we'll touch on cross the boundaries between commercial and government agencies, the corporate and enabling decisions that enable an organisation to sustainably operate as an organisation. We briefly describe these in Table 3.1, disaggregating into five decision types: (1) human resources – decisions relating to the hiring, conditions, and termination of the organisation's employees; (2) procurement and contracts – decisions to enter a market, select vendors, and enter commercial arrangements with individuals and other organisations; (3) benefits, entitlements, and grants – awarding, refusing, or terminating benefits and entitlements for employees, contractors, and other recipients; (4) financial and audit – decisions relating to the organisations' finance allocations, such as payment of invoices;

TABLE 3.1 Enabling Decisions Typologies

Decision Type	Description	Examples
Human Resources	Decisions relating to the hiring and termination of the organisation's employees. These decisions can be undermined by nepotism, cronyism, or biases or could be used to infiltrate the organisation.	• Hiring • Job offer • Termination • Performance review
Procurement and Contracts	Decisions to enter approach market, select vendors, and enter commercial arrangements with individuals and organisations. Conflicts of interest and corruption can result in a non-competitive selection of vendors.	• Procurement plan • Vendor selection • Set contract conditions • Contract termination
Benefits, Entitlements, and Grants	Awarding, refusing, or terminating benefits and entitlements for employees, contractors, and other recipients.	• Bonuses • Overtime • Incentives
Financial and Audit	Decisions relating to the organisations' finance allocations, such as payment of invoices.	• Invoice payments • Reconciliations • Audit findings
Grants	Awarding, refusing, or terminating conditional grants or accepting that the conditions of the grant have been met.	• Awarding grant • Refusing grant • Terminating grant • Accepting grant Conditions have been met

and (5) awarding, refusing, or terminating conditional grants or accepting that the conditions of the grant have been met.

Object-decision relationship

The final aspect of decision assets that must be considered to create a standard classification that can enable better targeting of insider threat is to set out the relationship between the decision and the "object" of that decision. Decisions themselves examined in the abstract are a choice of

- applying a positive outcome;
- applying a negative outcome;
- later rescinding the decision;
- overturning that rescission;
- the omission to apply any of these decisions; and
- the application of the decision in circumstances in which it should not be applied.

The object of the decision is the "what" that those decisions apply to:

- Any kind of permission (object) can be granted, refused, or terminated or the termination overturned. For example, border clearance (object), the act of permitting a person or a good to enter national borders can either be granted or refused, or once it has been granted it could be terminated or if terminated that termination of permission could be overturned. Equally the permission to participate in a carbon market (object), a quite different decision asset, can equally be granted, refused, and so forth. The same is true for any permission type "object".
- Any kind of condition (object) can be applied, not applied, or removed or the removal overturned. For example, the conditions on a visa could be applied or not applied; they could be removed or that removal overturned. Similarly, tariffs on goods could be applied to those goods, not applied (in both scenarios, either properly or improperly), and so forth.
- Any kind of information, report, or statement (object) can be accepted or not accepted, or the acceptance later removed or that removal later overturned. For example, if a grant or contract requires evidence that certain activities have been undertaken, the report or statement of that activity could be accepted, not accepted, and so forth.
- Any kind of instrument, security, or benefit can be granted, not granted, or rescinded, and so forth. For example, granting a carbon equivalent unit in response to abatement activities can be granted or refused, or at a later date rescinded.

The above examples are naturally repetitive, which illustrates that they are systemically applicable across a range of decision-object relationships across very different organisations.

The value of setting out these structures is that it provides a consistency in the objects and the decision types, which enhances analysis and understanding of the relative importance and threats to different objects and decisions. As a practical example, a visa could be improperly granted to people who do not qualify or alternatively; they could be improperly cancelled rendering a person an unlawful non-citizen – the object is the same but the decisions are quite different and, in reality, may be subject to very different decision controls. The question for the organisation is then, Which of these two decision types contribute most to the organisation's objectives or, if improperly made, would result in the greatest level of harm?

With this relationship established we can determine both which decision objects in aggregate are most at threat and for that object which decision type is most at threat or would result in greatest harm.

Information and data

Arguably information and data are the new commodities of the 21st century, with an estimated 90% of the world's data created in the last two years (U.S. Chamber of Commerce Foundation, 2022). The growth of information and data production is still growing, arguably exponentially. Data has become a key asset for organisations to create and multiply value, enhancing their understanding of market demand, competition, performance, and enabling more adaptable organisations. For government, information and data collection enable greater refinement in policy analysis to provide better and nuanced inputs to developing policies to address a multitude of economic, social, and environmental harms (Yang et al., 2023). Equally, big data and modern analysis and analytics techniques (such as machine learning) are enabling better and more targeted interventions to manage regulatory risks at a transactional level (Jarmin & O'Hara, 2016), feats which would not have been possible using traditional risk management mechanisms (Yeung, 2017).

These data are, therefore, of significant value to organisations in pursuit of their objectives. These same data and information may equally be of great value to outsiders who can use information to inhibit the objectives of the organisation or, independently, benefit from the information for illicit or criminal purposes.

Information typologies

Like organisational decisions, prioritising information assets requires the classification of information types into logical groupings, which enable relative importance to be assessed and modelled. Table 3.2 provides guidance on potential classifications.

Semantics and data models

Table 3.2 represents a high-level classification for information and data types, to provide a logical basis for assessing the level of exposure to insider threat and the level of harm that would be caused by the realisation of those threats. It provides the framing for management-level discussions on exposures and risks to business. However, in order for information threats and risk controls to be understood at a granular level, there is a need to align risk models with the data models, taxonomies, and ontologies of the organisation.

In a data science context, semantics refers to the understanding of meaning and structure in information without concern as to where in the enterprise it may be stored (e.g. which systems or databases). The scope of semantics might be roughly described as the combination of the following:

- *Terms and concepts:* The concepts/objects used in the business, the terms used to describe them, and the definitions. Visa, license, report, approval, assessment, client are examples.
- *Taxonomies:* The relationships and hierarchies from general to specific – such as reports and financial reports.
- *Relationships:* The relationships between different concepts. For example, a client may submit a report on a date. At the data level, these relationships are set out in general terms representing all permutations of these potential relationships.
- *Ontologies*: These set out domain-specific concepts, terms, and relationships particular to a part of the business, field of study, or world. For example, ontologies for biology versus economics, using the same terms and relationships for different meanings.

Within an organisation the development and organisation of these concepts is generally undertaken in order to maximise the business value delivered from data captured and held by the organisation or to assist with streamlining and integration of information and communication technology systems. From an insider threat management perspective, this work (where it exists in mature organisations) provides a rich structure for organising the key organisational concepts which are key to managing risk. That is, key pieces of information, such as personal information and commercial information, will already be captured in such a data model. Rather than creating new semantics for insider threat management, it is better practice to re-use the concepts and models of the enterprise, thereby maintaining consistency with other concerns. The benefits of such an approach are:

- Semantics are used for other purposes within the organisation, for example, corporate level reporting and risk management. This provides for

TABLE 3.2 Information Typologies

Information Typology	Description	Threat	Examples
Personal Information	Information directly or indirectly pertaining to an individual or class of individuals	Personal information can be utilised for a range of criminal purposes including identity theft, blackmail, and sale on black market platforms. In a range of jurisdictions personal information is also protected under legislation, creating penalties for unauthorised disclosure at an individual and organisational level.	• Government identifiers • Account numbers • Identity details • Personal history • Photos • Demographic data • Health information
Operational Information	Information pertaining to the mode of operation, capabilities, processes, and activities of the organisation.	This information can be used to identify vulnerabilities in an organisation's strategies and tactics to gain an advantage. This could relate to bypassing government regulation, gaining competitive advantage or military superiority. In many jurisdictions this information carries special secrecy protections under law, creating penalties for individuals and organisations for unauthorised disclosure.	• Procedural information • Records of activity and action • Risk assessment inputs • Strategies and plans • Concepts of operation • Countermeasure information • Control placement (e.g. sensors, CCTV) • Building plans

(Continued)

TABLE 3.2 (Continued)

Information Typology	Description	Threat	Examples
Organisational Information	Information pertaining to the structures, functions, and conditions of the organisation.	This information can be used to identify sources of formal and informal power and influence within the organisation and identify points of disruption (e.g. restructures/bankruptcy).	• Internal structures • Personnel • Centres of power/influence • Governance structures and practices
Intelligence Information	Information pertaining to the organisation's assessments of the capability and intent of its competitors and adversaries.	This information can be used to take a strategic or tactical advantage over the organisation by understanding its perceptions of its own threat environment. In many jurisdictions, severe legal penalties exist for disclosing national intelligence information.	• Intelligence assessments • Intelligence priorities • Threat discovery plans • Intelligence sources/collections • Targets
Financial Information	Information pertaining to the entity's financial records, ledgers, and accounting.	This information can be used to gain a financial advantage or to enable theft or embezzlement of financial assets.	• Accounts • Tax information • Salary information • Ledgers • Statements

(Continued)

TABLE 3.2 (Continued)

Information Typology	Description	Threat	Examples
Commercial Information	Information pertaining to commercial offerings, products, and services of vendors, partners, clients, regulated entities, and stakeholders.	This information can be used to gain competitive advantage over external commercial entities. In many jurisdictions, this information when collected in the course of business or government activity is protected by law and unauthorised disclosure may carry penalties for individuals and organisations.	• Product information • Production and supply chain information • Pricing structures and schedules • Trade volumes • Business plans • Marketing strategies • Business models
Intellectual Property (including R&D)	Creations for which exclusive rights are or would be recognised.	This information can be used to gain competitive advantage in the marketplace against the organisation or partners/vendors.	• Plans • Methodologies • Product designs • Source code • Templates • Software
Market Competition Information	Information which is likely to create fluctuations in pricing for publicly listed commodities, stocks, and securities.	This information can be used to facilitate insider trading, often due to access prior to the information being made publicly available to all traders.	• Statements and forecasts • Government statistics • Pricing adjustments • Product performance • Losses • Mergers, acquisitions, and restructures • Bankruptcy information

easier communication of insider threat information to audiences already familiar with key information terms and definitions.

- The semantics are often mapped to databases and applications. This provides a ready alignment for undertaking information risk assessments as detailed in forthcoming chapters. For example, understanding the application or database security controls will provide immediate visibility of the level of risk associated with those data elements held within that database or application.
- The modelled relationships between concepts can provide additional insights on the level of risk associated not only with the individual information object, but with the related elements and ontologies associated with those information objects. For example the concept of "name" on its own may have little risk; once it is associated with other concepts such as "address", "date of birth", or "biometric" the information becomes more valuable and hence at higher risk of compromise.

Information threats

The threats to an organisation's information may, *prima facie*, appear to be highly multivariate, based upon the diversity of case types associated with the improper access and use of information (such as those set out in the following).

At a systemic level, the threats to information can be reduced to six core typologies:

1 *Improper collection (or omission):* Improperly collecting information. For example, where the collection of such information and data is governed by legislation, rules, and policies, or the reverse, a failure to collect the relevant information as required.
2 *Improper creation (or omission):* Improperly creating records which could be used to obfuscate other improper activities or misdirect operational activity or failure to create records in accordance with business processes and requirements. This might again be done to obfuscate other activities or protect a person against whom a record might be made.
3 *Improper storage:* Storage of information in a manner which contravenes rules and policy, either deliberately or inadvertently, contributing to the loss of the information.
4 *Improper modification:* Improper modification of a record or component of a record.
5 *Improper disclosure and use (including theft):* Improper disclosure of information or data to a third party or alternatively theft (which is effectively self-disclosure). We combine into our definition the use of the information insofar as the value of the theft or disclosure is only realised when

the information is used for a purpose. When considering the harms of disclosure, it is important to consider the uses the information would/could be put to.

6. *Improper destruction:* Improper destruction of information, data, and records, including corruption of data files or otherwise rendering the information inaccessible.

These typologies provide a consistent framing for analysing threats across the breadth of the organisation's information holdings and aggregation of threat information to identify key vulnerabilities. For example, there may be higher levels of vulnerability of destruction of information across information holdings, while disclosure may be tightly controlled. The ability to draw a line of sight across vulnerabilities can enable more systemic treatments and controls.

Code: the nexus between decision and information

Since the advent of commercially available computing, ICT support to business and government has grown exponentially, initially to support humans to compute simple problems and to store data and results consistently and accessibly. Recent growth in computing power and technology has enabled computer applications to take a more prominent role in decision-making, making simple or low-risk decisions, and assessing risk prior to referral to a human decision-maker. In addition, the advent of machine learning and development of artificial intelligence has improved our ability to make nuanced assessments and decisions which often exceed human capability.

Underpinning the ability of computer programmes to execute actions and make decisions is the application's code base, a sequence of instructions which can be executed or interpreted by a computer (Silberschatz, 1994). Application code, particularly proprietary code, is an asset that, by its very nature, crosses the boundaries between information asset and decision asset and from a threat/risk perspective needs to be considered from both perspectives.

As an information asset

Computer code can fulfil a range of functions as pure information, mapping to our classifications above. Code may constitute the following:

- *Operational information:* To the right audience, the revelation of code, particularly source code (interpretable by people), can reveal a range of operational information that would be valuable to a motivated adversary, including business activities, risk assessment methods, decision hierarchies, and points of vulnerability. As an example, border agencies profile goods and people entering their country based on a set of risk rules. Access to these computing rules would reveal the profiling methodology and therefore enable smugglers to attempt to bypass those risk rules.

- *Commercial information*: Code information could reveal business models and practices for generating business profit, enabling a competitive advantage.
- *Financial information*: Code may set out the accounting standards and practices which could highlight vulnerabilities to financial exploitation.
- *Intellectual property*: The code itself may be a commercial asset to the organisation from which it earns a profit by providing it as a product or service.

As a decision asset

As set out above, the code constitutes a set of instructions on how an automated decision is to be made. As such the "role", which is responsible for making this decision, is the relevant computer application which has been given responsibility for such a decision. In many jurisdictions these decisions may be formally delegated to the computer programme, through an instrument of decision-making.

The threat associated with these decision types is equivalent to human-made decisions, in that they will be incorrectly made according to the risk and policy settings or omitted to be made at all. This may occur due to incorrect encoding of the instructions (and subsequent failure to adequately test that the system is performing as expected), incorrect policy assumptions governing the decision, or deliberate manipulation or hacking of the code to deliver a different outcome. An organisation's code and systems, therefore, need to be considered through the lens of the decision, with computers effectively fulfilling a "role" which can be under threat and can equally be a repository for information held by the organisation.

Example 1: AUSTRAC and The Commonwealth Bank of Australia

In an Australian context, The Commonwealth Bank of Australia settled a case brought forward by its anti-money laundering and counter-terrorism financing regulator, The Australian Transaction Reports and Analysis Centre (AUSTRAC). The case cost the bank AUD700 million in agreed penalties. One key factor that the case hinged on was a failure by the bank to report threshold deposits of AUD10,000 made into its newly rolled out "Intelligent Deposit Machines" (IDMs) over a period of almost three years. The reason for this reporting omission is that the bank had failed to properly encode the threshold reporting processes into the IDMs and transactional systems, which resulted in transactions being settled without the legislative reporting requirement being fulfilled (AUSTRAC, 2022).

Example 2: Computer hackers are helping illegal loggers destroy the Amazon rainforest

Greenpeace (2008) published an article declaring that computer hackers were helping illegal loggers destroy the Amazon rainforest by hacking the Brazilian government's timber tracking system and altering the records with the purpose of increasing logging allocations. These alterations allegedly enabled the allocation of protected Amazon rainforest tracts, thereby resulting in the illegal logging and destruction of these areas, contrary to domestic and international environmental protection covenants.

Example 3: Proprietary source code theft sends company out of business

U.S. company Ellery Systems, Inc., was a company that designed computer systems and were jointly funded by the U.S. Department of Defense and NASA to build a range of software applications (Cole & Ring, 2006). The estimated return on investment for these applications ran in to the tens of billions of dollars. An employee of the company stole the source code and sold it to a Chinese-controlled corporation, which rendered the software valueless and ultimately drove the company out of business. This example demonstrates the value of computer code as intellectual property information and underscores the value of it as operational information. The reason the software lost value once it was shared with strategic rivals is that it provided the basis for understanding and potentially exploiting operational vulnerabilities.

Physical, intangible, and financial assets

An organisation's assets are inputs to achieving its objectives. These assets are used to, for example, enable production, logistics, risk identification, research, and development. They may also represent the value holdings of the organisation, such as currency and securities.

The typologies of assets are highly varied across different organisations, and as such we will not attempt to provide a detailed classification for these asset types. However, to manage threats to these assets, it is critical that organisations have registers of these assets and how they are acquired, held, and stored. Like code, many intangible assets cross the boundary between physical and information asset. Finances, securities, and derivatives held in ledgers by the organisation or on behalf of others are held within information systems and electronic platforms which enable transactions and holding of units of value.

In a government context, market-based regulatory schemes create units of cost/value for externalities to production or assets of public value, for example water usage credits, carbon units, renewable energy certificates, chlorofluorocarbon trading permits. These kinds of assets have been demonstrated to be equally at threat. This is illustrated by a major case of theft in the European Union where hackers stole an estimated USD4 million in carbon credits from European Union emissions trading accounts, following an elaborate phishing scam targeting employees of companies required to participate in the European carbon market (Zetter, 2018). Such a case illustrates the need to consider and classify both tangible/capital assets and intangible ones to ensure that the organisation values and protects the broadest range of assets that deliver its mission and objectives.

Asset value and prioritisation

With the organisational assets classified as a reference list or model, it is imperative to assess the value of the asset. As depicted in Figure 3.3, we propose a two-axis assessment:

- *Assessing the **mission criticality** of the asset:* To what extent does the asset contribute to achieving the vision/mission/objectives of the organisation and, if it were compromised, to what extent would the achievement of those objectives be compromised?
- *Assessing the level of harm of compromise:* To what extent would compromise to the asset contribute to other forms of harm to the organisation's other priorities, stakeholders, and other entities (e.g. privacy, safety, reputational/brand)?

As set out in Figure 3.3, these two factors enable the prioritisation of the value of the asset to the achievement of the overall objectives of the enterprise.

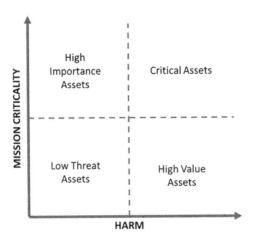

FIGURE 3.3 Assessing Value of Asset

This results in four quadrants of relative priority from those assets, which are critical to the delivery of the enterprise objectives to those which are of high individual value but of less criticality, or conversely those which are of low financial value and yet contribute significantly to the mission.

Mission criticality

As set out in Chapter 2, organisational assets are key inputs to the value streams and capabilities of the organisation. Some assets are, however, of more critical importance than others to the delivery of objectives, whether they are critical decisions, information holdings, or physical assets. These assets should be robustly protected from insider threats. The level of criticality is a matter for the individual organisation. However, we propose that a three- or five-scale model can assist organisations to quantitatively assess and score the criticality of their assets. Table 3.3 sets out an example model.

Importantly, Table 3.3 can be tailored to the needs of the specific organisation and its business model. But in any context, it provides a point of reference for scoring the importance of the asset that the organisation aims to

TABLE 3.3 Scoring Criticality of Assets

	1: Insignificant	*2: Important*	*3: Critical*
Decisions	Decision type is incidental to achieving the mission/objectives of the organisation.	Decision type contributes to achieving the mission but as part of broader suite of decisions.	Decision type is central to achieving the mission/objectives of the organisation.
Information	Information which is incidentally created or collected but does not contribute as an input to the mission/objectives of the organisation.	Information which is created or collected and contributes as part of a broader range of information.	Information which forms an input to critical capabilities, decisions, or processes that achieve the mission/objectives of the organisation.
Physical/ intangible	The asset is incidental to organisational capability.	The asset is an important input to capability but is part of a broader set of inputs.	The physical or intangible asset is a critical input to organisational capabilities, processes that achieve the mission/objectives of the organisation.

protect from insider threat. Using our notional border agency from Chapter 2 to illustrate, decisions to grant a person a visa or to clear a person or goods at the border, if systemically falsely made, undermine the core mission of the organisation to protect its nation from the harms of illicit goods or from inappropriate people entering the nation. On the other hand, the decision to select a particular vendor to undertake a refresh of desktop hardware is important to the organisation, but the awarding of a contract due to pay-offs would not undermine the mission of the organisation.

Harm

The notion of harm relates to the effect of the realisation of an insider risk on other organisational priorities that do not necessarily undermine the achievement of its mission and objectives. Assets that, if compromised, could cause a high level of harm to the organisation or its partners/stakeholders equally need to be elevated in priority. We propose again a three- or five-scale model to assist in prioritising these assets (see Table 3.4). The table sets out different domains which deliver or protect value for the organisation, such as its reputation, the privacy of information, the continuity of its operations, its compliance with legislative obligations, the health and safety of its employees and customers, and financial impacts. The impacts on each of these elements can range from insignificant to catastrophic to enterprise objectives.

Most mature organisations have a well-developed risk management framework, and in these circumstances the "harm" categorisation very much mirrors consequence tables contained within risk management frameworks. If the organisation does have such a framework, rather than creating a new framework for insider threat, it is better to use the organisational standard to ensure that insider threat is aligned and consistent with other risk management domains of the organisation.

Protecting the right assets

The purpose of the above assessments is to enable the organisation to assess the relative priority of its assets, enabling it to invest finite resources at the correct level across controls and focus on identifying vulnerabilities to the most important assets. For the purposes of rolling out the framework proposed in this book, the prioritisation of assets also provides guidance on prioritising the further analysis we propose in the forthcoming chapters, with focus first going to the critical assets and subsequently to high-value and high-impact assets, as set out in Figure 3.4. This illustrates how the quadrants of priority we established above can be utilised to effect this form of prioritisation.

TABLE 3.4 Prioritisation of Assets

	1: Insignificant	2: Moderate	3: Catastrophic
Reputation/ Brand	Minor inconvenience for clients/ stakeholders resulting in low-level annoyance.	Loss of brand requiring investment of effort to repair.	Irreparable impact on brand and client–stakeholder relationship.
Privacy	Release of incidental or de-identified information pertaining to clients/ stakeholders.	Breach of client/stakeholder privacy requiring recovering and triggering notification requirements.	Irreparable and major breach of privacy of multiple clients/ stakeholders.
Business Continuity	Minor lapse in continuity below three days.	Breakdown of system or asset creating a lapse in capability over three days.	Irretrievable breakdown of system or asset.
Compliance	Minor breach of internal policy.	Breach of legislation potentially resulting in civil action or pecuniary penalties between USD1 to USD1 million.	Major breach of law potentially resulting in criminal prosecution or pecuniary penalties over USD 1 million.
Health and Safety	Minor or transient injury.	Major injury requiring recovery and rehabilitation.	Fatality, life threatening or ongoing injury.
Financial	Minor financial losses below USD50,000.	Financial losses between USD50,000 and USD1 million.	Major financial losses over USD1 million.

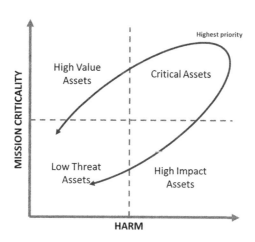

FIGURE 3.4 Prioritising Assets Based on Value

It is worth noting that the above prioritisation model assumes a level of organisational complexity. This involves a range of different decision, information, and physical asset types that contribute to achieving organisational objectives. Multinational companies, banking and financial institutions, and government service delivery and regulatory agencies are examples of this complexity. Simpler organisations will no less need to set out their key assets. However, prioritisation may be less complex and more readily assessed without the need for matrix models to guide prioritisation.

Roles and assets: a critical link

As we set out in Chapter 2, assets are only one component required to understand the complexities of insider threat. The critical link between the asset and the human or non-human actor that is enabled to make a decision, access information, or manage a physical or intangible asset also needs to be established. We suggest drawing on existing organisational structures and role typologies to draw the link between the roles in the organisation and the asset. As we'll set out in subsequent chapters, the link to roles is critical to assess the risk to the asset by reference to the role and the opportunities for insider threat that the role provides. In Chapter 11, we demonstrate this linkage and its impact on the level of risk in different scenarios in considerable detail.

Assets and location

The physical or non-physical location in which information is held or a physical asset resides is an important risk management consideration, in particular highlighting the location in which controls will need to be implemented in order to protect that asset. Location may be no less important for decisions, particularly where the same decision may be made in different locations. However, the local conditions or business processes for making that decision may be different. As such, the threat to that decision may vary depending on where it occurs. In multinational companies or agencies with multiple locations domestically or abroad, the location of assets should equally be captured as data to inform the assessment of risk is based on location. For instance, if a decision to grant a loan in Country A is governed by a lax set of rules and processes, whereas the rules applying to the same loan decision are stricter in Country B, then the risk of insider threat in Country A is likely higher and therefore warrants more attention.

Case studies

Case study 1: Two contrasting cases of migration fraud

In the first more typical case of migration fraud, a U.S. State Department employee at the U.S. embassy in Prague facilitated the fraudulent granting of visas in exchange for bribes from visa brokers. Examining this case through the lens of *assets*, this official held a role which had access and control over the visa decision asset. As we've set out in our imaginary organisation, these decisions are of high value to those wishing to enter a particular country, in this case the United States (sufficiently so that visa brokers would be willing to pay bribes to have these decisions made in their client's favour) (Cole & Ring, 2006).

A contrasting example also comes from the United States, where a U.S. Department of Agriculture employee facilitated visa fraud. In this case, the person was responsible for identifying and certifying other nationals to come to the United States to meet, exchange information, and establish agreements. Instead, the official decided to conspire with brokers to assist them in obtaining visas for persons who would not have been able to obtain legitimate visas. He did this by writing falsified recommendations based on fake biographical details that these individuals held agricultural qualifications and would be attending meetings in the United States (Cole & Ring, 2006).

The contrast here is that while the outcome was the same, visa fraud against the United States, the organisational asset used to deliver this outcome was very different. In the first case it was direct access to the visa decision itself; in the second it was access to the decision or ability to make a recommendation in relation to an individual that would enable them to be granted a visa, as well as access to the official letterhead enabling these false recommendations to look legitimate.

Case study 2: Theft of company stock

In this example, a financial analyst and an accounting manager conspired to steal almost USD8 million in company stock using their intimate knowledge of the system used to manage stock options for the company (Cole & Ring, 2006). The theft was only detected due to raising suspicions as a result of their newfound wealth, having bypassed the usual auditing controls within the system. This case highlights the vulnerability of the *physical*, *intangible*, and *financial* assets that insiders, through their roles, have access to and/or intimate knowledge of the accounting and auditing practices.

Case study 3: A compromise of information leads to lottery fraud

In this case, a security guard gained access to a list of all manufactured lottery tickets, thereby enabling him to pinpoint the location of winning lottery tickets each worth USD2 million (Cole & Ring, 2006). Working with others, all the lottery tickets including the winning ticket were purchased from one location. This raised the suspicion of authorities and ultimately resulted in the detection of the fraud and the insider activity. In this case the security guard was given access to sensitive and highly valuable commercial information, which enabled the fraud against the lottery operator. This case is also illustrative of the potentially tenuous link between the role and the information where controls are weak; *id est* there was no reason for a security guard to have access to the information in the course of their duties. As we'll explore in the next chapter, this case is an example of the compromise of information, which is the asset. Here, access created *opportunity*.

Chapter key points

- Assets are inputs to realising the organisation's mission and objectives. They are also the target of insider threats.
- Assets are systemic and, therefore, provide a solid and enduring reference for analysing insider threats.
- Classifying the assets by type, criticality, and harm provides a point of reference for prioritising which assets the organisation most needs to protect from insider threat.

References

Association of Certified Fraud Examiners. (2018). *Report to the nations: 2018 Global study on occupational fraud and abuse.* https://www.acfeinsights.com/acfe-insights/2018/9/28/key-findings-from-the-2018-report-to-the-nations-government-edition

AUSTRAC. (2022). *AUSTRAC and CBA agree on $700m penalty.* https://www.austrac.gov.au/austrac-and-cba-agree-700m-penalty#:~:text=An%20agreement%20has%20been%20reached,(AML%2FCTF)%20laws.

Cole, E., & Ring, S. (2006). *Insider threat: Protecting the enterprise from sabotage, spying and theft.* Syngress Publishing.

Financial Action Task Force. (2019). *International standards on combating money laundering and the financing of terrorism & proliferation.* FATF. http://www.fatf-gafi.org/media/fatf/documents/recommendations/pdfs/FATF%20Recommendations%202012.pdf

Gelles, M. (2016). *Insider threat: Prevention, detection, mitigation and deterrence.* Butterworth-Heinemann.

Greenpeace. (2008). *Hackers help destroy the Amazon rainforest.* https://storage.googleapis.com/gpuk-archive/blog/forests/hackers-help-destroy-amazon-rainforest-20081212.html

Herald Sun. (2019). *Customs broker couple may have been used as pawns.* https://www.heraldsun.com.au

Iannuzzi, E., & Berardi, M. (2010). Global financial crisis: Causes and perspectives. *EuroMed Journal of Business.* https://www.emerald.com/insight/content/doi/10.1108/14502191011080818/full/html?skipTracking=true

Jarmin, R. S., & O'Hara, A. B. (2016). Big data and the transformation of public policy analysis. *Journal of Policy Analysis and Management, 35*(3), 715–721.

Manning, M., Wong, G. T. W., & Jevtovic, N. (2020). Investigating the relationships between FATF recommendation compliance, regulatory affiliations and the Basel anti-money laundering index. *Security Journal.* https://doi.org/10.1057/s41284-020-00249-z

McKibbin, W., & Stoeckel, A. (2009). The global financial crisis: Causes and consequences. *Asian Economic Papers, 9*(1), 54–86.

Monahan, G. (2000). *Management decision making: Spreadsheet modeling, analysis, and application.* Cambridge University Press.

Orbach, B. (2012). *What is regulation? (12–27).* https://papers.ssrn.com/sol3/papers.cfm?abstract_id=2143385

Rowe, E., Akman, T., Smith, R., & Tomison, A. (2013). Organised crime and public sector corruption: A crime scripts analysis of tactical displacement risks. *Trends and Issues in Crime and Criminal Justice, 444.*

Silberschatz, A. (1994). *Operating system concepts* (4th ed.). Addison-Wesley.

Sparrow, M. (2011). *The regulatory craft: Controlling risks, solving problems, and managing compliance.* Brookings Institution Press.

Sparrow, M. (2012). Policy essay: Crime reduction through a regultory approach. *Criminology & Public Policy, 11*(1), 345–359.

United States Attorney-General's Office Central District of California. (2023). *Customs broker arrested on superseding indictment alleging new $2 Million fraud committed after his release on bond in original fraud case.* https://www.justice.gov/usao-cdca/pr/customs-broker-arrested-superseding-indictment-alleging-new-2-million-fraud-committed

U.S. Chamber of Commerce Foundation. (2022). *Big data and what it means.* https://www.uschamberfoundation.org/bhq/big-data-and-what-it-means#:~:text=In%20the%2021st%20century%2C%20digital,transforming%20the%20world%20around%20us

Witzel, M., & Warner, M. (2015). Taylorism revisited: Culture, management theory and paradigm-shift. *Journal of General Management, 40*(3), 55–70.

Yang, Y., Tan, X., Shi, Y., & Deng, J. (2023). What are the core concerns of policy analysis? A multidisciplinary investigation based on in-depth bibliometric analysis. *Humanities and Social Sciences Communications, 10*(190).

Yeung, K. (2017). 'Hypernudge': Big data as a mode of regulation by design. *Information, Communication & Society, 20*(1), 118–136. https://doi.org/10.1080/1369118X.2016.1186713

Zetter, K. (2018, February 3). Hackers steal millions in carbon credits. *WIRED.* https://www.wired.com/2010/02/hackers-steal-carbon-credits/

4

UNDERSTANDING OPPORTUNITY

Introduction

Insider risk emerges when an individual is motivated to act unethically (for whatever reason) in order to take advantage of an opportunity for their own gain. However, for this to occur, an opportunity must be presented through process or operational flaws, such as the lack of a capable guardian, the presence of a motivated offender, or access to a suitable target (Cohen & Felson, 1979). Frequently, criminal opportunity is not initially planned but rather stumbled upon by witnessing the mistakes of others or individual slip ups, which are subsequently exploited to commit longer-term fraudulent or corrupt activity (see for example Operation Heritage, where airport security measures were subverted to transport increasingly large amounts of illicit drugs through the Australian border) (Australian Commission for Law Enforcement Integrity, 2013).

In this chapter, we explore a possible framework for systematically describing how insider risk opportunity presents itself as a confluence of five factors: (1) authority; (2) access; (3) visibility; (4) transparency; and (5) certainty. Using real-world examples, we explore the definitions of these factors and how they operate to provide the opportunity for systemic fraud and corruption to occur without being detected.

Opportunity: the key to action

Insider threat emerges when a motivated actor has access to a suitably valuable organisational asset, whether a decision, information, or a tangible or intangible asset. However, to take advantage of that asset an opportunity needs to present itself that enables the threat against that asset to be realised

DOI: 10.4324/9781003055716-4

and for it to occur covertly, thereby reducing the probability of detection by the organisation. It is, therefore, the presence of an opportunity that enables a malicious actor to shift from passive preparedness or motivation to act against the organisation, to the ability to act on that motivation. In our view, opportunity is the most critical enabler or driver for insider risk, insofar as the other elements we outline in later chapters, such as motivation and the interaction with a potential beneficiary, rely fully on opportunity before they can drive an insider incident.

Much of the literature tends to present opportunity (see for example Gelles, 2016) as a diffuse set of factors which are specific to the organisation and its mode of business. These present each occurrence of corruption as diverse, placing the focus on the human actors who have committed the corrupt or fraudulent act, rather than examining and structuring the elements of the business processes that have enabled the act to be undertaken. The weakness of this approach is that human actors are themselves much more diffuse and non-systemic than the processes they interact with as part of their roles within an organisation. The examination of the actors therefore creates significant and, in our view, unresolvable challenges in developing a more systemic approach to understanding insider risk.

As we'll set out there are key systemic and measurable factors which exist across all organisations, and which can consistently provide the opportunity to commit malicious or inadvertent acts which harm an organisation. Apart from helping to identify risk, these opportunity factors also provide a point of reference for designing appropriate risk controls which reduce the availability of opportunities, while equally minimising impacts of those controls on business operations.

The slippery slope: from identifying opportunity to acting on opportunity

The reason why opportunity is so important is twofold:

1 Research indicates that insider threats tend to emerge by accident, when a suitably empowered insider stumbles over an opportunity to covertly commit an act of corruption or fraud (Cole & Ring, 2006). As this opportunity is identified and tested and the malicious acts go undetected, the inside actor may initialise further action, thereby increasing organisational losses. This evolution from inadvertent and incidental opportunity towards motivated and systemic activity highlights that opportunity is a key factor in enabling insider threat to emerge and grow within an organisation. The clear outcome here is increased losses and the potential for increased reputational damage.

2 The literature highlights that deliberate planting of individuals by governments, competitors, and organised crime may be increasing as a *modus operandi* for gaining commercial or strategic advantage over opponents (Cole & Ring, 2006). Such plants may work for many years observing and gaining a unique understanding of the organisation's insider threat opportunities. Again, this serves to illustrate the importance of opportunity as a key factor in the development of insider threats, in this case with an actor deliberately identifying systemic opportunities and vulnerabilities to exploit.

Opportunity factors

As we set out in Chapters 2 and 3, organisations are structured around a set of organisational capabilities, which deliver value and achieve the organisation's mission and objectives. These capabilities are underpinned by a set of organisational assets that enable that value to be delivered through decision-making, information, and other assets. This is true of all organisations and can therefore provide a consistent point of reference for assessing the risk of malicious or inadvertent insider threat. We argue that the opportunities which enable those threats to manifest are equally consistent. This consistent model enables us to build a far more nuanced model for determining the likelihood of insider threat against the organisation's assets, based on the aggregated level of opportunity against that asset. We identify five opportunity factors that act together to increase the likelihood that malicious insider action could be undertaken against an organisational asset:

1 **Authority**: The level of authority that the role associated with the asset has over that asset (e.g. the authority they have to make a particular decision).
2 **Access**: The access that the role or roles have to the asset (e.g. can everyone access the asset or is it restricted to certain people?)
3 **Visibility**: The level of real-time visibility that other people have over the actions that the role undertakes in respect of the asset (e.g. can other people consistently watch them make a decision or access money?).
4 **Traceability**: The level of traceable and auditable record of what action the role has taken and why the action was taken (e.g. the record of a decision and the supporting evidence).
5 **Certainty**: The level of certainty that the role will be able to access a specific asset they have an interest in (e.g. the ability to access a decision in relation to a friend or family member).

Similar to routine activity theory, which stipulates three necessary conditions for most crime (i.e. a likely offender, a suitable target, and the absence of a capable guardian), coming together in time and space (Cohen & Felson,

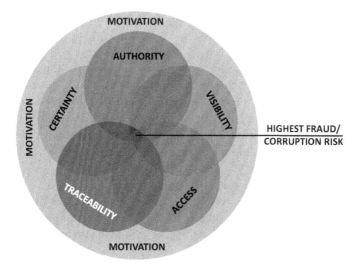

FIGURE 4.1   Opportunity Factors That Increase the Likelihood of Malicious Insider Action

1979), we propose it is the confluence of the above five factors, in the presence of the motivated offender, where we expect the likelihood of insider incidents to be high (see Figure 4.1). Figure 4.1 sets out these five factors, which we will discuss individually and in detail.

Authority

The ACFE Report to the Nations (Association of Certified Fraud Examiners, 2022) indicates that since 2012 the majority of detected corruption has involved perpetrators occupying roles of higher seniority/authority. Over the period 2012–2022, the proportion was found to be 62% of all detected corruption cases globally. Setting aside other variables that may give rise to this growth, such as changing and maturing detection methodologies and growing corruption awareness globally, evidence nonetheless illustrates the obvious link between authority and the opportunity to perpetrate malicious acts against the organisation. While the level of seniority within an organisational structure may signify a greater level of decision-making authority and access to the organisation's assets, authority for decision-making is often more distributed and delegated across management and operational roles within the organisation (Stickney & Johnston, 1983). While empowerment has been empirically demonstrated to foster employee's creativity, quality of work and life, spirit of teamwork, and organisational effectiveness (Vu, 2020), it is necessary to acknowledge the authority factor. The authority factor here refers to the relationship between the role and the asset and the level of authority that the role exercises over the asset:

- For decisions: does the role have individual authority for the decision or is there a separation of decision-making duties?
- For information: does the role just have authority to access or do they have authority to create, modify, or dispose of data and information?
- For physical and intangible assets: do they have the authority to access and use, or to purchase, stocktake, and dispose of the asset?

The level of authority that a role is granted over a particular asset enables them to act independently in respect of that asset and reduces the amount of scrutiny that their actions are subject to. This, thereby, increases the opportunity to act, which is to their own benefit rather than to the benefit of the organisation.

Examples of authority

1 Using our imaginary border agency, an individual officer is delegated the responsibility to assess the evidence that a person qualifies for a visa to enter the country and to make that decision. The delegation is to the individual and does not require a second person to review the decision before it is made. As such the officer has a relatively high level of authority in respect of the decision to grant or deny the visa.
2 When the organisation receives an invoice for payment the receiving officer confirms that the invoice is correct or incorrect but is not authorised to effect the payment. The approval for payment is referred to the finance area, which effects the decision to pay the invoice. In this case, the receiving officer has a relatively low level of authority for the decision as there is a separation of duties between the officer and a second person required to make the decision to pay on the recommendation of the first officer.
3 The chief finance officer has sole responsibility for a particular grant account including making payments from the account. They therefore have a very high level of responsibility for this particular decision.
4 The systems engineer has the authority to overwrite certain data types directly within the organisational systems. They have a high level of authority over these data.
5 The stock manager has authority to purchase and write off assets. They have a high level of authority in respect of those assets.
6 The building authority CEO has power to approve lucrative building allocations and land-use requirements. They have a very high level of authority.

As these examples above illustrate, the level of authority exercised over different decision typologies does not necessarily mirror the level of seniority within the organisation. Instead, the authority exercised is more closely linked to the roles, what purpose they serve, and what they are empowered to do.

Assessing authority

From a risk management perspective, the level of authority is a relative rather than an absolute measure. As such, a sliding scale is the most appropriate model for setting out relative levels of authority over the organisational assets, as illustrated in Table 4.1.

TABLE 4.1 Authority Scale

	Authority Scale			
	1: Low	*2: Moderate*	*3: High*	*4: Very High*
Decisions	Initiator of decisions with separation of duties, providing an initial decision or recommendation to ultimate decision-maker.	Decision-maker on decision with separation of duties generally guided by decision policy or guidance.	Individual generally delegated authority possessed with discretion within parameters and guided by decision policy or guidance.	Sole authority possessed by individual with high level of discretion and low level of decision policy or guidance.
Information	Authority to access and disclose information.	Authority to create, store, and disclose information.	Authority to collect, create, modify, store, disclose, and destroy information.	Authority to collect, create, modify, store, disclose, and destroy information, including access to code and/or audit logs.
Physical/ Intangible	Authority to use the asset.	Authority to account for and manage the asset.	Authority to purchase and manage the asset.	Authority to purchase, account for, and dispose of the asset.

When assessing authority there are several factors which affect the level of authority:

- Hierarchical authority: where authority is based on seniority within the organisation;
- Collective authority: where authority is distributed across roles, through separation of duties or collective decision-making (e.g. board and committees)
- Centralised authority: where a single role has multiple forms of authority in relation to an asset (e.g. purchasing, stocktaking, and disposal).

The scale of the organisation may also play a significant role in the level of authority, with smaller organisations potentially providing greater authority to individuals to promote better use of a smaller number of human resources.

Access

The second key factor is access to the asset of interest. There are several different scenarios in which access to assets becomes an opportunity for insider threat against the decision/information/physical or intangible asset:

- A specific role has a defined level or type of access to an asset. For example, the role is a delegated decision-maker and therefore has access to the decision types that they are delegated to perform; or the role requires a particular tool or information to undertake the role and individuals performing that role are given access to the tool or information required to undertake the role.
- While only specific roles have access to the particular asset, the access controls can be compromised to gain access to the asset.
- The asset is generally accessible to all roles within the organisation, for example, physical assets that are generally stored in common areas, general delegations, or generally accessible information.

The level of access that is granted to an asset will determine both the level of insider threat to that asset and the level of risk associated with a particular role type depending on their level of access to the asset.

Examples of access

- An assessing officer is delegated decision-making authority in relation to qualification to receive social welfare payments. The role accesses the decision via an online portal which is accessible to them and all assessing officers via a password authentication. Other roles are not able to access the decision. General access to buildings and facilities is restricted to working hours. They have moderate access to the decision.

- An intelligence officer has access to intelligence information and assessments which are stored on a secure network. Access is controlled via two-factor authentication involving passcode and biometric fingerprint authentication. They have moderate access to the information; however, the information itself has a low level of general access.
- In a border or police organisation, goods that are detained in relation to customs or criminal offences (such as drugs, weapons, or contraband) are held within detained goods stores. Access to the stores is permitted to certain classes of officers through personal identification and pass access. The store is managed by a detained goods manager who grants access to the physical safes and lockers. The officers have a moderate level of access to the assets, and it is likely the detained goods manager has a very high level of access.
- In a small organisation all officers have access to make credit card payments up to a limit of $5,000 per day. Here is a very high level of access.

Assessing access

As with all opportunity factors, from a risk management perspective, the level of access to an asset whether general or role specific resides on a sliding scale from low to very high (see Table 4.2). Access to an organisational asset that is entirely unfettered to any person or is unfettered to a particular role substantially increases the level of insider threat to that asset. For example if any person within an organisation is able to access sensitive information without any information security access controls or the application of a "need to know" principle, then every staff member of the organisation potentially is a risk to the information. If information is restricted to certain officials but they have access to substantial information that is not compartmentalised, then the broader employees are a lesser risk. However, those officials represent a significant risk to the organisation.

When defining an appropriate scale for an organisation to self-assess its level of risk, several lenses should be considered:

- *Personal:* limits on the people or roles that can access the asset.
- *Temporal:* limits on the time that an asset can be accessed.
- *Geospatial/geographical:* limits on the place in which an asset can be accessed.

While we will expand on the means of controlling these features of access in Chapter 7, for now they provide a point of reference for scaling the level of access and exposure a particular asset has to insider threat.

TABLE 4.2 Access Scale

	Access Scale			
	1: Low	*2: Moderate*	*3: High*	*4: Very High*
Decisions	Access to the decision is restricted in terms of physical or ICT access control.	Access to the decision is controlled in terms of physical or ICT access control.	Unfettered access to the decision within confines of working hours or fulfilling a particular activity.	Unfettered access to the decision at any time.
Information	Access to the information is restricted in terms of physical or ICT access control.	Access to the information is controlled in terms of physical or ICT access control.	Unfettered access to the information within confines of working hours or fulfilling a particular activity.	Unfettered access to the information at any time.
Physical/ Intangible	Access to the asset is restricted in terms of physical or ICT access control.	Access to the asset is controlled in terms of physical or ICT access control.	Unfettered access to the asset within confines of working hours or fulfilling a particular activity.	Unfettered access to the asset at any time.

Visibility

For a malicious insider act to be undertaken, it is not only the possibility or opportunity to commit the act, but the ability to conceal that act (to avoid detection) and a consideration of the potential consequences (albeit bounded). While there is not yet consensus as to whether the severity of punishment or the probability of detection play a stronger role in inhibiting malicious and criminal acts (due to controversies surrounding the nature of the data used) (Friesen, 2012), it is likely that both play at least some role in deterring those acts (Manning, 2019). Therefore, for an insider to engage in dishonest or illicit activities they must have some confidence that their activities will go undetected. There are, of course, exceptions and what we present here is a simplification of the economics of the crime model, as presented by Manning (2018). However, we do note that the level of visibility and the enhancement of natural surveillance are important factors, which when underpinned by the theory of crime prevention through environmental design (CPTED) (Jeffery, 1971) act upon an individual's tendency to act in a malicious way (Perry, 2017).

The visibility factor we present here refers to how easily observable an interaction with an asset is in *real time*, that is at the time the interaction occurs rather than at some other later time. To illustrate, active closed-circuit television (CCTV) involves the active monitoring of camera feeds which capture activity of interest, while passive CCTV involves the recording of footage so it can be referred to later. Active CCTV increases the level of visibility of an activity while passive CCTV (though also making that activity observable) does not increase its real-time visibility. The level of visibility of an activity can act as a deterrent against illicit activity or increase the speed at which it can be detected and responded to. This ultimately reduces the harm to the organisation. Either way, research demonstrates that CCTV is associated with a significant and modest decrease in crime (Piza et al., 2019).

Examples of visibility

- Entry and exit of a secure zone within the building where sensitive information is created or access is monitored by guards over the CCTV system. The level of visibility is relatively high.
- During business hours, visa processing officers work together in proximity, creating a moderate level of visibility. However, outside of work hours there are few to no officers in the office, thereby reducing the level of visibility to low.
- National security organisations observe office staff to monitor a range of information feeds including border movements, intelligence assessments, and human source information. They work in an open, active, and close-quarters work environment to enhance visibility and reduce opportunities for concealment. The level of visibility is relatively high.

Assessing visibility

Unlike authority and access, which have a positive scale, visibility factors require an inverse scale, where the higher the level of visibility, the lower the likelihood of insider threat to that particular asset (as depicted in Table 4.3).

There are several factors that influence the level of visibility of the interaction with assets; examples follow:

- The physical plan of the organisation or location: for example, open plan offices with high levels of visibility of peers and colleagues versus isolated offices or concealed locations within goods stores.

TABLE 4.3 Visibility Scale

	Visibility Scale			
	1: Very High	2: High	3: Moderate	4: Low
Decisions	The allocation and making of the decision are monitored in real time.	The environment in which the decision is taken is intermittently monitored.	The environment in which the decision is taken is incidentally visible to others if they are present or active within the relevant system.	The environment the decision is taken in is concealed, remote, and/or is not visible to others within ICT systems.
Information	Access to the information is monitored in real time.	Access to the information is intermittently monitored.	Access to and use of the information are incidentally visible to others if they are present or active within the relevant system.	The information can be accessed in a manner which is concealed and not visible to others within ICT systems.
Physical/ Intangible	Access to and use of the asset are monitored in real time.	Access to and use of the asset are intermittently monitored.	Access to and use of the asset are incidentally visible to others if they are present or active in the relevant system.	The asset can be accessed and used in a manner which is concealed.

- The ICT environment: for example, shared decision queues provide visibility across teams of what peers and colleagues are working on and the status of their work or alternatively to managers.
- Monitoring activities: such as CCTV (as above), or active security monitoring by guards.

In addition to considering general visibility, it is necessary to consider the level of visibility. Here it is worth considering whether the level of visibility could be reduced by an actor. This could occur through, for example, active concealment of an activity or by undertaking an activity at outside of normal work hours when visibility may be reduced due to the decreased number of peers and colleagues.

Traceability

The traceability factor refers to the ability to observe or trace back the inter-action with a particular asset later. Essentially, it refers to the capturing of a record or evidence of the interaction with the asset, for example recording of decisions and the supporting evidence for the decision in an IT system or in hardcopy files. Using the above example, while active CCTV increases the level of visibility, passive CCTV, by providing a record of activity, increases the level of traceability of activity recorded by the CCTV camera.

Like visibility, high traceability may have a deterrent effect on the actor insofar as it can increase the risk of detection and provide a source of evidence in the event of investigation and prosecution. Equally important, high levels of traceability can provide the basis for better detection of anomalous behaviour. For example if a decision is date and time stamped, then it will be possible to identify officers who make a large number of decisions outside of normal working hours, a potential indicator of illicit decision-making.

Examples of traceability

- The financial services counter is covered by a passive CCTV system that records the activities and interactions of financial services staff and clients. The CCTV records are overwritten in two months. Client interactions are also recorded on a client services system. In this scenario, the CCTV provides a moderate level of traceability; however, this is likely to be lifted to high by the recording on the client services system.
- License applications are submitted in a centralised system. When an application is processed by a processing officer, actions taken including time stamps and audit trail are all recorded. System rules ensure that supporting information must be attached to the application before it is finalised. Records are stored for seven years. The traceability is very high.
- The financial management system is used by accounts officers to affect the payment of invoices. While the financial details are included within the payment record, such as the vendor, amount, and time, the system does not require the invoice to be attached to process the payment. The level of traceability is high, but is not very high, due to the lack of consistently recorded evidence.

Assessing traceability

Like visibility, assessing traceability requires an inverse scale (Table 4.4), where higher levels of traceability act to reduce the probability of systemic insider threat, while lower levels of traceability can enable ongoing insider threat activities to occur and potentially go undetected.

TABLE 4.4 Traceability Scale

	Traceability Scale			
	1: Very High	2: High	3: Moderate	4: Low
Decisions	Complete decision and supporting evidence are recorded, including automatic audit logging. The record is stored for at least three years.	Decision and supporting evidence are consistently and completely recorded albeit at the discretion of the decision-maker. The record is stored for less than three years.	Decision and supporting evidence are inconsistently or incompletely recorded or if consistently recorded the record is stored for less than two months.	The decision and supporting evidence are not recorded.
Information	The interaction with the information is completely recorded, including what action taken (e.g. access, modification, disclosure). The record is stored for at least three years.	Interactions with the information are consistently recorded, albeit at the discretion of the decision-maker. The record is stored for less than three years.	Interactions with the information are inconsistently or incompletely recorded or if consistently recorded the record is stored for less than two months.	Interactions with the information are not recorded.
Physical/ Intangible	Interactions with the asset are automatically and completely recorded.	Interactions with the asset are consistently and completely recorded, albeit at the discretion of the decision-maker. The record is stored for less than three years.	Interactions with the asset are inconsistently or incompletely recorded or if consistently recorded the record is stored for less than two months.	Interactions with the asset are not recorded.

When assessing traceability, it is important to consider the completeness of the traceable record. This can be achieved by analysing the record created of the interaction with the asset using basic information gathering questions; examples follow:

- **Who** undertook the interaction?
- **What** was the interaction?
- **How** was the interaction undertaken?
- **Why** was the interaction undertaken?
- **When** did the interaction occur?
- **Where** did the interaction occur?

This assessment of completeness (the **6 Ws**) assists in determining the level of quality of the record and whether it would be sufficient to act as evidence in the event of an investigation or whether it could be analysed to detect insider threat activity already under way.

Certainty

The final factor we have identified is the certainty factor. This refers to the level of chance/probability that a malicious actor will be able to access a *specific* asset they have an interest in. For example, if they are receiving pay-offs for making a decision in favour of an outside entity, they must be capable of accessing the specific application of the entity. If they cannot access that application, they will not be able to offer the entity any benefit whatsoever. As such, *certainty* plays a very significant role in insider risk where a <u>specific</u> asset is of interest to a malicious asset, as opposed to interchangeable or fungible types of assets, such as money. In those circumstances, the higher the level of certainty that the insider can access a specific decision of interest, the greater the probability they will both be able to engage in a specific act of fraud or corruption and be able to engage in more systemic malicious acts. Reducing the level of certainty equally plays a very potent role in preventing these kinds of fraudulent and corrupt acts, by virtually eliminating the opportunity for the actor to access the asset they are interested in and thereby curtailing the activity entirely.

Examples of certainty

- In an airport, all air passengers pass through a single marshalling point staffed by a sole marshalling officer. The marshalling officer has a very high level of certainty that they will be able to make the decision about where to direct a specific passenger. This certainty could enable them to facilitate the importation of drugs through the border.

- License applications are randomly allocated to different officers within a large processing team. The certainty that a particular officer will receive a specific application is low. On the other hand, the team leader can allocate decisions from the queue to themselves. The team leader role therefore has a very high level of certainty that they can access a particular application.
- Visa applications are generally randomly allocated to different processing officers. However, there is one specialist who is an expert in a particular complex visa type and therefore all applications of this kind are allocated directly to this officer. They have a high level of certainty.
- The auditing and clearance of financial statements is undertaken by a small group of five auditors. While the statements are randomly assigned, there remains a relatively high certainty that an auditor will be allocated a particular financial statement.

Assessing certainty

Assessing the level of certainty involves determining the relative probability an individual occupying a role will be able to interact with a *specific* asset. This could be done on a percentage basis or an equivalent ratio basis, setting out threshold levels of probability on a normal positive scale. While it is logical and undeniable that certainty plays a role in determining the level of insider threat, more research is needed to examine whether there is a threshold at which lower levels of certainty effectively prevent malicious acts that involve specific assets. The question remains, At what point does the probability become too low for an actor to be able to effectively commit malicious acts? We now present a certainty scale (Table 4.5).

The level of certainty hinges on several identifiable factors:

- Consistency of role: Does a person always occupy the same role or do roles rotate?
- Centrality of role: Is the role central to a process, meaning that all assets interact with the role?
- Specialisation of role: Is the role specialised and therefore interacts consistently with a class of assets?
- Selection of asset: Is the role able to select the asset that they want to interact with?

Assessment of opportunity

The five opportunity factors outlined above work in concert to increase the likelihood of malicious or inadvertent insider threats to the organisational assets (as outlined in the previous chapter). The purpose of setting these factors out in a systemic way is to enable the relative level of risk to each asset or

TABLE 4.5 Certainty Scale

	Certainty Scale			
	1: Low	*2: Moderate*	*3: High*	*4: Very High*
Decisions	A less than 1:20 chance of being able to make a decision in which the role has a personal interest.	Between 1:20 and 1:10 chance of being able to make a decision in which the role has a personal interest.	A 1:10 or higher chance of being able to make a decision in which the role has a personal interest.	A 1:1 chance of being able to make a decision in which the role has a personal interest.
Information	A less than 1:20 chance of being able to access information in which the role has a personal interest.	Between 1:20 and 1:10 chance of being able to access information in which the role has a personal interest.	A 1:10 or higher chance of being able to access information in which the role has a personal interest.	A 1:1 chance of being able to access information in which the role has a personal interest.
Physical/ Intangible	A less than 1:20 chance of accessing an asset in which the role has a personal interest.	Between 1:20 and 1:10 chance of accessing an asset in which the role has a personal interest.	A 1:10 or higher chance of accessing an asset in which the role has a personal interest.	A 1:1 chance of accessing an asset in which the role has a personal interest.

asset type to be assessed consistently. This, in turn, enables the organisation to focus its efforts on enhancing controls to the most vulnerable assets.

While we will provide much more detail on risk controls in Chapter 7, it is important to note that there is effectively a relationship between the assessment of the level of opportunity and the controls that manage opportunity. In risk management theory, inherent risk refers to an assessed level of "raw" untreated risk (Monahan, 2008), which is comprised of the inherent likelihood and consequence of the risk event occurring. In contrast, when considering opportunities, it is more useful to consider the current state, including all current controls when determining the level of opportunity associated with an asset. The controls themselves form part of the definitions of each level on the scales we outlined above: for example when discussing the level of visibility or traceability, we referred to active and passive CCTV monitoring, which in themselves are controls. Similarly, when discussing certainty, we highlighted random allocation of decisions, another control which modifies this opportunity factor. As such the opportunity assessment should be viewed as a "baseline" assessment of the current level of opportunity, to which new controls could be added if they are cost effective.

The rationale for considering these controls when assessing opportunity is that it is rare that the analysis won't be conducted on an organisation that does not already have some form of control in place to manage insider threat. Developing a "baseline" level of opportunity thus focuses the assessment on actual vulnerabilities (rather than theoretical ones) to which new risk treatments can be applied.

Decisions

Using the scaling methodology that we outlined above, the assessment of opportunity relative to the decision assets of the organisation must separate out the elements of the decision assets (outlined in Chapter 3) (Figure 4.2).

Under this logic, the decision object is separated from the decision type, and the opportunities relate specifically to the decision type (approval, refusal etc.). Here, scores are based upon the scale for each opportunity factor and aggregated for each decision type against the decision object:

Decision Object 1

Decision Type A Opportunity Score = (Authority Score A) + (Access Score A) + (Visibility Score A) + (Traceability Score A) + (Certainty Score A)
Decision Type B Opportunity Score = (Authority Score B) + (Access Score B) + (Visibility Score B) + (Traceability Score B) + (Certainty Score B)

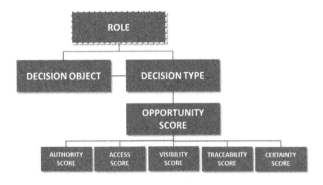

FIGURE 4.2 Relationship between Role and Opportunity: Decisions

Using this method will provide a differential view of each decision type against the *same* decision object, enabling relative vulnerabilities to be assessed consistently for the object. We use Figure 4.3 to illustrate.

In Figure 4.3, we use a colour scheme to represent the aggregate opportunity scores for different decision objects and related decision types. So, for example, the improper approval or refusal of a license has a higher aggregate score than the cancellation of the same license. This would denote that there are additional controls in place to manage the cancellation of a license when compared to approving or refusing the licence. For example, an officer may be able to grant the license in their own right (high authority) but the cancellation of a license involves a separation of duties (low authority). Figure 4.4 illustrates the decomposition of the assessment elements.

As illustrated in Figures 4.3 and 4.4, we can create a readily consumable heat map showing those decision objects and decision types which are most vulnerable to insider threat (*at this stage based solely on the opportunity factors*). This method will enable better targeting of resources to enhance controls around the most vulnerable assets and/or focusing control assurance resources on more critical controls.

Information

The decomposition method to assess the opportunities in relation to organisational information assets follows the same pattern as for decisions – a decomposition of the information type and the type of action that is undertaken in relation to the information providing a differential scoring for each action type against the information type.

As illustrated in Figures 4.5 and 4.6, a heat map can equally be produced highlighting the opportunity vulnerabilities against each information type.

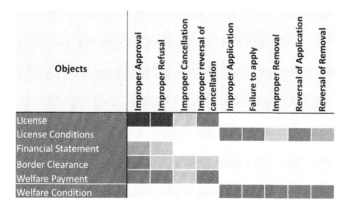

FIGURE 4.3   Example Opportunity Heat Map: Decisions

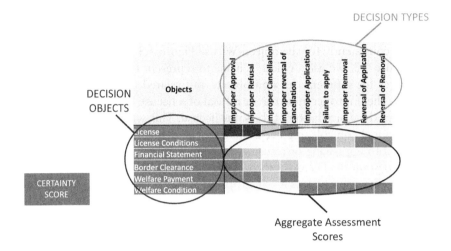

FIGURE 4.4 Decomposition of the Opportunity Heat Map

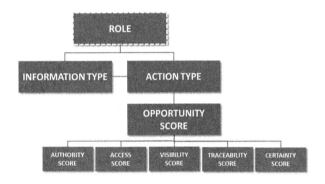

FIGURE 4.5 Relationship between Role and Opportunity: Information

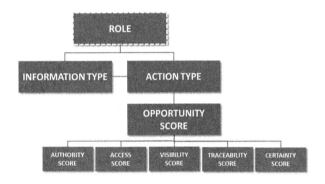

FIGURE 4.6 Example Opportunity Heat Map: Information

While we have adopted a very high-level decomposition of the information types, in reality it would be advantageous to decompose these types into more detailed information types. The above example highlights a pattern of opportunity for improper disclosure of information, which may warrant the organisation's examining systemic controls to manage the opportunity to disclose information.

Physical and intangible assets

Again, the assessment for physical and intangible assets follows the same decomposition pattern, with the asset type separated from the action which can be taken in respect of the physical or intangible asset (Figures 4.7 and 4.8).

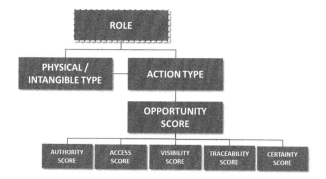

FIGURE 4.7 Relationship between Role and Opportunity: Physical and Intangible Assets

Objects	Improper Acquistion	Improper Creation	Improper Modification	Improper Destruction	Improper Use	Improper Storage	Improper Write-off	Omission to Acquire	Omission to Create	Omission to Modify
Bearer Bonds										
X-ray Machine										
Carbon Credit										
Physical Currency										
Aeroplanes										
Microscopes										

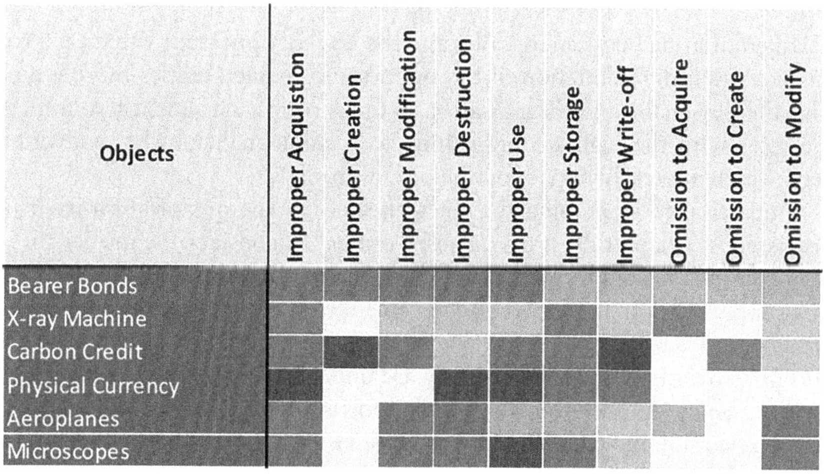

FIGURE 4.8 Example Opportunity Heat Map: Physical and Intangible Assets

Figures 4.7 and 4.8 set out an equivalent opportunity assessment for physical assets. The diversity of physical and intangible assets in the first column serves to highlight the way this assessment could be applied in a wide diversity of organisations, with very different physical or intangible asset types.

Roles

In each of our models presented (Tables 4.1–4.5) we highlight another feature that must be considered as part of the opportunity assessment: the role which interacts with the asset. Roles may be granted different decision-making powers, levels of access to information, or authority over assets. For assets where this is the case, a separate assessment should be captured for each role type: for example for decisions:

Role Alpha
Decision Object 1

> Decision Type A Opportunity Score = (Authority Score A) + (Access Score A) + (Visibility Score A) + (Traceability Score A) + (Certainty Score A)
> Decision Type B Opportunity Score = (Authority Score B) + (Access Score B) + (Visibility Score B) + (Traceability Score B) + (Certainty Score B)

Role Beta
Decision Object 1

> Decision Type A Opportunity Score = (Authority Score A) + (Access Score A) + (Visibility Score A) + (Traceability Score A) + (Certainty Score A)
> Decision Type B Opportunity Score = (Authority Score B) + (Access Score B) + (Visibility Score B) + (Traceability Score B) + (Certainty Score B)

Differentiating between the roles and the level of opportunity that each role has enables a differentiation of the opportunity vulnerabilities by role type. This thereby enables the organisation to focus risk management resources on the roles with the highest opportunity to commit malicious or inadvertent acts, which adversely impact on the organisation.

In addition to examining the roles effected by the organisation itself (as discussed in Chapter 2), it may also be critical to consider the insider threat opportunities related to roles effected by partner organisations or elsewhere in a supply chain that affect the achievement of the organisation's objectives. Drawing on our example from Chapter 2, a postal officer has *access* to and *authority* over mail items before they are under the control of our imaginary border agency. As such they have the opportunity to misappropriate or redirect mail containing prohibited items before they reach the border agency for profiling and intervention, effectively bypassing border controls entirely. As such, while this role is not strictly an "insider" within the organisation itself, they are an insider within the *broader supply chain* and their opportunity to undermine the organisational objectives should also form part of the risk assessment.

Location

For organisations with dispersed geographical footprints, another element that may warrant consideration is location. Location can also be a modifying factor in relation to the level of opportunity for insider threats. This is true where the environmental situation in various locations differs. For example, if a particular location has a very low number of staff processing applications, then the level of certainty will be increased relative to a larger office where there are more staff. Different business processes effected at different locations may have a similar effect on the risk: for example, where there is a separation of duties for a decision, while in another location the same decision may be made by a single officer.

Physical and technical infrastructure variations will also play a role, where highly secure locations may reduce the level of access enjoyed by staff to information of physical/intangible assets, while less well-equipped locations will enable higher levels of general access. As such, the assessment may also involve the following:

Location X
Decision Object 1

Decision Type A Opportunity Score = (Authority Score A) + (Access Score A) + (Visibility Score A) + (Traceability Score A) + (Certainty Score A)

Decision Type B Opportunity Score = (Authority Score B) + (Access Score B) + (Visibility Score B) + (Traceability Score B) + (Certainty Score B)

Location Y
Decision Object 1

Decision Type A Opportunity Score = (Authority Score A) + (Access Score A) + (Visibility Score A) + (Traceability Score A) + (Certainty Score A)

Decision Type B Opportunity Score = (Authority Score B) + (Access Score B) + (Visibility Score B) + (Traceability Score B) + (Certainty Score B)

We will go into more detail in Chapter 11 on how to structure and record the variables that influence risk.

Corruption crime scripts

Case studies

U.S. border patrol and customs agents smuggle drugs

In this example a border patrol officer, working under the supervision of a customs special agent, conspires to import marijuana into the United States. They facilitate the import of drugs by calling ahead and declaring that they have an "official controlled delivery of narcotics", thereby causing the inspection officers at the border inspection point to leave the area. They subsequently use a key issued to them to access the gate through the border. This case highlights several opportunity factors: firstly, the border officer role enabled a high level of *access* to open the border gate. Effectively by issuing the key, the border officer was provided unfettered access to pass through the border. The *authority* to declare an official controlled delivery also enabled the customs officer the ability to reduce the security at the border and thereby reduce the *visibility* and arguably the *traceability* of their actions at the border.

Chapter key points

- Opportunity is a key driver for insider threat, working in concert to increase the likelihood that a motivated actor will be capable of committing a deliberate or inadvertent act.
- A scaled and systemic model for decomposing opportunity factors against the organisational assets provides the ability to readily analyse relative risks and better direct effort to manage it.
- This decomposition draws from the breakdown of the organisational value streams, objectives, and assets outlined in preceding chapters.

References

Association of Certified Fraud Examiners. (2022). *Occupational fraud 2022: A report to the nations.* https://legacy.acfe.com/report-to-the-nations/2022/

Australian Commission for Law Enforcement Integrity. (2013). *A joint investigation of alleged corrupt conduct among officers of the Australian customs and border protection service at Sydney International Airport (interim report).*

Cohen, L., & Felson, M. (1979). Social change and crime rate trends: A routine activity approach. *American Sociological Review, 44*(4), 588–608.

Cole, E., & Ring, S. (2006). *Insider threat: Protecting the enterprise from sabotage, spying and theft.* Syngress Publishing.

Friesen, L. (2012). Certainty of punishment versus severity of punishment: An experimental investigation. *Southern Economic Journal, 79*(2), 399–421.

Gelles, M. (2016). *Insider threat: Prevention, detection, mitigation and deterrence.* Butterworth-Heinemann.

Jeffery, C. R. (1971). *Crime prevention through environmental design* (Vol. 91). Sage Publications.

Manning, M. (2018). A baseline model of deterrence. In B. Leclerc & D. Reynald (Eds.), *The future of rational choice for crime prevention.* Routledge.

Manning, M. (2019). Economics. In R. Wortley, A. Sidebottom, N. Tilley, & G. Laycock (Eds.), *Routledge handbook of crime science.* Routledge.

Monahan, G. (2008). *Enterprise risk management: A methodology for achieving strategic objectives.* John Wiley & Sons.

Perry, M. (2017). Influence of physical design. In L. Fennelly (Ed.), *Effective physical security* (pp. 55–65). Butterworth-Heinemann.

Piza, E. L., Welsh, B. C., Farrington, D. P., & Thomas, A. L. (2019). CCTV surveillance for crime prevention: A 40-year systematic review with meta-analysis. *Criminology and Public Policy, 18*(1), 135–159. https://doi.org/10.1111/1745-9133.12419

Stickney, F., & Johnston, W. (1983). Delegation and a sharing of authority by the project manager. *Project Management Quarterly, 14*(1), 42–53.

Vu, H. M. (2020). Employee empowerment and empowering leadership: A literature review. *Technium, 2*(7), 20–28. https://doi.org/10.47577/technium.v2i7.1653

5

UNDERSTANDING AND CATEGORISING BENEFICIARIES

Introduction

Generally, insider risk has a nexus to an external party who benefit from the fraudulent or corrupt behaviour. This is particularly true in view of the rise of more complex organised crime activities, which actively target the services of government and private sector entities, especially financial services providers (Australian Criminal Intelligence Commission, 2017; Smith et al., 2018).

In this chapter, we outline an approach to systematically classify beneficiaries and their relationships with organisations. This classification is vital as it enables one to target the relationships between insiders and external parties that really matter to insider risk, to develop a body of knowledge about the *modus operandi* of different corrupting entities, and to develop enhanced screening and due diligence processes for staff. In the context of the financial sector and border control organisations, there is a breadth of different entities who interact with these systems: for example migration agents, customs brokers, financial managers, mortgage brokers, visa applicants, legal professionals, accountants, and remittance services. A structured approach is necessary to make sense of these entities and their interactions with public and private entities charged with preserving the integrity of border control and financial systems.

Why are beneficiaries important?

As previously highlighted, organisational systems are vulnerable to insider threats given the value of the *assets* they possess and the *opportunities* available to exploit these assets. We must, therefore, turn to the question of who will exploit opportunities. As touched on in Chapter 2, organisations are

DOI: 10.4324/9781003055716-5

focused externally. In a commercial setting they provide services to clients and customers, whilst generally in competition with other parties for market share. In government, they regulate the behaviour of market players to mitigate the economic, social, and environmental harms that flow from market failure. Equally, organisations work in partnerships and within supply chains that, in sum, create value to customers or to society at large. As such, relationships with external entities are key to the achievement of organisational objectives and outcomes.

However, these entities may also have an interest in undermining or taking advantage of the assets of the organisation for their own benefit and to the detriment of the organisation. Where it is easiest and most cost effective to do so, they may enlist the assistance of insiders, who are able to facilitate malicious activity given the *assets* they interact with and *opportunities* available to them (as we've covered in previous chapters). In extreme cases, entities such as organised crime groups or market competitors may go so far as to actively infiltrate regulators or competing companies to take advantage of the opportunities that an insider presents. For example Dokko and Shin (2019) found that almost 85% of cases of industrial espionage are committed in cooperation with company insiders.

Given the breadth of typologies and interactions of potential beneficiaries with the organisation, a systemic approach is needed to identify and target the highest level of risk. This focuses the organisation's efforts on monitoring those beneficiaries who are most likely to engage in corrupting insiders and to those that will most grievously harm the mission and objectives of the organisation.

We propose a four-element model to categorise and assess the threat posed by beneficiaries through insider activity (Figure 5.1).

- **Group:** To systemically assess the threat and risk, the potential beneficiaries must be grouped into typologies relevant to the organisation and its operating environment. It is to these groups that each of the other elements is applied.
- **Interaction:** This element describes the way that the beneficiary interacts with the organisation and the roles within it – is it, for example, a systemic and ongoing interaction or a point in time interaction?
- **Intent:** This element describes the reason or interest that the beneficiary has when engaging with an insider. For example, organised criminal intent versus pure personal interest.
- **Capability:** This element describes the capability of a potential beneficiary engaging an insider and using them for their own benefit, for example, organised crime entities with substantial resources and *modus operandi* for infiltration or corrupting insiders, or well-resourced lobby groups who have the resources and connections to influence decision-makers. On the

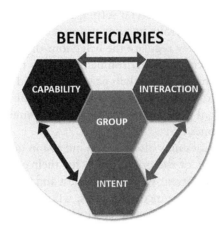

FIGURE 5.1 The Beneficiary Model

other hand, an individual applicant for services may be able to bribe an individual officer, but their capability is likely more limited.

It is worth noting that this part of the model is relevant to those forms of insider threat which involve and are to the benefit of external parties. On the other hand, in many settings the insider themselves may be the beneficiary of their actions, for example if they defraud the organisation or embezzle its funds.

Group classification

As discussed in Chapter 2, the decomposition of the organisation involves identifying the key value streams through which it creates value to clients or to society more broadly, and the interaction of those clients, regulated entities, and stakeholders across those value chains.

There are countless typologies and classifications of entities which interact with organisations and their objectives. As such, we will not attempt to provide an in-depth classification system for all typologies. It is advantageous for this analysis to be undertaken specifically for a given entity to ensure that the classification is developed in organisationally relevant language and, therefore, comprehensible by the organisation and its decision-makers. However, we propose some broad lenses which can assist an organisation to determine and classify entities of interest.

- **Clients:** Entities to which products/services are specifically provided and to whom some form of value is delivered.
- **Partners:** Entities who work in deliberate or incidental collaboration to create value across value chains.

- **Regulated entities:** Entities to which rules are applied by government organisations in accordance with legislation and regulation.
- **Commercial associates:** Entities which work under mutually agreed contracts and agreements to deliver products and services which further the organisation's mission and objectives.
- **Competitors and adversaries:** Entities who compete with the organisation, or whose interests run contrary to the mission and objectives of the organisation: such as criminal groups.

In our imaginary migration and border agency example from Chapter 2, we outlined one key value stream which grants and controls entry into the country. Along this value chain we identified different groups of entities (Figure 5.2) which interact with the organisation:

- Different classes of applicants, including visitors, workers, families, students, and residents.
- Agents who act on behalf of applicants to secure them the permission to enter the country.
- Sponsors who sponsor applicants: for example employers who sponsor workers to enter the country to work.
- Carriers who transport the travellers to the country.
- Airport (and potentially seaport) corporations that facilitate entry into the country at the first port of entry.

If we expand on the legitimate entities that interact with our imaginary organisation, we could also add criminal entities who may seek to smuggle goods or people across the border for criminal benefit (e.g. human trafficking).

This classification system will provide the backbone for assessing the relative risk created by the potential beneficiaries and the organisation. The

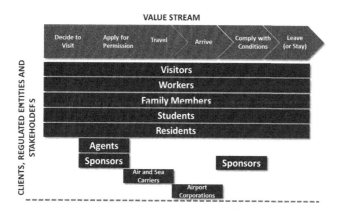

FIGURE 5.2 Value Stream and Group Decomposition

beneficiary classification (Figure 5.3) should be elaborated by reference to the organisational assets, by identifying those external entities that directly or indirectly interact with the organisation's decision, information, or tangible/intangible assets.

Some examples follow:

- For all permission decisions, the classes of applicants to that permission would be beneficiaries, along with secondary beneficiaries: for example agents who charge for their assistance to obtain the permission.
- Information assets have value to criminal entities who might seek to use them for the purposes of fraud and identity theft.
- Tangible assets would have value to competitors who seek to reverse-engineer a company's product/s as a means of competing.

FIGURE 5.3 Beneficiary Classification

These are simple examples, yet they illustrate the need to explore beneficiaries through the lens of the organisation's assets as well as its value streams and business model. As we touched on in Chapter 3, rather than creating new semantics or data models for the classification of the core elements of the organisation's business model (as opposed to those which are specifically related to insider threat), it is more beneficial to maintain alignment to the semantics that the organisation already uses to describe the external entities it interacts with as part of its operations.

Interaction

To benefit from insider activity, the beneficiaries must have some form of interaction with the organisation through its assets or the people occupying roles that work with those assets. The types of interactions that these entities have with the organisation will change the character of the insider threat and their ability to use an insider to achieve their purposes.

For an insider to be utilised by a beneficiary, a relationship must be formed between the two. The loss or harm flowing from insider threat activities increases the longer it is allowed to continue. The higher-consequence insider threats will therefore be those of an ongoing and systemic nature which are maintained over time. Additionally, the most serious forms of collusion between insiders and external beneficiaries requires a relationship of trust, that each actor will do their part to enable whatever the scheme is, and that they will not expose the other parties. So, from an interaction perspective, it is those features of the interactions between beneficiaries and insiders which most enable the formation of sustained and ongoing relationships which create the greatest threat.

As we consider these connections between beneficiaries and potential insiders it is useful to apply two key lenses: formal and informal interactions.

Formal

Formal interactions denote those exchanges that occur between a beneficiary and the organisation, represented by its staff, during business, that are part of the business processes. Within those formal interactions, between the beneficiary and the role, several factors should be considered to determine the level of likelihood that the beneficiary will be able to form a relationship with an insider:

- How close or distant does the potential insider interact with prospective beneficiaries? For example, working on the wharf front, a border officer works in close and repeated contact with other individuals working in this environment including stevedores, shipping crews, and logistics employees. Conversely, officers who assess license or visa applications and are based in offices are far more distant from the applicants: their interaction is likely to be over the phone or email and relatively infrequent.

- How transient or repeated is the interaction? For example, an applicant for a visa may interact very few times with the agency when initially applying to visit. They then may decide to work, followed by a decision to seek permanent residency. There are a limited number of interactions between the applicant and the agency, let alone any single processing officer. On the other hand, migration agents are solely focused on procuring visas for their clients and will interact with the agency on a consistent and ongoing basis, providing a much better foundation for creating a relationship with one or more processing officers.
- Does the role provide any form of agency or representation on behalf of a prospective beneficiary? For example, case officers may provide representation for individuals or organisations within an organisation, helping to facilitate their access to products and services.

Higher-order relationships between roles within the organisation and prospective beneficiaries will increase the likelihood that they are able to form a relationship to take advantage of the organisation's assets. The continuing nature of these relationships can also create ongoing opportunities for potential collusion which can increase losses, harms, and consequences to the organisation depending on the level of risk (see Table 3.4). In contrast to informal interactions (as set out below), formal interactions (classified as low, medium, or high, as shown in Table 5.1) are defined by the practices of the organisation and are, therefore, more straightforward to identify and therefore easier to control to mitigate the threat of insider risk.

Informal

Informal interactions, by contrast, concern interactions and relationships that may exist between a potential insider and a beneficiary in the course of their personal lives. These relationships can be established prior to the employment of a person by the organisation or may be established at a later point once the person has already been employed by the organisation.

Examples of informal interactions are as follows:

- Family relationships
- Friendships
- External commercial/business relationships
- Identity relationships: such as cultural and linguistic, socio-economic, religious, community, or values identities
- Criminal relationships

TABLE 5.1 Risk Scale: Formal Interactions

	1: Low	*2: Moderate*	*3: High*
Formal Interaction	Distant relationship with no direct formal interaction between the role and the beneficiary or transient interaction for a limited number of interactions.	Repeated though distant interactions between the role and the potential beneficiaries.	Close and repeated interactions between the role and the potential beneficiaries as part of the normal business of the role. The role may also act in an agency or representative capacity for the potential beneficiary.

Given these informal relationships are independent of the organisation, they are less readily assessed. They do not have a systemic relationship with a particular part of the business and, as such, relationships of concern could occur anywhere across the business. It is also possible that these relationships will develop after a person has been employed by the organisation. They are nonetheless important relationships, and the organisation should have in place controls to either limit illicit relationships and avoid infiltration by other organisations or detect where informal relationships may be compromising the integrity of the organisation and its staff. We will explore controls and their linkages to this area of analysis in more depth in Chapter 7.

A case study: ABS insider trading scam

ABC news, in 2015 (Vines & Carlyon, 2015), reported on a pair of university acquaintances, one employed with the Australian Bureau of Statistics and the other working within a major bank as a trader, that began Australia's largest insider trading scheme. The "informal" relationships they had developed while at university, coupled with the positions each of them held, enabled them to access sensitive labour force data (the asset in our model) which was used to make trades on the currency market. This relatively simple exchange of information became the largest insider trading scheme in Australian history, netting upwards of AUD$7 million before the scheme was uncovered by authorities (see Chenery, 2021 – full story on the crime).

In this case the detection of the relationship was made not by the organisation that employed the insider but separately by police investigating unusual trading patterns by the bank employee, including investigating potential connections within his social media accounts. Neither the connection nor the leaking of information was detected by the Australian Bureau of Statistics, in part due to a failure to recognise the value of the information assets they possessed for the purposes of trading, or for which beneficiaries may be able to use. The example illustrates the importance of understanding the potential informal beneficiary connections which could increase insider threat, which enables better prevention and monitoring of those threats. We can surmise that if the Australian Bureau of Statistics had considered relationships with traders to be of importance, alongside the value of labour force data, the organisation may have been able to put in place additional measures to manage the threat, such as mandatory declarations of relationships with traders, monitoring arrangements, and deterrent education and communication programs.

Intent

This element of the model explores the reasons that the beneficiary targets an organisational asset and what they have to gain from compromising that asset. There are two broad categories of intent that assist in focusing the organisation's effort on the greatest threats to its integrity – a pure benefit intent versus adversarial intent.

Pure beneficial intent refers to the beneficiary benefitting from the organisation's assets and potentially causing loss, but without directly opposing the organisation's purpose, mission, or objectives. In contrast, adversarial intent is in direct opposition to the organisation's purpose and the outcomes it is trying to achieve.

Examples

Example 1: Theft of rail lines

An employee of a rail company who is responsible for purchase and stocktake of steel rail lines is informally associated with a steel manufacturer. Together they conspire to steal a proportion of rail lines which can be melted down at a large profit to both, while covering up the losses through false stocktake and invoicing documents.

In this example, the beneficiary and the insider are benefiting from the rail company assets, and the company is facing a loss. The activity is not undermining its core purpose as a rail company (*pure beneficial intent*). On the other hand, if the insider and beneficiary were conspiring to sabotage rail lines, directly impacting on the conduct of its business, these activities would be in direct opposition to its organisational purpose (*adversarial intent*).

Example 2: Illicit drug importation

A border agency's purpose is to restrict the entry of people and goods that will cause economic, social, or environmental harm, such as drugs and weapons. In this example, border officers are conspiring with criminally affiliated wharf workers to facilitate the entry of drugs into the country without detection. In this instance, the beneficiary's *adversarial intent* is in direct opposition to the purpose of the border protection regime. On the other hand, if there was a scheme to utilise the border agency's data for insider trading which for some commodities correlates very strongly to the stock market pricing for those commodities, then this would potentially cause reputational damage but would not directly affect the organisational purpose (*pure beneficial intent*).

Example 3: Illegal waste disposal

An environmental regulator is responsible for preventing industrial waste from being dumped into river systems. The regulator monitors industrial activity, including through remote sensing and onsite audit activity. A company is colluding with an insider to adjust records enabling it to avoid more costly waste disposal processes and, therefore, provide it a competitive advantage compared to its peers. This is in direct opposition to the environmental goals of the regulator (*adversarial intent*).

Example 4: Money laundering

A criminal organisation utilises insiders within a financial or gambling institution to facilitate the laundering of its illicit funds. In this instance, the intent is *not adversarial* to the core mission and objectives of these organisations; in fact these organisations may benefit from the additional cash flow the money laundering may result in. This example illustrates that non-adversarial intent may still have high impact, as in this case it could trigger serious regulatory consequences for the organisation, assuming a sound national anti-money laundering regulatory regime is in place.

The other distinction worth making is between systemic ongoing or organised intent as opposed to temporal intent. In a similar vein to ongoing interactions, which can increase the systemic nature of insider threat, if the intent is one that is ongoing rather than limited to a point in time then the insider threat is likely to be more systemic and enduring, thereby creating more harm and loss to the organisation. For example, if the interest is a personal interest relating to a specific product or service, such as an application, then once that transaction is concluded, the risk will be reduced (noting of course that the risk will still exist across the cohort of applicants). By contrast, an organised crime entity who seeks to import drugs on an ongoing basis will continue to have that intent over time and therefore poses an ongoing threat to the organisation, thus creating threat/risk warranting a higher level of investment to manage on an ongoing basis.

The importance of outlining these distinctions is to support a more nuanced analysis of the relative insider threat. As depicted at Figure 5.4, the adversarial intent results in a higher level of consequence insofar as the beneficiary is working directly against the objectives and interests of the organisation and thereby creating more material harm to those objectives, as opposed to incidental losses, such as financial ones.

An ongoing intent will contribute to both an increase in risk likelihood and a consequence. If the intent is continuous, then its threat will also continue resulting in more systemic impacts on the organisation and greater losses. Similarly, the ongoing intent will result in a higher likelihood that that beneficiary will seek to corrupt the relevant insider role and that they will maintain that relationship, thereby creating a higher likelihood of the insider threat typology eventuating (see Table 5.2).

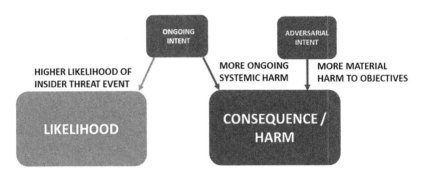

FIGURE 5.4 Effect of Beneficiary Intent on Likelihood and Consequence of Risk

TABLE 5.2 Risk Scale: Intent

	1: Low	*2: Moderate*	*3: High*
Interest	Non-ongoing or temporal intent which is non-adversarial to the organisation's mission and objectives.	Non-ongoing or temporal intent which is adversarial to the organisation's mission and objectives *Or* ongoing intent which is non-adversarial to the organisation's mission and objectives.	Ongoing adversarial intent against the organisation's mission and objectives.

Capability

This element of the model refers to the means or capability of the beneficiary to engage and use insiders to pursue their objectives. Alongside intent, capability is a critical component for externally motivated insider threat. As noted by Betts (1998),

A threat consists of capabilities multiplied by intentions, if either is zero the threat is zero.

The potential beneficiary groupings we identified above will have differing abilities to engage an insider ranging from rudimentary, opportunistic capability to much more sophisticated methodologies to plant, conscript, convince, or intimidate an insider into engaging in malicious insider activity.

As part of a modelled analysis of the threat type and level of capability of different potential benefit, groups must be examined to determine how the potential beneficiary is likely to approach corrupting an insider. The focus here will be on resources towards managing the risks involving high capability entities and determining the best mechanisms to mitigate the risks which draw on those capabilities.

Typologies

We now identify elements of capability – by no means exhaustive – that can serve as a guide when considering the capabilities of potential beneficiaries of insider threat to different types of organisations.

Financial capability

Conducting ongoing and systemic corruption may require access to substantial financial or other resources to pay off insiders to act on their behalf. This is particularly the case where a scheme requires coordinated efforts on behalf of multiple actors and which may require substantial resources. Corruption of senior public officials and politicians may also require substantial financial or other incentives.

- *License applicants* for example may be able to offer a modest bribe to the assessor to fast-track or approve their licence. They have a relatively low level of capability to engage in more substantial forms of corruption or insider threat.
- *Business competitors*, on the other hand, may have substantial financial assets to incentivise an insider to steal intellectual property on their behalf or even to plant a person or people within a rival organisation.
- *Organised criminal entities* have substantial funds and resources to incentivise insiders to facilitate the movement of drugs and other illicit goods

through the border. They also have the capability to launder the illicit funds on behalf of the insiders.
- *Multinational companies and lobby groups* may have substantial assets to engage in bribery of public officials and politicians to provide favourable contracts or general policy settings.

Method capability

Certain beneficiaries may have established *modus operandi* associated with their activities including activities potentially associated with engaged insiders through means other than financial. Examples include coercive techniques such as intimidation, social engineering, threats of violence, blackmail, honey trapping (i.e. a practice involving the use of romantic or sexual relationships for interpersonal, political, or monetary purpose), and manipulating addictions such as drug or gambling addictions. While these methods may be mostly associated with organised criminal groups, there are at minimum alleged examples of legitimate businesses engaging in these kinds of activities to benefit from favourable political environments, gain competitive advantage, or undermine rival firms (see for example Graham-Harrison et al., 2018). In contrast, individuals with unsophisticated or unrefined means have far less capability to corrupt insiders.

Role capability

Beneficiaries may hold a role within society, business, or politics, which may provide them with the capability to work with insiders for mutual benefit. For example, wealthy and powerful individuals may be able to provide favours to public officials and politicians in return for political and legislative benefits. In our Bureau of Statistics example above, the trader can facilitate the activity that provides the financial return on behalf of both parties. "Fences" may provide a similar benefit, enabling stolen assets to be sold and benefits shared from sales. Another aspect of role capability is the social influence of the beneficiary. An example of this may be religious influence, group influence, socio-economic hierarchies, and other social constructs which provide authority, influence, or obligation. Like formal interactions, the level of capability can be classified as low, moderate, or high, as depicted in Table 5.3

Tactical displacement

Initiatives to regulate market behaviour or control criminal activity have the potential to create a displacement effect, which triggers changes to the *modus operandi* of the regulated community or criminal entities. This effect could be temporal, locational, tactical or relate to the target of the non-compliant

TABLE 5.3 Risk Scale: Role Capability

Capability Scale		
1: Low	*2: Moderate*	*3: High*
The beneficiary has limited assets at their disposal to induce an insider to act on their behalf. The beneficiary has limited or no general influence or authority.	The beneficiary has access to resources and connections to influence insiders though restricted to limited interactions or domains of the organisation or would primarily be opportunistic.	The beneficiary has broad and systemic access to resources which can facilitate influencing or planting of insiders within the organisation.

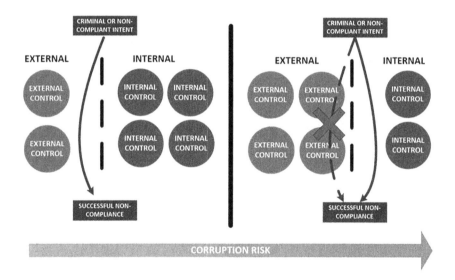

TACTICAL DISPLACEMENT

FIGURE 5.5 Tactical Displacement: Insider Threat

or criminal behaviour (Guerette & Bowers, 2009). Insider threat and corruption can represent a tactical displacement from "external non-compliance", that is non-compliance that does not involve an insider, to a change of *modus operandi* that involves insiders. As presented in Figure 5.5, this shift in tactics can occur where the intent to achieve some benefit through non-compliance persists, but achieving that non-compliance becomes more challenging as the regulatory or target organisation strengthens its ability to control non-compliance. For example, for our border agency, if it replaces its fleet of

X-ray scanning technology with newer technology capable of more readily and accurately detecting the presence of drugs within consignments or grows its workforce at border checkpoints leading to an increase in detections of contraband material, this will increase the losses to an organised criminal entity in its drug importation activities. As such, it may become more profitable to shift its tactics towards engaging insiders who can undermine the new control measures and reduce seizures/losses.

Organisations are constantly enhancing and improving their measures to control external risk to their objectives. Few evaluations have been conducted measuring the displacement effect of organised crime prevention initiatives, and thus observing potential displacement is difficult (Levi & Maguire, 2004). However, it remains plausible that such tactical displacement is in fact occurring. The implication, therefore, from an insider threat perspective is that when strengthening the external control environment, organisations must also assess the extent to which different entities/actors are affected by the changes in control mechanisms. Further, it is necessary to examine whether the change in the control environment is likely to create a tactical shift towards corruption of insiders to achieve their intent or objective. In the event of a capable and motivated actor (beneficiary), the strengthening of the external control environment will need to be complemented by a strengthening of the internal control environment. We explore the typologies and development of controls in more detail in Chapter 7. The following examples illustrate the shift in tactics by a motivated actor and how an organisation can strengthen its internal controls in parallel.

Examples of tactical displacement in context

Example 1: U.S. customs and border protection

Over a period of several years, through a combination of technology advancements, financial investment, and infrastructure development, the United States Customs and Border Protection (CBP) has strengthened its controls of the land and sea borders of the United States. However, a report by the Homeland Security Advisory Council claims that "arrests for corruption of CBP personnel far exceed on a per capita basis such arrests at other federal law enforcement agencies" (Homeland Security Advisory Council, 2015, p. 6). Arguably, this surplus of corruption can at least in part be attributed to a tactical displacement whereby the strengthening of border controls into the United States has made it more worthwhile for organised crime groups to attempt to co-opt border officials to facilitate the smuggling of drugs, weapons, and people into the United States. Regular and ongoing bribes of officials can drastically reduce the chances of detection and thereby reduce the potential losses to profit motivated criminal activity.

Example 2: General regulation and corruption

Research conducted by the World Bank (Amin & Soh, 2020) examined the correlation between the level of regulation on firms and the level of corruption, perhaps unsurprisingly finding that greater regulatory burden does indeed lead to higher overall and petty corruption. The implication is that the mere imposition of new rules and regulation can alone create a type of tactical displacement towards corruption/insider threat. Arguably, therefore, the corruption risk/insider threat needs to be considered as part of the design of any new regulatory framework.

Example 3: Information security and access

Numerous international studies have reported a dramatic increase in phishing attacks over the past two to five years (see for example Alkhalil et al., 2021). While the increase can likely be attributed to numerous different factors, including socio-economic factors, access to Internet, and the pandemic, one arguable cause is the growing measures to combat cyber-threats. Here we point to the external penetration of systems to harvest or corrupt data. Such penetration creates a tactical shift towards social engineering activities to obtain access to systems through inadvertent insiders or, worse, through active engagement of malicious insiders to harvest data and information to support organised crime or gain a competitive commercial advantage.

Risk assessment: Using intelligence

Intelligence is simply a set of information collection and analytical techniques which apply inductive reasoning to make inferences about the capability and intent of other actors ("threat" in intelligence jargon) and assess the impact of that threat on objectives. From the perspective of insider threat, the utility of intelligence is to understand the capability and intent factors we have outlined above, to understand the threat that potential beneficiaries may pose to the organisation from a corruption or insider perspective.

The process of intelligence consists of a cycle of activities:

1 Setting requirements: establishing where the intelligence should focus and what the key issues, questions, and actors are that are going to affect the achievement of the organisation's objectives. This sets the direction for where intelligence should focus efforts on information collection and analysis.
2 Planning: focusing on planning what information to collect and how that information should be collected (e.g. human sources, open source, signals). Planning happens both in terms of specific pieces of analysis and on

a broader systemic level, focusing collection efforts on longer-term threats to the state or organisation.

3 Collection: a broad-based set of activities to collect the relevant information for analysis to determine the threats.

4 Processing and exploitation: a set of activities to convert the collected information and data into a usable format for analysis. Such activities could include structuring and ordering data or translating from foreign languages.

5 Analysis and production: this consists of applying a variety of analysis techniques to draw inferences from incomplete data or information collected. These techniques are designed to explore and limit bias and apply inductive reasoning to make inferences about the probability that a threat exists.

6 Dissemination: assessment to decision-makers who can use the intelligence to guide a wide variety of strategic, operational, and tactical decisions.

Published intelligence reports highlight the issue of insider threat and corruption as a key enabler for a broad range of criminal activities and regulatory non-compliance (Europol, 2021). However, based on our research, these reports are generally produced by central policing or criminal intelligence organisations. There appears to be a dearth of intelligence analysis from within organisations that are the target of corruption and insider threats, even for organisations that publish assessments of risk and threat.

It is plausible that organisations remain focused on applying an external lens to the threat environment and are yet to consider the level of threat they are exposed to by insiders. Intelligence collection and analysis activities are,

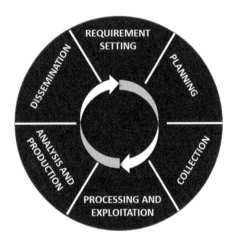

FIGURE 5.6 The Intelligence Cycle

therefore, focused on understanding the capability and intent of actors in respect of their general criminal or regulatory behaviour. But their capability and intent to corrupt insiders remains an intelligence gap.

This case may be illustrated utilising our above border agency example. If the agency's intelligence collection and analysis efforts are focused on understanding the capability and intent of criminal actors to import drugs, it might focus on collecting and analysing information about its production and supply chains, import routes, and mechanisms for trying to conceal drugs within legitimate shipments. However, it could very well neglect to consider and therefore collect information regarding the criminal actor's capability and intent to corrupt their staff or the staff of other actors at the border. The agency's decision-making regarding managing threats will most likely be focused on those threats that it has identified. However, it remains exposed as it is potentially being undermined through insiders working within the organisation to facilitate imports whilst undercutting the agency's mechanisms to detect and therefore disrupt drug importation.

Strategic, operational, and tactical intelligence

Understanding insider threats consists of understanding the threat associated with an individual entity as well as the systemic patterns that give rise to threat in a broader context. From an intelligence perspective, this is expressed in terms of strategic, operational, and tactical intelligence levels.

Strategic intelligence relates to analysis which is required to form policy or strategies at a whole of organisation, national, or international level. From an insider threat perspective, this consists of understanding the broad patterns and drivers which give rise to insider threat at an organisational level or on national/international scale. This would include analyses of broad socio-economic changes, political and attitudinal changes, and technology advances, among other megatrends which could shift the systemic threat of corruption to the organisation. The purpose of such intelligence is to inform the highest-level investment decision-making on where the focus should be to mitigate the threat to the organisation.

Operational intelligence, in contrast, focuses on a contemporary understanding of current actors and their capability and intent. Assessments in this realm of intelligence assists the organisation in understanding which assets are being targeted, for what purpose, and the level of capability of actors that could engage insiders to enable criminal activity, regulatory non-compliance, or illicit approaches to market competition. The purpose of these assessments is to direct resources towards target areas for insider threat and to understand capabilities and *modus operandi* so that controls can be designed to mitigate and disrupt that modus operandi. This domain of intelligence also assists the organisation to identify and understand tactical displacements (as outlined above).

Tactical intelligence relates directly to an entity or a specific activity of the organisation and provides inputs to immediate decisions relating to that entity or activity. This may be, for example, related to a specific investigation or operation in relation to a person or entity of interest.

With intelligence becoming a mainstream function for many organisations in government and the private sector, it is our assertion that intelligence activities must form part of any mature insider threat management approach. Strategic and operational intelligence, in particular, provides insights on the systemic capability and intent of potential beneficiaries to utilise insiders in pursuit of their objectives.

Chapter key points

- Insiders are at risk of being corrupted by external entities that benefit from the organisation assets that the insider has access to.
- Understanding the capability, intent, and type of interaction that different entities have within the organisation determines the level of risk associated with each entity type.
- Strengthening controls against an entity can create a tactical displacement towards corrupting insiders to achieve their purpose/intent.
- Intelligence, which is already used to underpin the understanding of external threats, is a vital input to assessing insider threat and risk.

References

Alkhalil, Z., Hewage, C., Nawaf, L., & Khan, I. (2021). Phishing attacks: A recent comprehensive study and a new anatomy. *Frontiers in Computer Science, 3.* https://doi.org/10.3389/fcomp.2021.563060

Amin, M., & Soh, Y. C. (2020). Does greater regulatory burden lead to more corruption evidence using firm-level survey data for developing countries. *The World Bank Economic Review*, *35*(3), October 2021, 812–828.

Australian Criminal Intelligence Commission. (2017). *Organised crime in Australia 2017.* https://www.acic.gov.au/publications/unclassified-intelligence-reports/organised-crime-australia-2017

Betts, R. (1998). Intelligence warning: Old problems, new agendas. *Parameters, 1*(1), 26–35.

Chenery, S. (2021). *The accomplice.* https://www.abc.net.au/news/2021-09-28/cracking-australias-largest-insider-trading-scam/100477328

Dokko, J., & Shin, M. (2019). A digital forensic investigation and verification model for industrial espionage. In S. I. A. T. E. Institute for Computer Sciences (Ed.), *Digital forensics and cyber crime*. Springer.

Europol. (2021). *European Union serious and organised crime threat assessment 2017.* https://www.europol.europa.eu/cms/sites/default/files/documents/report_socta2017_1.pdf

Graham-Harrison, E., Cadwalladr, C., & Osborne, H. (2018). *Cambridge analytica boasts of dirty tricks to swing elections*. https://www.theguardian.com/uk-news/2018/mar/19/cambridge-analytica-execs-boast-dirty-tricks-honey-traps-elections

Guerette, R. T., & Bowers, K. (2009). Assessing the extent of crime displacement and diffusion of benefits: A review of situational crime prevention evaluations. *Criminology, 47*(4), 1331–1368.

Homeland Security Advisory Council. (2015). *Council reports & recommendations 2015*.

Levi, M., & Maguire, M. (2004). Reducing and preventing organised crime: An evidence-based critique. *Crime, Law and Social Change, 41*(5), 397–469.

Smith, R., Oberman, T., & Fuller, G. (2018). Understanding and responding to serious and organised crime involvement in public sector corruption. *Trends & Issues in Crime and Criminal Justice, 534*, 1–16.

Vines, H., & Carlyon, P. (2015). *'Greedy' pair Lukas Kamay, Christopher Hill jailed over $7 million ABS insider trading scam*. https://www.abc.net.au/news/2015-03-17/pair-sentenced-over-abs-insider-trading/6324526

6

THINKING ABOUT MOTIVATION

Introduction

Much research has been undertaken to understand why people commit fraud and corruption. Examples of recent scholarship undertaken include the work of Iyer and Samociuk (2016), Tickner (2017), D. Archambeault et al. (2015), Mohamedbhai (2016), and Brooks et al. (2017), to name a few. This chapter builds on that research and proposes that people's motivation for fraud and corruption is comprised of three components: pressure, inducement, and rationalisation. These components help us better understand how and why people do the wrong thing, and thus assist government, non-government, and not-for-profit organisations to create preventative controls and ethical standards, which can address the motivating factors. The chapter also proposes that focusing on people's motivation is inherently less effective for managing insider risk, because people's motivations are so individualised that countermeasures cannot be effectively created in a systemic, repeatable, and reliable way.

Corruption and insider risk are inherently human concerns. As we have previously articulated, they emerge within systems of activity. Humans remain the primary actors within those systems, both effecting the tasks and activities that the system demands to achieve its higher order outcomes and acting on their own behalf to achieve personal and individual gain (or expected or desired outcomes) (Manning, 2018, 2019). The examination, therefore, of what motivates individuals to act against the system that they are part of has been core to much of the research on corruption and malicious insider threat. This research seeks both to identify the reasons that people act in a corrupt manner and from that basis to develop mechanisms

DOI: 10.4324/9781003055716-6

which counteract either the drivers for decisions or the effects of those drivers on decision-making.

There is much merit to these endeavours as motivation remains an important element of the risk equation, which gives rise to insider risk and, therefore, warrants additional examination and continual investment. However, in our view, there is a danger in taking an excessively anthropocentric approach to managing the risk: humans are highly individualised and while their actions may be the same and some inputs to those actions may be generalised, these generalisations are inherently less systemic and, therefore, less systemically controllable than other aspects of the organisation's operating model.

Why is motivation important?

As outlined in Chapter 4, opportunity is a major contributor to corruption and insider risk. However, the risk is not realised by opportunity alone. An actor must capitalise on that opportunity for the risk to eventuate. To analogise, a door may be left open but theft is only realised by a person walking through that door and stealing from the house. The motive that causes them to walk through that door and commit that act is, therefore, a key component to the realisation of the risk, not simply the door having been left open. Leaving aside other aspects of our model (such as assets and beneficiaries) the active part of the insider risk can be described as the multiplication of the opportunity by the motivation, insofar as if either is zero, the risk will not occur. Taking a page from Cohen and Felson's (1979) routine activity theory, even the greatest opportunities (a suitable target), if not coupled with a motivated actor (or likely offender) and/or the lack of a capable guardian, will not likely result in risk eventuating and thereby creating harm for the organisation. We will go into significant detail about the "system of capable guardians" that we propose as part of our model in Chapter 11.

Motivation is important in the risk equation in part because there are areas in which opportunities cannot be reduced because, as we outline further in Chapter 8 regarding *control impact*, attempting to control opportunities comes at too high a cost to the organisational objectives. As a result, mitigating motivation becomes our other viable alternative to address insider risk. As we touched upon in earlier chapters, the management of risk involves the relative investment of finite resources against the greatest areas of risk, thereby minimising harms overall (rather than an absolute activity designed to mitigate risk and uncertainty in a complete way). Therefore, understanding where in the organisation that motivation is mostly likely to occur and therefore to interact with opportunity provides a mechanism for more cost-effective investment of resources to mitigate both opportunity and motivation.

To inform the assessment of the risk, we need a model which can describe the elements of motivation in the context of insider risk. This enables the understanding of where those features are present within the organisation and the definition and design of controls which manage the motivational driver for risk (as outlined in Chapter 7).

The downside of the assessment of motivation to inform the management of insider risk is that humans are not very systemic and equivalent to one another. Upbringing, values, personal circumstances, peer groups (see for example Homel, 2005), and precipitating events (Wortley, 2016), and so forth are highly varied and will all play a role in the way an individual will think and act when presented with a set of circumstances. Indeed, even if their actions turn out to be the same, the motivation and "reasons" or drivers for exhibiting that behaviour can be highly diverse. For example, let's propose that a range of different people embezzle funds from their employer. The act or modus operandi itself may be the same (redirecting funds to their own accounts); however, their reasons and rationale for committing the act of embezzlement can be highly diverse. Examples include supporting an illicit drug habit, to punish the organisation for a perceived wrong, to meet the costs for a sick loved one, and to meet a political goal. Additionally, these potential motivating factors may present for two different individuals: one will act on the motivation while the other will not, for entirely personal reasons. As a result, the presence of motivating factors outlined in the literature such as "financial pressures" (Cressey, 1953) are not highly reliable indicators such that the absolute correlation or causation between motivational factors and malicious insider activity is therefore assured. Nonetheless, as we outline in this chapter, the analysis of motivation provides an additional input to a nuanced understanding of insider risk and an avenue for developing another layer of risk control.

The motivational factors

In 1958 criminologist Donald Cressy first developed the Fraud Triangle (see Tickner & Button, 2021), in which he described the elements that he considered contributed to the commission of fraud both external and internal to an organisation (e.g. embezzlement). The Fraud Triangle sets out three elements: opportunity, pressure, and rationalisation. The Triangle remains both influential and instructive for our examination of motivation insofar as two of the elements go to the motivations of the individual to commit fraud: namely pressure and motivation. Indeed, we propose these motivational elements are applicable to insider risk more broadly (the third element "opportunity", already discussed in Chapter 4). Cressy's focus is on the elements that enable an individual to commit fraudulent activity and, as such, the lens that is applied is by the individual facing the factors which will enable or encourage them to act fraudulently. Other researchers have criticised Cressy's Triangle for focusing too heavily on individual-level factors, which are unable to explain more socio-systemic triggers of fraud (Suh et al., 2020).

Our analysis, instead, attempts to link these individual-level factors with the broader system. Further, we examine the problem from the "system lens", which we propose provides a stronger means of developing broad-based controls and countermeasures, as we set out in Chapter 7. As a result, we seek to develop a deeper model that sees pressure and rationalisation as part of a motivation process which acts on the individual, while opportunity is separate and is primarily focused on the system of organisation.

In the context of insider risk and corruption, in a series of seminal examinations of corruption and its causes, Adam Graycar's studies appear to confirm that pressure and rationalisation apply equally to the study of motivation in corruption (Figure 6.1).

We argue that a third motivational element should be added: inducement. The reason for its inclusion is that it is distinct from pressure and rationalisation and provides for a further classification of controls which are specifically designed around managing the inducements that drive a person to commit malicious insider acts, whether through the acts themselves or through a third-party beneficiary (see Chapter 5).

The above-described elements provide a framework not only for identifying and understanding the factors which give rise to corruption and insider risk; they also provide a basis for designing controls, as we set out in substantial detail in the next chapter.

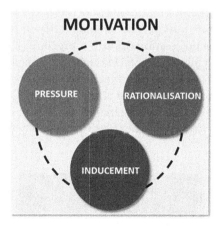

FIGURE 6.1   Motivation Model

Pressure

At the centre of the examination of insider risk motivation is the simple question: why do people commit corruption or other malicious insider actions? Examining a range of case studies, Cressy sought to answer this question by undertaking a holistic situational analysis of the people involved in these activities and identify systemic themes on what drove their behaviour. Similarly, Graycar and Prenzler (2013) utilise case studies which were, importantly, drawn from countries where corruption and bribery would not normally be considered to be a routine part of the operating environment. Hence, acting in corrupt ways in these countries could be considered a deviation from normal and acceptable behaviour rather than activities which have become culturally normalised. These actions, therefore, require an additional element of motivation beyond the learning and repetition of behaviours within a system or cultural framework. They require an active step to motivate a person to step outside the norms and accept the personal risk that may come from that deviation from acceptable behaviours.

Cressy's body of research, beginning with a seminal early piece (Cressey, 1953), outlined the fact that corrupt actors often (though not always) are subject to some form of personal pressure that caused them to act in a particular way. Gambling addiction, financial debts, drug dependency, and sex addiction, for example, can create the circumstances in which a person will act on when an opportunity is presented to them to contribute to resolving that pressure. Embezzlement of company finances, for example, would assist a person to resolve their financial debts, thereby providing a release valve and lessening the psychological stress associated with the acquired debt.

In our view there are three possible lifecycles: a *Simplex lifecycle, Pressure–Resolution lifecycle, Pressure–Resolution–Adaptation lifecycle.*

At its simplest, the relationship between the pressure motivator and the act might be the immediate resolution of a short-term pressure. We refer to this as the *Simplex lifecycle* insofar as it is unidirectional: once the pressure has been resolved there is no creation of further pressure (Figure 6.2).

An example of the Simplex lifecycle might be immediate peer pressure to make a temporal or unique decision in a friend's favour, for example using discretion to waive a speeding fine for a friend or family member. These kinds of behaviours could be considered circumstantial and temporal, and therefore not part of a systemic view of risk. This is true when being considered

FIGURE 6.2 Simplex Pressure

FIGURE 6.3 Pressure Resolution Cycle

at the individual level. However, these simplex behaviours, when perpetrated by many actors within the system, can nonetheless raise the level of risk and indeed create corruption-sympathetic cultural norms (see also Chapter 10, on culture).

In many circumstances, the resolution to the stressor might be short lived, thereby creating an ongoing *Pressure–Resolution lifecycle* (Figure 6.3).

For example, in the case of gambling addiction, the stealing of corporate funds might resolve the initial pressure but is similarly an enabler for ongoing gambling behaviour. In the absence of a real risk of detection, this becomes a lifecycle whereby the insider behaviour relieves the pressure that was its original catalyst. However, by relieving it enables the behaviour that led to the pressure (in this case gambling), thereby continuing the pressure on the individual.

Pressures that give rise to the Simplex lifecycle may also evolve into the *Pressure–Resolution lifecycle*. Using our example above, providing a benefit to friends and family members may stem from or create an expectation that family or friends will receive the same favours that the person is able to give by virtue of their role. If they can, for example, grant a visa for entry to a country and there is a family or community expectation that this favour will be granted, then the demand – and therefore pressure – for this service to be provided is likely to increase once this favour has been granted to one friend or family member.

Finally, in other circumstances the pressure factor may only be a cata-lysing agent which, in combination with the opportunities we discussed in Chapter 4, creates a pressure–resolution–adaptation lifecycle. In this case the psychological distress created by the pressure creates the initial catalyst for taking advantage of the opportunity presented to resolve the psychological distress caused by the pressure. Once the pressure has been resolved, how-ever, there is an adaptation which occurs which transforms and progresses the pressure.

Again, using the example of theft of company funds, financial debts may provide the catalyst for a decision to commit the theft and indeed either immediately or over a period could resolve those debts. Assuming that the pressure is at the centre of a rational decision-making process to address those debts and assuming there are a number of precipitating factors (i.e. prior events that lead to the rational decision but shape and influence the decision) and situational forces that regulate behaviour by the opportunities they present (see Wortley, 1998), then we would assume that once the pressure of those debts is resolved, then the theft activities will cease. This, in reality, is not what consistently or typically occurs. Our case studies highlight that there is, instead, an adaptation element that may occur. This is where the pressure has been resolved, but the corrupt behaviour has been normalised and the behaviour enables or activates a second separate set of pressure-like motivators. In this case the theft of funds is initially used to pay off the debts. However, once the debts are paid, the opportunity (or the situational forces that regulate behaviour) still exists. Here, previous behaviour is manifested to perpetuate other behaviours such as growth of personal wealth and living beyond ones means.

Using Maslow's (1943) theory of human motivation and hierarchy of needs, this lifecycle could be considered to be an adaptation up the hierarchy of needs. With the personal benefits of the fraudulent or corrupt behaviour initially providing for physiological and psychological safety, once that safety is achieved and the behaviour has been normalised and rationalised (see below), it subsequently provides a means of achieving other needs such as belongingness and esteem (e.g. buying expensive cars and jewellery). Here, the potential and realised criminal goes through the phases of pressure, resolution, and adaption (see Figure 6.4).

The differences in these lifecycles have implications for the level of risk associated with motivation by different individuals as well as the kinds of controls that are required to manage the differences in the lifecycle. By comparison with the Simplex lifecycle, the pressure–resolution and pressure–resolution–adaptation lifecycles can be anticipated to give rise to more systemic and ongoing insider risk by a single individual or set of linked individuals. This is because these lifecycles provide for continuous motivation over time, either through the continuation of the pressure or through the adaptation of the pressure into different forms of need and desire. By contrast, the Simplex lifecycle is time bound and in response to a specific stimulus. That being said,

FIGURE 6.4   Pressure, Resolution, Adaptation Lifecycle

the simplex lifecycle can give rise to systemic and ongoing risk where behaviour is normalised across the organisation or parts of an organisation. For example, if nepotism or cronyism in hiring decisions is considered normal practice, even though the motive may only be present for an individual in respect of a particular hiring decision, across the organisation this norm can nonetheless have deleterious effects.

The lifecycles also have implications for the design of controls that manage the motivational drivers for insider risk. There are two key typologies of controls which act directly on motivation – prevention controls, which aim to prevent the motivation from occurring, and detection controls, which aim to detect or identify the motivational factor or indicators of that factor (see Chapter 7 for a detailed examination on the concept of controls).

In the case of the pressure element of motivation, drug use or addiction might be a driver for the commission of insider risk, whether deliberate or inadvertent. Drug-related policies which prevent the hiring or retention of addicts are one form of preventative control in that they ensure that people subject to drug use are not employed by the organisation at the outset. Drug testing, on the other hand, is a detection control for drug use or addiction, identifying it once it has occurred rather than preventing it from occurring in the first place.

The implication of the different pressure lifecycles is several-fold. Under a Simplex lifecycle, pressure is limited to the life of the stimulus of that pressure. Preventative controls may prevent a person from acting on the stimulus: for example employee assistance programs that provide support to employees to manage and resolve issues may work to prevent a person from acting on the pressure and assist them to find other solutions to manage the pressure. These kinds of controls will operate effectively across all three lifecycles, insofar as they manage the pressure prior to the commencement of other stages of the lifecycle. By contrast, pressure detection controls operate after the pressure stimulus exists or has been acted upon. Under the Simplex lifecycle, the pressure is temporally limited until it is resolved. For example, a debt, once paid off, is no longer a pressure that will motivate a person to act, and therefore the behaviour will come to an end (unless it goes through adaptation). Consequently, the detection control to identify the debt as a motive would need to operate during the period while the debt exists; otherwise there is nothing further to detect.

As a practical example, financial status assessments are conducted to assess whether a person is in financial difficulty and, therefore, may be motivated for insider risk. Such a test would identify financial difficulties while the debt was outstanding but will not (unless it looks at past circumstances) detect financial difficulties once the debt is repaid. As a result, the effectiveness of such a detection control may be more limited. By contrast, under a pressure–resolution lifecycle, the resolution of the pressure perpetuates further pressure stimulus: that is the ability to repay the debt creates an incentive to enter more debt, thereby perpetuating the pressure over a more extended period. The implication is greater opportunity for detection of those debts which increases the chances of detection – the downside is that the risk is more systemic and ongoing and, therefore, likely to create greater financial harm.

Finally, under the pressure–resolution–adaptation lifecycle, the pressure which motivates the initial insider activity (the debt) might remain. Although the debt is repaid, the pressure evolves into a pressure to maintain and perpetuate a more lavish lifestyle. The effect, in this case, is that the detection control for financial debt will be viable only during the first phase of the lifecycle. But following the adaptation, an additional control will be needed which detects the person living beyond their financial means.

Internal and external pressure

The other salient element of all the motivational factors is that they may be driven by dynamics within or outside the organisation. The importance of this distinction is that, inherently, organisations are more capable of controlling the dynamics within the organisation than those that are external to it. This is because they have control of the assets, culture, and structures within the organisation which set "the way things work" (within the organisation). Drug use, gambling habits, debts, and lifestyle expectations are all factors which occur outside the confines of the organisation's structures and activities. As such, the only way the risk can be controlled is through the people that are subject to these factors: for example, by limiting the level of security clearance a person can hold if they are not able to pass financial due diligence assessments or by detecting financial hardships of individuals within the organisation.

Organisations can, however, generate internal conditions which give rise to pressures which equally increase insider risk. Incentive structures within organisations reward certain kinds of behaviours above others. In risk-averse and risk-conscious organisations, we would expect to see incentives such as promotion, remuneration, and status tied to the conscientiousness and management of risk across business operations. For example, insurance agencies who focus on actuarial assessments of insurance risk to reduce the likelihood of paying against their policies can be expected to have risk management as the core of their organisational psyche. Government auditing and financial institutions can be expected to be the same with high focus on conscientiousness and mitigation of financial risk. By contrast, high competition organisations, which place an emphasis on sales and marketing goals, are likely to reward sales performance potentially at the expense of other goals. A striking example of how this pressure can result in an increase in risk is the 2008

TABLE 6.1 Internal and External Pressure Factors

Internal		External	
<u>Workload Strain</u> • Unrealistic work volume • Unrealistic work complexity <u>Management Strain</u> • Unrealistic span of control • Complex staffing/ performance issues	<u>Internal Status</u> • Promotion • Influence <u>Internal Incentives</u> • Bonuses • Training and development • Career support	<u>Addictions</u> • Drugs • Gambling • Sex • Gaming • Etc. <u>Debts</u> <u>Lifestyle</u> • Home • Vehicle • Possessions	<u>External Status</u> <u>Cultural</u> • Family and friendship expectations <u>Exposure</u> • Taboos • Unlawful behaviour

financial crisis. The crisis was arguably brought about, at least in part, by sub-prime leasing driven by risk-taking lenders aiming for high sales targets during the fair-weather economic conditions preceding the crisis (Iannuzzi & Berardi, 2010; McKibbin & Stoeckel, 2009; The Reserve Bank of Australia, 2021). The sales performance targets created a pressure on employees. This pressure motivated brokers to make increasingly risky lending decisions, ultimately culminating in the collapse of several major financial firms. While changes in external conditions were equally important, the insider risk element is the weaknesses in lending practices which were exacerbated by motivating factors which were entirely brought about by the organisations themselves.

On the flipside to incentive structures, workload strains, whether ongoing or temporary growth in demand, can equally create pressures on individuals, for example to cut corners to keep up with workload or manage the complexity of workloads. This cutting of corners can create the initial catalyst for poor behaviour and performance by an individual or by teams and, if left untreated, can evolve into more problematic insider risks. Table 6.1 sets out some examples of internal and external pressure factors.

Inducement

The concept of pressure implies some mechanism to relieve that pressure which is derived from perpetrating a malicious insider act. Indeed, our addition of the pressure lifecycles includes a resolution that must flow from the pressure either to immediately resolve it (*simplex*) or to create the conditions for further acts (*pressure–resolution* and *pressure–resolution–adaptation*). The "relieving" mechanism is, therefore, a separate concept to the pressure itself. Hence, we propose the addition of inducement to Cressy's model to describe those mechanisms which, in conjunction with pressure, form the basis for malicious insider acts.

When we examine pressure and inducement together, pressure equates to the latent readiness or primer to behave in a certain manner. Inducement is the trigger or activator which stimulates the behaviour, which is then intended to relieve the pressure. As a result, pressure and inducement may often be paired with the same underlying stimulus. For example if the pressure is drug use, then the inducement to commit theft of the detained goods storage may be the drugs themselves. Likewise, if the pressure is around performance in an organisational context while under unrealistic workloads, the inducement would be the achievement of a key performance indicator (KPI) or performance measure, which may induce a person to cut corners in the quality of work and thereby expose the organisation to additional risk.

Commutability

As set out briefly in our examples above, the stimulus of inducement may be directly related to the pressure, thereby creating a direct and logical relationship between the pressure and the resolving inducement: for example, drug use and drugs or sexual addiction and sexual services. These forms of inducement are effectively non-commutable, in that the inducement has the direct relationship and cannot be converted into another form to satisfy a logically separate pressure.

To illustrate, the opposite proposition is money. Money is commutable in that it can be converted into other assets which may satisfy the pressure. So, for example, a person who has a problem with drug abuse may nonetheless be induced by money which can subsequently be used to purchase additional drugs to satisfy their drug habit. By contrast, using another outcome we've outlined above, the achievement of KPIs may act as an inducement to cut corners, but it is non-commutable, in that it cannot be converted into another stimulus to relieve any other form of pressure. We propose three levels of commutability:

- Non-commutable: These inducements cannot be converted or transferred to any other form of value. Examples of not commutable inducements are KPIs, sexual favours, and negative inducements (which we will outline below): such as threats of exposure. They are non-commutable insofar as they have value only to the individual rather than broader value to others.
- Semi-commutable: Inducements that can be converted into other forms of value in a limited way. For example, drugs or firearms taken from a goods store may be used directly to satisfy a pressure, such as drug use or self-defence against a threat. They may also be sold or traded for other forms of value including money.

- Commutable: These can be readily converted into other forms of value to satisfy other pressures. The most manifest example is money, which can be converted to any number of goods or services to satisfy many different forms of pressure, such as debts, gambling, drug use and addiction, sex addictions, and lifestyle desires, such as vehicles, houses, and other possessions.

Commutability of the inducement is relevant to the model insofar as commutable inducements provide an inducement across a broad range of pressures, while non-commutable ones are limited to more niche pressures. This has relevance to the level of investment that is put into the prevention and detection of the inducement. There is high value in preventing inducements that have a broader spectrum, insofar as they will limit risk under a wider variety of conditions. Niche inducements will only be relevant to a specific person or situation. For example, internal performance or performance bonuses will be an inducement in areas where there are high levels of workload pressure or that bonuses are offered for performance, but not be relevant in other conditions. By contrast the attraction of highly commutable inducements such as money will be organisation-wide, increasing risk in non-specific areas of business. For example, the detection of unexplained wealth of staff in the organisation will be of relevance, irrespective of which business activity that person is involved in, whereas anomalies in performance data, which might indicate that a person is artificially inflating their performance, will only be relevant to the specific area of business that anomaly relates.

Passive and active inducement

In Chapter 5, we discussed the role of beneficiaries in the risk equation for insider risk. Beneficiaries are, themselves, motivated by the assets of the organisation and therefore may seek to corrupt or take advantage of insiders within the organisation to pursue whatever objective they may have: personal, organised, or criminal. One means that the beneficiaries may pursue is to use an inducement to persuade an insider to take an action that will benefit them. This process of inducement is, therefore, "active" insofar as a third party is actively attempting to induce the insider to perform the act. As we discussed in Chapter 5, beneficiaries have different levels of capability to induce insiders to act on their behalf. A very simple example is bribery, the bribe forming the inducement to act on the beneficiary's behalf. Beneficiaries with higher orders of capability may instead target an individual's pressures to identify those inducements to which they will be particularly vulnerable.

For example, there are emerging cases of organised criminal groups identifying and using online nude photographs to threaten people to act on their behalf either as insiders or generally as agents for criminal activity – sometimes referred to as sextortion (Metropolitan police, 2023). More pernicious still, digital and artificial intelligence alteration of legitimate photographs (deepfake) have been used to create bogus nude photographs which are equally used to threaten people to act on the criminal's behalf (CBS News, 2023; Federal Bureau of Investigation, 2023). Drug use may also be a vulnerability that is used by criminals to induce a person to act – either by providing or by alternatively withholding drugs in exchange for actions on their behalf. The Home Office (2023) provides a range of scenarios in which children, young people, and vulnerable adults are exploited, for various reasons, to undertake criminal acts.

Social engineering, through a range of mediums from social settings to social media, is also an example of where cognitive biases (effectively a form of generalised pressure) are utilised to breach organisational defences (McNaughton, 2023). This can involve deceptive inducements such as providing access to information or passwords by imitating legitimate authorities, or by building trust with the insider to induce them to enable access to a particular organisational asset.

Under these active scenarios, the insider either is a willing participant or may equally effectively be the victim of a dishonest and deceitful beneficiary. By contrast with active inducements driven by a third party, passive inducements are driven by the insider themselves and the object of the inducement is sought by them. For example, if a staff member has access to organisation funds (which is an asset), they may passively induce the person to misappropriate those funds to relieve the pressure.

The salient difference between active and passive inducement comes back to the controls which are required to regulate against those inducements. Preventing active inducement includes countermeasures such as providing employee assistance programs (e.g. to provide employees support if they are threatened or to deal with issues such as drug use). Prevention of passive inducement is targeted solely at the person who might be induced. This may be, for example, by increasing the sense of threat of detection through information and education.

Detection of active forms of inducement will involve active monitoring of the relationships and activities between potential beneficiaries and officers (e.g. to detect a bribe paid by the beneficiary). Detection mechanisms for passive inducements naturally only focus on the individual activities of the singular person, for example detection of unexplained wealth. Finally, and importantly, response controls for active and passive inducement may differ significantly due to the specific nature of the motivation or intent for perpetrating the malicious act. Passive inducement is driven by the actor themselves and, as a result, the responses tend to be more punitive in nature, as any behaviours driven by passive inducements will naturally be deliberately motivated. By contrast, there are a class of active inducements where the internal actor could equally be the victim, for example where an inducement to act relies on deception and the intent of the action is not deliberate harm to the organisation. Providing a password to access the organisation's information or assets to a fraudulent support centre number is based on deliberate social engineering and deception. The response controls, in this case, are likely to be primarily educative, given that the insider has not deliberately provided access to the organisation's assets.

Positive inducement and negative inducement

As we touched on above, bribery is a form of inducement to influence the actions of a person, in the form of a transfer of value to that person. In effect, it influences that person's behaviour through a positive reward for the action which advantages the beneficiary. By contrast, a less explored form of inducement is negative inducement. Instead of providing a reward, negative inducement involves the threat of an adverse outcome to influence action. Threats of violence to the person or family members, threats of exposure of secrets or illicit activities, or withdrawal of a benefit such as promotions are all means by which a beneficiary can actively seek to influence the actions of insiders.

Consideration of both positive and negative inducements is important to managing the risk, due to the logical relationship between the inducement type and the controls that manage that type of inducement (as we'll explore in greater detail in Chapter 7). For example, a person may be bribed to unlawfully grant licenses or alternatively the same person could be threatened with violence or some other detriment again to induce them to grant those same licenses. A control to detect the bribery might be detection of unexplained wealth, a control which is effected by organisations in conjunction with financial service providers and financial intelligence agencies. This control may identify anomalies in a person's financial status, which would warrant further investigation and, thereby, identify the bribery and corrupt grant of the licences. By contrast this control will have little to no effect if the person is being threatened, even though the corrupt activity is exactly the same (granting licenses).

The appropriate control to detect threats might be Security Reporting, a mechanism which enables employees to report and seek support in respect of threats to personal security. While this example is simple, it illustrates the utility of ensuring that both positive and negative inducements are considered when designing and investing in insider threat controls. The alternative is investment in an incomplete insider risk control set (see Table 6.2 and Appendix A, which sets out a relatively complete control set including controls for positive and negative inducements).

TABLE 6.2 Examples of Positive and Negative Inducements

Positive	*Negative*
Bribes	Threat of violence
Kickbacks	Threat of exposure
Discounts or inflated sales prices	Financial loss
Workplace benefits	Withholding of workplace benefits
• Promotion	Restrictions on freedom
• Pay	
• Benefits	
• Training	
Gratuities	

Rationalisation

The final component drawn from Cressy's model is the concept of rationalisation. The essence of rationalisation is that corrupt actors will deal with the cognitive dissonance which arises from committing an act which is considered "bad" or deviant by rationalising the act. Geva (2006) defines rationalisation as "the assignment of logical or socially-desirable motives for what people do so that they seem to have acted rightfully" (p. 143). Fundamentally, for our purposes, this involves finding a logical or positive explanation to explain why the harmful insider act is acceptable and why there was a "good" reason for committing it. Alternatively, this may be by neutralising or obfuscating the negative outcomes generated by the corrupt act. Many empirical studies have reconfirmed that rationalisation is a mechanism that exists across and perpetuates a wide spectrum of harmful, illicit, and criminal behaviours – including insider risk and corruption (see for example Archambeault & Webber, 2018; Gannett, 2015; Geva, 2006). Successful rationalisation of corrupt acts has equally been demonstrated to lead to repeated unethical acts (Bazerman & Gino, 2012; Geva, 2006). Rationalisation as a psychological feature of corruption is a key mechanism at an individual level that can lead to systemic and ongoing corruption which, as we've explored in previous chapters, will create higher levels of harm to an organisation's goals and objectives than ad hoc or opportunistic insider actions.

In examining rationalisation in the context of business ethics, Geva (2006) proposed five classifications for the rationalisations used to justify unethical actions:

- Genuine dilemma-based rationalisation: This involves the creation of a dilemma where two goal or moral objectives conflict and both cannot be satisfied. Politically based motives for corruption are an example of this rationalisation, for example facilitating access to information to support political allies.

- Compliance based: In this case the rationalisation is on the basis that the actor is following orders or directives whether implicit or explicit. For example, in a policing context, Klockars et al. (2000) found that rather than being a deviation of some officers, corrupt behaviour is fostered and shaped by corrupt cultures and incentive structures. In the context of rationalisation, personal responsibility, for example, can be abrogated where there is an excuse that superiors may admonish those who do not participate in systemic bribery.
- Moral laxity: This form of rationalisation involves the pretence of addressing a behavioural or ethical issue, but not actually tackling the problem. Geva (2006) provides context through the use of phrases such as "promising adequate consideration . . . don't worry, we are aware of the problem, and we are working on it . . . or . . . let's appoint a special committee" (p. 143). From an insider risk perspective, where the organisation is serious about addressing insider risk, this rationalisation can reveal a disjunct between organisational goals and attitudes when compared with local level attitudes. If this rationalisation occurs at a higher structural level within the organisation, it indicates a much more fundamental issue where an organisation may not be committed to addressing the risk at all.
- No-problem-based rationalisation: In this form of rationalisation, unethical acts are a result of the business culture and system. Corrupt officials blame the organisation's interests as the basis for their actions. On the flipside, individuals may also blame the organisation for a perceived wrong or unfairness perpetrated by the organisation against them. Examples of script here include "well the organisation didn't look after me, so it is fine that I don't look after it".
- Euphemisation rationalisation: Geva's final classification of rationalisation is where unethical actors rename their acts to suppress their anxieties. From an insider risk perspective this might manifest as bribes being relabelled as contributions or donations.

Gannett and Rector (2015), drawing on Geva's model, examined the five classifications in the context of political corruption. Geva further recognised the classifications in the responses provided by convicted corrupt officials, distinguishing two strategies that individuals follow to rationalise corruption. The first highlights the positive intentions behind corrupt actions and the other obfuscates or reduces the negative intentions (Gannett & Rector, 2015; Rabl & Kühlmann, 2008). Gannett and Rector (2015) further noted that the second form appeared to be more common in their study than the first.

Rationalisation: harm proximity

The second overall form of rationalisation indicates that part of the mechanism of rationalisation is reducing the perceived level of harm or separating the malicious or unethical act from its consequences as a means of preserving psychological safety. Gannett and Rector (2015) provide an interesting insight into this form of reasoning by a corrupt official who had been convicted of nepotism in hiring practices. When asked whether nepotism could ever be good for society they replied

> I really probably would answer that, that I don't think that it's a totally negative thing. I think it depends on the position and what you are actually doing in terms of the public. That's what I think. . . . . . I don't think that it's always a bad thing. I'll put it that way. You have families that have done great things. The biggest example of nepotism not being so negative is the Kennedys.

In this statement, we see several interesting characteristics. Firstly, the heuristic confirmation bias, drawing on an anecdotal example of "the Kennedys", lessens the impact of the unethical activity and therefore an avoidance of harm. When asked whether they had committed corruption the same interviewee also responded:

> I would say that because I was put under the umbrella of corruption when really what I did was give somebody a job that was destitute.

In our view this demonstrates another element to the rationalisation equation, which is the proximity of the harm to the unethical act. In this case study, nepotism was perceived and rationalised as being of benefit to the destitute individual, a very proximate and directly causally related benefit. By contrast, the harm of nepotism is not necessarily directly causally related to a single act of nepotism. The harm, instead, accrues where nepotism becomes a systemic part of the hiring process, weakening merit, skills, and diversity of workforces and risking the achievement of organisational objectives. Like economic externalities, the price for nepotism is indirect and not paid by either the perpetrator or the beneficiary of the transaction, or indeed immediately perceptible in the transactional activity.

It is our view, then, the differential in proximity between the perceived or rationalised benefit and the real harm of the unethical act contributes also to the successful rationalisation of that act. Some examples showing the lack of harm proximity for different unethical actions include the following:

- Bribery: The proximate benefit is rationalised as some additional money for an "already underpaid police force". The harm in terms or protection for criminal behaviour, unfair allocation of law enforcement resources, and the economic and social harms flowing from bribery are much more systemic and distant from the individual act of accepting the bribe.

- Unlawful grant of visa: The proximate benefit might be the ability of the person to enter the country unlawfully, while the arguable social and economic harms of uncontrolled movement of persons across state borders is distant from the individual act.
- Illicit grant of fake license: Again, the proximate benefit might be the inducement provided in exchange for the license, while the harms of the potential identity crimes are more distant and conceptual.
- Using protected information for insider trading: The benefit might be the financial reward, while the harm of the individual trades can easily be minimised. However, the broader economic harm of systemic insider trading is substantial but again much less proximate to the individual trading activity.

The implication for countermeasures against rationalisation of the disjunct between the act and the proximate harm may then be that increasing the perception or recognition of the harm can make successful rationalisation more challenging to the actors. For example, this might involve, within merit-based recruitment guidelines or publications the following: (i) a statement about the harms that accrue from nepotism and cronyism in hiring: thereby forcefully creating a link between the harmful act and its consequences, for example the broader social harms and systemic disadvantage that may occur as a result of individual small acts of nepotism and cronyism and (ii) using an example drawn from our fictional border agency, the immediate and proximate effects of enabling the importation of drugs through the border: these may be limited and, therefore, are likely to have limited effects on the ability of an actor to successfully rationalise the act of facilitating importation. However, there are substantial societal impacts on hospitalisations, neonatal drug problems, violence, and motor vehicle accidents (MacDonald et al., 2005), which could be highlighted through internal communication channels to make it more difficult for a person to successfully rationalise it as a minor or inconsequential act.

The effectiveness of such measures in countering insider acts is a worthy one for further research. Restorative justice research provides some potential indicators, insofar as there is research demonstrating that restorative justice measures reduce recidivism by providing the criminal actor direct visibility of the effects and consequences of their criminal acts (Braithwaite, 1998). Piggott and Wood (2019), however, highlight the fact that the effectiveness of restorative justice measures remain subject to significant uncertainty, due to a high level of heterogeneity in definitions of restorative justice and in research methods into restorative justice. A similar dearth of clear research exists in the effect of countermeasures against rationalisation.

Motivation as part of the risk equation

The reason for an exploration of motivation in this work is to integrate the models of motivation into factors which influence the likelihood and consequences of an insider risk event and, through that understanding, develop countermeasures against motivation (which we'll discuss in detail in the following chapter). The benefit of including any element into the risk model is that there will be a differential between motivation in one context and, in another context, guiding investment towards the higher area of risk. In an organisational context, this would mean identifying functions and capabilities of the organisation where motivation factors are inherently greater than in others. This would mean that the organisation could logically invest more in those productive countermeasures, functions, and capabilities.

Given that motivation, while having some common elements (as set out in this chapter), is individualistic, it is likely that the organisational context for motivation is likely to be relatively individual as well. It would, therefore, not be of value to define or model those contexts. Rather it is more prudent to highlight that the consideration of motivational factors should guide the understanding of risk by the organisation (we'll explore this in more depth in the final chapter, which brings together all elements of the model). However, there is value in providing some examples of where those differentials may occur.

Politically contentious activities

Activities of an organisation that are politically contentious, or where there is a low level of general consensus, increases the risk that a person may be subject to politically motivated pressure and rationalisation in pursuit of the functions of the organisation. For example, functions related to suppressing terrorist groups will be more inherently at risk (i.e. discounting the controls that organisations have in place) to sympathisers with the political cause (Vorsina et al., 2019) than functions that enjoy general consensus: for example general street policing activities.

Adversarial intent

As discussed in Chapter 5, beneficiaries to insider acts may have adversarial intent. That is, their goals and interests run directly contrary to the goals and objectives of the organisation. In such circumstances the need and incentives to coerce insiders to assist them meet their objectives is greater, and consequently their investment in creating or exploiting pressures and rendering inducements is also greater. For example, cross-border drug importation, which runs directly contrary to border agency remits, creates a functionally higher risk for external pressure than management of internal funds within financial services areas of the organisation.

Workplace satisfaction

There is some evidence of the role that workplace satisfaction plays in the loyalty of people to their organisation's goals and objectives (Neveu & Kakavand, 2019; Ogungbamila & Ojogo, 2020). Some workplace functions are likely to be met with low levels of staff satisfaction. Such low satisfaction within the role or function is likely to create an environment where actors rationalise their actions using a "no problem based rationalisation" (according to Geva (2006) model) or are influenced by others – differential association (Sutherland, 1972) – effectively placing the blame for their actions on the lack of workplace satisfaction brought about by poor culture, systems, or processes.

These examples illustrate the potential for systemically greater levels of motivation within one part of the organisation as compared to another. These differentials provide the basis for relative levels of investment by the organisation in countermeasures against rationalisation. They also provide a basis for the design of those countermeasures, which are most apposite to the motivational risk within that organisational function. For example, as above, if the risk of politically motivated activity sits within one function, then the appropriate countermeasures are those which deal with political motivation as opposed to countermeasures which manage individual financial motives.

Relationship to opportunity

As set out in Chapter 4, it is our view that the key systemic enabler for insider threat is opportunity. This can be structured into a series of systemic and distinguishable factors that can be used to develop clear countermeasures (as set out in the following chapter). This being said, for insider risk to eventuate, opportunity cannot operate alone. A motivated actor must take advantage of that opportunity for the risk to be realised. Whilst, we argue, the removal of opportunity through control has a higher certainty of success because there is a clear relationship between the mechanism of opportunity (e.g. low visibility) and the mechanisms of control (active CCTV, which raises the visibility), due to the availability, cost, and impacts of controls, it will not always be possible or desirable to remove an opportunity. As a result, managing motivation becomes more important in these circumstances.

While not explicitly discussing opportunity in the same terms as we have, Ping (2017) draws on a range of philosophical, psychological, and neuroscientific research frameworks to develop a model which illustrates the relationship between opportunity and systemic corruption at the individual level. In

Ping's model, once the opportunity is encountered and exploited, the behaviour of taking advantage of that opportunity is gradually encoded in the neural pathways of the person committing the unethical act. This encoding enables the person to continue to act unethically when encountering that stimulus, thereby creating a systemic feedback loop for the corrupt or unethical actions. Ping's research demonstrates a clear link between opportunity, ongoing motivation, and systemic risk at a deep behavioural level. This being said, in reverse, it is our view that an excessive focus on motivation and the question of "why do people act unethically?" creates significant weaknesses when used as a basis for managing risk in the absence of other more systemic factors.

Weaknesses

As we observed in the examples provided above, motivation is highly individualised. Effectively, the simple answer to the question "why do people act unethically?" is "for a variety of reasons". The weakness inherent, then, is that the examination of motivation, short of the general factors we've outlined, is highly particularised. A person may act unethically for political reasons, for personal financial gain, to protect themselves or a loved one, to deal with an addiction, to take revenge on a person or the organisation for a perceived wrong, amongst many others. As set out in Figure 6.5, the

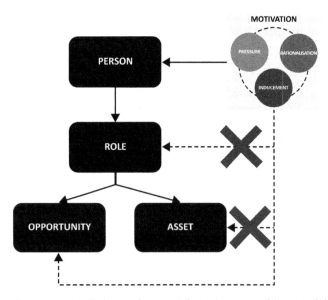

FIGURE 6.5 Motivation's Relationship to Other Elements of the Model

motivational factors conceptually connect directly only with the individual who occupies a role. Two people who occupy the same role can have an entirely different set of motivators, one of which may give rise to unethical acts while the other will not. As a result, motivation is an element that the organisation only has limited control over when compared with other factors such as how a function is effected in a way that reduces the opportunity for unethical acts.

Equally, a person's motivational context is not static. The accrual of debts, breakdown of marriage, newfound addictions, and so forth may change over the lifetime of the employment of the person within the organisation. Very few of these factors are within the control of the organisation and they may not even have visibility of those changes in circumstances which give rise to greater risk within that individual. By contrast, the roles, assets, and opportunities are dictated by the way that the organisation designs its operating environment and processes. As such any change in opportunity that arises is directly within the control and visibility of the organisation, and changed risk, as a result, can be managed by reassessing the risk and adjusting controls to meet the changed environment.

From an investment perspective, therefore, there is benefit in focusing on opportunity as the central enabler. This is because there are few more standard control types that can manage this element of risk. Managing opportunity risk at sufficient granularity would require investment in individual controls around each individual within the organisation. For large organisations, such an approach would be completely unworkable. Additionally, for the motivational elements we have outlined to be useful from an investment perspective, there would need to be a strong and preferably exclusive relationship between the motivating factor and the unethical activity. For example, many law enforcement organisations invest in drug testing as a means of detecting and mitigating potential corruption (in addition to other issues). The use of drug testing as a means of dealing with broader corruption issues may be ineffective, as it assumes a strong and exclusive correlation between drug usage and corrupt acts. Given the range of different motivations for unethical acts we have outlined above, plainly such a strong association does not exist. There are drug users who (though they may be engaged in illegal behaviour) are not corrupt and equally there are corrupt individuals who do not use drugs. The strength of such an association will determine the utility of countermeasures against a particular motivation. If the correlation relationship is weak, then measures to prevent or detect that motivational factor will be of limited effectiveness, effectively producing both type I and type II errors. It is our view that there remains opportunity for more research into the direction and strength of associations between specific motivational elements (such as drug use) and other forms of unethical behaviour.

Chapter key points

- Motivation is a key element that drives the risk of unethical behaviour.
- We identify three motivational factors *pressure, inducement, and rationalisation.*
- These factors enable the assessment of risk to different functions of an organisation, but equally provide the basis for the design of controls.
- Motivation is, however, highly individualised and particularised. Excessive focus on motivation undermines a more systemic approach to managing insider risk, which should focus more on systemic opportunities.

References

Archambeault, D. S., & Webber, S. (2018, April). Fraud survival in nonprofit organizations: Empirical evidence. *Nonprofit Management & Leadership, 29*(1), 29–46.

Archambeault, D. S., Webber, S., & Greenlee, J. (2015). Fraud and corruption in US nonprofit entities: A summary of press reports 2008–2011. *Nonprofit and Voluntary Sector Quarterly, 44*(6), 1194–1224.

Bazerman, M. H., & Gino, F. (2012). Behavioral ethics: Toward a deeper understanding of moral judgment and dishonesty. *Annual Review of Law and Social Science, 8*(1), 85–104.

Braithwaite, J. (1998). Restorative justice. In M. Tonry (Ed.), *The handbook of crime and punishment* (pp. 323–344). Oxford University Press.

Brooks, G., Tunley, M., Button, M., & Gee, J. (2017). Fraud, error and corruption in healthcare: A contribution from criminology. In M. Mikkers, W. Sauter, P. Vincke, & J. Boertjens (Eds.), *Healthcare fraud, corruption and waste in Europe* (pp. 25–44). Eleven Publishers.

CBS News. (2023). *Deepfake nude images of teen girls prompt action from parents, lawmakers: "AI pandemic".* https://www.cbsnews.com/news/deepfake-nude-images-teen-girls-action-parents-lawmakers-ai-pandemic/

Cohen, L., & Felson, M. (1979). Social change and crime rate trends: A routine activity approach. *American Sociological Review, 44*(4), 588–608.

Cressey, D. R. (1953). *Other peoples' money: A study in the social psychology of embezzlement.* Free Press.

Federal Bureau of Investigation. (2023). *Malicious actors manipulating photos and videos to create explicit content and sextortion schemes.* https://www.ic3.gov/Media/Y2023/PSA230605

Gannett, A. (2015). The rationalization of political corruption. *Public Integrity, 17*(2), 165–175.

Gannett, A., & Rector, C. (2015). The rationalization of political corruption. *Public Integrity, 17*(2), 165–175.

Geva, A. (2006). A typology of moral problems in business: A framework for ethical management. *Journal of Business Ethics, 69*(2), 133–147.

Graycar, A., & Prenzler, T. (2013). *Understanding and preventing corruption.* Palgrave Macmillan.

Home Office. (2023). *Criminal exploitation of children, young people and vulnerable adults.* https://assets.publishing.service.gov.uk/media/65322ad1e839fd0014867 20d/2023_FOR_PUBLICATION_-_Criminal_exploitation_of_children_young_ people_and_vulnerable_adults_county_lines1.pdf

Homel, R. (2005). Developmental crime prevention. In N. Tilley (Ed.), *Handbook of crime prevention and community safety* (pp. 71–106). Willan Publishing.

Iannuzzi, E., & Berardi, M. (2010). Global financial crisis: Causes and perspectives. *EuroMed Journal of Business*. https://www.emerald.com/insight/content/doi/10.1108/14502191011080818/full/html?skipTracking=true

Iyer, N., & Samociuk, M. (2016). *Fraud and corruption: Prevention and detection*. Routledge.

Klockars, C. B., Ivkovich, S. K., Harver, W. E., & Haberfeld, M. R. (2000). *The measurement of police integrity*. NIJ Research in Brief.

MacDonald, Z., Tinsley, L., Collingwood, J., Jamieson, P., & Pudney, J. (2005). *Measuring the harm from illegal drugs using the drug harm index*. Home Office Online Report 24/05.

Manning, M. (2018). A baseline model of deterrence. In B. Leclerc & D. Reynald (Eds.), *The future of rational choice for crime prevention*. Routledge.

Manning, M. (2019). Economics. In R. Wortley, A. Sidebottom, N. Tilley, & G. Laycock (Eds.), *Routledge handbook of crime science*. Routledge.

Maslow, A. H. (1943). A theory of human motivation. *Psychological Review, 50*(4), 370–396.

McKibbin, W., & Stoeckel, A. (2009). The global financial crisis: Causes and consequences. *Asian Economic Papers, 9*(1), 54–86.

McNaughton, C. (2023). *Mitigating the risk of social engineering on insiders through monitoring activity*. https://www.linkedin.com/pulse/mitigating-risk-social-engineering-insiders-through-mcnaughton/

Metropolitan police. (2023). *Sextortion*. https://www.met.police.uk/advice/advice-and-information/sexual-offences/sextortion/

Mohamedbhai, G. (2016). The scourge of fraud and corruption in higher education. *International Higher Education, 1*(84), 12–14.

Neveu, J. P., & Kakavand, B. (2019). Endangered resources: The role of organizational justice and interpersonal trust as signals for workplace corruption. *Relations Industrielles, 74*(3), 498–524.

Ogungbamila, B., & Ojogo, B. F. (2020). Perceived organizational injustice and corrupt tendencies in public sector employees: Mediating role of life satisfaction. *Romanian Journal of Psychology, 22*(2), 42–50.

Piggott, E., & Wood, W., (2019). Chapter 24. Does restorative justice reduce recidivism? Assessing evidence and claims about restorative justice and reoffending. In T. Gavrielides (Ed.), *Routledge international handbook of restorative justice*. Routledge. (Original work published 2018.)

Ping, A. C. (2017). Levelling the score: The role of individual perceptions of justice in the creation of unethical outcomes in business. *IAFOR Journal of Ethics, Religion & Philosophy, 3*(2), 1–6.

Rabl, T., & Kühlmann, T. M. (2008). Understanding corruption in organizations – development and empirical assessment of an action model. *Journal of Business Ethics, 84*, 477–495.

The Reserve Bank of Australia. (2021). *The global financial crisis*. https://www.rba.gov.au/education/resources/explainers/the-global-financial-crisis.html

Suh, I., Sweeney, J. T., Linke, K., & Wall, J. M. (2020). Boiling the frog slowly: The immersion of C-suite financial executives into fraud. *Journal of Business Ethics, 162*(3), 645–673.

Sutherland, E. H. (1972). *The theory of differential association*. Columbia University Press.

Tickner, P. (2017). *Fraud and corruption in public services*. Routledge.

Tickner, P., & Button, M. (2021). Deconstructing the origins of Cressey's fraud triangle. *Journal of Financial Crime, 28*(3), 722–731.

Vorsina, M., Manning, M., Sheppard, J., & Fleming, C. M. (2019). Social dominance orientation, fear of terrorism and support for counter-terrorism policies. *Australian Journal of Political Science, 54*(1), 99–113.

Wortley, R. (1998). A two-stage model of situational crime prevention. *Studies on Crime and Prevention, 7*(2), 173–188.

Wortley, R. (2016). Situational precipitators of crime. In R. Wortley & M. Townsley (Eds.), *Environmental criminology and crime analysis*. Routledge.

7

DESIGNING AND STANDARDISING CONTROLS

Introduction

Current methods for preventing and mitigating insider risk tend to focus on the individual/people aspects of fraudulent and corrupt behaviour. Measures of prevention and mitigation include the following: (1) building ethical and cultural values within organisations; (2) profiling potential fraudulent actors based on demographic characteristics; and (3) providing education to help people identify and report suspicious behaviour (Larmour & Wolanin, 2001). While these measures are important, we argue that controls, which operate on business processes, can be defined and designed consistently, thus providing a more reliable tool for mitigating insider risk. Adding a layer of structure to insider risk controls promotes logical thinking about where those risk controls are most effectively implemented. Given the volume and complexity of financial transaction and cross-border movement and screening processes, a structured approach is vital to ensure that controls on processes are in place and operating effectively.

Risk and control

Previous chapters have focused exclusively on understanding and assessing insider risk using a structured model that decomposes the elements of risk. In this chapter, we shift to examining the other key element of risk management, the treatment of risk, which is the development of strategies and mechanisms to modify the inherent level of insider risk associated with an activity of the organisation.

DOI: 10.4324/9781003055716-7

As we touched on in Chapter 2, risk refers to the effect of uncertainty on objectives. In the context of this book, it is the uncertainty of where and when malicious or inadvertent insider activity will emerge and harm the objectives of the organisation. Treatment of the risk, therefore, refers to positioning some strategy or action that will alter the level of uncertainty in a way that reduces the impact on the objectives of the organisation.

Treatment of the risk in any meaningful and ongoing way requires the investment of finite resources and may also impact on the achievement of other business objectives. As such, we contend that it is critical that organisations can apprehend the different control options available to modify different characters of risk and to understand the relative return on investment for different forms of treatment options. Such actions thereby enable more nuanced investment decision-making.

When we examine the relevant literature on insider threat, it is notable that a few key treatment options are emphasised. However, we note the absence of a formal structured model to describe treatments. The Association of Certified Fraud Examiners (2018a) and Larmour and Wolanin (2001) both emphasise the value of tip-offs as a means of identifying (or detecting) insider fraud and corruption, alongside education to help people recognise and report suspicious behaviour that might indicate fraud or corruption. While these measures are indeed valuable, they by no means represent the breadth of treatment options for insider threat, and are subject to some recognised weaknesses such as the bystander effect (Darley & Latané, 1968), which impact on their reliability as a means of treating insider threat.

Here, by decomposing the elements of risk, we demonstrate that it is possible to equally decompose and align relevant risk treatments to mitigate different risk drivers which contribute to the realisation of the risk.

Risk treatment

As articulated in Chapter 2, once the risk has been assessed the organisation needs to make decisions about whether the relative probability and impact of the risk warrants intervention; and/or whether the risk should be accepted as part of the cost of business for the organisation. If the risk warrants treatment according to the International Organization for Standardization (2004) (ISO) standard, several options are available:

- Avoidance: achieved by avoiding the activity that generates the risk entirely.
- Sharing: through partnerships, contracts, or other agreements the risk is shared and managed across partners.
- Controlling: investing in establishing measures and activities, which modify the likelihood/probability and/or impact/consequence of the risk.

In the context of insider threat, avoidance and sharing of the risk are not often viable options. An organisation is not likely to discontinue a business activity due to its exposure to insider threat, and government organisations are under legislative mandates to undertake activities which entail risk.

Sharing the risk is not practical, insofar the risk will only be of concern to the organisation if the harm accrues to that entity (organisation). To the contrary, if the organisation outsources an activity, and that activity is subject to insider threats albeit by insiders of the contracted organisation, then the organisation will retain an interest in managing the risk and assuring itself that effective controls are in place. (We will touch on this in the section Partnered Controls.) Thus, our focus for this chapter is on mechanisms to control the risk.

Control definition and typologies

Controls are defined as measures or strategies which modify the likelihood or consequence of the risk occurring. As set out in the international risk standard ISO31000 (International Organization for Standardization, 2004), there are three broad kinds of controls which can be put in place to mitigate risk, by modifying its likelihood/probability or its impact/consequence (see Figure 7.1):

- Preventative: Controls which modify the probability of the risk event, ideally preventing it from occurring altogether.
- Detective: Controls which discover and identify the risk event: either prior to or after its occurrence.
- Responsive: Controls which react after the risk event has occurred to minimise the harm or damage.

As outlined in earlier chapters, insider risk is complex and multifactorial, driven by different features of organisations, including its assets of value,

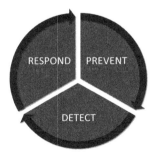

FIGURE 7.1 Overall Control Typologies

business practices and processes, and the stakeholders to its products and services. As a result, no single control is effective to manage the risk. The challenge for organisations, then, is to select the most effective suite of controls to manage insider risk, at the lowest cost and while minimising the impact on its business objectives.

The decomposition of the available controls against the drivers for insider risk provides an analytical and evaluative model to enable control investment decisions. As a comprehensive reference, a complete decomposition of controls is provided in Appendix A.

Preventative controls

The first order of controls is designed to preclude insider threat events from occurring, thereby reducing or eliminating the losses or harms of those events. As we've touched on in previous chapters, the cost of insider events to an organisation can be significant, particularly when the insider activity is systemic and organised. The Association of Certified Fraud Examiners (2022) estimates a global loss of approximately USD3.6 billion – an average loss per case of approximately USD1.8 million. This figure, however, does not consider the other costs and harms which may flow from a single insider threat case, for example, the loss of intellectual property resulting in loss of market dominance or reputational/brand damage. Prevention, therefore, should be considered a critical element of a risk management approach to limit the damage caused by insider activity before it occurs.

The model we proposed in previous chapters enables a logical definition of each control typology that relates to the relevant risk drivers. We can, therefore, define a set of preventative controls which relate directly to the individual driver type, thereby providing a reference model to assess the completeness of prevention controls against the identified risk drivers.

Preventative controls are designed to diminish the likelihood of the insider risk event occurring by impeding one or more of the drivers of the risk. If you recall in previous chapters, the drivers for insider risk are opportunity, motivation, and beneficiaries related to a particular organisational asset which is interacted with by a role. In an insider risk context, therefore, prevention controls impede or eliminate these factors and their effect on the likelihood of an insider risk. For example, if the inherent risk of an insider making an unlawful decision (the asset) is due to a low level of visibility and traceability (the opportunity factors) and low morale in the relevant part of the organisation, then putting in place CCTV cameras will impede the opportunity factors. Further, establishing staff support programs will impede the motivational factors, thereby diminishing the likelihood of insider risk associated with the decision.

Preventing opportunity

As we discussed in Chapter 4, a key and systemic driver for insider risk is opportunity, which can be decomposed into five opportunity factors: authority, access, visibility, traceability, and certainty. These singularly and concurrently drive the level of insider risk associated with a particular organisational asset. The utility of undertaking this decomposition of risk drivers is that it enables controls to be designed and defined specifically to target the relevant driver of the particular risk being managed. As such, when controlling the opportunity, an organisation is effectively controlling one or more of the opportunity factors outlined above.

- Authority controls: are controls which reduce the level of authority that a role may exercise in relation to a particular organisational asset, thereby limiting the opportunity to engage in malicious or inadvertent insider threat activity. Examples of authority controls include the following:

  - *Separation of duties*: Under separation of duties, a decision cannot be made or action cannot be taken by a single individual. For example, a license application with separation of duties involves an assessing officer to analyse the evidence justifying the granting of the license and making a recommendation to a separate decision-maker. As a result, the authority over the decision is diminished and for an insider threat to eventuate, collusion between both roles would be required.
  - *Collective asset management*:[1] Under this arrangement, physical assets are managed by a collective of individuals responsible for receipting, stocktaking, and writing off assets. No individual has singular authority for the processes and relevant decisions.

- Visibility controls: These are controls which increase the level of visibility associated with an organisational asset, thereby increasing the difficulty of undertaking malicious activity without being detected. Examples of visibility controls include the following:

  - *Centralised decision queue*: This involves a centralised visible decision queue for all decisions of a certain type, for example, approval of a bank loan. The queue and activities on this action are *visible* to all officers involved in those types of decisions both enabling workload management and enabling anomalies to be identified quickly: for example, an officer self-allocating a certain application, or approving an application that normally would not be approved.

- Traceability controls: These are controls which increase the quality of records associated with the interaction between the role and the asset, such as automated recording of the officer who made a particular decision.

The increased traceability plays a dual role, potentially deterring or preventing malicious activity but providing a clear record of action which can enable the detection of anomalous activity with respect to an asset. Examples of traceability controls include the following:

- *Complete decision recording*: This involves the creation of a complete record, including *who made the decision, what was the decision in respect of, what evidence was relied upon, when was the decision made, where was the decision made, why was the decision made, how was the decision made*? This provides a complete and auditable record of the decision, enabling any anomalies to be detected: for example, decisions which are consistently made outside of business hours, which may indicate insider risk.
- *Asset continuity recording:* This provides a complete record of the chain of custody and state of an asset "from cradle to grave", again enabling anomalies to be detected or evidence to be gathered in respect of who had custody of an asset when it was misappropriated or misused.
- *Body camera:* This provides a complete and auditable record of operational activity by a police officer.
- *Floor management*: This involves a roving floor manager who is responsible for facilitating the flow of work and resolving issues, risk, and exceptions and providing guidance to officers in the conduct of their duties. For example, in X-ray screening centres for border agencies, a floor manager may monitor and assist screeners and manage the allocation of screening tasks. This provides the floor manager visibility across the activities of all officers, thereby increasing the risk of detection and deterring malicious activity.

- Access controls: These are controls which restrict or eliminate access to a particular asset; this reduces the quantum of persons or roles that can access and, therefore, misuse the asset at risk. Examples of access controls include the following:

  - *Biometric access control:* This requires the enrolment of a biometric such as fingerprint or iris scan and restricts access to enrolled biometrics. This plays a dual role in restricting access to authorised officers, and in the event of an insider incident it provides a chain of evidence in respect of those who accessed the misused asset.
  - *Role-based access:* This restricts access to an asset based on roles which are authorised to access the particular asset, thereby reducing the number of people who would be able to misuse that asset.

- Certainty controls: These are controls which reduce the level of certainty that a role will be able to interact with a *specific instance* of an asset: for example, to make a decision in respect of an application of a family member or friend. The reduced certainty can drastically reduce the likelihood that a corrupt person will be able to make decisions in respect of applications they have a direct interest in, thus, significantly reducing the insider threat. Examples of certainty controls include the following:

- *Random decision allocation:* This involves decisions from the decision queue being randomly allocated to assessing officers/decision-makers, thereby reducing the probability of an individual officer receiving a specific application, with the probability being inversely proportionate to the number of officers. This reduction in certainty substantially reduces the value of the officer to a potential beneficiary and corrupting influencer.
- *Daily workforce redeployment:* This involves officers being deployed to different roles on a daily basis, with no certainty of what role they will be allocated each day (or in intervals less than a day). For example, in a border agency, an officer might be deployed to different locations to clear passengers through customs.

These are just examples drawn from a more complete control model provided in Appendix A. The examples are, however, illustrative of the ability to utilise the model to identify the drivers of risk to a particular asset and provide a logical link to appropriate controls to manage those drivers.

Preventing motivation

As discussed in Chapter 6, while motivations of individual insiders are far less systemic than the business processes and practices that they interact with, there are some recognisable key elements that motivate insiders to commit malicious or inadvertent insider activity. We identified three factors which contribute to motivation by insiders: pressure, inducement, and rationalisation. Preventing motivation then consists of a suite of measures which reduce the presence of each of these factors within the organisation.

- Pressure prevention controls: These are controls which reduce the likelihood of a pressure being present within the workforce. These controls may operate by excluding a class of persons from employment (such as drug users) or by creating recognition and resilience against internal pressures (e.g. through education and support). Examples of pressure prevention controls include the following:
  - *Drug and alcohol policies:* These act by excluding from the workforce individuals who are not prepared to undertake or who fail a drug and alcohol test. Such policies, therefore, reduce the potential for people working in relevant roles from succumbing to alcohol or drugs as an

inducement to insider threat, or as a cause for inadvertent threats, for example, to safety when operating heavy machinery.

- *Employee assistance and support:* Support systems act by providing support to employees when experiencing potential pressures, such as gambling addiction, family crises, or other issues that may increase the likelihood of insider threat. These services may create recognition and resilience within employees against the pressures which can create a risk of insider threat.

- Inducement prevention controls: These are controls which prevent or deter the role/officer from accepting an inducement to act against the organisation. These controls operate by raising awareness of the capabilities and methodologies used by beneficiaries to a decision, or the presence of detection mechanisms or of the consequences of accepting an inducement (such as a bribe). Examples of inducement prevention controls include the following:

  - *Adversary training:* Trains officers to identify the methodologies used by high-risk beneficiaries to induce insiders to act on their behalf and provides officers with procedures for managing these situations, for example how to recognise a honeypot scheme or how to manage blackmail and threats.

  - *Gift policy:* A policy or set of policies that set clear and enforceable guidelines for the acceptance of gifts and offerings up to a determined value and creates reporting and registration requirements. This acts to deter the acceptance of gifts without following the policy and in the event that a gift or inducement has been accepted creates a clear breach of organisational policy.

- Rationalisation prevention controls: These are controls which prevent or reduce the likelihood of factors contributing to officers rationalising their commission of malicious insider activity. These controls act by creating loyalty to the organisation and raising awareness of the potential impacts of malicious insider activity on the organisation's objectives and/or its clients and stakeholders, thereby creating a dissonance with acting against the organisation's interests. Examples of rationalisation prevention controls include the following:

  - *Leadership:* Positive leadership has a demonstrable impact on the level of motivation of the workforce to achieve the mission and objectives of the organisation and create loyalty to the organisational unit and/or the broader organisation (Sashkin, 1987). This *esprit de corps* may limit an individual's ability to rationalise the commission of acts, which run contrary to the organisation's interest and mission. In contrast poor leadership has the opposite effect, creating an environment where individuals feel lower organisational loyalty, creating a potential hotbed for insider threat.

- *Corruption impact case studies*: These are published case studies which may set out the nature, approach, and impact of corruption on organisational and personal interests: for example, highlighting the impact on other team members or social outcomes. Such case studies can act to mitigate the rationalisation that the corrupt action does not have a material impact on issues of importance to the organisation or individual/s.

Preventing beneficiaries

As discussed in Chapter 5, beneficiaries can play a role in corruption-related insider threat, inducing insiders to act on their behalf and to the detriment of the organisation. The threat elements related to beneficiaries are their *capability*, *intent*, and *interaction*. Capability and intent are both features of the beneficiary entity itself and, therefore, under limited control from a prevention perspective by the target organisation. From a more systemic national level, law enforcement controls may exist to disrupt the capability of beneficiaries; for example anti-money laundering measures which impact on cash flow for bribery. Similarly, beneficiary intent to elicit corruption may be deterred by legal penalties and the threat of detection (see discussions by Bun et al., 2020; Yezer, 2013). In contrast, the interaction between organisational roles and potential insider risk event beneficiaries is under the control of the target organisation.

- Interaction prevention controls: These are controls which prevent or limit the interaction between roles in the organisation and potential beneficiaries. It must be noted that the interaction between potential beneficiaries and the organisation or role is often legitimate and an element of the usual business of the organisation: for example the relationship between license applicants and license assessing officers. In legitimate circumstances, interaction controls may limit the systemic nature of the interaction between a role and potential beneficiaries: for example by limiting the timeframe for the relationship or the number of possible interactions that may occur within a timeframe. They may also limit the closeness of physical interactions: for example by creating separate physical spaces, particularly in operational zones such as wharves and depots. Illegitimate interactions, in contrast, are not undertaken in the normal course of business: for example meeting to exchange sensitive information with organised criminal entities. These controls, therefore, work to limit the development of such relationships. Examples of rationalisation prevention controls include the following:

- *Workforce redeployment*: The redeployment of workforce to different roles after a period of time limits the extent to which relationships can develop between the occupant of an organisational role and potential beneficiaries or will limit the extent of harm that relationship can create to the term in which an individual occupies the role. We have outlined this control above as an opportunity control, against the *certainty* factor. This highlights the fact that some controls may control multiple drivers of risk.
- *Employee screening:* This involves the screening of employees prior to or during employment to identify potential connections to organised crime or other entities of interest such as rival companies. This control may limit the employment of persons who have inherent conflicts of interest against the organisation or identify such conflicts so they can be managed through other controls, such as limiting the roles they are able to occupy.

Detection controls

The second major control typology concerns those controls which either detect insider threat events or detect the presence of indicators that the opportunity factors, motivation factors, or beneficiary factors are realising an insider threat event against an organisational asset. As we discussed in previous chapters, the ACFE (Association of Certified Fraud Examiners, 2018a, 2018b, 2022) has, through their survey studies, concluded that tip-offs remain (through several years of survey) the most common means of detection for insider threat and corruption incidents; and "nearly three times as many cases as the next most common method" (Association of Certified Fraud Examiners, 2022, p. 4).

The ACFE's observations can be interpreted in two ways: firstly, that tip-offs are a highly effective mechanism for detecting insider activity or, alternatively, that organisations are overly relying on tip-offs as a mechanism for detecting insider activity. Under the second scenario, the ACFE data is inherently biased insofar as it is based on those cases which have been detected, and that tip-offs remain the most significant mechanism utilised by organisations. It is natural, then, that the highest number of detections will be derived from tip-offs. This by no means demonstrates that tip-offs are an effective means of detecting the occurrence of malicious insider activity.

In Chapter 3 we touched upon the inherent weaknesses of tip-offs as a control for detecting insider activity, namely their reliance on individual observation and the fact that they are subject to heuristic biases, such as *confirmation bias* (i.e. that what has been observed is not illicit activity) and *bystander non-intervention* (i.e. that another person will report the observed behaviour). Tip-offs also may involve an unpredictable level of chance, insofar as they rely on a competent observer being present to detect the insider behaviour, while insiders themselves act to reduce the chances of detection by other individuals.

Therefore, we propose an alternative explanation, that organisations do not have systemic mechanisms for defining and designing controls to detect potential or actual insider activity. This theory is borne out through or review of relevant literature, in which there is a dearth of structured examination of detection methodologies for insider threat. The value of our model lies, again, in its ability to provide an analytical structure for defining and designing internal controls again by reference to the risk factors we have identified earlier.

Effective detections controls are critical to managing insider threat, insofar as the organisation can only respond to or mitigate losses from risk events that it is capable of detecting. The absence of effective detection controls or controls which are not consistent detectors of insider activity will increase the losses to the organisation. In addition, the absence of detection controls may also contribute to confirmation biases in the assessment of risk, by focusing attention on detected incidents rather than the inherent risk involved with the organisational asset.

We propose four types of detection controls: *opportunity detectors*, *motivation detectors*, *beneficiary detectors*, and *incident detectors*. We also suggest two lenses through which detection controls should be designed: *lead detectors* and *lag detectors*, that is detection controls which can detect the indicators of a risk event prior to its occurrence, thereby enabling or triggering prevention controls, versus detection controls which detect the occurrence of a risk event thereby enabling or triggering response controls.

Detecting opportunity

Opportunity factors equate to vulnerabilities within organisational processes and practices which can be exploited by motivated actors. The detection of opportunity is, therefore, the detection of behaviour or activity that is indicative that those vulnerabilities are actually being exploited.

- Authority detection controls: These detect where an authority is improperly exercised. For example, a financial delegation is contravened or a role makes a decision, in their own right, in circumstances where that decision is subject to separation of duties. Examples of authority detection controls include the following:

  - *Initiator: Decision-maker matching*: This is a control which identifies a match between the initiator and the decision-maker for a transaction (assuming that this is not prevented by a prevention control). This control identifies where a person has exceeded the authority of the role to make a decision individually.

- *Delegation anomaly detection:* This a control which detects anomalies in the level of delegation exercised by a person or role in respect of a decision, or the access or use of information or a physical asset.

- Access detection controls: These detect the unauthorised or unusual access to a system, data, physical, or intangible asset. Examples of access detection controls include the following:

  - *Access/leave data matching:* This is a control which detects where an individual has accessed a location, system, or asset while officially on leave. This is a potential indicator of insider activity which can be detected through this matching process.
  - *Tamper-proof seals:* These enable the detection of access to an asset, for example, physical evidence held by a law enforcement institution. While this mechanism may not identify the perpetrator, it will identify that the asset has been improperly accessed, which may trigger a response, such as an investigation.
  - *Access anomaly identification:* This identifies anomalies in access by an individual to a location, decision, information, or asset, for example, the regularity of access or a sudden change in access behaviour.

- Visibility detection controls: These are controls which detect actions which diminish the level of general visibility over decision-making or actions. Examples of visibility detection controls include the following:

  - *Out-of-hours-work-pattern anomaly identification:* Working outside of normal business hours may diminish the level of visibility over decision-making or activity by an insider actor, because of other staff not being present to observe those activities. This control would identify anomalies in the work pattern of staff to highlight those who are potentially undertaking insider activity while visibility and the threat of detection are lowered.
  - *Peer review anomaly identification:* This is a control to identify anomalies in the level of peer review of decision-making or activity in circumstances where peer review is required in the relevant process.

- Traceability detection controls: These controls detect actions which diminish the level of traceability of a decision or action: that is the completeness of the record associated with the action or decision. Examples of traceability detection controls include the following:

  - *Corrupted record detection*: Corruption of digital records is a methodology to reduce the level of traceability associated with a decision or action, preventing a review of the decision or confirmation of the

relevant evidence. This control would detect systemic issues around corruption of records associated with a potential insider.
- *CCTV gap identification*: This is a control to identify gaps in passive CCTV recording which may be indicative of insider activity which has eluded detection through CCTV.

- Certainty detection controls: These controls detect actions which increase the level of certainty that an insider will have access to a specific decision that they have a malicious interest in. Examples of certainty detection controls include the following:

  - *Self-allocation detection:* Some roles, such as team leaders, may have the ability to self-allocate a decision for review or quality purposes. However, excessive self-allocation of decisions may be indicative of attempts to bypass the usual random allocation of decisions to gain certainty that a particular decision can be made by the person. This control would identify where a person is self-allocating decisions at an unusual rate.
  - *Shift-swapping log:* Swapping shifts with other officers, to occupy a particular role, is a methodology for increasing certainty and being present to make a time-bound decision, for example, clearing a particular person or goods that will arrive on a given day. This control identifies unusual patterns in shift-swapping activity.

Detecting motivation

As discussed in Chapter 6, while the motivations of individuals are not systemic, there may be indicators at an individual or a systemic level of circumstances which increase the likelihood of malicious insider intent. Motivation detection controls are designed to identify those individual or systemic indicators of insider threat.

- Pressure detection controls: While not a consistent factor in insider threat, pressures on the individual, such as gambling and drug addictions, debts, and obsession with status, may generate the intent to maliciously exploit a vulnerability within the organisation. Controls to detect such pressures include the following:
  - *Drug and alcohol testing:* In addition to presenting other risks to the organisation, such as health and safety risk, drug and alcohol use may create pressure on the individual. Random drug and alcohol testing, which is common across many organisations, may act to detect individuals who are more prone to committing malicious insider activity.

- *Financial examination:* Debts and poor financial management can create pressures on an individual. Many organisations undertake financial testing, particularly for a higher level of security or higher risk roles. These financial examinations and credit checks can identify debts or generally poor management of finances, which may motivate a person to engage in malicious insider activity.

- Inducement detection controls: These are controls which detect an inducement which has been provided to an insider to prompt them to engage in malicious insider activity. Inducements may be positive, such as bribes, or negative, such as threats or blackmail. Inducement detection controls include the following:

  - *Unexplained wealth detection:* Unexplained wealth may be detected through the observation of a person "living beyond their means" (see for example National Institute of Justice, 2011). Alternatively, in many jurisdictions with anti-money laundering regulators, government agencies may receive and examine reports on suspicious transactions or unexplained wealth.
  - *Blackmail reporting:* Providing staff with a means to report if they are subject to threats or blackmail, including providing protections and confidentiality, will enable detection of this negative inducement.

- Rationalisation detection controls: Rationalisation of insider threat may happen at a systemic level in organisations with a poor "integrity culture", low motivation, or disengagement from the workplace. Rationalisation detection controls include the following:

  - *Attrition analysis:* This uses human resource or surveys to identify work units within the organisation which are subject to high levels of attrition, potentially indicating lack of engagement and motivation. These factors can create an environment where insider activity can develop.
  - *Unplanned absenteeism analysis:* Similar to attrition, unplanned absenteeism is a potential indicator of lack of engagement in an organisational unit, creating an environment for insider activity. Analysis of unplanned absenteeism can identify parts of the organisation where engagement is low.

Detecting beneficiaries

Beneficiaries to corruption and malicious insider activity must interact with key roles within the organisation in some form to pursue their goals to the detriment of the targeted organisation. As described in Chapter 5 higher risk beneficiaries will have an ongoing interest in the organisation's asset, thereby creating an environment for systemic forms of insider threat. In an insider threat setting, beneficiaries are characterised by four characteristics: *group*, *capability*, *intent*, and *interaction*. Beneficiary detection controls are, therefore, designed to detect the capability, intent, and instances of interaction of each group or typology of beneficiary.

- Capability detection controls: These controls are designed to detect instances where a particular beneficiary capability has been or is being deployed for the purposes of insider threat: for example, detection of criminal entities and their changing methodologies for blackmail such as online targeting and deepfake image production for blackmail. Capability detection controls include the following:

  - Operational intelligence (adversary capability): A control which examines and analyses secure or open-source information regarding the capabilities and intentions of external entities, including adversaries such as rival corporations or organised criminal entities.
  - Financial intelligence: This is a control which can detect the financial capabilities of external (generally criminal) entities.

- Intent detection controls: These controls are designed to detect where a particular corruption intent is occurring and creating malicious insider activity. These controls identify the emergence and changing character of the intent of actors. For example in the context of organised criminal entities, the criminal activity may shift from drug importation to weapons importation, creating a different intent. This shift of intent may result in the use of a different import pathway, shifting from air to sea, for example. Intent detection controls are similar or equivalent to capability detection controls and include the following:

  - *Operational intelligence (adversary intent)*: This involves operational intelligence analysis of secure and open-source information to infer the intentions of external entities, including potential corruptors.
  - *Tactical intelligence*: Intelligence provided by officers in direct contact with potential beneficiaries will outline the specific entity's behaviours and the likely intent at a transactional level.

- Interaction detection controls: These controls are designed to detect illicit interactions between beneficiaries and the organisational roles. As discussed in Chapter 5, interactions may be formal or informal and detection controls can be designed to detect both forms of interaction between role and beneficiary type. Interaction detection controls include the following:

  - *Interaction frequency anomaly detection:* This is a control which identifies where the frequency of interaction between an entity and an individual within the organisation is unusually frequent or persistent: for example, if an agent always or very frequently interacts with a particular processing officer, which is out of the ordinary course of business.

- *Targeted surveillance*: In a law enforcement context, targeted surveillance (both physical or online) may be utilised to detect the interaction between a government employee and organised criminal entities.

Incident detectors

The previously discussed detection controls focus on the detection of instances of the drivers for insider threat. These forms of detection controls provide indicators of potential insider activity, but are not designed to identify insider activity with absolute accuracy. For example, we outlined above the fact that the corruption of records or creation of false records may be an indicator of attempts to avoid traceability when undertaking malicious activity. However, there are likely to be entirely legitimate reasons for records to be corrupted. These controls, therefore, are designed to detect circumstances where corruption and insider threat are more likely, thereby enabling the targeting of resources towards further investigation and resolution. These controls also focus on detecting single risk factors, such as detecting a specific inducement. In reality, corruption and insider threat occur as the result of or through a combination of multiple factors occurring or being affected.

Scenario

An insider is induced through bribery to create fake licenses for a criminal entity. The insider here undertakes their work on a greater-than-average basis outside of work hours to reduce visibility and self-allocates decisions to a far greater rate than other officers, thereby bypassing controls to reduce certainty. Additionally (in our imaginary scenario), some license applicants will have criminal alerts applied to them. In the normal course of work, these alerts are identified after accepting the application for processing. However, our insider checks whether any alerts are present before accepting or self-allocating the application to ensure they don't trigger an internal alert when granting the license to a known criminal.

In this scenario, we could assume a range of detection controls that we've outlined above may be triggered. Equally, the behaviour might be recognised by another person within the organisation and detection occurs through a "tip-off" (which is an incident detection control). Additionally, however, in this scenario a control could be designed to identify the characteristics of this *modus operandi*:

1 Checking for alerts against an applicant prior to accepting a case
2 Self-allocation of a decision
3 A positive decision outcome

Assuming that there is an audit log of these various steps then this *modus operandi* could be identified through analysis or computer analytics of the audit log. This is an example of an incident detection control, insofar as it does not detect the emergence of risk factors but detects a known incident typology.

Unlike the detection controls set out above which are designed to identify the emergence of risk factors indicative of insider threat and corruption, based on the risk assessment, incident detectors are designed to detect the incidence of corruption or insider threat directly. We suggest two forms of incident detection controls: *broad-based* and *specific*.

- *Broad-based incident detection controls:* Notwithstanding the weaknesses we have previously outlined with over-reliance on tip-offs as a means of detecting insider threat, tip-offs remain an integral part of the control system for insider threat. Tip-offs are an example of broad-based incident detection controls. The control is broad based insofar as through human observation and analysis tip-offs can identify a wide range of insider risk behaviours rather than being specific to a modus operandi or risk factor. Another example is tactical intelligence, which is a structured form of analysis at the individual or entity level, which is capable of identifying specific instances of insider threat. For example, intelligence analysis of the behaviours of a particular criminal organisation may identify that it is capable of corruption and that there is going to be a meeting at a time and place: likely for the exchange of a bribe. This identification would enable surveillance, disruption, and response to the particular incident.
- *Specific detection controls* are, as outlined in the earlier example above, designed to detect the incidence of a particular recognised *modus operandi*, which may have been identified through risk assessment or through a previously detected incident and deconstruction of the *modus operandi*. In line with our example, specific incident detection controls will be subject to a wide degree of variation depending on the nature of the organisation and its assets.

Detection control design

Prevention and response controls (which we'll set out below) enjoy a relative level of standardisation irrespective of the organisation. For example, to prevent a high level of decision making a separation of powers will be equivalent across organisations. Similarly, response controls such as investigation and penalty will have equivalence across organisations.

In contrast, while there is a relative level of standardisation (as we've set out in Appendix A), detection controls can be subject to a greater degree of design and bespoke development based on the organisation and its asset types. Hence, there is value in discussing the relationship between the risk factors and the design and definition of detection controls.

Risk factors and design

Set out above are examples of the detection controls by reference to the risk factor that drives the insider risk, such as detection of factors indicating an increased level of certainty. It is precisely this defined disaggregation of risk factors which guides and aligns the design of detection risk controls, providing a target action or state that requires detection.

The risk assessment for the organisation identifies that asset at risk, which opportunity factors they may be subject to, which beneficiaries would benefit from the particular asset, their capability, intent, and interaction. This assessment, therefore, provides a rich source of information to define what the detection control is intended to detect, and a logical framework for determining whether it will be capable of detecting the event or state. This is the value of the decomposition of the risk factors.

Modus operandi

As set out in the example of incident controls above, incident detection controls can be designed around the identification of specific *modus operandi*. Such *modus operandi* may be identified through detected insider threat activity. That is, once an incident has occurred and been detected through some other means (such as a tip-off) the modus operandi can be deconstructed to create detection controls to identify past or future instances of the modus operandi. In our example above the pre-checking and self-allocation activities are indicative of insider activity and can, therefore, be structured into detection controls to identify other incidences when the modus operandi may have been utilised.

Modus operandi may also be identified *in potentia* through the risk assessment process, by identifying the confluence of vulnerabilities that could give rise to an insider incident and designing controls to identify whether the modus operandi has previously occurred or to detect its future occurrence.

Data and data analytics

The ubiquity of data produced through business transactions and interactions provides a growing asset for the detection of insider threat. Where previously reliance had to be placed on static records and human analysis and observation, the collection and aggregation of mass data in organisations provides opportunities to design and deploy computer analytics to detect likely or actual insider threat activity. Some considerations for detection control design include the following:

Anomaly detection: We provided several examples of detection control above relating to anomalies in behaviour. The systemic detection of these anomalies becomes possible through the availability of data, particularly audit log data, pertaining to the activities on personnel within the organisation. Anomaly detection may be designed to detect known vulnerabilities. For example, we identified that frequent out-of-hours work is a potential indicator for insider threat, given it lowers the "visibility" of the activities that personnel may be involved in.

Examining access and usage logs for outlier individuals relating to work hours and access can be undertaken, as viewed through simple analyses as shown in Figure 7.2.

Figure 7.2 reveals an obvious clustering of working times, which fits the "normal" pattern. There are a small number of outliers who start and/or end work at significantly different times compared to the main cohort. While all these individuals may not be corrupt, this simple analysis can assist in identifying targets for further analysis and surveillance.

In addition to identifying known patterns of behaviour, anomaly detection can be utilised to identify other unknown outlier patterns. Here further analysis can be undertaken to identify whether they represent a threat of any kind related to insider threat, external fraud, compliance risk, and so forth. Under these models, anomalies involving outlier activity to the norm or sudden shifts in behaviour can be identified for further investigation and, where threats are identified, for refinement to target specifically the threat behaviours.

Machine learning: Machine learning algorithms can identify and learn patterns in large and complex datasets. From a detection perspective machine learning techniques may be used in two key ways: identification and prediction. Identification involves presenting the algorithm (or set of algorithms) with known instances of corrupt transactions and utilising the algorithm

FIGURE 7.2 Example Anomaly Detection Chart: Logging On/Off Times

to identify the factors that contribute to or indicate the corrupt conduct, thereby enabling a better understanding and analysis of the insider risk in the business activity. Prediction involves utilising the identified indicators to predict other transactions where corruption is likely to have been a factor in the decision or activity of an individual. As a practical example, data pertaining to the provision of a series of fraudulent licenses may be exposed to the machine learning algorithm: assuming the data set is sufficiently large. The algorithm could identify the combination features such as the time of year, time of day in which an application is lodged or decided upon, and suburb address that are correlated with the corrupt grant of a license. Assuming there are statistically relevant indicators, the machine could then predict, for similar decisions, that there is a likelihood of corruption on other existing or future decisions.[2]

Automated alerts: Automated alerts can complement analytical techniques. Where an anomaly detection or machine learning algorithm identifies outlier behaviour (e.g. a modus operandi, predicted corruption), systems can generate internal alerts to bring those threats to attention for response action. Alerts can, therefore, enhance detection and response velocity when compared to human-driven analysis or analytics.

Intelligence prioritisation

We previously touched on strategic, operational, and tactical intelligence as a suite of detection controls for insider threat risk, including assessing the capability and intent of beneficiary actors and detecting insider incidents. Intelligence analysis consists of the collection and analysis of incomplete information to make inferences about the threat environment.

In contrast to detection controls, which are "embedded" within processes (e.g. the collection of data for anomaly detection relating to personnel attendance is collected as part of their attendance in offices spaces or access to systems), intelligence requires the collection of information from different sources, which is then analysed by trained intelligence personnel. As such, intelligence is a resource-intensive control requiring prioritisation for the allocation of those resources to the highest risk.

In the context of insider threat, therefore, collection and analysis priorities should be structured around the highest risks. These are identified through the analysis we've outlined in previous chapters, that is those risks focused on those organisational assets which are of greatest value to the organisation, subject to opportunity for corruption, by beneficiaries with a malicious intent. Intelligence efforts may also be directed towards the higher risk roles, that is those with high opportunity and interacting with those assets of greatest value.

The risk model, therefore, in addition to structuring and providing a logic relationship between risk and control, in the case of intelligence activity, also provides the means to determine insider threat intelligence priorities and deploy finite resources to the highest areas of risk.

Response controls

The final group of controls responds to a detected instance of insider risk to resolve that incident. In contrast to prevention and detection controls, there is no direct logical relationship with the risk factors. However, the risk levels should determine the allocation of finite resources to supply intensive activities. We identify three key typologies of response controls: resolution, harm aversion, and mitigation.

- Resolution controls: These are designed to resolve and conclude the specific incidence of insider activity. Controls of this type include investigation, prosecution, referral to law enforcement, application of penalty, asset recovery, information recovery, and reversal of decision. The controls deal directly with the individual instance of corruption or insider activity. In addition to responding to the insider threat, some of the controls serve as specific or general deterrence mechanisms, such as the application of penalties including termination of employment or criminal penalties such as pecuniary penalties and imprisonment.
- Harm aversion controls: These controls are designed to avoid the harm of the insider threat incident if the incident has been detected prior to the harm accruing. These controls largely consist of cancelling the action that has been taken by the insider. For example, if the insider has facilitated fraudulent financial transactions but the money has yet to be transferred, then the transaction can be cancelled before the harm has been accrued. Or, if the insider has illicitly granted a permission (e.g. a visa) and it has been detected before the permission is used to enter the country, then the visa can be cancelled prior to the person entering the country and causing whatever economic, social, and/or environmental harm that might flow from it.
- Mitigation controls: These are designed to minimise future losses or risks by targeting the weaknesses or vulnerabilities that have been exposed through the detected insider incident. These controls include modus operandi review, control effectiveness assessment, future loss mitigation, and control strengthening. The purpose of mitigation response controls is to ensure that there is a process for continuous strengthening of the control environment in response to known incidents.

A capability-based approach

In the preceding sections of this chapter, we outlined a structured approach to defining controls. We provided a line of sight between the risk factors, which give rise to insider threat, and the controls, which reduce or eliminate those risk factors. In addition to setting out a control structure and definitions, we contend that controls should be viewed through a capability lens in their own right. As outlined in Chapter 3, the basis for our model is the contention that organisations are structured as a group of "capabilities" which enable them to achieve their purpose. These units of capability are comprised of inputs, which may variously be described. But for our purposes we will use *people, Organisation, process, information,* and *technology.*

A weakness we have observed in insider threat management systems is that controls are described within risk assessments but may be described either as documents or as policies. For example, an internal fraud prevention policy may be described as a control. The danger of such an approach is that it creates a sense that risk has been managed due to the number of policies in place while no "physical" instantiation of control is in place. As a result, the insider threat vulnerabilities remain unencumbered by control.

In contrast, considering each control as an organisational capability ensures design of each of the inputs is undertaken. This approach also enables an auditable set of design criteria for that control. For example, we have identified *interaction frequency anomaly identification* as a control. Viewed through a capability lens, this control might comprise a data analyst (*people*), undertaking a process of analysis (*process*) of interaction data (*information*) within a data analytics platform (*technology*) from within an independent corruption analysis centre (*organisation*). These elements describe the physical instance of the control, both to provide assurance of its actual existence and to provide a point of reference for audit and assurance of its efficacy. This physical description of the control also allows for it to be included in costing, which enables assessments of its return on investment and cost effectiveness as a means of managing insider risk. We will explore this aspect of the model in the following chapter.

Control balancing

The controls we have described above are not intended to be implemented in isolation. A single control against a complex risk is unlikely to mitigate that risk and will, by definition, create a single point of failure in the risk management approach. Controls therefore must form part of an ecosystem of prevention, detection, and response. Investment decisions must, therefore, be made on where the balance of control investment should be placed. It is tempting to conclude that all investment should be directed towards prevention controls, therefore abrogating the need for detection and response controls. In practice, however, controls are not intrinsically positive. Controls may also involve downsides, such as cost or productivity impacts that must be considered as part of control investment decisions, alongside considerations regarding their effectiveness under different risk conditions. We will explore these concepts further in Chapter 8.

Partnered controls

In previous chapters, we have highlighted the fact that insider risk needs to be examined and assessed through a broader lens than simply within the organisation itself. Insider risk within partners, direct suppliers, and other entities further up or down supply chains may threaten the mission and objectives of the organisation. Using our imaginary border agency from Chapter 3, stevedores at ports who are responsible for transporting goods for examination to the border agency may be able to divert those goods before they are rendered to the agency, thereby facilitating the importation of illicit goods. As a result, the insider threat within the stevedoring company creates a threat for the border agency that is realised, undermining its mission to prevent illicit goods entering the country. As a result, in order to protect its objectives, the agency needs to not only understand the risk posed by the stevedores (as we've discussed previously), but to further have visibility of and assure itself of the controls which exist within its partners and suppliers to mitigate these risks.

We argue, therefore, that insider risk needs to form part of agreements or rules that underpin these partnerships. In a commercial setting, assurance around the controls of interest must form part of legally enforceable contractual agreements. In a government setting, further regulation may be required to impose controls and protections within organisations that may not be regulated. This is to ensure that insider threat does not undermine other regulatory regimes by enabling facilitators within supply chains to bypass existing regulatory regimes. The utility of the control model in the early part of this chapter is that it provides a structure to subsequently assess where, in a supply chain, controls should be placed to achieve the maximum effect on protecting the organisation's mission, objectives, and assets.

Controls in a changing context

Organisations, their missions, objectives, capabilities, and assets are not static. As their environment changes, to maintain their commercial viability or regulatory effectiveness, they will need to constantly subject themselves to change and improvement. This changing context equally changes the insider risks they are subject to and the controls that are required to manage those risks. Equally, changes to improve business practices to enhance competitiveness or effectiveness may inadvertently remove vital insider threat controls.

As a simple example, removing a separation of duties in decision-making may result in higher productivity to meet increased demand. But this will equally potentially increase insider threat related to the decision-making process, and indeed the increased threat and losses may be greater than the return.

Insider threat assessment and control design, therefore, needs to be part of the processes that organisations use to define and execute change. As shown in Figure 7.3, an organisation needs to modify its strategy to minimise insider risk by firstly re-assessing insider risk based on new potential threats, followed by defining and planning new or adapted insider risk controls, embed these risk controls into the executive structure, and evaluate the efficacy of the new controls.

As organisations change their business strategies to maintain or grow their effectiveness in a changing environment, those changes will modify the external and internal threats they are subject to. For example, they may change the following:

• Product suite and/or business activities, thereby creating new or changed organisational assets (and targets for insider risk);
• Target market/clients, thereby creating or changing the potential beneficiaries of insider threat;
• Business processes, thereby changing the potential insider threat opportunities;
• Industrial relations policies (or they may retrench staff), thereby potentially creating the circumstances for motivation and rationalisation of insider activity; and
• Business locations, thereby potentially changing all the risk drivers for that location.

As such, when changing organisational strategy and designing the specifics of the change, organisations need to reassess the risk in a changing context. Further, using the reassessed risk, determine whether current controls will be sufficient to effectively manage the risk, or whether new or modified controls

FIGURE 7.3 Organisational Strategy Lifecycle

will be required to manage risk in the new business state. If new or changed controls are required, then controls should be defined and embedded as part of the process of changing the organisation from one state to another, and subsequently evaluated to ensure they are functioning correctly (Figure 7.3).

We will explore the process of governance and investment in control further in Chapter 11.

Chapter key points

- Treatment of risk involves development of strategies and mechanisms (controls) to modify the inherent level of insider risk associated with an activity of the organisation.
- Understanding the drivers for risk provides a logical structure for defining how to treat and control risk.
- There are three core types of control: preventative, detective, and responsive, which are used in concert to mitigate the likelihood of the risk occurring or reduce its consequences if it occurs.

Notes

1 Both control types are also "visibility controls" – in that they also increase the level of visibility associated with the activities, while simultaneously diminishing authority.
2 We do not intend to set out a full analysis on the use of machine learning for detection. In addition to the opportunities we have outlined, application of machine learning and anomaly detection must guard against data confirmation bias, that is, where the machine learns only from detected issues, without a random quality sample, and "snooping" where, for example, data is updated or collected due to the knowledge that corruption is involved in the transaction (e.g. the inclusion of investigation data).

References

Association of Certified Fraud Examiners. (2018a). *Report to the nations: 2018 Global study on occupational fraud and abuse.* https://www.acfein sights.com/acfe-insights/2018/9/28/key-findings-from-the-2018-report-to-the-nations-government-edition

Association of Certified Fraud Examiners. (2018b). *Report to the nations: Global study on occupational fraud and abuse.* https://www.acfe.com/report-to-the-nations/2018/

Association of Certified Fraud Examiners. (2022). *Occupational fraud 2022: A report to the nations.* https://legacy.acfe.com/report-to-the-nations/2022/

Bun, M. J., Kelaher, R., Sarafidis, V., & Weatherburn, D. (2020). Crime, deterrence and punishment. *Empirical Economics, 59,* 2303–2333.

Darley, J. M., & Latané, B. (1968). Bystander intervention in emergencies: Diffusion of responsibility. *Journal of Personality and Social Psychology, 4*(1), 377–383.

International Organization for Standardization. (2004). *ISO3100: Risk management.*

Larmour, P., & Wolanin, N. (2001). *Corruption and anti-corruption.* Asia Pacific Press.

National Institute of Justice. (2011). *Comparative evaluation of unexplained wealth orders.* NCJ Number 237163.

Sashkin, M. (1987). A new vision of leadership. *Journal of Management Development, 6*(4), 19–28. https://doi.org/10.1108/eb051650

Yezer, A. (2013). *Economics of crime and enforcement.* ME Sharpe.

8

UNDERSTANDING CONTROL EFFECTIVENESS AND IMPACT

Introduction

When investing in controlling insider risk, organisations need to ensure that the investment is being made against controls that are effective to manage that risk and do not excessively adversely impact on their business objectives or costs of operations. In this chapter we discuss the importance of building a corpus of knowledge around the factors that make controls effective or ineffective in certain circumstances and how controls negatively impact on business from a cost, efficiency, or productivity perspective. In the context of financial services and border control, the need to ensure that control is cost effective and does not hinder the ability to operate in a high-volume transaction environment is critical.

As we have explored in the previous chapter, implementing controls is the most critical element of managing risk. This is no less true when managing insider risk. However, the application of controls within the business of the organisation requires careful investment whether in terms of personnel, systems, data, and organisational process. It is, therefore, crucial that investment is made against controls which are genuinely effective at managing insider risk and that the thresholds of that effectiveness are understood and monitored. Similarly, controls are not uniquely "good". It is tempting to assume that more control equates to better management of risk and, therefore, it would be reasonable to simply invest in all available controls and thereby to maximise the mitigation of insider risk. In reality, however, controls create impacts on the objectives of the organisation. They create new costs to maintain and may reduce efficiency or productivity of processes where additional checks and balances are required.

DOI: 10.4324/9781003055716-8

We propose that to develop and implement a systemic approach to managing insider risk, there is a need to analyse the factors that make different typologies of control effective. Further, organisations should examine those factors which create negative impacts on their objectives. In addition to setting out a structure of controls, Appendix A sets out these effectiveness factors and impact factors for each identified control.

Control performance

As discussed in the previous chapter, insider risk controls are capabilities established within the organisation to mitigate the likelihood or the impact of harmful insider activity within the organisation. In practice, controls are designed to prevent, detect, or respond to insider risk events, thereby mitigating the actual or potential harm to the organisation's objectives. They do this by creating a logical structure for defining and designing controls and aligning those controls to the risk factors they mitigate. This may take the shape of, for example, describing controls which prevent an opportunity from emerging.

Controls are comprised of a logical set of relationships between the assessed risk and its drivers (opportunity, motivation, beneficiaries), the purpose or desired effect of the control, what inputs are required to realise the control, the activities which make up the control in action, outputs produced (such as decision reviews, or audits), and the actual effects of the control (Figure 8.1).

Performance of the control (and the controls in concert) describes the quality of the relationship between these different elements:

- Effectiveness describes the relationship between the desired effect of the control (or set of controls) as defined by the logical model and the actual effect. For example if the control is designed under the logical model to prevent opportunity, effectiveness is the extent to which it does, in fact, prevent that opportunity.
- Cost effectiveness describes the relationship between the inputs and investment into the control against its actual effect. This relationship

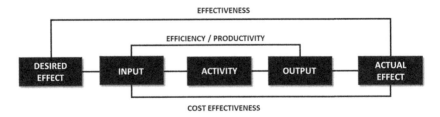

FIGURE 8.1 The Efficiency–Effectiveness Model

establishes the relative value of investing in a particular control relative to other controls (assuming we are comparing like controls, that is, apples for apples) that may have the same effectiveness, but with a lower level of investment.

- Efficiency and productivity are both factors in the relationship between the inputs into a control and its outputs. These consider either the amount of output for a level of input (productivity) or, in the counter direction, the amount of input required to achieve a level of output (efficiency). This relationship is important given that accomplishing controls carries a cost to the organisation.

Considering performance in terms of productivity and efficiency enables opportunities to reduce costs or enhance productivity of controls at the same level of cost. As an example, financial audit is a form of detection control. Enhancing training and automation of processes for auditors could improve the productivity of producing audit reports and improve findings, including identifying corrupt and fraudulent transactions.

Input and cost

When describing efficacy, it is worth outlining how inputs and costs of a control are represented. As we described in the previous chapter, control can be designated as organisational capability, with fundamental inputs being described in terms of people, process, information, technology, assets, and facilities. These elements of input, therefore, provide a basis for costing the control and thereby deriving measures of efficiency and productivity (e.g. the cost per unit of audit report, relative to the number and salary of auditors, amortised cost of audit software, facilities, and ICT equipment). In other words, they enable the measurement of cost effectiveness, again using the cost of these inputs relative to the control's actual effect in managing insider threat.

Describing effectiveness

The most critical element of the performance of insider risk control is the effectiveness of the controls. A highly efficient or productive control that does not control insider risk has no value. As such, a cost-effective control must first be an effective control. As such we turn our attention to describing the elements of control effectiveness.

We suggest there are two elements which enable us to design, describe, and assess the effectiveness of insider risk controls and thereby make sound investment decisions and continuously improve the management of insider risk: *effectiveness factors* and *effectiveness thresholds*.

Effectiveness factors

Effectiveness factors describe the necessary inputs or precursors to an effective control, within a broader typology of controls or for a specific control. To illustrate, *workforce redeployment* is an opportunity prevention control which prevents certainty. That is, if a person is redeployed to different roles within the organisation, then they will not have the certainty of being in a position on a particular day to make a decision to the benefit of a beneficiary. Take for example the redeployment of border officers to different roles within an airport. This action reduces their certainty that they will be in a role that is able to clear passengers for entry and thereby illicitly facilitate the importation of drugs. An effectiveness factor for this control is "randomness". For example if the redeployment were predictable (if roles were rotated on a regular basis resulting in the border officer being in a favourable role every Wednesday), then the control would not be fully effective. This is because the drug importation activities could simply be delayed until Wednesday when the officer is in the relevant role. As such the randomness of the redeployment and the attendant lack of predictability therefore forms a crucial factor for the effectiveness of the workforce redeployment control.

Using another example, separation of duties is a control which both prevents individual authority over a decision and increases the visibility of that decision. However, the hierarchical relationship between the two roles across which the decision-making duties are split can influence the effectiveness of this control. If, for example, the initiator of the decision is more senior in the organisational hierarchy than the decision checker/finaliser, then it is reasonable that the second person will simply validate the decision of the initiator. Take for example the process of signing off an invoice that has been fulfilled. Many organisations will require a senior officer to be the point of sign-off, while more junior officers will be given the task of validating and executing payment against the contract. In these circumstances the more junior officer is not a genuinely competent authority to limit the authority of the more senior person. As such the level of seniority is an effectiveness factor for the separation of duties control.

Effectiveness thresholds

Effectiveness thresholds describe the boundaries or limits within and outside of which a control will be effective. For example, *supervision* is a control which limits individual authority and increases the level of visibility of the activities of the personnel under supervision. Supervision can be through pure management control. For example, on factory or operational floors there may be floor managers who oversee and manage a physical space, managing both the activities undertaken within the space and the space itself. In these scenarios, several effectiveness thresholds exist. The first threshold is the ratio of people to supervisor. The second is the size of the space to be supervised. Finally, it is the number and complexity of activities undertaken. At a certain ratio of personnel to supervisor, the effectiveness of the supervision will diminish. Let us assume that the threshold ratio is 1:20: 1 supervisor to 20 personnel. Once that threshold is exceeded, the control will no longer be as effective as it had been when the ratio was 1:10 or 1:15. Similarly, if the size of the space that the supervisor must oversee impacts on a level of visibility they can exercise over a workspace, there will be a negative impact on the control.

Substantial research has been put into different forms of crime prevention controls examining the circumstances and mechanisms by which different crime prevention mechanisms operate and the limits of their effectiveness. Here we refer the reader to the work undertaken by Johnson et al. (2015), in which the authors describe the EMMIE Framework. EMMIE has five dimensions: "effect of intervention, the identification of the causal Mechanism(s) through which interventions are intended to work, the factors that Moderate their impact, the articulation of practical Implementation issues, and the Economic costs of intervention" (p. 459). For results relating to crime prevention initiatives rated by EMMIE see College of Policing (2016).

Considering the breadth of controls we have outlined in the previous chapter and Appendix A, in our view, there is considerable opportunity for further research into the thresholds of effectiveness for different insider threat controls.

Describing control impact

For the purposes of our model, impact describes the "negative" effects of an individual or set of controls. Across risk management studies there appears to be a lack of examination on the downsides of risk controls. To make informed decisions about investing organisational resources and minimising impacts on the objectives of the organisation requires consideration of the negative effects of controls and a model through which to identify and consider those effects.

We therefore identify several lenses through which organisations can identify and assess the relative impact of controls when making decisions in relation to implementation:

- *Cost*: These controls require resources for their design, implementation, and ongoing evaluation within the organisation. Resources that are invested in these controls could otherwise be invested in other activities that achieve the organisation's objectives. There is, therefore, a cost impact to each control. For example, implementing *key access* to secure areas has costs for the creation of secure areas, maintenance, and protection of keys and locks. These costs could otherwise be allocated elsewhere, while accepting the higher risk of security breaches for assets which would then be protected within a key only access zone.

- *Efficiency/productivity*: Given the relationship between efficiency and effectiveness/productivity, as outlined above, it is worth considering these elements together. Some controls impose additional inputs or steps into business processes. These may reduce the efficiency of those processes by requiring those additional inputs to achieve the same level of productivity. Alternatively they may, for a fixed level of input, reduce the level of productivity. An example is separation of duties under which at least two people are required to complete a decision. If, for example, we enacted a separation of duties for decisions to the grant of licenses (which is typically a high volume activity), then either

  - we would need more officers in order to grant the same number of licenses in the same amount of time, because each license now involves two people, which would have an impact on the efficiency of the process; or
  - we keep the same number of officers; however, the officers can tentatively produce only two thirds as many licenses in the same time period.

- *Cultural*: While evidence exists that insider threat is prevalent within most organisations (Association of Certified Fraud Examiners, 2022), it is noted, in spite of the significant harm to organisations, that it is perpetrated by a minority of individuals. The controls that are imposed on all individuals or classes of individuals within the organisation impact on those individuals whether they are inclined or not inclined to engage in insider activity. These controls can create a form of cultural dissonance impact within the organisation. As an example, the introduction of drug and alcohol testing as a means of preventing and detecting potential pressure factors for individuals can create a broader perception of a lack of trust in all staff within an organisation, which can impact on staff engagement, motivation, attraction, and retention (Neveu & Kakavand, 2019).

- *Personnel*: Some controls will modify the practices under which personnel approach their work, requiring modifications to their training or conditions of employment. For example, workforce redeployment means that personnel will occupy different positions within the organisations on a rotational or random basis. This approach to deployment of personnel will require specialised workforce conditions and role descriptions and require training across the multiple different roles within the operational setting.

- *Relationship*: Some controls will create impacts on relationships with other organisational stakeholders and partners. This occurs as the organisation imposes new or changed requirements on their partners, often affecting the delivery of services to clients and customers. In a border control setting, for example, officials may work in the same physical space as wharf operators. Here, authorities, access controls, drug and alcohol testing, employment screening may be all applied by the border agency for personnel of the other organisation to operate in shared zones. The imposition of these controls may impact on the relationships between these organisations.

- *Infrastructure*: Some controls will require new or changed infrastructure to implement and support their ongoing operation. For example, the establishment of active or passive CCTV requires the purchase and set up of the CCTV cameras. It also requires networking, data capture and storage, and dedicated space and fixtures for placement.

Considering these impacts provides a basis for making decisions about whether there is value in controlling the risk and the ideal mix of controls to control the insider risk while minimising costs and impacts on the priorities of the business. We'll examine the concept of *control balancing* further, which is the concept of balancing which controls to put in place relative to their benefit and impact.

Control typologies

Let's turn now to considering control effectiveness and impact across the different control typologies we identified in Chapter 7.

Preventing opportunity

At the highest level, and self-evidently, the test of the effectiveness of a prevention control is its ability to *consistently* prevent a driver of risk from eventuating. In the following chapter, we will explore the assurance of the effectiveness of controls. But, in short, a prevention control must statistically prevent the risk driver from occurring to a greater than random level, and from an effectiveness perspective to a level required to prevent the insider threat and the losses which would occur.

Access preventers

Preventing access across all control types involves restricting access to assets through physical or cyber-security barriers. The factors which determine the effectiveness of these controls may be described as "soundness". In a physical sense, this may be conceptualised as the thickness and impenetrableness of the physical barrier and the inability to breach the barrier. In a computing environment, this may be the impenetrableness of the information environment, encryption protocols, firewalls, and so forth.

In order to do business, however, the assets to which access has been initially prevented must eventually be accessible. Therefore, access points must be created, whether physically (e.g. access doors, ports) or virtually (e.g. computer access interfaces), to provide controlled access to those assets. This allows those that have authorisation to access the asset/s but in a secure yet monitored environment. Factors determining the robustness of controls may include the difficulty of bypassing the control. For example, if an area is accessible through pass card access, the theft of a pass would enable access to the area. In contrast, a biometric access point, such as fingerprint or retina scan, restricts access to the specific individual to which access was granted.

The impact of access controls is, for example, the *cost* of establishing the secure walls and vaults to protect assets. This may, for example, include *infrastructure* costs in the form of physical barriers, access points, and access mechanisms. Such impact will affect the *efficiency/productivity* insofar as accessing the assets requires the additional time and effort to access the assets before they can be used for the purposes of pursuing the organisation's objectives.

Authority preventers

Authority preventers act to reduce the level of individual authority held by a role. The general effectiveness factor of authority prevention controls is forced interaction, that is when separating or reducing the authority that the other elements of authority are vested within a person of equal rank an interaction takes place. This interaction is between the person of authority and the decision referrer. For example, a license is referred by an assessment officer to a decision-maker. For illicit reasons the decision-maker overturns the recommended action by the referrer. The model of separating or reducing authority promotes interaction between the two parties (referrer and the decision-maker) whereby, in our example, the referrer then has the capacity to question the decision. This may act as both a deterrent and a detection mechanism against illicit decision-making (assuming the referrer has the opportunity to interact with the decision-maker). In contrast, an invoice is received by a senior contract managing officer for services which have not been rendered, whereby they sign the invoice off stating that the services have been rendered. The invoice is sent to a central processing area with junior finance staff making the "decision" to pay the invoice on the basis of the sign off by the contract managing officer. In this case, while there is technically a separation of the invoice approval and payment authority, in practice the disparate seniority coupled with the lack of any interaction between the two officers undermines the effectiveness of the separation of duties.

The impact of authority prevention controls is that by separating authority across more than one person, there is an associated *cost* and *efficiency/*

productivity. By this we mean that to undertake the same number of decisions would necessitate more staff to maintain the same level of decision-making – if separation of duties were introduced. Alternatively, if authority prevention controls are introduced within the same resourcing profile, then the total number of decisions which could be made would be reduced.

Visibility preventers

Visibility controls are designed to raise the visibility of the interaction between a role and an organisational asset. Across these controls the factors which make them effective are the level of consistency of visibility. For example, space and person ratios may create infrequent visibility by others during the day. Equally, blind spots, which enable activity to go on unseen, reduce effectiveness of these controls.

In an ICT environment, visibility refers to the extent in which other officers can see and observe the activities of their peers within computer applications. This is often done to manage shared workloads and allocation of effort. The factors that inform the effectiveness of these controls is the depth of visibility within the system, that is, how many activities and reasons for activities or decisions does the system enable other users to see and observe. If the information is only basic or cursory, such as who is currently holding a particular case, rather than the reasons or mechanisms by which they were allocated the case, then the opportunity, for example, to illicitly self-allocate a case will be higher.

The impact of increased visibility may be *personnel* related, insofar as creating open plan working environments creates change and a potentially disruptive working environment. This can affect *efficiency/productivity.* Active CCTV monitoring also carry *cost* and *infrastructure* requirements.

Traceability preventers

Traceability controls prevent *low* traceability of the interaction between roles and organisational assets. Across traceability preventer controls the factors that determine their effectiveness are the following:

- The completeness of the record of an interaction between a role and an asset. For example, the record captures the time, circumstances, person, role, and so forth of the interaction. For decision assets, evidence leading to the decision is also captured. For passive and active CCTV, blind spots or the ability to obfuscate the field of view of cameras reduces their effectiveness.
- The mandatory nature of capture or collection of the record. For example, if a decision can be effected without saving the evidence or completing the

record, then later determining the reasons behind the decision or detecting that the decision was illicit will be significantly more challenging.
- The length of storage of the record. If a record is only stored for a finite period, then it will not be effective beyond that period.

The impact of traceability preventer controls includes the following: (i) the cost of systems of record and record storage whether physical or digital and (ii) the *efficiency/productivity* of processes, which will involve the additional burden of collecting and storing of record information. Controls such as CCTV may also have *personnel*, *relationship*, and *cultural* impacts, by effectively placing staff and other stakeholders under surveillance.

Certainty preventers

These controls prevent certainty of interaction between a role and a specific asset of interest. The factors which contribute to the effectiveness of certainty preventers is the level of the following factors:

- *Unpredictability*: For example, if decisions are allocated in an unpredictable manner, thereby ensuring that an officer cannot engineer the process to receive a decision of interest.
- The *ratio of people to assets*: For example, though decisions may be allocated randomly, if the ratio of officers to the decision is low, then their probability of landing on a specific decision will be higher than for a decision asset with a high ratio of officers to decisions. As discussed above, the threshold at which the effectiveness of random allocation diminishes is worthy of further research.

The impacts of certainty preventer controls are *personnel* related in that they require officers to be capable of randomly managing different assets or decision types; or more acutely for random workforce redeployment, they must be capably trained to fulfil multiple different roles competently.

Preventing motivation

Preventing motivation involves implementing systemic broad-based controls that act on the desires and motivations of individuals. As such, the effectiveness of motivation prevention controls is their ability to mitigate the desire of insiders to commit acts against the organisation. Across the three typologies of motivation prevention controls, pressure preventers (discussed in the following), inducement preventers, and rationalisation preventers (discussed in the following), there are two general forms that each of these controls take. They either (i) act on the individuals to mitigate motivations by creating behavioural and psychological resistance to those motivating factors or (ii) act on the environment by removing the stimulus that creates the motivation, for example, detecting and controlling the use of drugs through drug-testing regimes or by excluding people who are already subject to those stimuli (i.e. not hiring drug-users in the first place, again by utilising drug-testing in the hiring processes). For (i) to be effective, it must create an assumed or actual change in behaviour when confronted with the motivating factors and opportunity to commit malicious insider acts. For example, bribes or threat are inducement factors which may convince a person to act against the organisation. Effective controls of the type (i) prevent a person from acting on the bribe, while effective controls of type (ii) remove the circumstances which enable the bribe or threat to be issued.

Davis et al. (2015), in a review of behavioural change for health outcomes, identified at least 82 theories of behavioural change. Psychology's theoretical models, which outline effective interventions to change actual or potential behaviour, are broad and varied, highlighting further opportunity for research into models which apply to insider threat behaviour. For our purposes, we prefer to consider examining this aspect of motivational control through a basic decision theory lens. A motivated decision by an individual to engage in malicious activity based on the presence of a motivating factor is comprised of the three components of a decision:

A *cognitive process* resulting in the *selection of a belief or course of action* based on available *information*.

These three elements provide our points of influence on the decision-making process. Effective interventions can influence the following:

- **The cognitive process**: For example through training, knowledge building and exposure to ethical questions and considerations, influencing the emotions that influence the irrational elements of decision-making. Equally, raising awareness of cognitive biases that may influence an individual's decision-making may not fully remove those biases but can enable them to consider potential biases when deciding. For example, optimism bias may influence a person in believing that their luck will continue and they won't be caught for their action. Highlighting this bias and its role in previously detected and prosecuted insider cases may influence future decision-makers to consider whether bias is influencing their decision.
- **The selection of options**: Here, the options available to a decision-maker are largely limited by the opportunity controls. However, where the option does exist to act maliciously, controls act to impact the perception of those options, for example, the perception of reward versus risk for the options of committing or not committing the act.

- **The available information:** Decisions can be influenced by the information available both generally and/or at the point of decision. For example, general knowledge regarding detection methods available to the organisation may act to deter action (as opposed to that same information being held secret). Information regarding the *modus operandi* of organised criminal entities and their approaches to corrupting individuals may help those individuals to recognise attempts to bribe or induce them.

Taking these elements into account, the factors that contribute to the effectiveness of the two typologies of motivation prevention controls are as follows:

Type 1: Normative and cultural qualities that influence cognition and selection, and quality factors for information such as completeness, correctness, and comprehensibleness.

Type 2: Effectiveness factors. These influence the ability of the control to exclude or mitigate the environmental stimulus or the individuals that may already be subject to that stimulus. We will explore these elements for each of the motivational factors. This examination will also highlight our central argument, that *while influencing motivation remains a component of a threat control system, acting to change the motivations of individuals is a less systemic and reliable approach.* This is highlighted by the difficulty in attaining precision in the description of those factors which render a control effective at changing the motives of the individual. In our view this is in part because the number of variables influencing individuals is large, containing many permutations of values, beliefs, knowledge, preferences, perceived rewards, and so forth. As such, this renders it difficult to create a precise descriptive model for describing effectiveness in relation to motivational controls. This does, however, provide an avenue for future research into motivation control building on significant research into motivation in both this work and others (see for example Graycar & Prenzler, 2013; Graycar & Sidebottom, 2012).

Preventing pressure

Following the logic above, pressure prevention controls either equip individuals to reduce or resist pressures and act in accordance with the organisation's objectives or exclude persons who are subject to particular kinds of pressure from occupying roles where those pressures may increase risk. Alternatively, they may exclude those persons from the organisation entirely. For example, people who fail drug tests, have gambling addictions, or have criminal connections may be unable to acquire the security clearance for certain roles, or may not be hired by the organisation in the first place.

For the first type, controls make individuals pressure resilient; the factors influencing effectiveness include the "reach", "frequency", and "quality" of information or cognitive influence, that is, influence across the organisation and, in particular, to those who are already subjected to a specific type of pressure.

Taking a specific scenario, an organisation may raise awareness that gambling addiction may cause reckless behaviour. Further, the organisation is routinely exploited by corruptors to gain inside information, and that the organisation has in place mechanisms to identify both the signs of such addiction (such as financial screening) and the activities of corruptors (such as tactical intelligence). This would be anticipated to influence the decisions of would-be insiders through both cognitive and informational influencers. However, if this information does not reach individuals that are at risk or only reaches them intermittently (such as through annual training regimes), then this information will not act as an effective control. Equally, if the information provided through whatever channel or means is incomplete or incomprehensible, then the information will not be an effective vehicle for modifying the response to pressures.

The second control type relies on the accuracy of the means of detecting pressures as well as the level of correlation between the pressure and the commission of an insider act. For example, using drug testing as a means of identifying potential corrupters and excluding them from the organisation assumes a high level of correlation between drug use and corruption. If this correlation is not statistically significant (assuming this is empirically explored) then this control will be of limited effectiveness. This follows the logic of our earlier proposition that while controls that act on people through motivation remain useful, they are generally of less systemic effect than controls on process, which are inherently designed to be systemic.

An additional effectiveness factor is the frequency of controls. If, for example, these exclusionary controls are only undertaken on entry into the organisation, then the assumption is that personal circumstances are static and do not change from the state at entry. In reality, circumstances do change and, therefore, the effectiveness of these controls is determined by whether they are able to prevent potential changes in circumstances.

Pressure prevention controls derive impact on the organisation. One example is cost. Drug testing comes at a very high cost, being generally outsourced to qualified medical corporations. Reviews of the pros and cons of such a regime are provided by Pidd and Roche (2014) and Shaffer and Kleiner (1992). There may also be personnel and cultural impacts to these controls. For example, the controls may invade the personal privacy of individuals by examining their private or personal circumstances, such as undertaking financial screening of the individual. These impacts have the potential to increase organisational attrition or impact on recruitment of new personnel, some of whom may be deterred by the time and effort to undergo checking regimes or drug testing prior to joining the organisation.

Preventing rationalisation

As with pressure, there are two broad forms of controls for effectively preventing rationalisation. Firstly, those which act on the individual to mitigate their motivation when faced with rationalisation factors. Secondly, those which act on the environment itself to remove the rationalisation effect. As set out in Chapter 6, poor work culture characterised by bullying and lack of supportive leadership and positive reward for effort create rationalising factors for malicious acts.

The factors that influence the effectiveness of controls are the quality of leadership and mechanisms to create an *esprit de corps* within the organisation, creating connection between individuals and the objectives of the organisation. The quality, comprehensibility, and timeliness of information about the objectives and the values of the organisation, along with modelled behaviours, will mitigate the rationalising environment itself. This, therefore, has the potential to mitigate the likelihood of malicious acts when confronted by opportunity. The proposition here is that resilient cultures, norms, and values can guide behaviour even where personal benefit may be at stake (Larmour & Wolanin, 2001). The factors that guide the effectiveness of these controls is the extent to which they are understood and consistently exhibited both by authorities within the organisation and by its staff; creating a normalisation of these values and expectation from others that these values will be upheld.

The other set of controls outlined in Chapter 8 act to mitigate the effect of the rationalising factors, even when they have not been excluded from the organisational environment. They do this by acting on the individual decision-making processes of the officer. As an example, in an environment of poor values and norms of behaviour (thereby increasing the risk of insider activity), the organisation may provide an employee assistance programme (e.g. providing a support hotline for staff experiencing work or personal difficulties). Such a hotline may mitigate the effects of the environment on individual decision-making. Factors influencing the effectiveness of such a control include its accessibility and norms and values about using it. Overall, the effectiveness of such controls is weaker in addressing rationalisation insofar as the control relies heavily on the individual taking some action to address their own reaction to the environment. One could argue that the insider threat activity might itself take the place of an investment by the individual in pursuing these actions.

In terms of control impacts, leadership controls, we believe, have minimal downsides. Creating sound leadership and culture is inherently beneficial to the productivity of the organisation (Chiok Foong Loke, 2001). The impact on insider threat is, in some ways, an ancillary benefit to values and behaviours that will already support the organisation to achieve its objectives. In contrast, the second set of controls, which act on the individual, involves cost, such as the costs in providing counselling and ethical support services for employees, noting that they may equally have an impact on employee productivity which offset their costs.

Preventing inducement

Finally, controls to prevent inducement follow the same pattern with effective controls acting on the individual and mitigating their actions when faced with a potential inducement or preventing the inducement from being rendered. For the first type, the factors that render the control effective act on the components of decision-making in respect of how to react to the inducement. Some examples follow:

- Providing personnel with information and awareness regarding the forms of inducement that may be used by certain beneficiaries may assist those personnel to identify and resist an attempt at inducement. For example, education in relation to "honeypot" schemes (Das, 2009) may help to identify and resist these methods (Srinivasan, 2021). Again, the completeness and correctness of this information will be critical to the effectiveness of such a control.
- Support channels and training in resisting in the event of threats may assist personnel to resist acting on such threats and thereby protect organisational assets. From a cognitive perspective, the effectiveness of such controls will be their ability to create psychological safety or resilience. Equally, the trust created in such services will be critical to their use by personnel in the event of a threat.

The second type of control which involves the prevention of the inducements themselves may include, for example, a mandatory declaration and forfeiture of gifts and hospitality, where these gifts or hospitality may be used to influence decision-making. For example, in many jurisdictions government employees are required to declare or decline gifts irrespective of whether those gifts are intended to directly induce action. The impact of both types of controls involve the cost of delivering training and messaging, personnel and cultural, and relationship impacts. For example, the mandatory declaration and refusal of gifts may impact on organisational relationships where gifts are considered a cultural norm, such as in China (HSBC, 2023).

Preventing beneficiaries

As discussed in the previous chapter, the mechanism through which the beneficiary element of risk can be managed is through the prevention of the *interaction factor* between beneficiaries and roles or persons occupying those roles.

Interactions may be limited in several ways:

- *Frequency*: The frequency of the interactions. Here, the effectiveness threshold needs to be considered. That is, how many interactions are required to enable the establishment of an illicit relationship? This is also a question warranting further empirical examination based on cases of corruption.
- *Temporal*: The length of time over which an interaction can take place. For example, if an officer is redeployed after a certain period of time, then the threshold for establishing an illicit relationship becomes a relevant consideration.
- *Physical/spatial*: Limiting the physical interaction between individuals, for example, by creating separate physical spaces and offices. The effectiveness factor is the level of physical separation and exclusion of the potential corruptor from the physical space.

In each of these cases, the control impact will be the extent to which the control limits the legitimate interaction or establishment of relationships that benefit the objectives of the organisation. For example, the establishment of long-term partnerships between government and industry may create efficiencies, new service opportunities, or the reduction of regulatory burden. If controls mitigate the establishment of relationships between individuals, then the organisation will need to invest in mechanisms to maintain continuity of relationships and partnerships where interactions between specific individuals is reduced through insider risk controls.

Risk velocity and control velocity

Before we explore the effectiveness of detection and response controls, it is worth outlining the twin concepts of *risk velocity* and *control velocity*. In Chapter 2, we discussed the concept that risk is comprised of the probability and consequence of an uncertain event. Risk velocity refers to the temporal relationship between the risk event and its consequence. A high velocity risk is one where the time interval between the risk event and its consequence is short, or even simultaneous. In contrast, a low velocity risk is one where the time interval is long. Examples follow: the risk event of theft is simultaneous with the financial loss suffered as a result. In contrast, if the event is the illicit grant of a permission, the harm only accrues where that permission is used: the harm of the illicit grant of a visa does not accrue until the visa is used to enter the country without legitimate permission.

Control velocity is a similar concept, referring to the time interval between the activation of a control and the effect of the control to mitigate the risk. For example, a control which detects anomalous and potentially fraudulent transactions in real time has a high velocity, whereas financial auditing, which may take substantial time to complete, has a low velocity.

The relationship between these two concepts is that a control whose velocity is lower than the velocity of the risk that it is intended to control will be ineffective. Equally or alternatively, a control which activates too late and whose effect therefore takes place after the harm has accrued will be equally ineffective. As set out below:

$Rv - Ta - Cv \geq 0$ is effective

$Rv - Ta - Cv \leq 0$ is ineffective

Where,
Rv is risk velocity,
Ta is time to control activation (which can be 0),
Cv is control velocity.

Applying this to an example outside of insider threat, if the effects of removing carbon from the atmosphere have taken significant time to have an effect (therefore the control velocity is slow), then even though the risk velocity might be slow (i.e. the time between the release of carbon and its effects on climate), the time to trigger the removal of carbon will have a significant impact on its effectiveness as a control.

These become key concepts in determining the effectiveness of both detection and response controls insofar as their effectiveness is determined, in part, by whether they are sufficiently rapid to mitigate the harms arising from insider activity.

Detection

As set out in the previous chapter, detection controls are designed to detect the exploitation of an opportunity. They identify either circumstances that would give rise to motivation or specific acts of inducement, and illicit interactions between roles or their occupants and the beneficiaries to malicious or inadvertent activity. In order to be effective, detection controls must avoid type 1 and type 2 errors, that is, false positives where a control is designed to

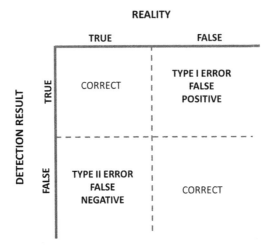

FIGURE 8.2 Type I and Type II Errors

detect an event, but that event is not or does not relate to an insider threat, or false negatives, where a control does not detect insider activity and the conclusion is therefore reached that insider activity has not or is not occurring (Figure 8.2).

Following the logic that effective detection controls are designed to reliably detect events which are indicative of insider threat, all typologies of detection control have equivalent effectiveness factors:

- *The level of correlation between the detected event and insider threat*: The higher correlated an event is with insider threat, the more effective the control that detects that event will be. For example, as we discussed, if a control detects the self-allocation of a decision, then for this control to be effective, self-allocation of decisions must correlate strongly with insider activity. If, on the other hand, self-allocation is a regular occurrence as part of the normal course of business, then detecting self-allocation will not be an effective identifier of insider threat. Rendering a control of this type effective may involve "tuning" the control to increase the correlation between the detected event and the insider threat. Continuing with the same example, if the rate of self-allocation plays a role in the correlation between self-allocation and insider threat (e.g. if the rate is above a certain number of self-allocation events per month), then setting the detection control at the threshold at which the correlation becomes strong will strengthen the control and reduce its false positives.

    Taking this example one step further, there may be multifactorial indicators that the self-allocation event is actually correlated with insider threat activity. Modern data analytics techniques may therefore assist in further enhancing the detection control, in two potential ways:

- *Anomaly identification*: Rather than understanding the specific elements that may correlate with insider threat, anomalies in the rate of self-allocation coupled with other elements of interest can be identified. Subsequently, the detected events can be tested for their correlation with insider threat activity. This technique potentially narrows down the particular events that need to be examined by differentiating "normal" incidents from statistically "abnormal", thereby enabling the abnormal ones to be more closely examined and therefore further correlated with insider threat through investigative activity.
- *Prediction algorithms*: Again, rather than understanding the specific elements that correlate with insider threat, if sufficient events have been detected, then predictive models can be developed to identify those factors that may have led to or are strongly correlated with insider threat activity. In our example, if sufficient people have been caught self-allocating and making illicit decisions, then other elements of data concerning those decisions could be fed into such an algorithm to identify other like cases: both in past and in future transactions. A few notes of caution, for this technique to be effective, are in order: there must be a statistically significant number of events; otherwise it is likely that no significant pattern will emerge. For example, if three people are detected self-allocating and making decisions, then it is extremely unlikely that there is a statistically significant pattern to identify. Next, if the events are detected through an initially biased process, then any prediction model will be subject to the same biases. For example, if the self-allocation is detected by some form of targeting, then the model would predict self-allocation events that would fit within the targeting sample but will not be exposed to data from those events that would not be targeted. This potentially creates a false negative for those events outside the targeting sample. This could be overcome, for example, if there were a random quality sample of self-allocation decisions in addition to the targeted sample. This brings us to our second broad factor of detection effectiveness.

- *The level of detection bias*: Because detection controls are rarely 100% accurate (almost by definition, if they were that accurate then they would have a very strong deterrent effect and the insider activity would not occur in the first place), their effectiveness is, in part, determined by the biases that affect their accuracy. There are a few key areas of bias that are worth identifying:

    - *Heuristic bias*: As we have discussed in previous chapters, human judgement is subject to a range of heuristic biases which may affect the assessment of risk, or in our current examination, the detection of risk events. Biases such as confirmation bias may impact on the detection of indicators of insider risk, thereby diminishing the effectiveness of tip-offs as a control. Other biases such as bystander non-intervention and group conformance norms may affect the reporting of a tip-off even if an individual has, in fact, detected and recognised insider activity, equally reducing the effectiveness of tip-offs.

- *Data biases:* There are a range of biases that can affect the data which is or could be used as the basis for detection controls. Using a targeted sample or events that have been detected through tip-offs as a means of creating detection controls risks a form of selection bias. This can create both false positive and false negative events. That is, the tip-off sample or targeted sample is overrepresented in the data and therefore detection controls, which are designed around them, will naturally target similar cohorts while ignoring those outside the sample. Similarly, completeness and quality issues in data can skew the results of detection. If data is incomplete, then any correlation between the "non-existent" data and insider threat will not be recognisable. Conversely if quality issues affect one part of the data in a statistically significant way, then they may skew detect towards or away from correlation with the low-quality data (e.g. incorrectly entered data which is consistently incorrectly entered).

  As a result, when designing effective detection controls, the biases that may be present in the data must be examined and mitigated during the design and implementation phase or incrementally by refining and correcting data quality issues.

The final effectiveness factor and effectiveness threshold element for detection controls is its *control velocity*. For a detection control to be fully effective it must be triggered and take effect prior to the accrual of harm to the organisation. Using our example above, if a decision to grant a person a visa to enter the country is illicitly granted (the event) using a self-allocation that is deemed anomalous and the detection control is triggered immediately before the person travels to the country (the harm), then this can enable the visa to be cancelled, thus preventing the harm from actually accruing. In contrast, if the same visa is illicitly granted but is detected through a quarterly audit after the person has travelled to the country (perhaps as part of criminal activity) then the harm has already accrued, and the detection control is only marginally effective.

Response

Response controls are designed to resolve the results of the insider incident after it has occurred. As set out in the previous chapter, there are three broad classes of response controls: *resolution*, *harm aversion*, and *mitigation*.

Resolution effectiveness

Resolution controls essentially resolve the insider threat incident through actions such as investigation and disciplinary actions against the individual. Determining the factors which contribute to their effectiveness then largely depends on the proposed purpose of such controls. If the purpose is incapacitation (i.e. preventing the specific individual from conducting the behaviour again) then the control is effective insofar as these controls, if carried out, will remove the person from the role which constitutes an integral part of the insider threat; *id est* it will incapacitate them from engaging in the same behaviour. See Braga et al. (2018) for a full discussion on the evidence associated with different forms of deterrence. If, on the other hand, the intention is that these controls have a general deterrent effect, then the question of their effectiveness and those factors contributing to that effectiveness is more challenging. For a full discussion of evidence regarding the effectiveness of general deterrence see Apel and Nagin (2011). The insider threat mitigation theory is still in its infancy, in that there is still no conclusive answer as to whether general deterrence is effective in this context. At best it appears, from our perspective, that deterrence is only effective in the presence of an effective detection control, as the threat of detection appears to have a higher deterrent effect than the scale of the penalty (Manning, 2018). As such, investment in detection controls remains more important than the investment in resolution controls.

Other elements that contribute to the effectiveness of these controls is the quality of investigative and evidence-handling procedures. These are critical to establishing the facts that will justify taking other resolution actions such as termination of employment in a way which is defensible at law. In terms of impact, these controls generally have a high cost and low return in that they react to the individual incident of insider activity, and investigative and prosecutorial activity remains resource intensive (see for example Gabor, 2015).

Harm aversion effectiveness

Harm aversion controls are designed to avoid the harm that would be caused by the insider event. For example, using our visa scenario, this would be cancelling the visa prior to the person travelling to the country. The main effectiveness factors to harm aversion controls are *trigger* and *control velocity*. If a risk aversion control is triggered earlier, then it provides more time for the control to operate within the risk velocity timeframe. Here, controls that are triggered directly by the detection control are likely to be more effective than those which require separate triggering or might operate alongside another harm aversion control. For example, an anomaly is detected indicating insider enabled fraud, but the detection is not entirely accurate. Rather than triggering a cancellation of the transaction it triggers the suspension of the transaction before it goes through an interim harm aversion control, thereby avoiding the harm. Subsequently, an investigation is undertaken which confirms fraud and the transaction is cancelled (the final harm aversion control). In this case the interim control is triggered within the risk velocity timeframe avoiding the harm, while the cancellation occurs only once fraud is confirmed. This tiered control approach is also designed to reduce control impact of simply cancelling the transaction without the benefit of confirming the fraud. If each transaction with internal fraud indicators was cancelled, then it would create significant relationship and productivity impact.

Mitigation effectiveness

Mitigation involves controls which review and improve the current control system. Given they are effectively a form of assurance of controls after failures or near misses necessitates discussion.

Effectiveness and impact measurement

As we touched on above, measurement of the effectiveness and impact of controls is an important element in establishing baseline effectiveness and either improving on that baseline or recognising negative deviations from the baseline, where a control's effectiveness diminishes or its impact increases. Assurance and measurement of controls are related concepts and as such we will further develop this aspect of the model in the forthcoming chapter.

Control balancing

Finally, sound investment in controlling insider risk means investing in those controls which are individually and collectively the most effective at managing insider threat with the lowest impact on other business priorities. The purpose of setting out the elements of effectiveness and impact in this chapter is that they inform investment decisions about the best mix or balance of controls to protect the organisation's assets from insider risk. These decisions should be taken in the context of governance of the system of insider risk control. We will return to the discussion about how effectiveness and impact factors inform decision-making under our model in Chapter 11.

Chapter key points

- An organisation needs to invest in the most effective controls and, to do so, must understand the factors that lead to effectiveness and the thresholds at which that effectiveness diminishes.

- Controls are not inherently "good". They also involve downsides, which we refer to as *control impacts*. They may negatively affect other organisational priorities such as productivity and relationships.
- The effectiveness of detection and response controls is, in part, determined by their velocity relative to the velocity of the risk.
- Decisions about the best mix controls can be made by considering the benefits and effectiveness of a control versus its control impact.

References

Apel, R., & Nagin, D. S. (2011). General deterrence: A review of recent evidence. *Crime and Public Policy, 4*, 411–436.

Association of Certified Fraud Examiners. (2022). *Occupational fraud 2022: A report to the nations.* https://legacy.acfe.com/report-to-the-nations/2022/

Braga, A., Weisburd, D., & Turchan, B. (2018). Focused deterrence strategies and crime control: An updated systematic review and meta-analysis of the empirical evidence. *Criminology and Public Policy, 17*(1), 205–250. https://doi.org/10.1111/1745-9133.12353

Chiok Foong Loke, J. (2001). Leadership behaviours: Effects on job satisfaction, productivity and organizational commitment. *Journal of Nursing Management, 9*(4), 191–204.

College of Policing. (2016). *Crime reduction toolkit.* https://www.college.police.uk/research/crime-reduction-toolkit

Das, V. V. (2009). *Honeypot scheme for distributed denial-of-service.* Paper presented at the 2009 International Conference on Advanced Computer Control, IEEE Computer Society United States.

Davis, R., Campbell, R., Hildon, Z., Hobbs, L., & Michie, S. (2015). Theories of behaviour and behaviour change across the social and behavioural sciences: A scoping review. *Health Psychology Review, 9*(3), 323–344.

Gabor, T. (2015). *Costs of crime and criminal justice responses.* Public Safety Canada Research Report: 2015-R022.

Graycar, A., & Prenzler, T. (2013). *Understanding and preventing corruption.* Springer.

Graycar, A., & Sidebottom, A. (2012). Corruption and control: A corruption reduction approach. *Journal of Financial Crime, 19*(4), 384–399.

HSBC. (2023). *A guide to China's business culture and etiquette.* https://www.businessgo.hsbc.com/en/article/a-guide-to-chinas-business-culture-and-etiquette

Johnson, S. D., Tilley, N., & Bowers, K. J. (2015). Introducing EMMIE: An evidence rating scale to encourage mixed-method crime prevention synthesis reviews. *Journal of Experimental Criminology, 11*(3), 459–473. https://doi.org/10.1007/s11292-015-9238-7

Larmour, P., & Wolanin, N. (2001). *Corruption and anti-corruption* Asia Pacific Press.

Manning, M. (2018). A baseline model of deterrence. In B. Leclerc & D. Reynald (Eds.), *The future of rational choice for crime prevention.* Routledge.

Neveu, J. P., & Kakavand, B. (2019). Endangered resources: The role of organizational justice and interpersonal trust as signals for workplace corruption. *Relations Industrielles/Industrial Relations, 74*(3), 498–524.

Pidd, K., & Roche, A. M. (2014). How effective is drug testing as a workplace safety strategy? A systematic review of the evidence. *Accident Analysis & Prevention, 71*(1), 154–165.

Shaffer, J. R., & Kleiner, B. H. (1992). Drug testing in organisations: Pro and con. *Equal Opportunities International, 11*(2), 10–13.

Srinivasan, V. (2021). Detection of black hole attack using honeypot agent-based scheme with deep learning technique on MANET. *Ingénierie des Systèmes d'Information, 26*(6).

9
CONTROL ASSURANCE AND EVALUATION

Introduction

Approaches to managing insider risk tend to focus on regular risk assessment processes, which can help identify what controls are in place (albeit often just on paper) and articulating what new controls could be introduced to further mitigate the risks (Commonwealth of Australia, 2017). What is often missing is a way of ensuring that the controls are actually in place and working effectively. This chapter will present an approach to developing an assurance program focused on the effectiveness of different controls, and how to focus the investment in this programme on the highest areas of organisational risk. We also argue that organisations should shift their insider risk investment from resourcing risk assessment activities to control assurance activities, which provide far greater return on investment.

As we outlined in previous chapters, the management of insider risks consists of a structured approach to understanding the relative risks to an organisation's assets, designing, and implementing appropriate preventative, detective, or responsive controls to mitigate the risk while minimising the impact on other priorities and objectives. From a theoretical perspective, this could be where the process ends, and indeed much of the literature on insider threat focuses exclusively on the risk elements or on the risk with some exploration of controls. There are few, if any, that systematically explore the mechanisms to ensure that controls are (1) in place; (2) functioning as designed; and (3) actually effective at managing the insider risk. These mechanisms, which we'll collectively refer to as control assurance, will be explored in this chapter. The purpose of this assurance is, firstly, to enable decision-makers to determine the value of their investments across the

DOI: 10.4324/9781003055716-9

complex system to manage insider threat. Secondly, identify areas of vulnerability or improvement opportunities. And third, correct deficiencies in the way that controls are effective in reality as compared to the theoretically described or prescribed operation of the control.

Why is control assurance important?

As worked through in previous chapters, organisations are exposed to insider threats potentially right across the spectrum of their business activities and organisational assets. This may be via *opportunities*, potential *beneficiaries*, and *motivations* for internal actors to act contrary to the organisation's interests. Managing these drivers of risk requires investment in a suite of controls that protect those assets depending on their value and the relative costs, benefits, and drawbacks. If, however, those controls are either (in reality ineffective) not properly executed or not actually present, then the investment in control is wasted and the organisation is no less exposed to risk than it was before the investment. Sunken investment in control is both wasteful and diverts resources which could be better utilised to advance the organisation's objectives or to manage risk elsewhere.

Why though would an investment in control remain ineffective, not be properly executed or in fact not be present? Shorrock (2021) provides a basis for understanding how organisational activity is perceived as opposed to the manner in which it is executed. Shorrock proposes a set of "proxies" for the way that work is executed in reality. In our case, the "work" we refer to is the execution of control against insider threats.

In the preceding chapters we explored the relationship between assessing the insider risk and defining or designing controls that mitigate the drivers for the risk to reduce its likelihood or impact individually or collectively. What the model below tells us, however, is that when those controls are implemented, there may be a gulf between what was defined or designed and the way that the control is affected (Figure 9.1).

According to Shorrock, that gulf may present itself in a variety of ways:

- *Work-as-imagined*: This refers to the perception or imagination of how a particular activity is undertaken, for example, the perception of what it is to be a fire-fighter and the reality of the work that fire-fighters actually undertake. This issue of perception applies equally to the perception by organisational decision-makers of how work is done versus its reality. In an insider threat scenario this imagined state can provide false confidence or assurance that risk is being managed, when in fact the work as done involves continuing vulnerabilities to insider threat.
- *Work-as-prescribed*: This describes work as it is designed and prescribed, for example through operating procedures, business processes and

FIGURE 9.1   Proxies for Work as Done

instructions. Following the insider threat model set out in this book, once risk has been assessed and appropriate controls selected, the next natural progression is to implement those controls through people, business processes, information, organisation, and technology. If though the prescription of how that control should be effected and the actual manner in which it is effected are different, this may undermine or render the designed control ineffective.

- *Work-as-disclosed*: This describes work as it is defined and communicated whether in written or in verbal form. The description of activity can easily be subject to biases and/or omissions that alter the perception of how work is perceived to be undertaken relative to how it is undertaken in reality. In an insider threat context, this can manifest as a false assurance that work is undertaken with particular controls associated with it. For example, if a decision-making process is described as occurring in an open plan space, then there may be confidence that there is a high level of visibility of that process. However, if the decision-making process also occurs in a second location where the visibility was not at the same level, this will provide a false level of assurance that insider risk is managed.
- *Work-as-analysed*: This describes work as it is modelled and synthesised. Again, using our insider threat model, we assume that the controls are synthesised and modelled to articulate how they act to mitigate insider

threat. If, however, those models differ from the way the control is effected in reality then this will affect the performance of the control.

- *Work-as-observed*: Here we describe how work may differ under observation as compared to its execution under normal circumstances. This is similar to the observer effect in physics, which posits that the act of observation creates a disturbance of an observed system (Sassoli de Bianchi, 2013). In relation to assurance, unlike other proxies, this may represent a pitfall to be avoided or managed in the conduct of assurance activities.
- *Work-as-simulated*: Here we describe the imitation of the real work. Often this may be the simulation of a future way of working such as a proof-of-concept or prototype operating model. In the context of insider threat controls, this may also refer to the simulation of a control in anticipation of its implementation. A good example is the simulation of automated controls within an ICT system: for example, the simulation of the operation of a detection algorithm as a means of testing prior to or through its implementation.
- *Work-as-instructed*: This describes work as explained or demonstrated as a means of describing how work is performed. This instruction may be to develop skills and capabilities in others to perform the work. Work as instructed may differ also from work as prescribed: for example, where local or personal practices emerge which are communicated and replicated by the group undertaking the work, though it does not follow the prescribed or designed work pattern.
- *Work-as-measured*: Here we describe work as it is quantified or classified with the aim of assessing the work in terms of efficiency or effectiveness. In terms of insider risk, any disparity between the measurement of the control and the actual way in which that control is effected is a pitfall for the assurance of controls. Additionally, the measurement is equally a form of observation and may, likewise, create an observer effect that modifies the way a control would otherwise be effected. For example, the act of measuring an element of a control, such as its efficiency, will tend to create an optimisation of that element, potentially to the detriment of other more important elements such as the effectiveness of the control.
- *Work-as-judged*: This describes the proxies by which work is assessed or estimated, similar to, or derived from, work as observed or work as measured.

In sum, these proxies indicate that the way a control (discussed in previous chapters) is effected is not necessarily aligned with the way it is designed. Conversely, the design may not, in fact, achieve the outcome that it was intended to, or may have unintended consequences that were not considered. A decision-maker investing in controls, therefore, cannot simply rely on the investment made without further checks and due diligence. Such checks ensure that the control is in place as anticipated, performs, and describes the level and the extent to which it creates impacts on other business objectives. These checking and due diligence mechanisms will collectively be referred to as *control assurance*.

An assurance system

Drawing back to our overarching model for insider risk management, the system of assurance is a key building block of the system which manages the risk by ensuring that controls are functioning as intended. Since assurance activities in themselves required the investment of effort, an equally systemic approach to developing, investing, and managing assurance activities is warranted. Such a system creates an efficient investment in assurance (Figure 9.2).

The Institute of Internal Auditors (2013) published a global position paper in 2013, titled "The Three Lines of Defense in Effective Risk Management and Control" and in 2017 the Chartered Institute of Internal Auditors (2017) published "The Three Lines of Defence". This model of risk management and assurance posits that there are three lines of defence that manage risk, ensuring the effective execution of controls (Figure 9.3). The model also delineates assurance functions which should not be executed by other lines of defence, as they may create conflicts of interest or dilute the responsibilities of the other lines of control (e.g. a person in the first line reviewing their own work).

- **First line:** The first line of assurance is local management, supervision, and quality control. This line of defence ensures the quality of controls by acting directly on or within the controls by directing the way the control should be executed. Quality control acts at a transactional level, providing control over each transaction and ensuring its correctness: for example, checking each instance of a credit card reconciliation to ensure it is correct.
- **Second line:** This line of control measures and analyses the activities of the first line, providing an independent and separate examination of exposures and gaps in the first line. Further, it communicates the findings of those analyses to address exposures and improve performance. The second line also includes quality assurance which, unlike quality controls, does not examine each transaction. Instead it analyses a statistically valid sample of transactions selected on a random and/or targeted basis.
- **Third line:** The third line is internal audit. This is an independent examination of the activities of the first and second lines to assess their accordance with design, standards, economy, and efficiency.

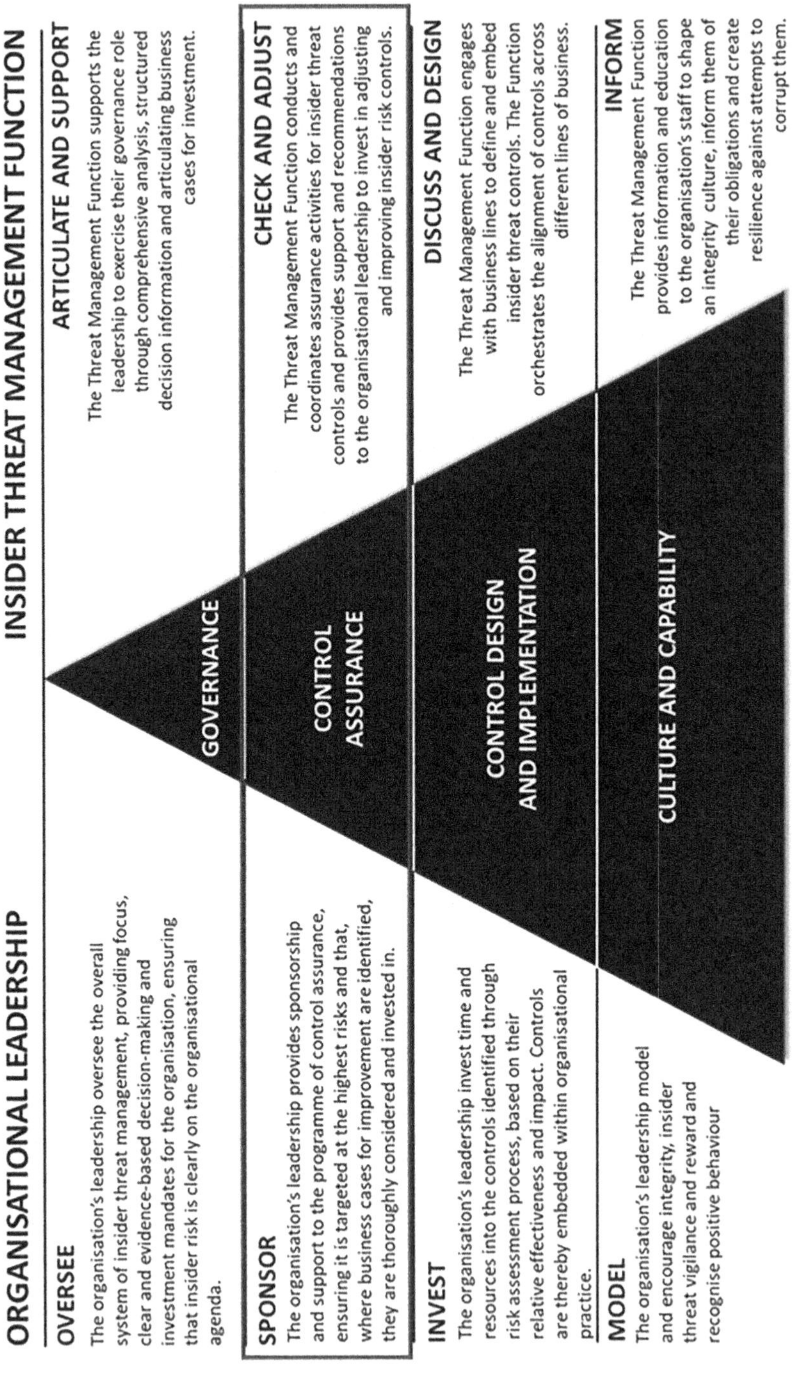

ORGANISATIONAL LEADERSHIP

INSIDER THREAT MANAGEMENT FUNCTION

GOVERNANCE

OVERSEE

The organisation's leadership oversee the overall system of insider threat management, providing focus, clear and evidence-based decision-making and investment mandates for the organisation, ensuring that insider risk is clearly on the organisational agenda.

ARTICULATE AND SUPPORT

The Threat Management Function supports the leadership to exercise their governance role through comprehensive analysis, structured decision information and articulating business cases for investment.

CONTROL ASSURANCE

SPONSOR

The organisation's leadership provides sponsorship and support to the programme of control assurance, ensuring it is targeted at the highest risks and that, where business cases for improvement are identified, they are thoroughly considered and invested in.

CHECK AND ADJUST

The Threat Management Function conducts and coordinates assurance activities for insider threat controls and provides support and recommendations to the organisational leadership to invest in adjusting and improving insider risk controls.

CONTROL DESIGN AND IMPLEMENTATION

INVEST

The organisation's leadership invest time and resources into the controls identified through risk assessment process, based on their relative effectiveness and impact. Controls are thereby embedded within organisational practice.

DISCUSS AND DESIGN

The Threat Management Function engages with business lines to define and embed insider threat controls. The Function orchestrates the alignment of controls across different lines of business.

CULTURE AND CAPABILITY

MODEL

The organisation's leadership model and encourage integrity, insider threat vigilance and reward and recognise positive behaviour

INFORM

The Threat Management Function provides information and education to the organisation's staff to shape an integrity culture, inform them of their obligations and create resilience against attempts to corrupt them.

FIGURE 9.2 Insider Risk Management Model: Control Assurance

FIGURE 9.3   Lines of Assurance Defence

Some organisations may also be subject to a fourth line of assurance: an external audit; for example government entities which are subject to audits by an independent government auditor or other external assurance function.

Assurance in insider risk

As we examined in previous chapters, managing insider risk in a systemic way involves the assessment of the organisational drivers of risk, including the assets, opportunities, motivations, and beneficiaries to insider activity. Subsequently, it involves using this analysis as a means of implementing controls which mitigate the likelihood or impact of the insider risk. Assurance, then, is a layered approach to ensuring those controls are in place and are functioning as anticipated.

Drawing on our border agency from Chapter 2 as an example, this organisation manages a value stream of commodities and entities entering the country through a range of permissions and conditions that reduce economic, social, and environment harm to the country or create economic benefits (e.g. in the form of customs duties) (Figure 9.4).

To put the layers of assurance in context, let's take several of the key assets of the organisation:

- *The permission decision*: which provides a person permission to enter the country or a commodity to be imported.
- *Detained goods*: which may be seized because they do not have the appropriate permission or are illicit and illegal.
- *Personal information*: the organisation holds a substantial repository of personal information collected through its permissions decision-making processes and stored as data within its information systems.

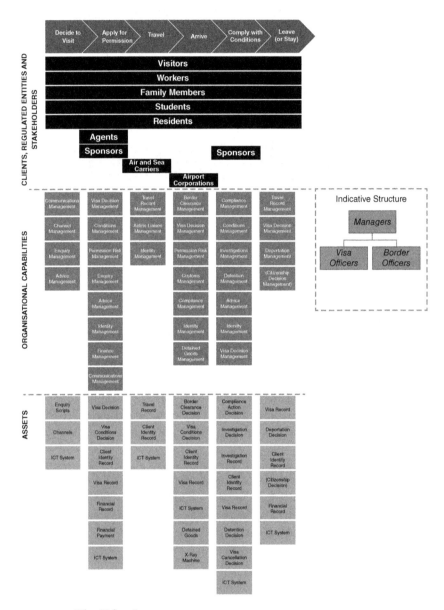

FIGURE 9.4 The Value Stream

Beginning with the permission decision, let's postulate that the means by which opportunity is controlled is through the following: (i) a separation of decision-making duties (thereby reducing *authority*); (ii) a random allocation of decisions; and (iii) a bar on the self-allocation of decisions (thereby reducing *certainty*): though some officers are still able to do this for legitimate reasons. An automated record is made of each decision and captures self-allocation actions (preserving *traceability*) and the decisions can only be accessed by authorised officers using a username and password (limiting *access*). These are coupled with a detection control, which detects anomalies in decisions through self-allocation.

The application of the lines of control to this scenario might be as follows: The line management of the permission function would be responsible for enforcing the separation of duties and a bar on self-allocation of decisions to ensure that these controls are effected as designed. Another, arguably, more reliable approach is that automated decision workflows enforce these controls by making it impossible for the same person to initiate and make a decision or enforcing the rule against self-allocation. Managers may also monitor for anomalies in relation to self-allocation, targeting these for further investigation.

The second line of control is independent from the management of the function and might consist of a periodic review of a sample of self-allocated decisions to ensure that the reason for self-allocation is legitimate. It may also involve checks of the automated workflows to ensure that separation of duties is in fact enforced. The second line might also test and measure the ratio of true to false positives in the anomaly detection process, thereby elucidating its level of effectiveness as a detection control mechanism (we will provide additional detail of the different typologies of second line assurance below). Second line controls could also examine whether access controls can be bypassed or penetrated.

The third line is again independent but might involve an audit of the entire process of decision-making to determine whether decision-making standards and guidance are in place. This requires examining whether the standards are being enforced by management and whether systems controls have been effectively implemented to ensure a separation of duties. The audit could also examine whether access is properly rescinded when an officer ceases employment in the decision-making role, thereby preserving access control.

Each of these assurance activities may serve functions other than in relation to insider threats. However, as set out above, they are applicable to ensuring that insider risk controls are in place and operational.

To further our example, let's turn to physical assets in the form of detained goods. In this example, let's assume that detained goods are seized from entities – both persons and corporations – and subsequently transported to a central holding facility to be used as evidence or destroyed. *Access* to the facility is limited through biometric fingerprint access to detained goods officers only. The goods are recorded within an information system to maintain a chain of custody. The record includes the type of good, the size, weight, and colour and hence provides a high level of *traceability*. The recording of this information is undertaken by two officers to increase *visibility* and reduce individual *authority* over the records. The first line of assurance, in this case, might be management control over the chain of custody and the recording of custody information. System restrictions might also act to ensure that two separate officers must log into a detained goods case to make the record.

The second line of assurance in our example includes random reviews of the detained goods records, independent detained-goods stocktake, and reconciliation of the goods held against records. Audits of biometric access records confirm that biometrics of authorised officers alone are provided access and that no access has been made by persons who no longer hold the *role* of detained goods officer at the time access was made. The third line of assurance in our example would undertake focused independent audits of the management controls in the first line and of the specialist independent reviews and quality assurance of the second line.

As a third example, let's turn to personal information held by the organisation. For the purposes of simplicity, we'll use the example of information which is held in information systems rather than physical file information. In this example let's assume that personal information is submitted through an online application system and held within a combination of system databases and a data lake, which is the organisation's overall repository of information in a combination of structured and unstructured formats. *Access* to the system itself is limited through password access control and a policy rule that information/cases must only be accessed where there is a business need (e.g. to assess the application), thereby limiting *authority*. Direct access to databases containing the data is limited through access to the data stores themselves alongside limits on access to subsidiary computing environments (e.g. development and testing environments). Access and changes to data are automatically logged and monitored, enhancing *traceability*. Copying of data is controlled with only a small number of roles with *authority* to copy or download data. Each download of client data requires a second person to assess and confirm the business need. First-line assurance controls would include management oversight which ensures that access to cases is only on an as-needed basis, thereby enforcing the policy rule. In the second layer, data assurance reviews might be undertaken to examine uncharacteristic access to client data. Random reviews of data copies and downloads are undertaken. The third line audit of the first- and second-line activities occurs to ensure conformance with assurance activities.

These examples illustrate the mechanics of the three lines of defence. Let's turn now to defining the standard assurance typologies focusing on the separate and independent assurance activities of the second and third lines.

Assurance typologies

While the first line of control largely consists of management control mechanisms and transaction level quality control checks, in contrast, the second and third lines involve a range of different mechanisms for providing assurance that controls are performing as designed and/or as expected. It is, therefore, worth systemically outlining the typologies of assurance within these layers.

Control tests

The first cluster of assurance activities involves direct testing of the controls to establish whether the control operates as anticipated and under what conditions. The testing of controls enables measurement of the controls' performance under controlled or simulated conditions. This approximates the conditions under which the control will be triggered and observes whether the control is able to manage the risk driver, as theoretically anticipated. Testing takes three broad forms which are not mutually exclusive and can be undertaken simultaneously: performance testing, threshold pressure testing, and impact testing.

Performance testing

Performance testing is designed to test the theoretical performance against the actual performance to establish whether the control is, in fact, effective. The outcome of this testing regime may result in one of three outcomes: the control is effective, the control is ineffective but can be remediated, the control is ineffective and cannot be remediated (and therefore either risk will need to be accepted or alternative controls will need to be established).

As an example, a control to increase visibility is the centralised decision queue. Here, all officers have access and visibility to a central queue of applications and decisions enabling them to passively monitor the activities of their peers and thereby reduce the likelihood and/or deter a malicious insider. Testing of this control could involve testers creating and assigning applications within the queue to establish whether the anomalous behaviour is noticed and reported by peer officers. This would establish whether the queue provides a basis for enhanced detection and, therefore, a probable deterrent to a motivated actor.

Methodology

To ensure that performance testing will result in a systemic and repeatable result, the test should be conducted with a defined methodology to ensure its integrity and replicability. We propose four elements to the testing process: planning and design, execution and validation, analysis, and dissemination.

In the *planning and design* phase, the controls to be tested should be identified including the theoretical and/or practical mechanisms by which they operate and their assumptions. These mechanisms and assumptions become the key elements that are to be tested. A testing plan will outline the means by which the control will be directly tested, either by simulating the control in a controlled environment or by alternatively testing the live control by introducing a simulacrum of the stimulus/driver that the control is intended to mitigate (such as in our example above: introducing fictitious applications into the queue). The plan will also set out how the data will be collected and analysed to make conclusions, along with any anticipated biases or errors which may need to be accounted for either statistically or in caveats around the findings and conclusions. Finally, a sound plan will also include considerations around ethics and communication.

Our example above requires that the officers undertaking the application decision activities be unaware of the test process; otherwise, it is likely that the test results will be biased. There are therefore ethical considerations that will need to be taken into account and protections implemented. The test in our above example may find that the central decision queue, while it does raise visibility, does not result in other officers recognising and sounding the alarm over anomalous behaviour. This result does not indicate that those individuals have failed, but that the control has failed and one of the ethics principles that might be adopted is a no-fault principle. Managing the ethical risk might also involve de-briefing and support mechanisms. These components are critical to an ethical approach to control testing.

In the execution and validation phase, the test is run using the processes outlined in the plan, and the test results are reviewed and validated. In the analysis phase, the findings and conclusions of the test are developed based on the validated data. In this phase it is important – as in any scientific analysis – to examine the implications and caveats of the data. Examples include the statistical validity for making broad-based conclusions about the effectiveness of the control, potential type I and type II errors, and analysing any skewing of the control which may occur because of simulating the control or through the observation of the control. To create value from the testing regime, the results must be disseminated to decision-makers to generate investment in improving the control or deciding that an alternative control is more cost effective or effective (assuming the absence of economic data).

Threshold pressure testing

As set out in our previous chapter, controls may be subject to effectiveness threshold: points at which their effectiveness diminishes or they become entirely ineffective. Threshold pressure testing establishes the minimum threshold at which effectiveness is diminished. This ensures that controls are implemented in a fashion which does not exceed their effectiveness thresholds under the circumstances those controls are most likely to encounter.

For example, active CCTV is a control which enhances visibility and deters malicious insider threat activity. In practice, a CCTV operator is in a control room observing several monitors. A threshold pressure test might examine the effectiveness of the operator at detecting a behaviour depending on the number of monitors being operated. Testing of this control might consist of randomly presenting a behaviour within a different number of CCTV monitors and increasing the number of monitors to be observed while measuring the accuracy of identifying the behaviour. Such a test was undertaken at the UK Police Scientific and Development Branch to examine how well CCTV operators could detect a person within a main street using a different number of monitors. The study found a decreasing level of accuracy: 85%, 74%, 58%, and 53% for operators monitoring one, four, six, and nine monitors respectively. Operators were also significantly less likely to detect targets at greater depth and/or in background areas when there were more monitors (Medium, 2019).

This type of test, therefore, establishes the relative threshold at which CCTV's effectiveness diminishes, thereby assisting a decision-maker to assess the acceptable level of detection for a level of required investment (e.g. in monitors and operators). However, another key critical element in this example that must be established is the context in which the control operates. As noted by our good friend Professor Nick Tilley, "context matters". In this example our operators are monitoring a main street, which experiences many simultaneous events, potentially high numbers of people, and a relative distance between the CCTV camera and the events (hence the different result for events at depth or in the background). Active CCTV can, however, be used in different contexts. For example, it might be used to monitor the entryway to a safe or vault as well as its inner areas. One would anticipate, therefore, that the operator is monitoring fewer interactions between people and the vault, with less frequent or complex activity and CCTV cameras are placed closer to the risk areas, thereby providing greater image detail to an operator. While the results of the above may be applicable in a general sense, it is highly likely that the threshold effectiveness for the CCTV applied to a vault would be quite different, given the context of the use of CCTV in this example. Design of threshold effectiveness testing, therefore, requires a sound design and planning process which considers the context.

Methodology

The process elements and methodology of threshold effectiveness testing are equivalent to performance testing, planning and design, execution and validation, analysis, and dissemination. The main differentiation is that rather than establishing the mechanisms by which the control is anticipated to operate effectively, for threshold testing, the variables that impact on the effectiveness of the control will be identified and form the basis for testing the thresholds relative to those variables.

Continuing with our active CCTV example, in the planning and design phases, the variables that impact on the effectiveness of the control should be identified. For CCTV, these would include the experience and training of the operator, the number of operators, the ratio of operators to monitors, the anticipated simultaneous events, and the number of people attending the monitored sites. As with any scientific test, the testing design then needs to control for a single variable enabling the impact of changes in that variable to be assessed. It may also be valuable to additionally test the interaction or compounding effect of multiple variables. For example information on the number of people attending the monitored sites against the ratio of operators to monitors is necessary to establish whether the effect of the two variables has a compounding effect on the effectiveness of the control.

The purpose of testing compounding effects is to deal with variables which are not within the control of the organisation. For example, in relation to CCTV used in a public area such as a main street, it is not plausible (without crowd control mechanisms) to control or restrict the number of people in that public area without good reason. Hence the impact of changes in the number of people present needs to be tested against variables which are within the control of the organisation, such as the number of operators and the ratio of operators to monitors. This enables the establishment of a probable range for the variable outside of control and the effectiveness threshold for the variable within control at different parts of the range. The testing plan will then set out the tests to be performed against each variable, data to be collected, and the means of evaluation for each variable, along with the means of testing the statistical validity of the results against each variable; noting that each variable will need to be tested several times to establish a repeatable and reliable result.

As above, the execution and validation phase involve running the tests as set out in the plan. Using our example of CCTV monitoring of a vault, tests might involve recreating a risk behaviour such as concealed appropriation of goods within the vault under different conditions, such as varying the number of operators, the number of people within the vault at any one time, and the time of day to establish the detection accuracy under each of these conditions, and collecting data on these results.

The analysis and dissemination phases involve the collation and analysis of the results and development of recommended actions to improve the effectiveness of the control, considering variables under control and variables outside of control. Using our example of the vault under active CCTV monitoring (if the threshold test established is using a single CCTV operator), once 5 people are within the vault detection area, accuracy diminishes, reaching close to zero, or purely random. With two CCTV operators, the accuracy begins to diminish once 10 people are introduced and reaches 0 at 15 people. In this simple example, two options emerge as a means of ensuring the effectiveness of the control: (i) restrict the number of persons entering the vault at one time (to less than 5); or (ii) increase the number of operators to 2 with a restriction on access to less than 10.

For a decision-maker, there becomes a relatively simple investment decision to determine the best course of action to ensure the continuing effectiveness of the control. Here, either the impact on productivity to restrict access to five people is acceptable to manage the risk of theft, or the cost of an additional CCTV operator is offset by the productivity gain of having simultaneous access by 10 people. Alternatively, the likelihood and impact of theft with a single operator and unrestricted numbers within the vault remains acceptable and no further investment is made. The value of threshold testing is that it establishes baselines and relationships that enable these classes of investment decisions to be made.

Impact testing

The third form of control testing is impact testing. This establishes the level of impact of a control as set out in the previous chapter. This form of testing establishes the actual impact versus the theoretical impact of the control or identifies additional unidentified impacts.

For example, workforce redeployment is a control on certainty, limiting an officer's certainty that they will be able to effect a particular decision or have access to a particular asset. As set out in the previous chapter, this control has a personnel impact in that it changes the way an officer would otherwise work and creates a need to train those officers on all roles to which they may be deployed. The changing of roles on a random basis may also create productivity impacts, as officers adapt to the role they will occupy on a particular day or may be required to travel to a different location to fulfil a different role. Impact testing would establish the level of impact on productivity and the personnel effects.

Methodology

The methodology follows the same pattern as for performance testing, and threshold effectiveness testing. In the planning and design phases, testing is designed around establishing the level of impact on an organisational priority with and without the control in place. In the case of workforce redeployment, the test might consist of deploying personnel to the same role over a consecutive period and measuring whether there is a noticeable change in productivity at the outset of a shift period. This would serve as a proxy for an officer occupying a position without redeployment. In the planning phase, the data collection plan could also be utilised to identify opportunities to reduce the impact of the control: for example, identifying the mechanisms which affect productivity and attempting to reduce those impacts. This test might examine whether an officer was more productive if given a day of prior warning regarding their upcoming deployment.

As with the other testing regimes, the execution phase involves the running of the actual tests and recording of results. In the analysis and dissemination phase, the conclusions and recommendations are developed focusing on establishing whether the impacts remain within the expected limits, whether impacts can be mitigated, and whether there are any additional previously unidentified impacts. Continuing our above example, assuming a forewarning of one day enables greater productivity, it potentially provides a level of certainty, albeit for a much shorter period of time. This period may, however, be sufficient to alert a potential beneficiary to facilitate a malicious decision on their behalf. As a result of the test, the decision-maker has additional information to determine whether by reducing the impact of the control a tolerable or intolerable level of risk has been introduced. Similarly, the test may identify previously unknown impacts; in our example let's assume that the productivity impact creates an impact on the organisation's clients and stakeholders, causing them to incur additional costs. Again, the identification of this impact through the testing regime provides new and additional decision-making information to determine whether the cost, benefit, and impact ratio is acceptable for the control.

We will further explore these decision-making processes in Chapter 11.

Application, benefits, and drawbacks of control testing

The principal application of control testing involves "physically" measurable mechanisms that have an *immediate or constant effect*. The controls set out in the earlier examples above all follow this pattern:

- The centralised decision queue creates a constant and "physical" or virtual visibility of the work on hand.
- Active CCTV provides immediate and ongoing visibility and involves physical componentry such as the camera and monitors, which provide immediately testable visibility to the operator and the ability to detect harmful behaviour.
- Workforce redeployment creates an immediate effect on the role undertaken by officers and provides an instant effect on certainty.

In contrast, other controls that work on personal predispositions or group dynamics such as education or leadership do not involve this immediate measurable effect. As a result, control testing does not provide an effective means of testing or measuring the effectiveness of these control types. This does not mean that measurement or assurance of these controls is not possible. Rather it means that a different measurement or assurance mechanism, as set out below, is better applied to these controls. Appendix A sets out our perspective on the control assurance and effectiveness mechanisms best suited to different control typologies.

The benefits of applying control testing on applicable controls is that the process provides an immediately measurable effect and feedback on the performance of the control, thereby enabling decisions around improvements to the control to enhance its effectiveness or mitigate any negative impacts. However, the cost of undertaking control testing activities is higher than other assurance mechanisms, requiring a dedicated investment in each of the planning and design, execution and validation, and analysis and dissemination stages of the testing regime. Such costs mean that it is likely prohibitive to apply this methodology across the entire organisation's controls. Therefore, the methodology is applicable to the most critical controls. In addition, due to the cost and time effort of applying control testing, the statistical validity of a realistic/affordable test sample and its meaningfulness to the overall transaction volume needs to be carefully examined as part of the analysis phase of the testing process.

As set out above, control testing may be considered to be examples of work-as-observed or work-as-simulated and hence may not be a "true" representation of controls as effected under normal circumstances outside of testing. Therefore, when undertaking testing it is important to assess and limit the effects of any distortions to the normal control environment: for example, ensuring that simulated environments are as equivalent to the real environment, or undertaking control samples when testing on a live control (e.g. not introducing the stimulus to a control and comparing the introduction of the stimulus against this baseline under observation).

There are also important ethical and cultural considerations that need to be considered when managing risk to the organisation's culture and people. As set out above, control testing may highlight control failures which almost invariably involve the performance of the people involved in effecting the control. Here, it may be tempting to penalise individuals for failures that may become apparent during the testing process. From our experience, this is likely to create greater harm to the organisation's overall culture and therefore impact on the trust and motivation which is at the core of organisational performance. Equally, as we've discussed in several chapters, humans are naturally subject to a range of heuristics that can impact their performance under a range of conditions. The purpose of a systemic approach to managing risk which we propose is to accept that these heuristics are an unavoidable element of any organisation and, therefore, controls need to be developed and improved to cope with the heuristics of the humans that effect controls. Even in the absence of penalisation, the recognition that a critical control has failed, whether under real or simulated circumstances, is likely to create psychological distress which needs to be managed. From an ethical perspective, it is important to establish principles around the management of testing which limit the perception of "fault" for participating staff and manage any distress that the testing process is likely to cause.

Control vulnerability assessments

The second broad type of assurance assessment practice we refer to is *control vulnerability assessments*. For the purposes of the model, these assessments consist of identifying assets of value to a beneficiary (through the risk assessment process), identifying the controls that protect the asset, and posing a simple theoretical question: "How could a motivated actor in an organisation (i.e. *place*) bypass existing controls (i.e. *guardian*) to successfully achieve their objective without being detected?" In short, answering this question becomes one of logical assessment: of whether there is a plausible means to bypass one or multiple controls that protect a particular organisational asset.

Let's assume, for example, that the granting of a license is protected through password access by authorised officers to the license system. The granting of the license is on a centralised queue, providing a relatively high level of visibility: the record of access to the system is automatically logged along with each action taken by an assessing officer (*automated access log*). The access and usage logs are analysed relatively infrequently and manually by a different officer. The organisation has in place processes to investigate and cancel improperly granted licences, if detected.

In this simple example a control vulnerability assessment would evaluate whether motivated actors could bypass the set of controls that protect that asset, using a logical assessment and understanding of the controls and their mechanisms. In our example let's assume that an officer can choose a license assessment from a queue of possible applications, which provides them with a relatively high level of certainty. While it is possible excess choosing of applications may be noticed by peers, if a motivated person limited the choosing of applications to a relatively limited number, it is plausible that it would go undetected. If the analysis of the logs is undertaken sufficiently infrequently, again, it's plausible that the behaviour might go undetected. From this perspective, if the activities cannot be detected, then the presence of investigation and license cancellation controls becomes significantly less relevant. This very simple logical exercise could be considered to be a rudimentary control vulnerability assessment, identifying the vulnerabilities or gaps in the control environment which might enable malicious insider activity to occur.

Methodology

Control vulnerability assessment consists of four practice steps: target selection, control identification, assessment and validation, and dissemination.

The *target selection* phase consists of identifying which organisational asset or assets will be assessed and what objective(s) the motivated actor is assumed to have. In respect of licenses, for example, the illicit objective might be to have licenses improperly granted or to steal blank license cards for separate forgery activity. The assets are related but different, as are the motivations and opportunities related to each asset. As a result, it is important to define the objectives of the actors involved, including the internal actor and potential beneficiaries, in order to undertake the exercise focused on the selected asset and controls and identify the likely modus operandi which will achieve the actor's objectives.

The *control identification* phase consists of identifying, in full, the controls which protect the organisational asset, which will be the subject of the assessment. Ideally, these controls will be identified as part of the risk assessment and control design components of the model. (Chapter 11 will also deal with the data structure and recording of the control environment, which, therefore, provides a ready repository of information on the full set of organisational controls.) The completeness of the identification of controls is critical to ensuring the assessment reflects the actual state of control investment to protect the relevant asset and provides a sound basis for assurance or recommendations for improvement.

The assessment and validation phase consists of undertaking the evaluation of the control environment based on logical actions which could be taken by a motivated (or inadvertent) actor to bypass the existing controls. In contrast to control testing, control vulnerability assessment can be undertaken as a "desktop exercise" assuming sufficient understanding of how the controls operate, or alternatively through interviews or roundtable discussions which explore how the controls operate in reality. Using our example above, the information regarding the controls and control gaps could, equally, be elucidated through discussion with those who effect the license assessments business processes within the organisation. In this phase, any assumptions regarding how the process and controls operate should also be validated to ensure they are correctly understood to avoid the pitfalls of "work as imagined" or "as-prescribed" being different to the controls as performed in reality.

Finally, as with other control assurance practices, the results of the assessment need to be disseminated to a decision-maker who is empowered to make investments to improve the control environment or judge any vulnerabilities to be acceptable for the organisation.

Application, benefits, and drawbacks of vulnerability assessment

The application of control vulnerability assessment is to examine multiple layers of control surrounding an organisational asset and assess the residual insider risk around that asset. The benefit from an assurance perspective is that this practice avoids decision-maker complacency, which may occur in an environment with multiple lines of control that are nonetheless subject to ongoing vulnerabilities in the system. Being a process which can be undertaken through a logical examination of the control environment as a desktop or roundtable review, the cost of undertaking a vulnerability is less than for control testing practices and can examine a larger number of controls with a manageable level of organisational investment.

The downside of vulnerability assessment is that while it can identify those vulnerabilities, it can be challenging to quantify their effects. This is because the process avoids the conundrum of statistical validity of results entirely by not directly testing the controls at a transactional level and therefore not providing quantified or statistical results in relation to the vulnerability. Instead, it takes a logical or inductive approach to assessing controls. From a decision-making perspective, therefore, the results of vulnerability assessments continue to require human judgement as to the likelihood that a vulnerability would in fact be exploited and therefore warrant investment to prevent the harm or loss of that exploitation.

Control exercises

The third broad category of second-line assurance mechanisms for countering insider threat is *control exercises*. Unlike control testing, which is designed to test the performance and limits of a particular control or set of controls, control exercises are designed to simulate the running of those controls to determine whether they will perform as required when needed. In simple terms, control testing attempts to break or breach controls while control exercises simply attempt to see what happens when they are triggered and whether improvements to performance or consistency can be made.

This type of assurance activity is most relevant for complex (involving different processes or activities), time-sensitive controls with a triggering event rather than ongoing controls. To illustrate the difference, as outlined above, separation of duties is a control to reduce authority and increase visibility: as a control it has ongoing effect applying to each transaction without any form of triggering event. By contrast, financial loss recovery and financial investigation are response controls. These controls are triggered by the detection of an actual or imminent financial loss created by an insider act. These controls are complex insofar as they may involve several discrete activities such as transaction searches, transaction cancellations or reversals, forensic accounting analysis, potential insurance claims, evidence-gathering and assessment, and development of briefs of evidence. To minimise losses, aspects of these activities are time sensitive and need to be activated prior to the losses being incurred (high control velocity as set out in the previous chapter).

Using these controls as an example, a control exercise would involve undertaking all these activities either as a desktop or as a simulated exercise to determine whether each of these activities is undertaken as prescribed, whether the velocity is sufficient to mitigate losses, whether any gaps in practice exist, and whether the two controls are coordinated successfully. Findings would then inform potential improvements in the control or set of controls.

Methodology

The methodology for control exercises consists of three phases: (i) scenario development and planning; (ii) exercise and evaluation; and (iii) dissemination.

The scenario development phase involves defining a control triggering scenario. In the case of our example above, the triggering scenario is the detection of a financial loss through internal fraud, corruption, or inadvertent action by an insider. This might be triggered by a recognised financial anomaly identified through transaction analyses. The development of the scenario enables the controls to be tested against realistic scenarios that may have yet to occur. It is also possible to design scenarios with additional levels of complexity, for example multiple potential losses in parallel which stretch the resourcing within the control or require additional coordination of activity within the control or set of controls. The planning element of this phase concerns planning how the exercise will be run, which roles need to be involved in the process, determining whether the exercise will be desktop or simulated and, therefore, what assets are required to conduct the exercise.

The exercise phase consists of running the exercise itself. This can be undertaken by fictitiously triggering the controls and observing or questioning the roles involved in the control about how the control is to be effected and analysing areas where the processes fail to act as planned or prescribed and the reasons why this occurs. As discussed in previous chapters, controls are in themselves organisational capabilities consisting of people, organisation, process, information, and technology. Weaknesses or failings in the control should be examined through these lenses, for example:

• Are staff sufficiently trained and knowledgeable?
• Does the organising model enable the control to operate as planned? For example if there is an incident control approach, does this work effectively?
• Is the process efficient and documented, and does it operate with sufficient velocity?
• Does information go to the right roles to enable the control to be effected as designed?
• Is information adequately collected and recorded?
• Does technology support or hinder effecting the control?

The final phase of the exercise, again, involves evaluating the results and defining recommendations to improve the relevant controls to enable a decision-maker to assess whether further investment is warranted.

Application, benefits, and drawbacks of control exercises

The application of control exercises, as set out above, is most beneficial to controls which are triggered infrequently and involve complex and time-bound processes. In the main, controls that meet these conditions are the response controls which are triggered by a detection control. Controls which are frequently triggered may not warrant investment in exercising, given that they can be observed in action. However, controls which are needed to protect assets and mitigate harm but are not frequently triggered benefit from exercises to establish whether they perform as designed and effectively.

The downside of these exercises is chiefly the investment required for design and running of the exercises, in terms of financial investment and investment of human resources which would otherwise be directed to other organisational priorities.

Control survey and interviews

Prevention controls, which act on the *motivation element* of the risk model, are not readily testable or exercisable insofar as there are complex individual psychological and normative mechanisms at play which are not readily observable. Given motivation controls require investment by the organisation, it is important that there is assurance that this investment is achieving the desired result in terms of reducing or mitigating the motivation to commit malicious or inadvertent insider acts.

As discussed in the previous chapter, we analyse motivation through a decision-theory lens, reducing decisions to three elements: the *cognitive process*, the *selection of options*, and the *available information* to guide that decision. Prevention controls, therefore, act on one or more of these three factors to determine how an actor can and/or will act in response to a decision stimulus. Assurance of these controls is, therefore, gaining an understanding about whether the factor has been modified and has that modification resulted in a change of behaviour compared to the baseline without intervention.

Given this change is initially a cognitive one, it is not readily observable in an organisational context. Hence, the best window on the cognitive change is to ask the relevant actors whether the relevant control has triggered a change in perception and whether that change in perception has resulted in a change in behaviour. Survey and interview methods provide the tools by which this information can be built and analysed to determine the effectiveness of controls. For example, adversary training is a control which mitigates pressure and inducement by enabling internal actors to acknowledge their own pressures and recognise the modus operandi of potential beneficiaries to exploit those pressures through various forms of inducement. This recognition of the modus operandi is intended to modify the cognitive process when confronted with inducing behaviour and provide additional information to change the decision (i.e. what the beneficiary's intent is). To assess the effectiveness of this training, a survey or interview could be undertaken to determine whether the training had indeed changed the perception of the behaviour of beneficiaries and therefore reduced the likelihood of acting on an inducement.

As with any social research survey, the design of the survey instrument remains equally critical in an internal organisational context. Questions need to be designed to (i) measure the motivational element it is intended to measure; (ii) not measure other concepts; and (iii) be unambiguous and mean the same thing to all respondents. The evaluation of responses equally needs to be repeatable and the sample size adequately sufficient to judge the reliability of the results. We will not further detail the practices of survey design given the existing literature available on this topic, but point you to the work of Fowler (1995) and Converse and Presser (1986).

Another source of information on the effectiveness of these controls may come from the testimony of those insiders who have been detected. It is in this context that interviews become an effective technique for collecting information regarding the effectiveness of controls on motivation and identifying opportunities for improvement based on instances where the control has failed.

Post-event analysis

The final domain of second-line assurance that we'll outline involves the analysis of controls following an event where controls have failed or where there has been a "near miss" where the control thresholds have almost been breached. Unlike the other forms of control assurance, which require an event to be simulated or imagined, post-event analysis provides reliable evidence of a control's performance: albeit in the context of a control or set of controls within the control environment failing to manage the risk.

The process for *post-event analysis* consists of identifying the controls which were intended to manage the risk through prevention, detection, or response and undertaking analysis of which control or set of controls has failed. Like *exercises* it is beneficial to examine controls through a capability lens, considering the people, organisation, process, information, and technology elements of each control to identify which elements have contributed to the failure of the control. As with all forms of assurance, the value of post-event analysis is only realised once the analysis informs the decision-maker on investments to improve the control or set of controls which have failed resulting in the adverse event.

Audit

As discussed above, an organisation's internal audit forms the third layer of control which independently assesses the activities of the first and second line to establish whether they are being effective in accordance with applicable standards and practices, or in accordance with internal procedural guidance. Given the extensive literature regarding the practice and standards of audit we will not dwell on the mechanisms of audit. Here, we point the reader to the work undertaken by the International Audit and Assurance Standards Board (2023) and the International Standards Organization (2018) literature.

From an insider threat perspective there are two elements which are worth elucidating in brief:

1 *Audit findings in relation to insider threat*: Internal audit activity takes a variety of forms including financial audits, information audits, information system and cyber-security audits, physical security audits, and so forth. All focus on the management of organisational controls to protect assets, manage risk, and uncertainty and/or achieve organisational objectives. Given insider threat emerges from the assets, capabilities, and practices of the organisation, internal audit has significant potential to independently identify insider threat vulnerabilities across organisational functions. In view of the investment that organisations make in internal audit activity, it would be valuable for insider threat to be formally included within audit standards and practices across different domains of audit.

2 *Audit standards for the second line*: Above, we outlined a series of practices for providing specialist second-line assurance against insider threat controls, including perspectives on the processes and practices that guide each of these assurance mechanisms and their application to different domains of controls. While we do not propose to do so here, there remains an opportunity to create specified audit standards around control testing, control vulnerability assessment, control exercises, control surveys, and post-event analyses to provide a standard basis for auditing organisational performance and maturity within each of these assurance mechanisms. This would provide a basis for ongoing research and improvement of control assurance mechanisms.

Chapter key points

- Independent assurance is needed to check that controls are operating as desired and anticipated and providing a platform for ongoing refinement and improvement to controls.
- Assurance activities can be organised into lines of control and different means of assurance are most effective for different analysing typologies of control.
- Assurance activities only realise their value when they become an input to risk and investment decisions by a competent decision-maker.

References

The Chartered Institute of Internal Auditors. (2017). *The three lines of defence.* https://www.icas.com/professional-resources/audit-and-assurance/internal-audit/internal-audit-three-lines-of-defence-model-explained

Commonwealth of Australia. (2017). *Commonwealth fraud control framework.*

Converse, J. M., & Presser, S. (1986). *Questions: Handcrafting the standardized questionairre.* Sage Publications.

Fowler, F. J. (1995). *Improving survey questions: Design and evaluation, applied social research methods.* Sage Publications.

The Institute of Internal Auditors. (2013). *The three lines of defence in effective risk management and control.* https://theiia.fi/wp-content/uploads/2017/01/pp-the-three-lines-of-defense-in-effective-risk-management-and-control.pdf

International Audit and Assurance Standards Board. (2023). *A new standard for audits of less complex entities.* https://www.iaasb.org

International Organization for Standardization. (2018). *ISO 3100:2018 Risk management – guidelines.* International Organization for Standardization.

Medium. (2019). *How many monitors should a cctv operator view?* https://news.umbocv.com/how-many-monitors-should-a-cctv-operator-view-10ef0e6f27b7

Sassoli de Bianchi, M. (2013). The observer effect. *Foundations of Science, 18*(2), 213–243.

Shorrock, S. (2021). *Work-as-imagined & work-as-done: Mind the gap.* chrome-extension://efaidnbmnnnibpcajpcglclefindmkaj/https://www.sintef.no/globalassets/project/hfc/documents/09-shorrock_-_waiwad_mind_the_gap.pdf

10

CREATING AND SUPPORTING THE ORGANISATIONAL CULTURE

Introduction

This chapter articulates how cultural norms and resilience play a significant role in managing insider risk by, for example, creating commitment to the organisation, normalising and rewarding integrity, and promoting transparency. We propose organisational approaches to developing a culture, which is appropriate for its exposure to risk and the importance of modelling behaviour through the leadership of the organisation. Financial and border control organisations provide interesting counterpoints on how these norms are expressed and modelled between public and private entities and how a core set of principles operate to determine the best cultural framework for each organisation.

There is a well-established body of sociological, anthropological, psychological, philosophical, and scientific literature which defines culture through a wide range of contexts and perspectives. From an insider threat and corruption perspective, there are two broad contexts to frame the context and ontology of culture: societal and organisational. The societal context is a broad ranging concept concerning the social behaviours, norms and institutions, knowledge, beliefs, customs, and habits, which may also be manifested physically through arts, literature, and capabilities found in human societies. This aspect of culture is important to the broader study of corruption and integrity insofar as it retains a level of acceptability or normalisation within societies. In some contexts, however, it is deemed to undermine the expressed values of society whose culture is encompassed within concepts such as the rule of law, independent bureaucratic institutions, and expectations of bureaucratic and organisational honest, integrity, and trust (Adolphs, 2003; Macionis & Gerber, 2011; Marien et al., 2019).

DOI: 10.4324/9781003055716-10

Given our examination is of insider threat at the organisational level, it is more meaningful to focus on the second, organisational context. In this context, culture refers to the norms, values, beliefs, and behaviours which codify acceptable conduct within an organisation and serves as a template for expectations within the organisational construct.

Harmful insider activity, whether deliberate or inadvertent, is a behavioural problem, insofar as the harm results from an empowered actor behaving in a manner which is contrary to the organisation's objectives or interests. As we've discussed in previous chapters, that behaviour can be curbed or modified through the creation of processes and controls which modify an individual's opportunities or individual motivations to act in a harmful manner. However, such a system of controls requires investment of finite resources to protect organisational assets. Given the finite nature of these resources, it is almost inconceivable that these controls provide a complete mitigation against the risk of harmful insider activity. Furthermore, as we discussed in Chapter 8, the impacts or downside of certain controls may outweigh their benefits in certain circumstances, therefore likely necessitating acceptance of gaps in the control environment by decision-makers.

The importance of culture, therefore, comes to the fore. Cultural norms that shape what is considered acceptable conduct acts in a normative fashion guiding behaviour in the presence and the absence of other forms of control. For example, Klockars et al. (2000) find little evidence to support the notion that police corruption is an aberration committed by individual officers. Rather, independent of other factors, corrupt behaviour is fostered and shaped by corrupt cultures and incentive structures within police forces. While this is framed in the negative, the opposite conclusion may also be true: if corrupt culture causes corrupt acts, then integrity culture will cause and shape more honest or conscientious behaviours.

Why is culture important?

Underpinning culture is the concept of cultural or social norms. This is commonly defined as shared standards of acceptable behaviour by and in groups (Finnemore, 1996). Culture may emerge spontaneously and informally through the interactions of individuals within a group (Young, 2015) or may be created, shaped, and transmitted deliberately by individuals seeking to establish new norms (Sunstein, 1996). The research of Klockars et al. (2000) highlights this emergence of norms supporting corruption through informal interactions, arguably due to the absence of countervailing norms. The importance of culture, then, is its capacity to create normative prescriptions and proscriptions to human behaviour.

From an insider threat perspective, an integrity culture can be anticipated to generate behaviours which protect the organisation's assets and objectives and disparage and diminish harmful conduct. The adherence to norms follows two forms of logic (Herrmann & Shannon, 2001), one around the consequences of acting against those norms on a rationale cost–benefit basis. Arguably the control environment we've discussed in the previous chapters sets the circumstances for a rational appreciation of the consequences through the deterrent effects of preventative, detective, and response controls. The second is that of appropriateness. In effect, people will adhere to a cultural norm of behaviour due to its social acceptability. Importantly, this adherence can occur *in the absence of control or the direct oversight of an authority*. Culture can be seen to be systemic insofar as the norms and values that are created consistently influence behaviour across the system, rather than being solely the purview of individuals pressures and preferences of the people within the system (Young, 2015). As a result, the creation of a set of cultural norms complements the formal control environment. We argue, therefore, that it must form part of a holistic model for managing insider threat.

Managing insider threat implies an active practice of protecting the organisation and its assets from the threats that insiders pose to its objectives. Indeed, the assessment of risk, investment in controls, and assurance are an active and conscious process under our proposed model. The creation and embedding of a threat-resistant culture is no different and equally requires a proactive and conscious approach, as demonstrated in Figure 10.1, at the bottom of the pyramid (Culture and Capability). In an organisational context, cultural and social norms may be created which are contextual and internalised to the organisation itself (Ravasi & Schultz, 2006). While broader societal norms may push against corruption and criminality, organisational and localised culture may nonetheless support it (Klockars et al., 2000). Equally, while broader society may hold these norms, the organisation provides the context and specificity for how those norms are to be observed, and indeed it is through teaching of these norms to new organisational members that frames their way of perceiving, thinking, and feeling within the context of the organisation (Schein, 2004). The organisation's leadership must, therefore, take an active role in advancing the culture that preserves its interests and objectives against threats, including insider threat.

Different approaches to understanding culture

In her seminal work on organisational culture, Martin (2013) argues that understanding culture is a complex vortex which cannot be viewed through a single lens. Further, previously espoused managerial approaches to culture create the promise that organisational managers could build a "strong culture", which would result in improved productivity and profitability for organisations. As Martin outlines, this assertion has proved to be overly simplistic and typically untrue, though organisations invest considerable resources in trying to create consensus of values and goals to achieve the promised enhanced competitiveness.

While our endeavour is to introduce a model for managing insider threat, rather than a deep study of organisational cultural theory, Martin's work provides a salient message that a simple, functional, or static deterministic view of culture does not reflect the reality of its complexities, internal conflicts, and evolving nature. We propose that there is no single perfect model for describing the operation of culture. A simple articulation of values, for example, represents only a small element of the system of norms, actions, thoughts, and perceptions and is certainly not on its own a determinant of them. Indeed, various examinations of culture recognise that culture is not uniform across an organisation. Instead, culture is comprised of sub-layers (subcultures) that are formed through local structures, beliefs, and responses to the different or unique organisational challenges or contexts. Taking a simple example of a policing organisation, the cultural attributes of "beat" officers compared to detectives and again compared to staff within corporate services and accounting are likely to be diverse. Diversity here is based on the activities they undertake, the norms that are built around challenges, and opportunity in those activities and the difference in training background (e.g. police training vs. accounting practice). Therefore, viewing culture as homogeneous and to be influenced as a whole is erroneous. Culture, instead, is a system comprised of a conglomeration of numerous elements in different states of flux. The achievement of an integrity culture should, therefore, be viewed not as a static end goal but rather the ongoing adjustment of a set of elements or levers which relatively, but not absolutely, shape thoughts and behaviours.

With a perfect model outlining the mechanics of culture thus far out of reach, in examining the literature on culture we prefer models which do not attempt to identify different typologies of cultures themselves and the makeup of those cultures. Instead, we examine models that identify different elements of culture which may serve as indicators or levers for influencing cultural and social norms.

Johnson et al. (2008) presented a "cultural web" as a means of understanding organisational culture as a set of interlinked elements. In our view, this tool meets our criteria of providing lenses through which to examine and influence organisational culture without being excessively prescriptive in describing cultural typologies or including value judgements around the reasons for the emergence of cultural norms in different organisations. Equally, the cultural web does not attempt to identify the elements of a "good" culture or a "bad" one. Equally, this is not what we propose to do. Instead, we prefer to provide the structure to examine culture and, for that structure, to guide the analysis and interventions in their real context, rather than a purely theoretical model of what a "good" or insider threat resistant culture looks like.

ORGANISATIONAL LEADERSHIP

OVERSEE

The organisation's leadership oversee the overall system of insider threat management, providing focus, clear and evidence-based decision-making and investment mandates for the organisation, ensuring that insider risk is clearly on the organisational agenda.

SPONSOR

The organisation's leadership provides sponsorship and support to the programme of control assurance, ensuring it is targeted at the highest risks and that, where business cases for improvement are identified, they are thoroughly considered and invested in.

INVEST

The organisation's leadership invest time and resources into the controls identified through risk assessment process, based on their relative effectiveness and impact. Controls are thereby embedded within organisational practice.

MODEL

The organisation's leadership model and encourage integrity, insider threat vigilance and reward and recognise positive behaviour

INSIDER THREAT MANAGEMENT FUNCTION

ARTICULATE AND SUPPORT

The Threat Management Function supports the leadership to exercise their governance role through comprehensive analysis, structured decision information and articulating business cases for investment.

CHECK AND ADJUST

The Threat Management Function conducts and coordinates assurance activities for insider threat controls and provides support and recommendations to the organisational leadership to invest in adjusting and improving insider risk controls.

DISCUSS AND DESIGN

The Threat Management Function engages with business lines to define and embed insider threat controls. The Function orchestrates the alignment of controls across different lines of business.

INFORM

The Threat Management Function provides information and education to the organisation's staff to shape an integrity culture, inform them of their obligations and create resilience against attempts to corrupt them.

GOVERNANCE

CONTROL ASSURANCE

CONTROL DESIGN AND IMPLEMENTATION

CULTURE AND CAPABILITY

FIGURE 10.1 Insider Risk Management Model: Culture and Capability

The cultural web

Johnson et al. (2008) identify seven interlinked elements or concepts which both comprise culture and represent its manifestation in real circumstances (Figure 10.2). These elements, therefore, can serve a dual purpose. Firstly, they support the analysis of the existing and prevalent culture and secondly, they serve as mechanisms to influence or change that culture.

The cultural web comprises the following elements:

- *The Paradigm* represents "the taken-for-granted assumptions, or paradigm, of an organisation and the behavioural manifestations of organisational culture" (Johnson et al., 2008, p. 201). The other elements of the cultural web provide a window into the cultural paradigm of the organisation and a way to shape that paradigm.
- *Power structures* deal with the way that power in the organisation is distributed and effected, in particular, the informal structure of power and resources and distribution of incentives. The most powerful groups in the organisation are likely to have greater influence on the values of the organisation or where those values conflict with the broader values formally adopted, they are more likely to be capable of resisting change.
- *Organisational structure* signifies the formal hierarchies and flow of effort and control through the organisation. The organisational structure is likely to, but not always, reflect power within the organisation, ranging from highly hierarchical organisations to flatter or highly devolved structures. Adding complexity, matrix-based structures combine vertical hierarchies with horizontal responsibilities for domains of business.

FIGURE 10.2   The Johnson and Scholes Cultural Web

- *Control systems* concern the processes, practices, and procedures which control what and how things happen within the organisation and where the focus of control is placed. This includes the measurement and rewards system of the organisation and its tendency to support or emphasise some values and behaviours more than others. For example, control and reward systems that emphasise fiscal conservative over risk-taking and innovation may protect financial assets but are less likely to support the development of new business strategies. Equally, organisations which reward individuals for sales are less likely to be successful at supporting team-based work.
- *Rituals and routines* refer to the *routine* activities and behaviours within the organisation: for example daily board meetings, regular communiqués. *Rituals* refer to the handling of particular or special events: for example the practices and rituals around hiring, rewards, and promotion. Routines and rituals may be embedded within formal processes but may be informal and simply the accepted "way that things are done". In a positive sense, they may be able to provide consistency to regularised activities where this consistency is needed for success. On the other hand, harmful routines will equally have a level of consistency; for example, the demand for bribes in exchange for particular services that, while not supported by the organisation, may become a routine within operational activities.
- Stories concern the narratives told within and outside the organisation. These stories highlight the organisation's core beliefs and values and flag important events, personalities, and archetypes. According to Johnson et al. (2008), "they typically have to do with successes, disasters, heroes, villains and mavericks [who deviate from the norm]" (p. 203). They serve to tell people what is important within the organisation.
- Symbols refer to the imagery which represents the organisation, such as logos and designs. Symbols also include uniforms and marks of status such as executive offices and special parking spaces. Further, symbols also refer to the terminology commonly used within the organisation, in particular related to its underlying meanings or associations. In an example outlined by Johnson et al. (2008), "the head of a consumer protection agency in Australia described his clients as "complainers". In a major teaching hospital in the UK, consultants described patients as 'clinical material'" (p. 206). These examples highlight underlying assumptions about these actors and may drive different strategies in relating to them.

Understanding and shaping the paradigm

Johnson et al. (2008) describe the paradigm in terms of the overall organisational paradigm, though recognising the existence of different subcultural paradigms within organisations. For our purposes, we are interested in exploring a sub-domain or culture. By this we mean a domain of culture which exists at the whole of organisation level (rather than part of the organisation) and indeed in itself needs to be a feature of sub-cultures. However, it does not represent the whole of the culture of the organisation needed to achieve other objectives or which may cause other forms of harm (e.g. a low safety culture). This sub-domain we will refer to as "integrity culture" or the "integrity paradigm".

The term "integrity" can be considered a broad term which encompasses honesty and moral principles. The term also encompasses other concepts such as the coherence, soundness, and robustness of the organisational system, with people (within the organisation) taking responsibility for the structural soundness of the system. This is, therefore, much broader terminology than "corruption-resistant" or "threat-resistant" culture. By taking a broader perspective, our hope is that this element of the model can be more broadly applicable to analysing and shaping culture in a diversity of organisations to which narrow definitions of culture may not be readily accessible.

What then might be the elements of a relatively generic integrity paradigm? While we do not wish to be exhaustive or prescriptive about the elements that might make up the paradigm for a particular organisation, some simple and generic plain-English terms that could comprise an integrity culture:

- *Honesty*: in terms of truthfulness and making choices with an honest intent;
- *Fidelity*: in terms of loyalty to the objectives of the organisation and an "esprit de corps" or loyalty to peers and others within the organisation;
- *Selflessness*: in terms of putting the organisation's overall interests ahead of personal interests in the event of a conflict between the two;
- *Diligence:* in terms of care and due diligence in fulfilling tasks and managing risks to the organisation; and
- *Vigilance:* in terms of being aware of risks, recognising and reporting insider threat issues if observed.

We use these terms insofar as they can convey or imply both a set of behaviours and the values that underlie those behaviours. However, we do not intend to express these terms as preferred or universal across all organisations, nor are they exhaustive. The preferred terminology for expressing the concept of integrity is a part of the cultural foundation itself and therefore in our view should be selected for the relevant organisational context. We use these terms to outline how these values and behaviours may be analysed and shaped using the cultural web model (Johnson et al., 2008).

As we briefly outlined above, cultural norms may emerge and be shaped organically through a range of stimuli including work activities, the individuals that make up groups and sub-groups, shared training, and educational backgrounds, and shared socio-economic cohorts or pressures. However, using culture as a means of protecting the organisation from insider risk means taking a conscious approach to shaping cultural norms and values. Shaping the integrity paradigm requires analysis of the alignment of the current paradigm through each of the elements of the cultural web and the creation of a preferred paradigm through each of those elements, in our case using the values above.

Let's turn then to look at this paradigm through each of the elements of the cultural web.

Control systems

As described above, the control system refers to the mechanisms for exerting control within the organisation including formal procedural controls and "soft" controls such as the rewards and incentive systems within the organisation. In terms of our integrity paradigm, arguably the establishment of the control and assurance system we outlined in Chapters 7–9 places emphasis on the value of the integrity system and would be a direct experience for actors across the organisation. However, delving deeper, additional questions can be asked in relation to our integrity culture value set above, for example:

- Does the control system reward honesty or silence it? The answer to this question might be observed through the way in which the organisation deals with internal complaints. A control system that seeks to suppress "inconvenient truths" is unlikely to create a culture of honesty in the event of internal threats.
- Does the control system emphasise fidelity to the organisation or individual competitive performance? For example, banking systems that devolve products sales including loans and insurance to individual brokers, emphasising sales performance to the exclusion of other priorities are likely, and perversely, to create a culture of self-interest which may undermine loyalty to the organisation's other objectives.
- Similarly, does the control system support selflessness or selfishness? Our example above equally illustrates a control system which promotes selfishness rather than selflessness.
- Does the control system support diligence? There are a range of ways in which the system might support or undermine diligence. It might simply be by rewarding diligence and attention to detail or conversely through indifference to the level of diligence displayed by individuals. In a more formal process sense, the control system might undermine diligence if it makes processes and practices unnecessarily complex or overloading individuals with more work than is realistically feasible with any level of diligence (thereby increasing the risk of mistakes or risky shortcuts).

Again, we do not want to be excessively specific in terms of a universal "good" culture. In terms of our integrity paradigm, a better control system is one that places emphasis on its insider threat control system and rewards the diligence of individuals. The rewards could indeed relate directly to some of the opportunity elements we outlined in Chapter 4; examples follow:

- Emphasising diligence and selflessness in the exercise of authority over a decision or asset;
- Rewarding diligence and honesty in recording and thereby enhancing traceability; and
- Stressing honesty regarding access to information and assets.

Organisational structures

In addition to the pure hierarchical structure of an organisation, the way in which authority is distributed may also be a strong indicator of the things that are deemed important. For example, an organisation might structure itself around its products, with a department for mobile phone design, development and sales, and another equivalent structure in respect of software design. It may structure itself around its different customer or market segments, for example, a bank with corporate and individual banking arms. It may structure itself purely around its different functions and capabilities with, therefore, a focus on efficiency and fiscal restraint. Each of these structural options emphasises the importance of those different elements to the organisation, its products, its customers, or its functions. The allocation of C-suite roles equally places emphasis on further elements which are cross-cutting within the organisation: such as the chief information officer, chief financial officer, chief operating officer, and chief technology officer roles, placing emphasis on each of these domains and providing authority to these roles through formal structures and governance.

In terms of organisational structure then, what might we observe that emphasises our integrity paradigm? We may observe structures with names including integrity, professional standards, and quality. Related to the power structures below, we may observe that these functions possess authority within the organisation rather than being perceived as a peripheral function. Equally, there may be a role of Chief Integrity Officer. Each of these elements sends cultural signals that the integrity culture is of importance within the organisational psyche.

Power structures

The power structures in an organisation might mirror, to some degree, its hierarchy or may differ with distinct types of person and roles commanding differentials of power both in organisational and in personal terms. The distribution of power provides a window on what is valued or deemed most important in the organisational context. Applying a policing example, there may be a differential of power between "sworn" police officers and civilian members of the police force, with power residing with sworn members even potentially in relation to more structurally senior personnel within the civilian part of the organisation. Similarly, police unions and union members may wield a differential of power within the organisation, potentially emphasising a form of police solidarity, which may also result in the well-researched "blue wall of silence" (Chin & Wells, 1997; Conway & Westmarland, 2021).

Observations we might make in terms of our integrity paradigm may include the following questions: does a professional standards or anti-corruption function appear to wield real power and authority within the organisation, and is this supported from the power centres at the top of the organisation? Is it staffed by people with recognised power (e.g. sworn officers, or conversely with officers not nearing retirement)? In terms of our integrity paradigm elements, Are individuals empowered to report or speak up on misconduct? Does power centre around those who display diligence or merit? Or is power and promotion distributed through cronies and informal networks?

Given these power structures do not necessarily reflect the organisational structure, a conscious approach to changing this manifestation of the organisational paradigm might involve the breaking and redistribution of power structures, with a greater emphasis on power aligning with the elements of our integrity paradigm.

Rituals and routines

The routines and rhythms of the organisation are reflected through its procedures but may also emerge through regularised informal actions or behaviours. Examples might include regular communiqués from the Chief Executive Officer, water cooler chats, weekly, monthly, annual planning events, or routines that are established by introduced methodologies such as project and programme management activities, involving routines around planning, scheduling, risk, and budgetary reviews.

In terms of our integrity paradigm, a simple and repeated routine might be the request and declaration of any conflicts of interest at the outset of all decision-making meetings. This simple routine puts value on the separation of personal from organisational interests. More complex routines may be the routine examination of insider risk as we posit in the earlier chapters of this book. Again, this puts emphasis on the fact that insider risk is taken seriously from a decision-making and action perspective. In a highly mature or resilient culture it would be reasonable to expect that the routine of considering insider risk would find its way into normal planning practices, procurement and contracting activities, recruitment considerations: as an encoded and habitual practice.

According to Johnson et al. (2008), rituals represent the more infrequent or "special" events that make up the rhythm of the organisation. For example, annual general meetings not only provide practical decision-making forums, but are also a demonstration of the cultural importance of corporate governance and shareholder primacy in a corporate setting. The planning processes which go into organising these sessions, inviting and preparation for the presence of normally distant shareholders, and the rituals around the way that particular people are welcomed and respected all emphasise what is important to the organisation and who is considered important. The investment of time and effort in these rituals, equally, is a demonstration of the organisation's cultural recognition of the theme or meaning that underlies the ritual.

In terms of creating an integrity culture, the observations we make is whether there are rituals that incorporate the integrity culture themes we have identified above, such as executive addresses or training events. Equally applicable is the observation of domestic or international events: for example the United Nations General Assembly designated 9 December to be International Anti-Corruption Day; this may again be a demonstration of the cultural importance of these integrity themes.

Conversely, in organisations which do not hold integrity values, we are unlikely to see investment either of time or of effort into these kinds of routines and rituals. Worse, we might expect to observe routines and rituals which are, in effect, a demonstration of the acquiescence to corruption of diminished integrity. For example, in a corrupt police force the regular route to collect "kickbacks" might effectively become a routine to which new recruits are effectively inducted. These routines commence as education about "how things are done" and progress to being entrenched and encoded into the routine of the organisation or part of the organisation. Great examples of such questions regarding policy integrity and corruption have been raised in Sue Gray's report on Downing Street parties during the COVID lockdowns (Newburn, 2022) and the recent report by the Commissioner of the Metropolitan Police Force (MET) that poor integrity and corruption will be rooted out of the MET as some officers face trial for crimes such as violence against women and dishonesty (Dodd, 2023).

Symbols

As discussed briefly above, symbols come in a wide variety of forms, such as physical symbols and designs that denote aspects of the organisation's values and objectives, for example, a ubiquitous brand or symbol used to denote specific activities, opportunities, or dangers, such as signage. These physical symbols can infer powerful messages about the organisation's values. For example, following the investigation into allegations of war crimes by Australian forces, the Chief of the Australian Defence Force moved to prohibit death imagery from the defence forces (such as the grim reaper and skull and cross-bones symbols) on the basis that these symbols were at odds with the values of the Defence force representing "a general disregard for the most serious responsibility of our profession; the legitimate and discriminate taking of life (Gaynor, 2020)". From this perspective, these physical symbols were deemed to undermine the integrity of this serious military responsibility.

Organisations are rich with symbols which Johnson (2000) highlights shape and influence the way that actors within the organisation perceive the nature of events and individuals. The culture of the organisation can both shape and be shaped by the meaning of these symbols. A police uniform may be a symbol of authority or responsibility. The way it is defined in the internal narrative will determine the behaviour of those in the uniform and those that interact with those in the uniform. If the uniform is defined as a sign of absolute authority, authority than can be indiscriminately abused. This, then, is the behaviour that will be exhibited, as evidenced in many countries globally which suffer from routine abuses of power by law enforcement agencies (see for example Igbo, 2017; McCarthy et al., 2020). In contrast, if the cultural symbol associated with the uniform is one of social responsibility and a source of pride in the uniform, then equally we would anticipate the behaviour, generated through this symbolic association, to closely resemble the elements of our integrity culture: that is vigilance, diligence, and loyalty.

Johnson et al. (2008) emphasise that the terminology of the organisation may also have a symbolic role. The implicit meaning or connotations of key words used within the organisation, likewise, shape the understanding and attitudes of the actors within the organisation in respect of the objects those terms refer to. Derogatory terminology to describe professional standards or internal affairs functions (e.g. the term "toecutters" used in Australia to denote this function of a police force) indicate that these functions are considered superfluous or at odds with the broader objectives of the organisation.

Stories

The final element of the cultural web goes to the stories and narratives that are told within the organisation. These stories and their repetition shape the perception of people within the organisation about the events and history of the organisation. How these events are portrayed or whether they are spoken about at all help people to make sense of what is important, what is taboo, and what is considered irrelevant.

Stories that present certain events as victories and others as failures highlight an organisation's sense of what success looks like and what the organisation and its people should aspire to or should avoid at all cost. The heroes and villains of those narratives help people to recognise the personal attributes and qualities that are considered to be desirable or objectionable, and those who are portrayed as mavericks, whether good or bad, provide the framing for what is considered to be within or deviate from conceptions of the norm.

Shaping an integrity culture is then about developing and sharing the stories that highlight the attributes that we've outlined above. Stories which accentuate diligence, vigilance, and honesty while deriding dishonesty and carelessness, according to Johnson and Scholes' model, is expected to bring out those behaviours within an organisation.

Shaping the paradigm

The cultural web sets out a model for observing, analysing, and understanding the attributes of cultures within organisations, which can help predict the behaviour of those within that organisation. More importantly though, the model provides a set of levers that can be used to shape and change culture. These levers influence the future behaviour of those within that cultural *milieu*. Shaping an integrity paradigm therefore means not simply understanding the current power structures, symbols, or stories, but proactively developing or influencing them to reflect the behaviours that will protect the organisation from insider risk.

It is the leadership and decision-makers of the organisation who have the resources and assets necessary to invest in shaping the organisation to address all facets of its risk environment, including its insider risk. With sound governance (which we will discuss in the forthcoming chapter), this power to shape the culture of the organisation comes with the accountability to shape it to the benefit of the organisation and supporting it to achieve its mission and objectives. Those with formal power and control of the organisation, whatever its scale and complexity, from company to multinational, to government organisation to the leadership of a nation, are responsible and empowered to adjust the cultural paradigm that drives the behaviour of people within it.

Driving an integrity culture to protect the organisations assets, and through them its mission and objectives, is then

- creating control systems which emphasise the value of those assets and embed practices to protect them, including the system of control which is set out within our model;
- establishing organisational structures which allocate responsibility and provide power and authority to identify, prevent, detect, and respond to insider risks, and through that authority to demonstrate a cultural norm and commitment to integrity of behaviour;

- embedding routines that protect those assets, routines such as risk assessments, conflict of interest or personal interest declarations, merit-based hiring practices, integrity, dialogue;
- creating symbols and terminology which denote or are associated with attributes of integrity, whether they are the symbols of the corporate brand or identity, or symbols associated with the inside risk management activities themselves; and
- choosing, carefully, the stories that will be shared at the organisation level, including shedding light on victories achieved with honesty and integrity, the narratives of those who have acted with or without integrity in the course of the work of the organisation, and the benefits and harms of those actions.

The reason the model is presented as a web is that no aspect of the web can be viewed in total isolation, culture remaining a nebulous and changing concept. The elements that shape the paradigm must be viewed together. Indeed, inconsistencies and conflicts between elements of the web can undermine the development of a beneficial culture. If, for example, the stories that the enterprise wishes to tell emphasise integrity, but power is held by those who do not display integrity then this is likely to undermine the impact of the stories on creating a cultural norm.

Identifying and managing conflicts between elements of the web is imperative to embed the cultural norms of an integrity culture. We briefly turn now to looking at some of the contexts in which those conflicts may occur.

General and sub-cultures

As proposed by Martin (2013), culture is not uniform or homogeneous across organisations. Cultural norms can develop at the macro-organisational level. They are also shaped by local conditions and stimuli within different functions of the organisation. Those stimuli can be created through a range of factors:

- *Role-based stimuli*: including the nature of the work, its stakeholders, and particular pressures, the difference between beat police interacting with petty criminals versus the accounting department managing financial revenues and outlays.
- *Leadership and management structures*: the personal characteristics and preferences of leaders in different parts of the organisation will shape the culture within their line of management.
- *Nationally or globally distributed organisations*: which create interactions with local cultural norms and hiring from within local cultural groups.

- *Team and structural evolution factors*: In other words, teams that are newly established will proceed through an evolutionary lifecycle which explores and normalises their way of operating. Cultural norms will be different at various stages across this lifecycle which may or may not reflect desired norms at the whole of organisation level.

These cultural variations or inconsistencies should not be considered inherently problematic since they can be adapted to local conditions or needs that assist the organisation to achieve its purpose. In the context of insider risk, however, the fact that variations occur means that the establishment of cultural norms cannot be solely focused on the whole of organisation level. Instead, organisational leaders need to be conscious of the actual or potential for inconsistencies in the cultural framework within different parts of the organisation and focus efforts on understanding whether those variations create risk at the sub-culture level. If for example, honesty and diligence are valued less in a part of the organisation – as evidenced through the analysis of the cultural web – then investment of effort should be put towards shaping new norms within that part of the organisational structure. Analysis and feedback loops that enable insights to be gleaned about the culture of the organisation need, therefore, also to be organised with the organisational structure and capability framework in mind (see Chapter 3).

Using our imaginary border control agency as an example, the value stream (see Figure 10.3) of the organisation involves interventions to manage risk along the process of decision to visit the country, to leaving, whilst complying with those conditions which create economic, social, or environmental benefit or mitigate equivalent economic, social, or environmental harm.

Across that value stream, the organisational structures and teams which undertake different interventions (e.g. grant of permissions, the clearance through an airport) are likely to have quite different cultural norms and frameworks. We can posit that the processing officers for grant permissions are primarily an office-based workforce, which consider and evaluate applications while clearance officers who work in an airport are in an operational environment in close operating proximity with other workforces including airport corporations and other regulatory agencies. Equally, they come into

VALUE STREAM

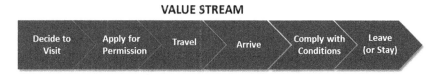

FIGURE 10.3   Example Value Stream: Travel and Migration

direct contact with agency stakeholders in that environment. It is almost inconceivable, given these different operating environments, that the cultural frameworks of these two workforces would be the same. However, from a whole-of-organisation perspective, it is indispensable that the elements of the integrity paradigm are part of both sub-cultures. Honesty, diligence, vigilance are necessary components of the stories, symbols, control structures, power centres, and so forth to protect against insider threat in both functional areas. Additionally, the risk profile of the two functions is different as we have explored in earlier chapters. Hence, consideration needs to be given by the organisation's leadership into the relative value of specific cultural interventions in the different functions based on the risk profile of the function based on its assets, opportunities, beneficiaries, and so forth. We will explore this further in Chapter 11.

Competing cultural objectives

At the whole-of-organisation level, different objectives can create tensions between cultural structures. Integrity describes the quality with which an objective is achieved rather than the objective itself. The cultural norms that help the organisation to achieve an objective may not integrate easily with norms that create integrity and protect its assets from insider risk. A salient and analogous example comes from the banking sector and its role and culture leading up to the 2008 Global Financial Crisis, the worst financial crisis since the Great Depression (The Reserve Bank of Australia, 2021). Numerous factors led into the crisis but a key one was the sub-prime lending practices. As a business, the banks are naturally motivated by financial profit. Under the favourable economic conditions leading up to the crisis, there was fierce competition between lenders driven by a combination of short-term housing investors and high prices for genuine homeowners. The culture within the sector emphasised a devolution of management of prudential risk and a chief focus on bringing on new lenders. Incentives, narratives, and organisational symbols were all geared towards the "heroes" who achieved high lending targets. This also incentivised the taking on of sub-prime borrowers, borrowing at or even above the price of houses on the market on the assumption of continuing fair-weather economic conditions, or borrowers who were demonstrably unable or at risk of being unable to repay those loans. In aggregate, the cultural incentives for short-term financial gain created a surge of prudential risk which eventually accrued causing the collapse of several major financial institutions (McKibbin & Stoeckel, 2010; Melvin & Taylor, 2009).

Drawing this back to our integrity culture example, the culture that was perceived to (and indeed initially was) achieve profit for the organisation did not involve diligence and vigilance against the prudential risk that was accruing in the background. A similar cultural framework in banks in Australia led to many of the same lending practices, but additionally led to one of the banks effectively inadvertently facilitating money laundering and eventually accruing the largest infringement ever issued in that country's history (AUS-TRAC, 2022; Australian Government, 2020). These examples illustrate that the benefits of the prevailing culture need to also be assessed by senior leadership with respect to the risks that they create, including systemic insider risk.

Culture and motivation

As we explored in Chapter 6, a fundamental component of our insider risk model concerns the motivations of the individuals within the system. While this element can be considered to be the least systemic element of the model in so far as motivation is genuinely individual and cannot be comprehensively modelled, substantial research has identified features that generally provide an answer to the question, "Why do people do the wrong thing?"

Building on that research, we identify three factors associated with insider risk motivation: pressure, inducement, and rationalisation. As discussed in Chapter 6, motivation can be highly individualised and extraneous to the organisation. For example, an individual who has accrued personal debt might be expected to experience pressures that may increase the risk that they will commit malicious acts. Beneficiaries may use a range of inducements to play on those pressures such as financial bribes or threats, and the acts themselves may be rationalised in a personal way. These motivational factors are not created by the enterprise itself.

The organisational culture may, itself, create motivation within the organisation that drives insider threats. Using our example above in the banking and lending sector, the culture within the organisation focused on competition between individuals in respect of the number and value of lending against targets. This cultural narrative would in its own right create pressures around performance: pressure which could very well lead to cutting corners to achieve targets and thereby exposing the organisation to risk. In government organisations, the culture and frameworks underpinning the relationship between public servants and politicians equally can create pressures to meet political goals at the expense of social and economic policy objectives of the enterprise. For example, in an Australian context the Royal Commission into the Robodebt Scheme (Australia Public Service Commission, 2023), a scheme designed to identify fraud through the linking of social security with taxation data found that the intense political pressure for results meant that the illegality of the scheme was at best ignored or at worst suppressed.

The distribution of power and status within the organisation can act as an inducement for behaviours that run contrary to the organisation's interest. For example, if promotion or other status can be granted by certain people within the organisation, then this may act as an incentive to please those individuals at the expense of care, due diligence, or merit in undertaking the activities of the organisation. Using our imaginary border agency as an example, if rewards and incentives were created around those who can clear the most individuals through the border, and the cultural stories presented them as "heroes" then naturally this social approval could act as a strong inducement to increase the velocity of border clearance at the expense of due diligence over the clearance decisions. In contrast if the cultural norms and incentives favoured due diligence and correctness, then this might provide more of an inducement for care and vigilance in the process.

Finally, the cultural framework of the organisation can play a crucial role in the rationalisation of malicious insider activity. If a culture normalises particular behaviours and routines that are, for example, corrupt (such as the acceptance of bribes) then this will equally enable the action to be rationalised as just "the way things are done around here". Likewise, cultures that tolerate other negative actions such as bullying and harassment may perpetuate other insider threats, with the malicious insider acts being rationalised as revenge against the organisation for mistreatment or failure to address mistreatment. In this way, organisations need to be conscious of whether aspects of their cultures, observable through the lens of the cultural web, might create flow on motivational factors that may increase their insider risk.

Why not culture unaided?

In this chapter we have argued that culture is a systemic element of the management of insider risk, insofar as it creates consistent behavioural attributes, and can act to normalise behaviour in places where controls cannot be implemented. A natural question arises then, Why not focus exclusively on culture and not invest in the other elements of the model? In our view there are two reasons.

Firstly, as we have discussed above, the control system of the organisation including its insider risk control system is a part of and manifestation of its culture. The presence of an insider risk control system, in its own right, shapes a culture that values integrity to its systems and processes, normalising and encoding behaviour that accord with risk controls.

Secondly, while cultural norms can encode relatively consistent behaviours based on either or both a consequence logic or an appropriateness logic, there will remain a small number of people who continue to deviate from social and psychological norms. For example, clinically diagnosed psychopaths will not be motivated by any logic of appropriateness, since their motivations for action are, for the most part, selfish. As argued by Hare (1999), psychopaths "selfishly take what they want and do as they please, violating social norms and expectations without the slightest sense of guilt or regret". Further, research by Sonne and Gash (2018) reveals that

> the underlying neural circuitry differs between psychopaths and altruists with emotional processing being profoundly muted in psychopaths and significantly enhanced in altruists; . . . [here] both groups are characterized by the reward system of the brain shaping [their] behavior.

Equally, consequences will only be around personal rather than any genuine or righteous sense of consequence. While Klockars et al.'s (2000) research suggests people fitting these personality profiles are not the main risk in relation to corruption and insider threat, they can, nonetheless, create significant harm if they have access to organisational assets and the opportunity to exploit them.

Our conclusion, therefore, is that culture is an important component of a systemic approach to managing risk but must complement other elements to be effective as part of a holistic system.

Chapter key points

- Organisational culture provides a normalising influence on behaviour within the organisation, including creating attributes of integrity.
- Culture should, therefore, be seen as integral to a systemic approach to managing insider risk.
- An integrity culture is a crucial component of the insider risk management system, protecting organisational assets from threats even potentially in the absence of other controls.
- The cultural web provides a means to both understand and analyse current prevailing cultural norms, and also as levers to influence cultural change.
- Culture cannot be looked at solely at the whole of organisation level or to the exclusion of other domains of culture within the organisation. Conflicts and inconsistencies between these cultural frameworks need to be managed by the organisational leadership.

References

Adolphs, R. (2003). Cognitive neuroscience of human social behaviour. *Nature Reviews Neuroscience, 4*(3), 165–178.

AUSTRAC. (2022). *AUSTRAC and CBA agree on $700m penalty.* https://www.aus trac.gov.au/austrac-and-cba-agree-700m-penalty#:~:text=An%20agreement%20 has%20been%20reached,(AML%2FCTF)%20laws

Australia Public Service Commission. (2023). *Robodebt Royal Commission.* https://www.apsc.gov.au/initiatives-and-programs/workforce-information/research-analysis-and-publications/state-service/state-service-report-2023/integrity/robodebt-royal-commission

Australian Government. (2020). *Westpac ordered to pay $1.3 billion penalty* [Press release]. https://www.austrac.gov.au/news-and-media/our-recent-work/westpac-penalty-ordered

Chin, G. J., & Wells, S. C. (1997). The blue wall of silence as evidence of bias and a motive to lie: A new approach to policy perjury. *University of Pittsburgh Law Review, 59*(2), 233–300.

Conway, S., & Westmarland, L. (2021). The blue wall of silence: Police integrity and corruption. In S. Starystach & K. Höly (Eds.), *Silence of organizations: How organizations cover up wrongdoings* (pp. 105–132). heiBOOKS.

Dodd, V. (2023). Two or three met police officers to face trial every week, commissioner predicts. *The Guardian.* https://www.theguardian.com/uk-news/2023/jan/25/met-commissioner-predicts-two-or-three-officers-to-face-trial-every-week

Finnemore, M. (1996). *National interests in international society.* Cornell University Press.

Gaynor, J. M. (2020). *Report of enquiry under division 4A of part 4 of the inspector general of the Australian defence force regulation 216 into questions of unlawful conduct concerning the special operations task force group in Afghanistan – part 1 the inquiry.* chrome-extension://efaidnbmnnnibpcajpcglclefindmkaj/https://www.defence.gov.au/sites/default/files/2021–10/IGADF-Afghanistan-Inquiry-Public-Release-Version.pdf

Hare, R. D. (1999). *Without conscience: The disturbing world of the psychopaths among us.* Guilford Press.

Herrmann, R. K., & Shannon, V. P. (2001). Defending international norms: The role of obligation, material interest, and perception in decision making. *International Organization, 55*(3), 621–654.

Igbo, E. U. (2017). The use and abuse of police powers and extrajudicial killings in Nigeria. *African Journal of Criminology and Justice Studies, 10*(1), 83.

Johnson, G. (2000). Strategy through a cultural lens: Learning from managers' experience. *Management Learning, 31*(4), 406.

Johnson, G., Scholes, K., & Whittington, R. (2008). *Exploring corporate strategy: Text and cases.* Financial Times Prentice Hall.

Klockars, C. B., Ivkovich, S. K., Harver, W. E., & Haberfeld, M. R. (2000). *The measurement of police integrity.* NIJ Research in Brief.

Macionis, J., & Gerber, L. (2011). *Sociology.* Pearson Prentice Hall.

Marien, H., Custers, R., & Aarts, H. (2019). Studying human habits in societal context: Examining support for a basic stimulus–response mechanism. *Current Directions in Psychological Science, 28*(6), 614–618.

Martin, J. (2013). *Organizational culture: Mapping the terrain.* Sage.

McCarthy, B., Hagan, J., & Herda, D. (2020). Neighborhood climates of legal cynicism and complaints about abuse of police power. *Criminology, 58*(3), 510–536.

McKibbin, W. J., & Stoeckel, A. (2010). The global financial crisis: Causes and consequences. *Asian Economic Papers, 9*(1), 54–86.

Melvin, M., & Taylor, M. P. (2009). The global financial crisis: Causes, threats and opportunities: Introduction and overview. *Journal of International Money and Finance, 28*(8), 1243–1245.

Newburn, T. (2022). The Metropolitan police's integrity is now at risk in the 'partygate' affair. *The Guardian.* https://www.theguardian.com/uk-news/2022/jan/30/the-metropolitan-polices-integrity-is-now-at-risk-in-the-partygate-affair

Ravasi, D., & Schultz, M. (2006). Responding to organizational identity threats: Exploring the role of organizational culture. *Academy of Management Journal,* 49(3), 433–458.

The Reserve Bank of Australia. (2021). *The global financial crisis.* https://www.rba.gov.au/education/resources/explainers/the-global-financial-crisis.html

Schein, E. H. (2004). *Organizational culture and leadership* (3rd ed.). Jossey-Bass.

Sonne, J. W., & Gash, D. M. (2018). Psychopathy to altruism: Neurobiology of the selfish–selfless spectrum. *Frontiers in Psychology, 9.*

Sunstein, C. (1996). Social norms and social roles. *Columbia Law Review, 96*(4), 903–968.

Young, H. P. (2015). The evolution of social norms. *Annual Review of Economics, 7*(1), 359–387.

11

GOVERNING THE SYSTEM

Introduction

This chapter argues that traditional approaches to developing risk registers are vastly inadequate for making sense of the complexity of organisations and the insider risks that present themselves across varied and multifaceted lines of business. Here, we also propose that this approach actively hinders good decision-making in relation to managing and mitigating insider risk. The chapter, instead, proposes an approach to modelling the data components of insider risk and assembling them in such a way to make sense to a wide variety of decision-makers and accountable parties throughout organisations. It also argues that this assembly of information is critical to making behavioural changes around the governance and investment in managing insider risk. In the context of financial institutions and border control agencies, the sheer number of products, processes, and services offered by these organisations makes it difficult, if not impossible, to provide central management and oversight of insider risk without better use of data to inform decision-makers of the risks and their options for investing in mitigating those risks.

In this final chapter, we will synthesise all the elements of the model to describe how the complete model enables organisations to better understand risk and thereby to make more cost-effective decisions to mitigate risk while minimising the impacts on other organisational priorities. The central concept of this chapter is governance, that is, the processes and mechanisms by which organisations make decisions and enforce decisions over the system of the organisation. As we set out in earlier chapters, insider threat is a complex organisational problem which arises in the many permutations of interaction between people, roles, organisational assets, processes, objectives, and

DOI: 10.4324/9781003055716-11

motives, within an overall context of uncertainty. Recognising the limitations of the human mind to calculate and consume these permutations (Manning, 2008; Manning et al., 2011, 2013; Saaty, 1990), models must therefore be constructed to create the correct linkages between the elements and to enable us to identify which are the most actually or probably common of those permutations: this is the likelihood component of risk. Similarly, those linkages will identify those permutations which create the most harm or opportunity: this is the consequence component of risk. Equally, the options for controlling the risk and the relative benefits, costs, and downsides of those controls are also complex.

To make sound, rational, and objective decisions in relation to managing insider risk, decision-makers need the data and information of the system to be structured in order to make sense of the options, cost–benefit, and relative merits of investment in different configurations of controls. The alternative is a reliance on heuristic decision-making devices, which draw on simplistic notions of where risks "might" be and/or which controls are familiar and appealing. As we've outlined in previous chapters heuristic decision-making, almost by definition, does not provide a sound basis for managing risk in a complex system.

The other key element that we will outline is the roles involved in decision-making. In a complex system, a singular point of decision-making and decision-making input is unlikely to yield the best decisions for the organisation. As we'll set out below, this is because responsibilities and accountabilities for different aspects and interests within the system are likely in conflict. The implementation of new controls on business processes may also create inefficiencies and impacts on productivity. For example, if the same person is given primary accountability for the operations of the business and achieving productivity levels and decisions regarding the investment in insider threat controls, unless these are equally valued, one will take precedence over the other potentially to the detriment of the organisation. Equally, excessive concentration of responsibility creates single points of decision failure, where devolved organisational responsibilities become manifestly challenging to oversee or balance against one another.

Why is governance important?

At all levels, organisations are complex systems designed to achieve an objective or set of objectives utilising finite resources in an uncertain internal and external environment. Governance, then, is the set of processes and practices of decision-making around the application of those resources to meet those objectives.

As we've set out in previous chapters, insider risk is an equally complex problem which emerges within organisations and impacts on its assets and objectives. As part of the overall governance of the organisation's objectives then, governance of the allocation of finite resources to manage insider risk, which may impact on those objectives, is critical.

Merely having the structures of governance in place is, however, not sufficient. The quality of governance is tied to the level of efficiency in the allocation of those resources to meet the objectives, and this is based on the structure and completeness of the decision-information, which is available to make rational and objective resource allocation decisions, based upon cost–benefit–impact factors. At its core, the goal of the model we've outlined in previous chapters is to enable enhanced systemic decision-making by organisational leaders by bringing together, in a structured model, all the information pertaining to insider risk and the mechanisms to control it. In the absence of sound governance, investment in insider risk management system will be more or less random or "hit and miss", dominated by simplistic or heuristic-based decision-making using intuition rather than evidence to guide decisions.

The governance model

Our model of governance of insider risk system is, in its own right, a system within a system, comprising different roles, activities, and organisational capabilities. As shown in Figure 11.1, governance sits at the top of the regulatory pyramid, with lower levels pertaining to earlier discussions regarding control assurance, control design, and implementation and finally culture and capability.

For the remainder of this chapter, we will outline the various components of the governance system and how it operates to better manage insider risk than those less structured systems of management.

The seven "capable guardians"

Graycar and Prenzler (2013) in their examination of corruption in different contexts, drawing on Cohen and Felson's (1979) routine activity theory, contend that corruption emerges through a combination of a motivated actor, a target, and the absence of a "capable guardian". In our earlier chapters we dealt with the motivated actor and the targets (along with other concepts such as the beneficiaries and the opportunities). However, the question remains, What is a "capable guardian'?

In the literature, the term "capable guardian" is used to denote a wide variety of actors including property owners, law enforcement entities, local supervisors, and regulatory entities. These examples signify the guardian in specific situations or contexts. We prefer instead to take a functional view of guardianship, that is, describing the functional roles of the guardians within

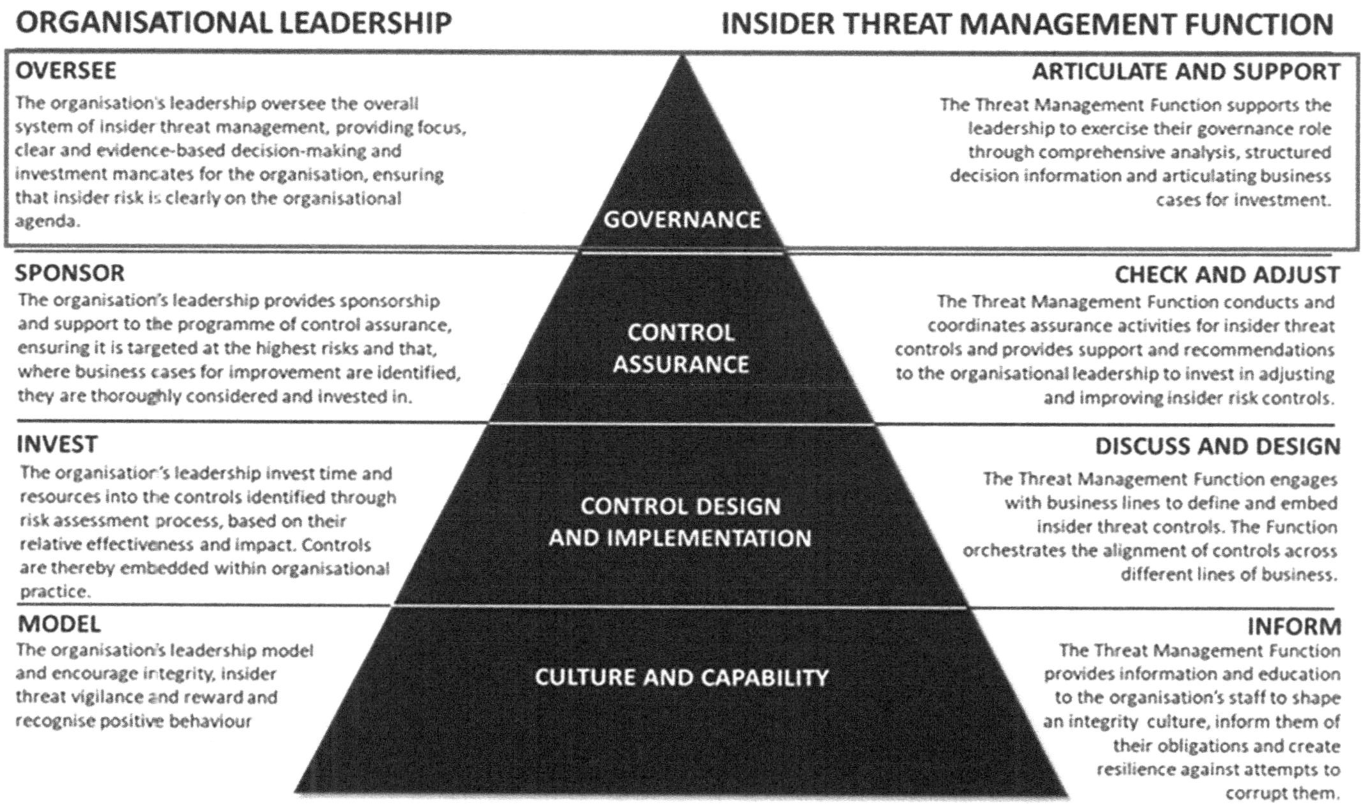

ORGANISATIONAL LEADERSHIP

OVERSEE

The organisation's leadership oversee the overall system of insider threat management, providing focus, clear and evidence-based decision-making and investment mandates for the organisation, ensuring that insider risk is clearly on the organisational agenda.

SPONSOR

The organisation's leadership provides sponsorship and support to the programme of control assurance, ensuring it is targeted at the highest risks and that, where business cases for improvement are identified, they are thoroughly considered and invested in.

INVEST

The organisation's leadership invest time and resources into the controls identified through risk assessment process, based on their relative effectiveness and impact. Controls are thereby embedded within organisational practice.

MODEL

The organisation's leadership model and encourage integrity, insider threat vigilance and reward and recognise positive behaviour

INSIDER THREAT MANAGEMENT FUNCTION

ARTICULATE AND SUPPORT

The Threat Management Function supports the leadership to exercise their governance role through comprehensive analysis, structured decision information and articulating business cases for investment.

CHECK AND ADJUST

The Threat Management Function conducts and coordinates assurance activities for insider threat controls and provides support and recommendations to the organisational leadership to invest in adjusting and improving insider risk controls.

DISCUSS AND DESIGN

The Threat Management Function engages with business lines to define and embed insider threat controls. The Function orchestrates the alignment of controls across different lines of business.

INFORM

The Threat Management Function provides information and education to the organisation's staff to shape an integrity culture, inform them of their obligations and create resilience against attempts to corrupt them.

GOVERNANCE

CONTROL ASSURANCE

CONTROL DESIGN AND IMPLEMENTATION

CULTURE AND CAPABILITY

FIGURE 11.1 Insider Risk Management Model: Governance

the system. Approaching the concept of the capable guardian from a systemic perspective enables us to define consistent personas which are applicable in all organisational contexts, rather than specific examples which are only applicable in a particular setting and hence do not outline the functions of that guardian as they would apply in other settings.

When considering guardianship in a systemic context we identify seven guardians that interact to operate the system of insider risk management: five internal guardians – the chief(s), the risk owner, the control owner, the insider risk steward, and the assurer – and two external guardians – the regulator and the enforcer.

The chief(s)

In earlier chapters we referred to the importance of the organisation's leadership, which both defines and drives the organisation's business objectives. The top leadership of the organisation is broadly made of the C-suite of executives including the Chief Executive Officer (CEO). Depending on the size and complexity of the organisation, the CEO may be supported by other C-suite roles such as the Chief Operating Officer, the Chief Financial Officer, the Chief Risk Officer, who support the CEO to manage a complex organisational system. From an insider risk perspective, the chief(s) provide the authorising environment that recognises insider risk as an important domain of risk for the organisation and invests part of the organisation's finite resources to manage that risk. Primarily, their guardianship consists of providing this sponsorship, creating and supporting an insider-risk-resistant culture and investing resources into controls to manage the risk.

For these guardians to be "capable" they must therefore be able to invest those resources effectively and efficiently within the organisation. In contrast, there are several ways in which a lack of capability may manifest itself:

- *Investment in controls that are not effective, either in an absolute or a relative sense:* In this scenario, investment of resources is made into controls which are not effective at all, or are not effective as other controls to manage insider risk. For example, in previous chapters we described "employee screening", which is done when a person is initially employed. Logically, this control may identify a person who is already corrupt in some way but will not identify individuals who are corrupted once in the organisation. Arguably the control is ineffective or at least there are more effective detection controls to identify corrupt activity than screening out people before commencement. For the guardian to be capable, they must be able to compare controls and their investment and make balanced decisions about which is the best set of controls (see "Control Balancing' below).

- *Under-investment in controls:* In this scenario the investment or direction of resources into a control or set of controls is insufficient for the control to work. As we articulated in Chapter 8, there are control effectiveness factors which determine whether a control is effective or not and sufficient investment is required to ensure that a control will, in fact, be effective. For the guardian to be *capable* they must be able to identify the level of investment which is required for the control or set of controls to be effective.
- *Incomplete investment*: Under this scenario, investment is made in effective controls against risks. However, there is an incomplete understanding of the risks which, therefore, result in investment in some controls but an incomplete investment in the full set of controls that would arguably manage the losses from insider risk to an acceptable level.

The chief(s) are at the centre of the organisational governance model and equally are the key actor in the governance of insider threat as they control the resources of the organisation. As the above examples illustrate, to be a capable guardian of the system, the chief(s) must have the information and knowledge of the complex system of the organisation in order to make objective and effective decisions in relation to the investment of resources to combat the risk. The chief(s) also set the cultural tone for the organisation. As we set out in Chapter 8, they must equally have the means of identifying and addressing cultural issues that may increase insider risk. In our view, being a capable guardian goes beyond a simple interest or ad hoc understanding of insider risk. It requires the ability for a deep understanding of the system and the cost and benefits of different investments of resources to manage risk to an acceptable level. As we will further outline below, the purpose of our model is to provide this capability. We do this by identifying and structuring the various elements of insider risk so that they can be consumed readily by the chief(s) to make sound investment decisions.

In addition to investment decisions about the control environment, the chief(s) also make decisions about the relative investment in assurance across the multiple lines of assurance described in Chapter 9. In order to make sound decisions, sufficiently nuanced decision information must be available to identify where investment (both current and potential) in assurance has and should flow to manage risk.

The risk owner

According to ISO 31000, a risk owner is a person who has been delegated the responsibility for managing a specific risk (International Organization for Standardization, 2018). In an organisational context, the delegation of this authority is made by the chief(s) and is often made along organisational structural lines. Returning to our fictional border agency, risk ownership for the incorrect grant of a visa (whether deliberate or inadvertent) would be delegated to the senior manager of the visa function. Similarly, the risk of an unauthorised entry through the border would be delegated to the senior manager of the border function. This is illustrated in Figure 11.2 in the bordered section titled Indicative Structure.

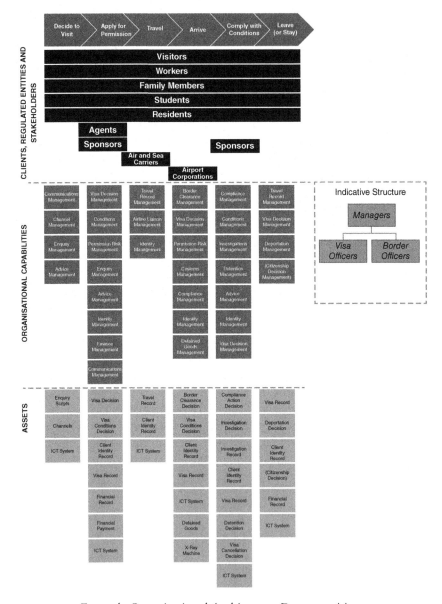

FIGURE 11.2 Example Organisational Architecture Decomposition

There will, therefore, be multiple risk owners within the organisation with responsibility delegated for managing specific areas of risk, most likely aligned to their functional responsibilities within the organisation. Put another way, the person with the overall accountability for the asset (we described in Chapter 3) is delegated with the responsibility for the management of risk to that asset, whether it is a decision asset, information asset, or physical/intangible asset. The more complex and numerous the functions and assets of the organisation, the larger the number of risk owners required to manage risks to the assets within their control.

The role of the risk owner from the perspective of insider risk is to oversee the risk assessment over the assets in their control by (i) identifying gaps in controls; (ii) overseeing the performance of controls to manage the risk, (iii) seeking new investment into controls where the investment is insufficient; (iv) trading off the impact of the risk versus the impacts of the controls within their delegated authority; (v) taking accountability when risk does eventuate; and (vi) evaluating control failures.

A capable risk owner is one that has a fulsome understanding of the elements of the risk and has line of sight to the controls that manage that risk whether they are in their direct control or not (see control owners below). In this way, the risk owner is capable of understanding and expressing both the probability and the impact of the inherent insider risk based on the following:

- The *opportunities* that their assets are subject to;
- Who the *beneficiaries* are and what their *capability* and *intent* and *interactions* are; and
- The systemic motivation factors, primarily *rationalisation* factors.

Equally, to balance the benefit of effective controls against the control impacts, the risk owner must have visibility of the controls, their effectiveness factors, and impact factors.

Finally, risk owners provide the support to the chief(s) to manage the overall risk environment by taking responsibility for a particular or several domains of risk. This includes ensuring the risk is being effectively managed within organisational tolerances, and where those tolerances are breached, escalating for further intervention. To achieve this, the risk owner must be capable of understanding the residual risk once controls are in place and whether that residual risk exceeds organisational tolerances. These capabilities are all enabled through the risk register and risk assessment, as we describe in the following.

The control owner

Control owners are responsible for the execution of the controls. As described in Chapter 7, controls must be organisational capabilities. That is, they are practical processes and activities, supported by resourcing and technology that create a deviation in the risk by reducing the likelihood of a risk event or its consequence (or both). Control owners are, therefore, responsible for executing those processes and ensuring that they are efficient and effective in terms of managing the risk, within the investment made in the control by the chief(s) and the risk owner.

To be a capable guardian in the system, the control owner must understand what risk the control is designed to mitigate and what control effectiveness factors are required and should be measured and the control impacts to be mitigated. The control owner must also be capable of escalating control failures or where a control is ineffective to the risk owner and/or the chief(s), for example, if additional investment is required to make the control effective. Risks will be mitigated by multiple controls and equally a single control may manage multiple risks. As a result, within an organisation there will be a significant number of control owners for each of the different controls (see for example Chapter 7 setting out all the different typologies of controls which operate against the opportunities, motivation, and beneficiaries).

The capability of the control owner also hinges on their ability to have line of sight to all the risks managed by the control and ensure that the control performs for each of the risks as intended. For example, active or passive CCTV will act as a control to increase visibility and/or traceability of actions and decisions for any assets that are monitored under CCTV cameras. If we propose that the CCTV monitors an evidence storage facility where like goods are stored together (drugs are kept in one area while seized weapons are in another) and one area is more obscured than the other, then arguably that control is less effective for the class of goods in the obscured area. It would be for the control owner to either remedy or highlight the deficit in the control to the risk owner in respect of the obscured assets.

The risk owner and control owner, therefore, operate in complex symbiotic relationships: on the one side owning the risk and ensuring that relevant controls are in place to manage the risk and on the other side effecting and maintaining performance of the controls themselves.

The insider risk steward

As the preceding chapters set out, the management of insider threat is a complex system, involving many elements which, in combination and permutation, create threats to organisational mission, objectives, and assets. In our view, a complex system of this nature requires a steward or owner who has oversight of the system as a whole and can coordinate and orchestrate the activities within the system to maximise the efficiency and effectiveness of the system as a whole. We refer to this actor as the insider threat management officer and envisage this as a function within the organisation, to which has been delegated the responsibility to oversee and organise the insider risk management system by the chief(s) (Figure 11.2).

In our view, this actor is at the centre of operationalising the model we describe throughout this book in a real-world organisational context. The steward takes responsibility for

- undertaking and coordinating the risk assessments;
- organising the risk register (which we describe below);
- framing the cultural context (per Chapter 10) with the chief(s);
- orchestrating the relationships between the risk owner and the control owners;
- maintaining a register of standard controls, control effectiveness factors, and control impacts;
- coordinating assurance and undertaking and undertaking second- and third-line assurance activities;
- reviewing control failures; and
- monitoring the overall performance of the system in protecting assets, mission, and objectives.

Our model is designed to enable the steward to be a capable guardian of the system, by providing a systemic and structured set of data and information that enables the system to be comprehended and analysed in a systemic fashion. It is through the comprehension and analysis of the system that the steward supports the chief(s) to (i) invest in controls that mitigate risk while minimising impact on the mission and objectives; (ii) support the risk owners to identify appropriate controls and work with control owners to mitigate risk; (iii) to support the control owners on design, execution, and measurement of controls; and, (iv) define the priorities for assurance for the assurer (below).

The assurer

As discussed in Chapter 9, ensuring that controls as executed reflect controls as designed and intended to operate requires investment in assurance over those controls. Within organisations, assurance runs across numerous lines of control, first-line controls embedded within the business processes to second- and third-line assurance that undertakes sample-based or periodic checking of the controls in operation. These activities require an assurer to take ownership of the planning, coordination, and investment case for those activities based on the risk managed by those controls.

To be a capable guardian, the assurer must have line of sight between the risk that the control is designed to manage and through what mechanisms the controls are intended to operate against the opportunities, motivations, and beneficiaries. Equally, the assurer should have visibility of the control thresholds and impacts. These provide the standards against which a control is tested by the assurer to ensure the control is performing as anticipated. A "capable assurer" is also one that has sufficient investment and ability to undertake the different typologies of assurance activities as set out in Chapter 9, thereby enabling them to choose the correct assurance tool for the control typology under evaluation.

The regulator

Insider risk within any organisation is effectively a market failure which can create or exacerbate economic, social, and environmental harms. This may be, as an example, because insider threat within companies threatens their market share (e.g. through industrial espionage) or through the undermining of regulatory schemes designed to minimise those harms (e.g. corrupt grant of logging permits in protected forests). As a result of these harms, jurisdictions globally have developed legislative frameworks regulating the internal control frameworks, including those that prevent, detect, and respond to insider risk. Equally, these legal frameworks create reporting and auditing requirements for organisations to ensure the functioning of their internal control environments (see for example the Sarbanes-Oxley Act in the United States or the Companies Act in the United Kingdom) (Rezzy, 2007).

Effectively, any regulatory system creates compliance requirements on organisations of all kinds. Where individual incentives exist for non-compliance with those regulatory frameworks, then there is an increased insider risk within those organisations in respect of those regulatory frameworks. For example, a business may have the intention to comply with environmental protection regulations, which require protection against pollution. However, if the incentive to pollute remains for individuals within the organisation, because they will be able to turn higher profits and achieve greater bonuses, then the absence or failure of the internal control system to prevent this will undermine overall compliance.

In addition to establishing regulatory obligations, those legislative and regulatory frameworks generally establish regulatory bodies to administer the legislation and ensure compliance by the regulated entities subject to that legislation. Examples of these regulators range from financial and securities, prudential, anti-money laundering, and environmental and safety regulators. These regulators indirectly regulate insider threat insofar as the compliance of the entity as a whole hinges on the compliance of the individuals within the organisation and the systems of control to manage their behaviours. In addition to the general regulators, specialist regulatory entities exist to directly regulate the insider risk control system, such as government anti-corruption and anti-bribery bodies.

The presence of these regulatory frameworks and their respective regulatory body creates complementary incentives for the strengthening of insider risk control systems, in addition to the internal incentives for insider risk to be managed guarding against harms to mission and objectives or profits.

The capability of the regulator can be defined in terms of the following:

- The sufficiency of the powers available to it to effect systemic change amongst its regulated entities: by systemically preventing, detecting, and responding to non-compliance with its legislative framework, including evidence-gathering, rights of entry and audit, enforcement, and sanction powers.
- Its focus on education and capability building (see for example Braithwaite's regulatory model) (Braithwaite, 2002). To build capability and capacity within organisations, the regulator needs to have a sound understanding of insider risk within a variety of different organisational contexts. Further, it requires an ability to articulate controls or undertake audit activity to identify whether the controls are sufficient to manage the risk within the regulated sector.
- Its performance in terms of using the various powers and resources at its disposal to effect systemic change of behaviour within its regulated population.

The implication of the link between external regulation and inside threat is that while the focus of our model is on examining insider risk from an internal organisational perspective, the model can also be a tool for regulators to better understand insider risk within a wide variety of regulatory schemes. The insider risk assessment and register set out below serves as a tool for regulators to better analyse insider risk within those regulated entities. These provide the basis for strengthened education and capability building as well as improved detection capability for vulnerabilities within the regulated organisations.

The enforcer

Finally, in respect of malicious and deliberate insider acts, the strength of a nation's law enforcement and prosecutorial bodies will play a substantial role in terms of creating the general and specific deterrent consequences for those acts. The capability of police forces and other enforcement agencies is dependent upon the level of resources, their ability to prioritise those resources against the highest impact criminal activity, the strength of their investigative capability, and the ability to compile evidence for successful prosecution of crimes.

In the context of insider crimes typologies, enforcement agencies may also require specialist investigative techniques given the wide-ranging insider typologies and methodologies across different organisations and the variety of different assets under threat, including decisions, information and tangible and intangible assets. Digital media, which holds much of the modern assets and the records of action in respect of those assets, requires a modern capability enforcer. This capability enforcer will incorporate digital forensics capability to retrieve, examine, and store data and information from digital devices to be used in investigations or the compiling of evidence.

The system of guardians

The purpose of setting out the guardians is not simply to enunciate different possible types of guardians, but instead to describe a set of inter-operative guardian actors in a system of governance and guardianship which mitigates insider risk.

The chief(s) have overall responsibility for the organisation and the achievement of its objectives. This includes the shaping of its strategies and plans, investment of resources into achieving those organisational objectives, future-proofing the organisation against market shocks and competition, and overseeing every domain of risk to those objectives: strategic, financial, prudential, safety, compliance, and so forth.

Insider risk is only one domain of risk to the organisation's objectives amongst a broader risk ecosystem, which is the purview of the chief(s) of the organisation. Excessive focus by the chief(s) on insider risk would not only be poor investment but would also be detrimental to their other responsibilities. However, as previously illustrated, underinvestment in managing insider risk equally increases the risk of harm to the broader organisational objectives and must, therefore, remain an element of the organisational control system.

The notion of span of control occupies a fundamental position in the study of the exercise of control through organisations. Traditional research has sought to determine the number of subordinates a supervisor can effectively maintain control (Urwick, 1956; Woodward, 1965). Later research into the domain seeks, instead, to focus on span of control based on the allocation of attention and effort to issues rather than in relation to the management of subordinates (Ocasio, 1997). Both thought models propose that there are limits to the number of subordinates, assets, or issues that a person can effectively focus on within an organisational context. The implication being that breaching this threshold diminishes the effectiveness of that person at managing the breadth of issues under their control.

However, the limits of span of control or span of attention do not limit the actual numbers of issues that senior managers must be able to exercise organisational control over. Under either model, therefore, the twin concepts of delegation and accountability accompany the exercise of span of control. More recent research has observed a shift in organisational management structure towards functional management structures (Guadalupe et al., 2014), with delegation both along vertical structural lines (e.g. production managers overseeing production lines) and across horizontal lines (e.g. a chief financial officer who has accountability for maintaining financial control across the organisation or chief information officer who has accountability for maintaining control of information, data, and technology assets and architectures of the organisation).

In the context of insider risk, the maintenance of management control over the risk system equally requires the delegation of functional responsibilities to different actors or, using Graycar's language, "guardians" within the organisation. Figure 11.3 provides an illustrative example of the systemic relationships between the guardians of the system.

The chief(s) have two incentives for maintaining effective control over insider risk to the organisation. First is quite simply the direct harm that insider risk has on the objectives of the organisation. In a business context these are financial losses or more broadly loss of competitiveness and/or market share; and in a public sector the undermining of market interventions designed to mitigate broad economic, social, and environmental harms. The second incentive is where the insider risk creates broader economic harms and therefore is itself the subject of regulation by government and administered through a regulator. In this context, the stimulus on the chief(s) is external and is determined by the capability of the regulator in terms of its ability to detect non-compliance with its regulatory regime and the level of disincentive derived from its enforcement of legislation, through pecuniary or other penalties (such as direct liability for the chiefs including direct fines or jail time for non-compliance).

As an example, let us take a theoretical importing business and our hypothetical border control organisation. The company will have a variety of assets including the products in its import lines, the infrastructure used for importation, commercially sensitive information, and its finances. As we outlined earlier, these assets are under threat from insiders all along the supply chains of the company and it is in the chief(s) of the company's interests to manage the direct threat to those assets, to avoid financial losses (from theft) or losses of market share (from the divulging of sensitive commercial information). As a result, the chief(s) have an immediate incentive to allocate their attention to managing risk to their overall company objectives.

The border agency serves as the regulator on importation, mitigating the economic, social, and environmental harms that would emerge from uncontrolled importation of goods. This may include collecting customs duties and detecting and enforcing the regulations prohibiting or controlling the importation of certain substances such as drugs or environmentally damaging

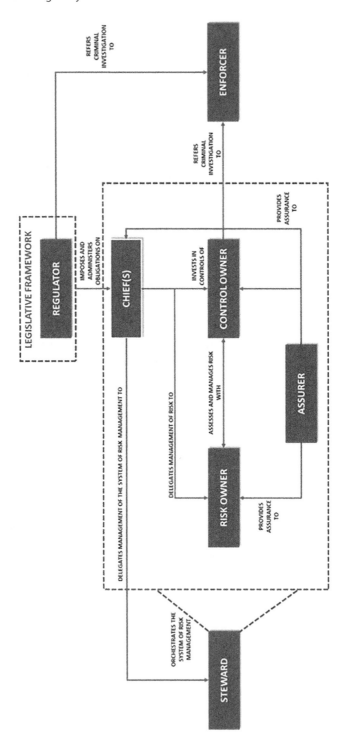

FIGURE 11.3 The Systemic Relationships between the Guardians of the System

substances such as asbestos. In addition to direct targeting of our theoretical importer's assets, insiders could instead attempt to use their supply chains as a means for importing controlled substances through legitimate networks. The incentive for the chief(s) to expend effort and attention on this area of risk derives from the strength of the regulatory regime and the regulatory posture of the border agency, including its effectiveness at detecting illegitimate imports and the strength of its enforcement actions. If those enforcement actions result in harms to the company's financial status in the form of pecuniary penalties or in brand damage affecting market share, then there is a strong incentive for the chief(s) to devote some of the span of their attention to managing this second form of insider risk.

Taking our example a step further, the border control organisation itself is subject to insider risk, with its officers able to facilitate the importation of controlled substances. Like the importer, the chief(s) have a direct incentive to manage this risk insofar as it directly impacts on the objectives and mission of the organisation. Let us also propose, then, that there is a national anti-corruption body that regulates government organisations, including our hypothetical border control agency. This then creates a further external incentive for the allocation of investment and attention to managing insider threat; again, on the premise that the regulatory body is sufficiently capable to incentivise compliance with anti-corruption measures.

These scenarios illustrate the key role that the chief(s) of the organisation have in initiating the system of risk management for insider risk. The role requires a recognition by the chief(s) of the risk to their objectives or the creation of external regulatory requirements to create energy into the insider risk management system.

Now that we have established the motivation for the chief(s) to invest attention and resources into managing insider risk, how then can they go about managing that risk without excessively consuming their span of attention? We propose that the system is then enabled by the delegation of accountability to the four remaining internal guardians.

Again, drawing on our hypothetical border control agency, let us propose that the functional manager for the border officers (for ease of reference let us refer to them as the Border Operations Manager [BOM]) is delegated the role of risk owner in respect of the risk that

> a border officer (the role) will make a border clearance decision (the decision asset) in respect of controlled substances.

In this scenario, the BOM is delegated the risk in alignment with their functional responsibilities within the organisation and their management control over the border officers. This being said, the risk owner is a functional role and could effectively be delegated to any person within the organisation provided that the delegation comes with the authority of the chief(s). Note also that the delegated risk, as outlined above, only articulates the role and the decision asset, rather than the risk driver elements, opportunity, motivation, and beneficiaries. The rationale for expressing the delegated risk in this manner is that the risk owner remains accountable for the all the permutations of the above risk: that is, all the variations that may occur in opportunity, motivation, and beneficiaries which may result in the border officer illicitly making a border clearance decision.

As risk owner, the BOM is delegated the responsibility for assessing and managing the risk. In practice, this means identifying the level of likelihood and the consequences of the different permutations of the risk and ensuring that the appropriate controls are in place to mitigate the risk to within the organisation's tolerance for risk to its objectives or compliance with external obligations. Where the risk exceeds the tolerance or resources delegated to them, the risk owner escalates the risk to the chief(s) for a decision on whether to invest further in managing the risk or to accept a higher level of risk than previously accepted (we will describe the mechanisms of the risk assessment and escalation in more detail below).

In some circumstances our hypothetical BOM will have the ability to directly implement and manage controls which mitigate the risk of a border officer making an illicit clearance decision. This is because they have direct control over the workforce and practice of the border clearance function, so they could, for example, implement daily workforce redeployment as a control to reduce certainty or create a separation of duties to mitigate authority and increase visibility. In this circumstance, the risk owner and the control owner are the same actor.

In contrast, let us propose that CCTV is used to monitor the activities of border officers to mitigate the risk by increasing visibility and traceability, and further suggest that the CCTV function is overseen by a role we'll refer to as the security manager. The notion of risk is largely conceptual (the effect of uncertainty on objectives); hence the delegation of the ownership of the risk could be delegated to any person. Yet controls have tangible physical manifestations; there are capabilities, changes to process, tangible objects, or digital code. As a result, it is more rational for control ownership to be delegated to the person with direct management of the control. In our example, therefore, the control owner would be the security manager, who has management control over the CCTV capabilities of our hypothetical organisation.

The fact that organisations do not fall into neat vertical structures is the reason for differentiating between the risk owner and the control owner, which may in reality be functional roles that reside in different parts of an organisational structure. There is a "useful tension" which is created between the role of the risk owner, who is incentivised to reduce risk down to the lowest possible level while minimising impact on their other objectives and priorities, and the control owner, who must affect the control within the investment provided to them by the chief(s). When fully realised by a capable chief, this tension has the effect of optimising the investment in controls.

To illustrate, the chief(s) have delegated accountability to the BOM to manage the above risk along with the delegation to manage the border operations and meet productivity targets. It is, therefore, within the risk owner's best interests to increase the controls on risk while trying to reduce the impact on their productivity targets. An option would be to seek additional CCTV cameras from the security manager to maximise the visibility of all parts of the border clearance area. In contrast, the control owner needs to be able to effect the control within the resourcing provided to them, and if their discretionary funding is insufficient to install new cameras, then an impasse is reached. We propose then that this impasse or tension then creates a point of escalation to the chief(s) because the parameters under which they have delegated the risk to be managed have conflicted with the parameters they have delegated for the controls (i.e. the budget for cameras). Since they have created this tension, from a governance perspective, it is the chief(s) that should resolve the tension, by either accepting the risk level without the cameras or investing further resourcing into the security manager to procure more cameras (amongst other options). In this way, the tension both draws from and enhances the "capability" of the chief(s) as guardians who manage exceptions where two delegated parameters cannot be simultaneously met.

As part of the system of capable guardianship, the chief(s) must be capable of exercising control over the management of insider risk, whilst limiting the impact on their span of attention. In part, this is achieved by delegating the management of risk and controls to the risk owners and control owners. However, they must also ensure that the assessment of risk and the administration of controls is effective at managing the risks, whilst equally limiting the effects on their span of attention. This is achieved by delegating accountability for assurance to the assurer.

As set out in Chapter 9, control assurance provides a system that examines controls and ensures that they are functioning as designed and that the design is effective at mitigating the targeted insider risk. There are two reasons for separating the assurer from the risk owner and control owner. The first is the practical maintenance of an effective span of control and attention. Using the above example, the BOM has a span of control and attention which is already dedicated to the management of the border operations of the organisation and to managing the risk. Bearing in mind the typologies of assurance activity set out in Chapter 9, the addition of delegated accountability for those assurance activities on the risks within the border functions would likely go beyond the effective span of control or attention of the risk owner. Secondly, there is an inherent conflict between the ownership of risk and control and the undertaking of assurance on the same risk and controls. In effect, if the risk owner relies upon the control environment to manage the risk and the control owner effects the control in a particular manner, then it is reasonable to presume that both consider that the risk is being effectively managed, and the relevant control is functioning as intended (and effectively). As we set out in Chapter 9, this is the reason for creating independent lines of assurance that can critically examine the assessment of risk and utilise the assurance tools and techniques we set out to evaluate the effectiveness of those controls and the limits of that effectiveness. It is for this reason that we classify the assurer as a separate guardian that operates in concert with the risk owner and control owner as part of the broader guardianship against insider risk. The assurer then provides assurance to the chief(s) that the control environment is effective or, where further investment is required to reduce the insider risk to an acceptable level, within the organisation's tolerances. Equally, such assurance provides direct insight to the risk owner and the control owner to enhance the control environment or the execution of a particular control.

In our hypothetical border control agency, the risk owner relies upon the CCTV to manage the risk of illicit border clearances, along with a detailed decision record that would enable the detection of anomalies in decision-making. Let us propose then that the assurer undertakes performance tests and threshold pressure tests on these controls. Such tests identify several problematic areas which could be used by malicious insiders to obscure illicit border clearances. Further, the decision records are so inconsistently recorded in the course of normal business that anomalies in decision-making would be statistically challenging to identify. The results of these tests would (potentially) build the business case for additional cameras to cover obscured areas, along with prompting the control owner (who in this case is also the risk owner: the BOM) to improve practices around decision-recording along with quality assurance sampling of decision records to ensure that record quality is improved. In this manner, the assurer provides guardianship to the system by providing the stimulus for ongoing improvements to the system and guarding against the gulf between work-as-done and the proxies for work-as-done that we described in Chapter 9.

Let us turn then briefly to the relationship with the enforcer. As we described in Chapter 7, there are a class of controls which are "responsive", serving to resolve the insider risk incident after it has occurred. These controls include measures for internal investigation and penalisation for malicious or reckless insider acts, along with controls which mitigate the harm of the action after it has occurred. In the case of organisations, which are in themselves not criminal enforcement agencies, in most jurisdictions the investigation and prosecution of criminal insider acts will need to be referred to policing organisations and prosecutorial agencies to pursue criminal charges. The relationship between the internal control owner and the enforcer turns then to the quality of the referral of criminal matters to the enforcer. The quality of evidence, the timeliness of referral, and to referral to the correct agency with jurisdiction will all reasonably impact on the effectiveness of criminal prosecution and the prospects for charges to be upheld. Additionally, for the enforcer to be a capable guardian, the quality of their evidence handling, investigative skill, and ability to present probative prosecutorial evidence will impact on the success and, therefore, the specific and general deterrent effects of prosecutions. Equally, other powers such as the confiscation of criminal proceeds may have a diminishing effect on the motivation for malicious insider activity.

In contrast, the absence of a capable enforcement agency would severely reduce the disincentives for criminal insider activities, limiting their investigation and abrogating any negative consequences for insiders beyond those consequences that a non-enforcement agency has the power to impose (such as termination of employment). Equally, the capability of the organisation's control owner responsible for the internal investigation and referral of matters to enforcement actors plays a role in the capability of the enforcer to detect and investigate serious or systemic insider threats which warrant criminal investigation and prosecution. An incapable organisation may not collect and handle evidence effectively or may not identify matters which warrant criminal investigation. These faults would ultimately diminish the capability of the enforcer and therefore the deterrent effect of their guardianship of the system.

Drawing again on our fictitious border control agency, let us propose that the organisation exists in one of the many jurisdictions in which corruption is criminalised, both in terms of the acceptance of a bribe to make an illicit clearance decision and, on the other side, the act of offering the bribe by the beneficiary. Firstly, the detection of such activity may primarily rest with the border agency itself through controls we identified in Chapter 7: such as decision anomaly detection, CCTV monitoring, and reporting channels for other staff. For the criminal activity to be reported to the law enforcement agency (the enforcer) these controls need to be sound and effective but also need to be complemented by the capability to refer matters to law enforcement effectively. This may consist of undertaking preliminary investigations and compiling evidence. Law enforcement agencies themselves must prioritise their resources against the highest value criminal investigations and prosecutions. These agencies use a variety of prioritisation tools to determine whether an investigation is worthy of pursuit, including triage and prioritisation matrices and resource allocation tools, for example, assessing potential cases against the level alignment to national criminal investigation priorities (such as drug crime and counter-terrorism, or against the value of losses and potential recovery of criminal proceeds). The capability of our fictitious border agency to present compelling demonstration of alignment to those priorities will determine whether investigation is pursued or not.

Logically then, high-value investigations could be foregone, or lower-priority investigations pursued based on the prioritisation tool, but equally on the basis of the capability of the organisation to develop a compelling case. The creation of a "capable guardian" of the enforcer, therefore, equally rests with the enforcer and the referrer, particularly in the case of insider risk which, though a systemic issue, is particular to the organisation, its assets, and vulnerabilities.

This brings us to the last of our proposed guardians: the steward. Given the breadth of responsibilities of the other guardians, it would be reasonable to conjecture on the need for a further guardian role within the insider risk management system. In our view, the need for the steward of the system is justified again because of the limits to the span of control and span of attention of the other guardians.

As set out above, we propose that the insider risk management system is a complex one. When considering a complex organisation there may be a significant number of permutations and risk relationships between the assets, roles, opportunities, beneficiaries, and motivations within the organisation, each creating a unique risk scenario for the organisation. The relationship between each of the risk typologies and the control environment is also not simple. A risk will be managed by a suite of different controls which collectively prevent, detect, and respond to the particular risk event. Controls themselves may control more than one risk: for example CCTV acting to mitigate illicit clearance decisions and also theft. Therefore, the permutations of relationships between risk and controls are also complex.

As illustrated in Figure 11.4, even with three risks only, there exists a complex set of relationships between the risks, risk owners, and a varied set of control owners.

This complexity of the system, in our view, has several implications for managing insider threat:

- The span of attention required to manage a system of this complexity is high, requiring investment of time and effort to understand the risks and their drivers and the control environment that mitigates the risk.
- At scale, the complexity requires a distribution of accountability; otherwise the span of attention and span of control would exceed an individual's capability for attention. Hence more complex organisations, in the same way that they will have more assets in more structural lines of accountability, will have more risk owners and control owners distributed across the organisation.
- The complexity requires a model to codify the body of knowledge around insider risk as we have done. This in turn requires a level of expertise to engage with such a codified body of knowledge.

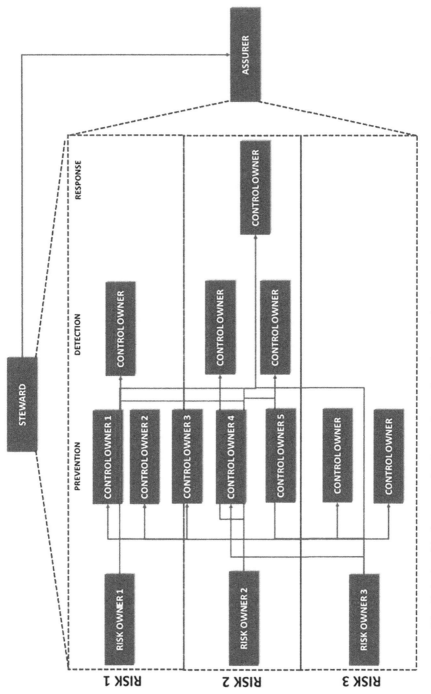

FIGURE 11.4 The Relationship between the Stewards: Risk and Control

The upshot is that managing the insider risk across an organisation along with the other domains of responsibility would, we argue, exceed the effective span of attention of the chief(s) if not with the support of another actor who would bring a dedicated span of attention to the management of the risk. We propose, therefore, that a systemic approach to insider threat must have a steward within the organisation with responsibility for the overall orchestration of the insider risk management system.

There is a strong rationale for a separation between the steward and the risk owners and control owners within the system. In respect of risk owners, as we've suggested above, this individual, ideally, would be the person with senior accountability for the asset at risk; this creates two compelling reasons for separation:

- The first is simply the span of control and attention. Given the risk owners' responsibility for a function of the organisation, we argue it would be ineffective for risk owners generally to develop the expertise and knowledge base to assess, manage, and evaluate risk without the support of a dedicated expert function within the organisation. Furthermore, given there are likely to be more than a single risk owner in any organisation of sufficient size, the distribution of risk assessment, management, and evaluation would create ad hoc discrete approaches without standardisation. As we'll set out below, the risk register we propose is a crucial tool for managing risk at a whole-of-organisation level, which relies on a standardisation of data ontology and taxonomy. A distributed approach to stewardship would therefore not function effectively.
- The second is that there is an inherent tension between the insider risk controls and other organisational objectives. As we set out in Chapter 9, the implementation of controls to protect against insider risk does not come without downsides, including direct costs, impacts on productivity, and client relationships. The risk owners, with responsibility for managing core business objectives, are arguably inherently more incentivised to achieve those business objectives given that the objectives are more certain than insider risk which, by definition, is the "effect of uncertainty". For example, if a senior manager can achieve a high output of license decisions, and the level of productivity for those decisions is measured, the imposition of a control which reduces productivity to manage an uncertain risk that a person may grant illicit licenses is arguably not well incentivised. There is evidence to support this proposition, where 81% of organisations modified their risk controls after an event had occurred (Association of Certified Fraud Examiners, 2022). Arguably, this is because the incentive to invest in those controls only became apparent through the losses accrued as a result of the event (at this point of course the new controls have inherently less value than they would have had if they had prevented

the losses). From our perspective then, a separate accountability for insider risk whose performance is measured on the success of insider risk controls creates a new set of incentives which are likely to enhance risk control within the organisation. This being said, such incentives equally create drawbacks. The role of the steward is to control the overall risk to an acceptable level. Arguably, this creates an incentive to impose as much control on the system as possible, which could be as damaging or more damaging to the objectives of the organisation, for example if it creates severe limits on productivity without a greater return in terms of reduced losses.

In sum, these rationales justify the need for a separate guardian delegated with oversight of the system as a whole by the chief(s) and independent from other organisational interests. The capability of this guardian is then defined by their expertise in systemically analysing risk and supporting the chief(s) to manage that risk with the lowest possible investment.

What then is the interaction between the steward and the other guardians in our proposed system of guardianship?

A systemic approach implies consistency of practice, ontology, and taxonomy across the organisation, which enables risk to be uniformly and coherently assessed. We contend that this requires a guardian to preserve and maintain the ontology of insider risk across the organisation, providing stewardship over the language which is used to describe the objects which comprise insider risk. As we've argued in previous chapters, the language of asset, opportunity, beneficiary, asset, and motivation, along with all the sub-components of these concepts, provides a coherent classification model for describing risk to the organisation and its objectives.

We contend that the preservation of the language and structure of insider risk requires an expert guardian, guardianship which is best delegated by the chief(s) and vested in the steward. Equally, as set out below, the undertaking of the risk assessment requires a consistent approach to classification and to the process, which results in a consistent model of relative risks for the organisation. The practice of setting and maintaining standards for the risk assessment, equally, then requires a guardian which, in our view, rests with the steward delegated by the chief(s) to oversee the insider risk system as a whole.

The application of these standards of risk assessment and risk ontology, in turn, inform the language that risk owners use to comprehend the nature of the risk and through that understanding to appreciate the most appropriate controls to manage the risk at the lowest impact on the organisation's broader objectives. Likewise, the relationship between the risk owner and the control may not be readily evident except in the context of the examination of risk.

For example, drawing from our hypothetical border agency, the risk of a border officer making an illicit clearance decision is owned by the border operations manager, while the CCTV is managed by the security manager. Arguably, in the context of business activities, their roles do not relate to one another strongly. Instead, the nomenclature of risk owner and control owner is a convention used to describe their relationship from a risk perspective, in this case with focus on insider risk. It is through the assessment of risk and the assignment of ownership that these roles and relationships are created. This implies that the delegation of these relationships must follow the assessment of risk, at least in an ultimate sense. Once risk owners have been identified this then may create a baseline from which change occurs, as opposed to the initial undertaking of the assessment. Given this, it makes sense that through the stewardship of the risk assessment, the steward is responsible for identifying the appropriate owners of risk and the owners of the controls which may treat the risk. Indeed, the relationship between the risk and the control establishes the relationship between the risk owner and the control owner.

The role of the steward is intrinsically linked with the application of the model to assess and manage risk under a systemic approach. The following sections express the practice of utilising the model. We do this to provide the reader with a deep understanding of risk and, from that understanding, examine how one may mitigate the risk at the lower practicable cost to the organisation and its objectives.

While we have set out the seven guardians in a way that implies they are different individuals, in reality they are simply different conceptual roles, some of which could be acquitted by the same individual. In a simple organisation, for example, the chief may decide to act directly as the steward of the system or may directly manage the risk.

Risk assessment and risk register

Risk assessment

As set out in Chapter 2, the concept of risk as "the effect of uncertainty on objectives" provides a foundation for exploring insider activity, recognising that its emergence in an organisational context is the uncertain confluence of valuable assets, opportunity, motivation, and beneficiaries. Given uncertainty is central to risk, there is no absolute measure of the risk of a specific event occurring unless that event is either entirely impossible or conversely is certain. All other events, therefore, occur on a continuum of probability and impact. Plainly the insider risk examples we have outlined, such as the improper grant of a license, or misuse of protected information are not entirely impossible given both have occurred in reality, nor are they certain to occur in a certain set of circumstances.

Risk instead is relative rather than absolute; the circumstances make an event more or less probable with more or less impact when compared with the following:

1. The same event occurring with a different set of circumstances: for example the improper grant of a licence is more probable where the opportunities to do so are greater and of greater impact where the license is used for organised criminal purposes.
2. Two different events whose relative probability and impact can be compared by using a standardised assessment: for example the harm of an improper grant of a visa whose probability is higher than the improper clearance of goods, but whose impact on the overall organisational mission is lower.

Our rationale is one of utility. The underlying purpose for exploring risk is the allocation of finite resources to mitigate the effect of those uncertain events. Arguably, with sufficient research, it may be possible to calculate the absolute probability of an insider risk event for a transaction based upon the volume of transactions along with opportunities and other factors. However, this absolute probability would not be of great use when determining whether to invest resources in mitigating the risk when compared to the option of mitigating an entirely different risk. The absolute probability would be noteworthy but would not be practically useful to mitigate risk at an organisational level.

In contrast, being able to describe an event as more probable or less probable than another event within an order of magnitude rather than at an absolute level and similarly to calculate impact on a relative scale will assist with decisions on allocating resources to risks with higher relative probabilities and impacts.

This logic then flows through to our approach to assessing insider risk, which we base on a scoring approach drawing on our analysis from the previous chapters. As we proposed earlier, setting out assets, opportunities, and beneficiaries (each acting as drivers of risk) allows us, in relative terms (using a simple scoring system), to convert the qualified assessment of the risk drivers into quantifiable data, whilst avoiding the pitfalls of attempting to determine absolute levels of probability and impact. The aggregate score of all the factors which create relative levels of probability and impact provides an overall relative level of risk for each permutation of risk for the organisation.

Methodology of assessment

Pure opportunity

The pure opportunity model for describing risk focuses on the two variables of the role and the opportunity in respect of an asset, thus providing a measure of the inherent opportunity for a specific role to commit a malicious or inadvertent insider action.

The methodology for assessing the risk can be described as follows:

For each combination of Asset and Role, the Opportunity Risk level OR_1 is equal to the sum of the likelihood/probability score L_1 plus the Consequence/Impact Score C_1:

$$OR_1 = L_1 + C_1$$

We would represent another combination of Asset and Role as

$$OR_2 = L_2 + C_2$$

L is calculated as the sum of the following:

- *The opportunity scores*: scores for each of the opportunity factors, Authority (Au_1), Access (Ac_1), Visibility (V_1), Traceability (T_1), Certainty (Ct_1).

C is calculated as the sum of the following:

- The asset value score (Av_1).

Thus, the expanded equation is

$$OR_1 = (Au_1 + Ac_1 + V_1 + T_1 + Ct_1) + Av_1$$

In relation to the Asset, it is worth recalling that this needs to be set out in terms of the Object–Decision or Object–Action relationship (as discussed in Chapter 3). Additionally, Asset value is the combination of the mission criticality of the Asset and the harm if it were compromised. We provide examples.

Example 1

OR_1 is the illicit grant (the decision) of a license (the object) by a license-processing officer (the role).

If the grant of a license has a high asset value of 4 (on a four-point scale) due to its mission criticality to the organisation and the potential economic and safety harms from unlicensed activities (of whatever kind), the opportunity factors are as follows:

- A high level of authority over the decision which is made under "delegated authority possessed with discretion within parameters and guided by decision policy or guidance", for an Au_1 score of 3 on a four-point scale (see Table 4.1).
- A moderate level of access where "access to the decision is controlled in terms of physical or ICT access control", for an Ac_1 score of 2 on a four-point scale (see Table 4.2).

- A moderate level of visibility involving an "environment in which the decision is taken is incidentally visible to others if they are present or active within the relevant system", for a V_1 score of 3 on a four-point scale (see Table 4.3).
- A high level of traceability where the "decision and supporting evidence is consistently and completely recorded albeit at the discretion of the decision-maker. The record is stored for less than 3 years", for a T_1 score of 2 on a four-point scale (see Table 4.4).
- Finally, there is a low level of certainty which is due to the random allocation of license decisions resulting in "a less than 1:20 chance of being able to make a decision in which the role has a personal interest", for a Ct_1 score of 1 on a four-point scale (see Table 4.5).

OR_1, therefore, is $(Au_1=3 + Ac_1=2 + V_1=3 + T_1=2 + Ct_1=1) + (Av_1=4) = 15$ of a total possible score of 24.

Example 2

For our second example let's change a single of our core variables, the role, which this time will be a license-processing team leader.

OR_2 is the illicit grant (the decision) of a license (the object) by a license-processing team leader (the role).

The license value is unchanged (high asset value of 4 on a four-point scale) due to its mission criticality to the organisation.

The opportunity factors are as follows:

- A very high level of authority over the decision which is made under "sole authority possessed by an individual with high level of discretion and low level of decision policy or guidance" with the team leader having greater authority to take on and make grant decisions to deal with infrequent circumstances with minimal guidance, for an Au_2 score of 4 on a four-point scale (see Table 4.1).
- An unchanged moderate level of access where "access to the decision is controlled in terms of physical or ICT access control", for an Ac_2 score of 2 on a four-point scale (see Table 4.2).
- An unchanged moderate level of visibility involving an "environment in which the decision taken is incidentally visible to others if they are present or active within the relevant system", for a V_2 score of 3 on a four-point scale (see Table 4.3).
- An unchanged high level of traceability where "decision and supporting evidence is consistently and completely recorded albeit at the discretion of the decision-maker. The record is stored for less than 3 years", for a T_2 score of 2 on a four-point scale (see Table 4.4).
- Finally, there is a very high level of certainty because the team leader has the ability to self-allocate decisions in order to deal with exceptional cases

and, therefore, has "a 1:1 chance of being able to make a decision in which the role has a personal interest", for a Ct_2 score of 4 on a four-point scale (see Table 4.5).

OR_2 is $(Au_2=4 + Ac_2=2 + V_2=3 + T_2=2 + Ct_2=4) + (Av_2=4) = 18$ of a total possible score of 24.

Example 3

For our third example, we retain the same decision object and the license, but this time rather than granting of the license the decision is the cancellation of the license.

OR_3 is the illicit or inadvertent cancellation (the decision) of a license (the object) by a license-processing officer (the role).

The license cancellation has a lower asset value of 2 on a four-point scale: licensing remains mission critical to the organisation and there would be a level of reputational harm for incorrect cancellations.

The opportunity factors are now as follows:

- A low level of authority where the license-processing officer is only the "initiator of decisions with separation of duties, providing an initial decision or recommendation to the ultimate decision maker", with the team leader finalising decisions, for an Au_3 score of 1 on a four-point scale (see Table 4.1).
- An unchanged moderate level of access where "access to the decision is controlled in terms of physical or ICT access control", for an Ac_3 score of 2 on a four-point scale (see Table 4.2).
- The fact that there is a separation of duties also raises the level of visibility providing "the allocation and making of the decision is monitored in real-time". This is because the team leader effectively monitors each decision through the separation of duties, resulting in a V_3 score of 1 on a four-point scale (see Table 4.3).
- There is now a very high level of traceability where "complete decision and supporting evidence is recorded, including automatic audit logging. The record is stored for at least 3 years". This is because the referral of a cancellation decision to a second decision-maker requires sufficient evidence to be presented for the final decision-maker to make the decision, for a T_3 score of 1 on a four-point scale (see Table 4.4).
- Finally, there is a moderate level of certainty because only a few of the officers can make cancellation decisions. However, the volume of these decisions is also low resulting in "a between 1:20 and 1:10 chance of being able to make a decision in which the role has a personal interest", for a Ct_3 score of 2 on a four-point scale (see Table 4.5).

OR_3 is $(Au_3=1 + Ac_3=2 + V_3=1 + T_3=1 + Ct_2=2) + (Av_3= 2) = 9$ of a total possible score of 24.

Example 4

In our final example we change our core variable completely. This time we will draw back on our repeated border clearance example.

OR_4 is the illicit granting (the decision) of border clearance (the object) by a border officer (the role).

In this example we assume that the border clearance has a high asset value of 4 on a four-point scale, due to its mission criticality to the border organisation.

The opportunity factors are as follows:

- A high level of authority over the decision which is made under "delegated authority possessed with discretion within parameters and guided by decision policy or guidance", for an Au_4 score of 3 on a four-point scale (see Table 4.1).
- A moderate level of access where "access to the decision is controlled in terms of physical or ICT access control", for an Ac_4 score of 2 on a four-point scale (see Table 4.2).
- A moderate level of visibility involving actively monitored CCTV cameras (albeit with some blind spots) and a high level of traffic to monitor at the border resulting in an "environment in which the decision is taken is intermittently monitored", for a V_4 score of 2 on a four-point scale (see Table 4.3).
- A moderate level of traceability where, due to the high volume and physical nature of the border inspection and clearance process, the "decision and supporting evidence is inconsistently or incompletely recorded", for a T_4 score of 3 on a four-point scale (see Table 4.4).
- Finally, there is a moderate level of certainty which is due to the random arrival of persons at the border, coupled with the border officer's ability to physically approach a person (including an insider beneficiary) to initiate the clearance, resulting in "a 1:10 or higher chance of being able to make a decision in which the role has a personal interest", for a Ct_2 score of 2 on a four-point scale (see Table 4.5).

OR_4 is $(Au_4=3 + Ac_1=2 + V_1=2 + T_1=3 + Ct_1=2) + (Av_1=4) = 16$ of a total possible score of 24.

As these examples illustrate, a change in the core insider risk variables of role and asset result in flow on changes in the opportunity factor variables. This highlights differences in the risk profile between different insider risks on a relative rather than on an absolute basis. While it is evident through our examples above, it is nonetheless worthwhile emphasising the following risk relativity between our risks: $OR_2 > OR_4 > OR_1 > OR_3$.

Based purely on the level of opportunity available to the different roles, we would conclude that the greatest level of pure opportunity risk is OR_2: "the illicit grant (the decision) of a license (the object) by a license processing team leader (the role)", while the lowest relative level of risk is OR_3: "the illicit or inadvertent cancellation (the decision) of a license (the object) by a license processing officer (the role)".

Importantly, the key concepts of this risk model can be applied to any form of organisation based on the classification of its assets and roles, and the assessment of the relative level of opportunity associated with each combination of those two variables.

Equally important, while we argue that the meta-elements of the model including the opportunity factors are complete and provide a structured model for assessing insider risk, the specific descriptions and quantification of those different factors can be tailored subject to further assessments and indeed further research into the effects of each of these factors on the likelihood and impact of insider risk. Furthermore, it is our view that additional research may also establish the weighted impact of these factors on the risk. For example, does a change in visibility have a higher or exponential impact on the likelihood of the risk when compared with the changes in the traceability variable. It is likely, for example, that the "certainty" variable has a disproportionate impact on the likelihood of insider threat for any risk requiring access to a specific asset: such as a particular decision.

We will outline the data model further below. However, before that it is worth noting that even the simple data above can be represented in different ways to provide different perspectives on insider risk. As above, we can illustrate the relative risk as a whole of risk (based purely on opportunity), that is, the relativity of all permutations of asset and role relative to opportunity. Equally though, the same data could be presented to illustrate the relative risk for each role type.

For example, as seen above, the risk associated with the role of license-processing officer is lesser than the license-processing team leader's for the same asset type. Conceived at a whole-of-organisation level, the relative opportunity risk associated with each role type may provide insight on the relative level of investment in general controls based on the level of risk associated with the role. An example could be applying additional levels of due diligence, security, and suitability screening to roles which are of a higher risk as compared to other roles.

Opportunity/beneficiary

As set out above, the pure opportunity model utilises the combination of asset and role to assess the variability of opportunity risk associated with those combinations.

The opportunity/beneficiary model is the inclusion of a third core variable to the risk equation, which then includes the beneficiary sub-variables to the risk equation. This model then enables not only the internal vulnerability perspective on the risk but, by including beneficiaries, includes an external threat perspective onto the risk assessment.

The methodology for assessing the risk under the opportunity and beneficiary approach can be described as follows:

For each combination of Asset and Role and Beneficiary the risk level OBR_1 is equal to the sum of the Likelihood/Probability Score L plus the Consequence/Impact Score C:

$$OBR_1 = L_1 + C_1$$

We represent another combination of Asset and Role and Beneficiary as

$$OBR_2 = L_2 + C_2$$

L is calculated as the sum of

- The opportunity scores: scores for each of the opportunity factors, authority (Au_1), access (Ac_1), visibility (V_1), traceability (T_1), certainty (Ct_1).
- The beneficiary capability (Cp_1) and interaction (It_1)

C is calculated as the sum of

- The asset value score (Av_1),
- The beneficiary intent score (In_1).

Thus, the expanded equation is

$$OBR_1 = (Au_1 + Ac_1 + V_1 + T_1 + Ct_1 + Cp_1 + It_1) + (Av_1 + In_1)$$

We use three examples drawing on our licensing example above to illustrate the addition of the beneficiary to the equation.

Example 1

Let us propose that OBR_1 is the illicit grant (the decision) of a license (the object) by a license-processing team leader (the role) for the benefit of an applicant (the beneficiary).

The license remains unchanged with a high asset value of 4 on a four-point scale due to its mission criticality to the organisation.

The opportunity factors are as they were previously:

- A very high level of authority over the decision which is made under "sole authority possessed by an individual with a high level of discretion and low level of decision policy or guidance" with the team leader having greater authority to take on and make grant decisions to deal with infrequent circumstances with minimal guidance, for an Au_1 score of 4 on a four-point scale (see Table 4.1).

- An unchanged moderate level of access where "access to the decision is controlled in terms of physical or ICT access control", for an Ac_1 score of 2 on a four-point scale (see Table 4.2).
- An unchanged moderate level of visibility involving an "environment in which the decision is taken is incidentally visible to others if they are present or active within the relevant system", for a V_1 score of 3 on a four-point scale (see Table 4.3).
- An unchanged high level of traceability where "decision and supporting evidence is consistently and completely recorded albeit at the discretion of the decision-maker. The record is stored for less than 3 years", for a T_1 score of 2 on a four-point scale (see Table 4.4).
- Finally, there is a very high level of certainty because the team leader has the ability to self-allocated decisions in order to deal with exceptional cases and, therefore, has "a 1:1 chance of being able to make a decision in which the role has a personal interest", for a Ct_1 score of 4 on a four-point scale (see Table 4.5).

The Beneficiary scores are as follows:

- In terms of interaction, the applicant has "a distant relationship with transient interaction for a limited number of interactions". Once the license has been granted to them, they have received the benefit they sought. This results in It_1 score of 1 on a three-point scale (see Table 5.1).
- In terms of intent, the applicant has a non-ongoing and non-adversarial intent. Their desire to receive a license is not directly adversarial to the organisation and their intent will come to a conclusion once the license has been granted. This results in an In_1 score of 1 on a four-point scale (see Table 5.2).
- Finally, in terms of capability, the applicant "has limited assets at their disposal to induce an insider to act on their behalf. The beneficiary has limited or no general influence or authority", resulting in a Cp_1 score of 1 on a three-point scale (see Table 5.3).

OBR_1 is $(Au_1=4 + Ac_1=2 + V_1=3 + T_1=2 + Ct_1=4 + Cp_1=1 + It_1=1) + (Av_1=4 + In_1=1) = 21$ of a total possible score of 34.

Example 2

For our second example, let's maintain the same role and asset. Thus, OBR_2 is the illicit grant (the decision) of a license (the object) by a license-processing team leader (the role), but this time for the for the benefit of a license agent (the beneficiary). We assume a license agent runs a business whose purpose is to facilitate the applications for and granting of licenses, and that increased grants result in more customers.

The license is unchanged and has a high asset value of 4 on a four-point scale, due to its mission criticality to the organisation.

The opportunity factors are again as previously described:

- A very high level of authority over the decision which is made under "sole authority possessed by individual with a high level of discretion and a low level of decision policy or guidance", with the team leader having greater authority to take on and make grant decisions to deal with infrequent circumstances with minimal guidance, for an Au_2 score of 4 on a four-point scale (see Table 4.1).
- An unchanged moderate level of access where "access to the decision is controlled in terms of physical or ICT access control", for an Ac_2 score of 2 on a four-point scale (see Table 4.2).
- An unchanged moderate level of visibility involving an "environment in which the decision is taken is incidentally visible to others if they are present or active within the relevant system", for a V_2 score of 3 on a four-point scale (see Table 4.3).
- An unchanged high level of traceability where "decision and supporting evidence is consistently and completely recorded albeit at the discretion of the decision-maker. The record is stored for less than 3 years", for a T_2 score of 2 on a four-point scale (see Table 4.4).
- Finally, there is a very high level of certainty because the team leader has the ability to self-allocated decisions in order to deal with exceptional cases and therefore has "a 1:1 chance of being able to make a decision in which the role has a personal interest", for a Ct_2 score of 4 on a four-point scale (see Table 4.5).

The beneficiary scores are as follows:

- In terms of interaction, the licensing agent has "close and repeated interactions between the role and potential beneficiaries as part of normal activities of the role. The role may also act in an agency or representative capacity for the potential beneficiary". Given their role is to seek the grant of licenses in an ongoing way, their interactions with individual license-processing team leaders is likely to be repeated. This results in a It_2 score of 3 on a three-point scale (see Table 5.1).
- In terms of intent, the licensing agent has an ongoing and non-adversarial intent. They will have an ongoing intent to for illicit licenses to be granted. However, their desire to receive licenses is not directly adversarial to the objectives of the organisation. This results in an In_2 score of 2 on a four-point scale (see Table 5.2).

- Finally, in terms of capability, the license agent "has access to resources and connections to influence insiders though restricted to limited interactions or domains of the organisation or would primarily be opportunistic". This is because the license agent has the resources to bribe or provide kickbacks to the team leader, resulting in a Cp_2 score of 2 on a three-point scale (see Table 5.3).

OBR_2 is $(Au_2=4 + Ac_2=2 + V_2=3 + T_2=2 + Ct_2=4 + Cp_2=2 + It_2=3) + (Av_2=4 + In_2=2) = 25$ of a total possible score of 34.

Example 3

In our final example, we maintain the same role and asset. However, we incorporate a new beneficiary. Therefore, OBR_3 is the illicit grant (the decision) of a license (the object) by a license-processing team leader (the role), but this time for the for the benefit of an organised crime gang (OCG) (the beneficiary). Let's assume the OCG seeks the licenses to facilitate other serious criminal activities that create harm to objectives of the licensing authority.

The license continues to have a high asset value of 4 on a four-point scale due to its mission criticality to the organisation.

The opportunity factors are again as they were in earlier examples:

- A very high level of authority over the decision which is made under "sole authority possessed by individual with high level of discretion and low level of decision policy or guidance" with the team leader having greater authority to take on and make grant decisions to deal with infrequent circumstances with minimal guidance, for an Au_3 score of 4 on a four-point scale (see Table 4.1).
- An unchanged moderate level of access with "access to the decision controlled in terms of physical or ICT access control", for an Ac_3 score of 2 on a four-point scale (see Table 4.2).
- An unchanged moderate level of visibility involving an "environment in which the decision is taken is incidentally visible to others if they are present or active within the relevant system", for a V_3 score of 3 on a four-point scale (see Table 4.3).
- An unchanged high level of traceability where "decision and supporting evidence is consistently and completely recorded albeit at the discretion of the decision-maker. The record is stored for less than 3 years", for a T_3 score of 2 on a four-point scale (see Table 4.4).
- Finally, there is a very high level of certainty because the team leader has the ability to self-allocated decisions in order to deal with exceptional cases and therefore has "a 1:1 chance of being able to make a decision in which the role has a personal interest", for a Ct_3 score of 4 on a four-point scale (see Table 4.5).

The beneficiary scores are as follows:

- In terms of Interaction, the OCG can have "close and repeated interactions between the role and potential beneficiaries as part of the normal business of the role". Given their intention is to seek multiple illicit licenses to further the criminal activities, it follows that there will be numerous systemic interactions. This results in a It_2 score of 3 on a three-point scale (see Table 5.1).
- In terms of intent, the OCG has an ongoing and adversarial intent. They will have an ongoing intent for illicit licenses to be granted. Their goal to receive licenses is directly adversarial to the objectives of the organisation. This results in an In_2 score of three on a four-point scale (see Table 5.2).
- Finally, in terms of capability, let's assume the OCG "has broad and systemic access to resources which can facilitate influencing or planting insiders within the organisation". This is because the OCG has significant resources to bribe, provide kickbacks, or threaten the team leader, resulting in a Cp_3 score of 3 on a three-point scale (see Table 5.3).

OBR1 is $(Au_3=4 + Ac_3=2 + V_3=3 + T_3=2 + Ct_3=4 + Cp_3=3 + It_3= 3) + (Av_3=4 + In_3=4) = 28$ of a total possible score of 34.

As the above examples highlight, the change of beneficiary within the risk assessment equation changes the underlying beneficiary variables creating a relative differentiation between the risk level even where the asset and the role remain fixed.

The simplicity of the equation belies its utility in being able to differentiate between risk areas and to focus control enhancement efforts on the highest level of risk. Additionally, adding a beneficiary layer to the model – as we'll see when we explore the data model – allows the relative comparison of risk by single beneficiary where they occur in association with different assets across the organisation. For example, the applicant and the license agent will only emerge in association with the license function of the organisation, whereas the OCG may have interests in a number of different assets including stealing financial assets or accessing personal information held by the organisation. This relatively higher risk may mean that countermeasures are directed more to these beneficiary actors, for example, directing more intelligence effort to infer their capability and intent, when compared with intelligence directed towards other actors.

Adding motivation

As set out in Chapter 6, while we consider that motivation is inherently less systemic than the other factors we have discussed throughout, motivation nonetheless provides a component which is worth considering through the risk assessment process to understand the relative risk of insider threat. The pressure and inducement elements of motivation occur at the individual rather than at the systemic organisational level (though they can be described consistently, which is valuable when describing controls as we did in Chapter 7). In contrast, the rationalisation factor may have some more systemic characteristics which we consider can be assessed and contribute to the understanding of risk at the whole-of-organisation level.

As argued in Chapter 6, rationalisation is "the assignment of logical or socially desirable motives for what people do so that they seem to have acted rightfully" (Geva, 2006, p. 143), which ultimately plays a role in the perpetuation of malicious insider actions. While the act of rationalisation in this context remains an individual one, the specific act of rationalisation may differ between individuals even given the same set of circumstances, for example, rationalising the grant of a benefit for political reasons versus rationalising the same grant of a benefit based on a perceived slight perpetrated by the organisation against the insider.

As discussed above, the role is a key variable in the risk equation, particularly changing the nature of the opportunity factor of the risk. Different roles will connect to differently valued organisational assets (the license and the license-processing officer versus the clearance decision and the border officer). These roles, in turn, are occupied by individuals and exist in an organisational structure and societal context. In our view, it is those contexts which may create a plausible differential in the potential for rationalisation which may contribute to a relative variation in the profile of the risk. For example, it is plausible that a politically contentious business activity, such as a foreign relations function, will create a greater level of politically motivated genuine dilemma-based rationalisation for insider actions than for example an uncontentious administrative function and the roles that fit within.

Similarly, as we touched on earlier, staff satisfaction, wellbeing, and engagement may be an indicator of an environment in which the "no-problem-based rationalisation" of malicious insider acts is more likely to be successful. As a result, staff satisfaction and engagements surveys routinely conducted by organisations take on another character when considered through the lens of insider risk. Here, for example, areas of an organisation which may be perceived by employees to be of less importance may also be environments in which insiders can successfully rationalise and, therefore, perpetuate harmful insider activity (as they may also perceive the risk prevention mechanisms to be a little lax).

As these brief examples illustrate, within an organisational context, the environment in which the roles operate may create a plausible and rational differential in the level of risk, based on whether the environment is one in which the likelihood of successful rationalisation is higher or lower. That being said, it is our view that the quantification of this rationalisation differential and inclusion within the risk equation we propose above would be of limited value. Further, *it* may skew the assessment of the risk. The reason for this judgement is that without further research, it is not clear whether the different forms and drivers of rationalisation create different calibres of motivation. For example, is a political motivation more likely to create and perpetuate malicious acts than workplace disgruntlement or a permissive culture towards minor corruption?

In addition to this gap in knowledge, rationalisation, as a variable, does not function in the same fashion as the other key variables in the model do – asset, role, and beneficiary – which create change in the dependent opportunity variables and beneficiary variables. Instead, rationalisation is a largely an independent variable which impacts on the potential risk associated with the individuals occupying a set of roles and their individual and collective likelihood of committing malicious insider acts. Additionally, the instances of the other key variables are mutually exclusive thereby creating different and distinctive risk scenarios: a particular role is distinct from another role, an asset is distinct from another asset, and a beneficiary type is distinct from another beneficiary type. While a single person could occupy two (or more) roles, or a single entity could be two (or more) beneficiary types, the risk profile, however, will be different depending on which role or beneficiary type those entities are exercising. For example, a person could potentially exercise the functions of both the licensing processing officer and the licensing processing team leader. Because our concern is the risk profile of the role rather than the individual, the relative risk between these two roles does not change.

If we concern ourselves with the individual, for example by implementing higher levels of security screening for higher risk roles, then the individual would be captured as higher risk by virtue of fulfilling the higher risk role rather than due to their personal characteristics. The same can be said for beneficiaries. Because they are typologies rather than individual entities, the risk profile of those typologies will remain and the risk profile and thus countermeasures/controls used to manage the specific entity risk would be applied to the entity based on both its beneficiary types and risk profiles. In these circumstances, both risk drivers do not co-exist: that is, the person exercises one role or another, or the beneficiary is acting as one or another type. From a data perspective, these data objects are independent while they may be characteristics of a single entity.

In contrast, instances of the rationalisation variables can co-exist; a workplace can be both of low morale and politically contentious. It is plausible that in some circumstances these co-existing variables will have a compounding impact, which would increase the overall risk. In other circumstances the factors may act independently on different individuals. As a result, it is our view that rationalisation factors are not clear and reliable indicators.

Rather, they should be viewed as an overlay on which a higher level of risk can instead be inferred. From a decision-making perspective, this intelligence about the threats within the organisation may still serve to inform the chief(s) about investment priorities within the organisation. We consider this aspect of the risk should serve only as an overlay to extrapolate a risk differential. This is particularly the case in large, more complex or geographically diverse organisations where there is more likely to be variations in rationalising factors within different lines of business.

Role of the steward: Risk assessment

To have a complete appreciation of the permutations of risk requires a model which can deal with the complexities of the variables which drive greater or lesser relative probability and impact of the insider risk. For such a model to operate effectively requires a level of standardisation of classification, taxonomy, and ontology of the elements and the application of those model elements to the organisational context: that is, the specific assets, roles, and beneficiaries of the organisation and the related assessments of the sub-variables.

Additionally, as set out above, the risk assessment itself involves the technical application of these concepts to determine the relative probabilities and impacts of the different combinations of key variables.

It is our view, then, that the maintenance of these standards of information and assessment requires an owner within the organisation; hence, this is a key role we ascribe to the steward.

Risk register

Above, we proposed a risk assessment model which uses a qualitative and quantitative approach to provide a relative assessment of the risks for the different combinations of key variables. Even in a relatively simple organisation there are likely to be several combinations, while in more complex organisations the number of combinations will be substantial. Capturing this information, therefore, requires a structured repository of the data elements that drive risk.

While our assessment reduces the risk to a quantification exercise, in reality, the qualitative data is equally or more important when moving from assessing the relative risk to investing in countermeasures against the risk. This may be due to several reasons; firstly two risks may be assessed to have the same relative risk score while that score is the result of different variables: for example, higher authority versus higher visibility. Given these risks would have different drivers, the mitigations against such risks would equally be different to mitigate the relevant driver. Secondly, the countermeasures themselves create a variability in the drivers: for example, a level of assessed "visibility" will depend upon whether active CCTV is installed. Hence, the data on those controls is also important to understanding the current assessment of the risk.

As discussed earlier, it is our view that risk registers that have been or are currently used in the assessment of many risk typologies are inappropriate to the task at hand. Further, they lack the necessary complexity and nuance of capturing our systemic approach to understanding insider risk. Instead, therefore, we propose that the risk register for insider risk requires a more sophisticated data model, as we will set out below.

Conceptual data model

We stated earlier that insider risk is comprised of a set of classifiable factors or objects. The objects, however, exist not in isolation but in a defined relationship with one another. It is both the objects and the relationships between them that conceptually define the data model that we believe most effectively describes insider risk at a systemic level, whilst considering all its permutations. Effectively, this conceptual data model is the crystallisation of the complete insider risk model we have described up until now.

Importantly, the objects we describe, as set out in Figure 11.5, represent the name of the container in which each of the instances of those objects fits: for example, "role" describes all different types of roles, while the "instances" are license-processing officer and license-processing team leader. The reason for describing the objects at this level is that the instances will be particular to the organisation in question and the value of the model is that it can be applied to any organisational context.

It is also important to highlight that the conceptual model is not intended to be a perfect representation that would enable the direct construction of a database to capture the risk model. It does, however, provide strong guidance on the development of such a database to capture risk systemically. To fully comprehend the model we set out below, we encourage the reader to cross-reference with the detail provided for each element as described in earlier chapters.

To describe the conceptual model then, let us start where we started with our description of insider risk in Chapter 3: "assets".

Each asset type interacts with a particular role or roles. For example, the role that is empowered to make a particular decision has access to information types or makes use of a tangible or intangible assets. A single role is likely to have interactions with multiple assets, such as the decision or decisions they are empowered to make and the information which informs those decisions. A single asset may also have multiple roles that interact with it: for example, the license grant decision and the license-processing officer and

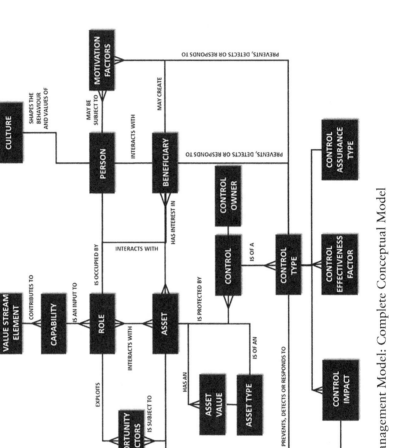

FIGURE 11.5 Insider Risk Management Model: Complete Conceptual Model

license-processing team leader. As a result, there is a many-to-many relationship between the asset and the role objects. Assets themselves then have a type: information, decision, tangible/intangible; they have a value based on their importance to the organisation.

The assets and the roles themselves are inputs (along with process) to the organisation's capabilities (as set out in Chapter 3). They are the enabling components that enable the organisation to execute a function. In turn, those capabilities contribute to the organisation's value streams which deliver value to customers or for public entities to deliver economic, social, or environmental value for society at large. This value creation then underpins the objectives of the organisation. The traceability between the asset to capability and the objective defines the value of the asset in terms of which assets contribute most to the achievement of the objective and which are more incidental to it.

The compromise of those assets (in our area of focus), due to insider activity, then creates typologies of harms: harms to the economy, society or environment, financial loss, reputational loss, harm to individual health and safety, privacy, and business continuity. The compromise of a single asset may create multiple harms and similarly in reverse a harm may be created by the compounding impact. There is, therefore, a many-to-many relationship between the assets and the harms. The harms then impact on the overall objectives of the organisation, either commercial or public.

The compromise to those assets is created when a person, who occupies a role, exploits the opportunities to successfully compromise the asset: for example, by illicitly granting the license. Different roles will have different interactions with the opportunity sub-variables (authority, access, visibility traceability, certainty), but each is unique in creating a one-to-many relationship. These data elements then also form the basis of the pure opportunity assessment of risk we have set out above.

The assets are protected from compromise by a set of controls of different types (prevention, detection, and response) and sub-types. The control sub-types are defined by the opportunity, beneficiary, and motivation sub-variables (e.g. prevent authority, detect intent, prevent rationalisation controls). These relationships provide traceability between the vulnerabilities of the assets and the controls which mitigate those vulnerabilities. The controls are also owned and effected by a control owner. The record of the control owner provides visibility of who is accountable for the operation of the control and any enhancements necessary should the control fail to per form as anticipated.

The performance of the control is determined by a set of control performance factors that place limits on the parameters or circumstances in which the control will perform effectively. A control type may have multiple effectiveness factors, creating a one-to-many relationship.

The measurement of the performance of the control is undertaken through a set of different control assurance typologies which are appropriate to the testing of the control type, for example, threshold pressure testing the number of CCTV monitors which can effectively be observed at once.

As we articulated in Chapter 8, in addition to positive effects, controls may have downsides or control impacts, for example, creating impacts on productivity or cost. A single control may have multiple control impacts, creating a one-to-many relationship between control and control impact. Those control impacts, in turn, create harms as expressed above, which again impact upon the organisational objectives. The comparison of the harms created by the compromise of the asset versus the harms created by the controls produces the basis for decision-making on the business case for a particular set of controls (as we will set out below).

Moving to the right side of Figure 11.5, beneficiary types will have an interest in the organisation asset with capability and intent. They will also have an interaction with the role, whether close or more distant, as well as potentially interacting with the person who occupies the role.

Motivational factors including "pressure", "inducement" and "rationalisation" may act to create the drive for the person to engage in harmful malicious or inadvertent insider actions. This may include inducements provided by the beneficiary. Control types provide countermeasures against the beneficiary's capability and interaction, along with the motivation factors, "pressure", "inducement", and "rationalisation". As before, these controls may create downsides, are subject to factors rendering them effective, and may be assured using different assurance methodologies. Finally, the person's values and behaviours are shaped by aspects of general societal culture, organisational culture, and local culture.

The relationships in the conceptual model then enable us to construct all permutations of the risk, effectively using the objects and relationships in the model as the "grammar" to construct sentences describing the risk as set out below in Figure 11.6.

This illustrative example demonstrates in the abstract how the conceptual model captures the permutations of risk, noting that we do not include every element as this would result in an even longer and more elaborate sentence. This is precisely the value of the model, in that capturing even a single permutation is complex, let alone all the combinations of the risk factors.

In addition to describing the risk permutations, the conceptual model can also be utilised to describe the control environment within the organisation (see Figure 11.7).

By describing the control environment in data terms, we can identify where controls are in place and where vulnerabilities remain, along with

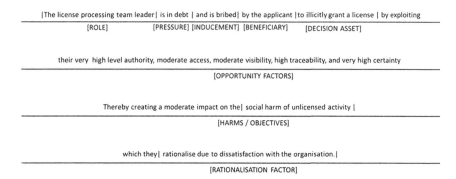

|The license processing team leader| is in debt | and is bribed| by the applicant |to illicitly grant a license | by exploiting

[ROLE]   [PRESSURE] [INDUCEMENT] [BENEFICIARY]   [DECISION ASSET]

their very high level authority, moderate access, moderate visibility, high traceability, and very high certainty

[OPPORTUNITY FACTORS]

Thereby creating a moderate impact on the| social harm of unlicensed activity |

[HARMS / OBJECTIVES]

which they| rationalise due to dissatisfaction with the organisation.|

[RATIONALISATION FACTOR]

FIGURE 11.6   Example Decomposition of Risk Using the Elements of the Model

making decisions on the best balance of controls for the protection of a particular asset. In this regard, the model is also employed to systemically understand the control performance, assurance, and impact landscape (see Figure 11.8)

The above three examples demonstrate only the elements of the model. In our view, the value is derived instead at the systemic level by creating a database capturing some or all of these model elements in order to interrogate the model (and all the permutations captured therein) to ask amongst other things:

- Which are the highest value and highest risk assets? Derived from the data and relationships linking assets, roles, opportunities, and beneficiaries.
- Which organisational capabilities, if subject to insider risk, would result in the greatest harm to objectives? Derived from data and relationships between capabilities, assets, and harms.
- Which are the highest risk roles? Derived from the data and relationships linking roles, assets, opportunities, and beneficiaries.
- Where are there gaps in controls? Derived from the data and relationships linking assets, roles, opportunities, and controls.
- Which controls have been recently/regularly assured? Derived from data and relationships linking controls and control assurance (including temporal data on date or frequency of assurance activity).
- Is the organisation expending more on prevention or responding to indi vidual cases? Derived from data on the balance of preventative versus responsive controls along with control effectiveness data.
- What downside impacts would implementing new controls have on the objectives? Derived from data and relationships linking controls, control impact, harms, and objectives.

|The license processing team leader| is prevented from accessing | other staff license decision accounts to illicitly grant a License |

[ROLE] [CONTROL TYPE] [DECISION ASSET]

through password authentication and Biometric authentication, low traceability is prevented through access and usage logs

[ACCESS PREVENTION CONTROL] [TRACEABILITY PREVENTION CONTROL]

along with comprehensive decision recording,| there are no controls on self-allocation|

[TRACEABILITY PREVENTION CONTROL] [OPPORTUNITY (CERTAINTY)]

however self-allocation is detected through self allocation anomaly detection, Bribes are detected through unexplained wealth monitoring,

[CERTAINTY DETECTION CONTROL] [INDUCEMENT DETECTION CONTROL]

And in the event illicit grant is detected the organisation can | investigate and terminate employment. |

[RESPONSE CONTROLS]

FIGURE 11.7 Second Example Decomposition of Risk Using the Elements of the Model

|The Border Officer| is prevented from low visibility by| CCTV monitoring|, which is monitored on a 4:1 ratio|

[ROLE]   [CONTROL TYPE]   [VISIBILITY PREVENTION CONTROL] [CONTROL PERFORMANCE FACTOR]

|at a cost of $250,000 per annum|, which is assured every six months through |threshold pressure testing|

[CONTROL IMPACT]   [CONTROL ASSURANCE]

FIGURE 11.8   Third Example Decomposition of Risk Using the Elements of the Model

By capturing the risk data at a systemic level, such a conceptual model when translated into a data model enables these and other questions to be answered at a whole-of-organisation level. This is the inherent purpose of data models, to capture complex relationships between different points of data and assist analysts and decision-makers to make sense of them. The model, therefore, "makes sense" of the risk to guide decision-making by the time- and attention-poor chief(s), enabling them to focus in on the aspects of risk that will affect their broader organisational objectives.

The location variable

In Chapter 2, we briefly touched on location as an element of the risk equation, as shown in Figure 11.9. Now that we have established the elements of the conceptual risk model, it is possible to clarify the role of location within the model.

For organisations that only operate or interact with a single location, location will not be a variable. However, for organisations that have geographical spread, whether physical or virtual, location may play a role in creating variation in the risk equation. In these circumstances, each of the conceptual

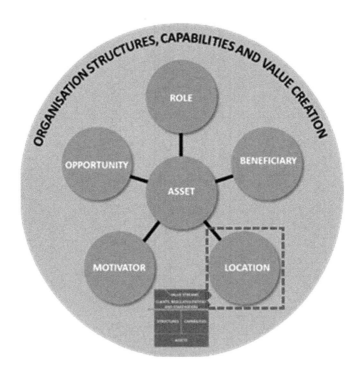

FIGURE 11.9 The Location Factor

model objects may have a relationship to location. For example, let us propose that a capability of the organisation, license decision-making, can be done in location 1 and location 2, and importantly the decision is made differently in each location. Let's say in location 1 all decisions come into a queue and are randomly allocated between a team of 20 decision-makers. The level of certainty is therefore 1:20. Whereas in location 2, the same random allocation from a queue applies. However, the office is much smaller and there are only 5 possible decision-makers creating a ratio 1:5, a significantly higher level of certainty in this location. The risk, therefore, in location 2 is demonstrably higher than in location 1.

Similarly, controls may be implemented differently in different locations. In our example, it would be possible for random allocation to exist in location 1 thereby reducing certainty. In location 2 there is no random allocation, thereby enabling a decision-maker to choose which application to process. Again, this renders location 2 at higher risk irrespective of the ratio of decision-maker to decisions.

In respect of the beneficiaries, it would be possible for the interaction between the beneficiary and the role to be distant in one location whilst closer and more repeated in another. Again, this creates a differential in the risk environment.

As we touched on earlier, culture and rationalisation factors can simultaneously exist at the local level within organisations. Culture in different "locations" in the enterprise, either functional or geospatial locations, have the potential to make parts of the organisation arguably more prone to insider risk.

Control impacts, performance, assurance, and harms may all be different depending on the location. In such circumstances, it is important that the conceptual model capture the relevant geospatial relationships for the organisation in question, where such geospatial relationships create changes in the risk variables we have outlined.

Third parties in the value stream

As we touched on in Chapter 2, the conceptualisation of what an organisation is comprised of according to its value stream may need to consider other actors who exercise capabilities on that value. These actors would not inherently be considered to be "insiders" (i.e. staff of the organisation) but can act as insiders from the perspective of the risk to the organisation.

We use, again, our border agency example to illustrate. Here, we propose that the value stream for a legitimate visit to a country involves the elements as highlighted in Figure 11.10.

Managing the risk of illegitimate visits and the economic, social, and environmental damage that may be created involves managing the risk of external

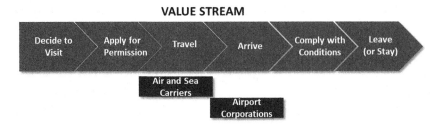

FIGURE 11.10   The Value Stream: Travel and Migration

parties complying with the conditions imposed (on visitation and insiders). For our example, let's say a person with a substantial criminal background travels as part of a drug importation exercise. When they arrive in country, they are checked and cleared by the border officer, which provides an intervention point to detect their unlawful travel to the country. However, when arriving at the border screening point, they will need to pass through the airport, which is owned by the airport corporation. It would be feasible for a staff member of the airport corporation, who had the proper opportunity factors (e.g. access to back doors of the building), to facilitate the exit of the traveller without passing through the screening point. In this example, the staff member of the airport corporation is not a border agency insider, nor are they a beneficiary (this is the traveller), yet a gap or vulnerability in the system of controls exists. In reality, airports are controlled through layers of security to prevent the above scenario from occurring. The border agency is, therefore, relying on the control environment of this other entity to manage risks to its objectives (as opposed to the airport corporation's own objectives, which are not at risk from the bypass by the traveller). Additionally, managing any insider risk arising from the border officer themselves would be a wasted investment if the insider risk is occurring before the value stream involves them as an actor.

In our view, when conceptualising the actors who are "insiders" – who contribute to the organisation's objectives and may then contribute to insider risk to the organisation – it is preferable to take a broad perspective, incorporating other actors within the value stream who contribute to the objectives. From a conceptual model perspective, this means incorporating the capabilities, roles, assets, and opportunities those actors present within the overall threat environment in the same way as would be done if the actor were a "staff member". Equally, it is important to incorporate and have visibility of the control environment of the other entities on the value stream. This means having visibility of gaps, if any, in the control environment of the airport corporation which would enable successful insider action.

In the broader governance context, the operationalisation of such a control environment, which is outside the investment control of the organisation, would require management through the relationship with a third-party organisation. This could be achieved through instruments of agreement or contracts or, in the case of government organisations, be managed through regulatory requirements. This creates a requirement for insider risk to be managed within the third-party organisation such that it mitigates risks to the objectives of our organisation (in our example, the border agency).

Role of the steward: Risk register

The application of the conceptual risk model to an organisational context in our view requires a technical understanding of the model. When captured as a database, the data equally requires a steward to maintain the standardisation of the data taxonomy and ontology and to manage the interrogation of the model. As set out above, we conceive the steward as the orchestrator of the risk management system, a role which has sufficient span of attention to comprehend the entire risk and control landscape. The conceptual model is effectively a representation of this landscape and, from our perspective, the management of that landscape is a role to be fulfilled by the steward of the system.

Equally, the interrogation of the model to understand specific aspects of risk or control requires a technical understanding of the sum total of the conceptual model to design the right queries. This requires a role, in our view, that necessitates a significant span of attention (available from our perspective only) to a role dedicated to understanding insider risk: the steward.

Role of the chief(s) and risk owner

It is also worth utilising the conceptual model to further highlight the roles we propose for the chief(s) and the risk owners. In respect of the chief(s), their role within the organisation is the achievement of the organisation's objectives, which in turn requires the management of risks that may impact on the achievement of those objectives. As such, the chief(s) own every permutation of risk that may occur within the system and impact on the objectives. Equally the chief(s) own the overall investment in controls within the organisation, ensuring they are cost effective and do not impact on the achievement of the objectives to a greater degree than they mitigate risks and harms. From a conceptual model perspective, then, the chief(s) become the overall "owner" of the model, in a high maturity state using the model to inform nuanced investment decisions based on business cases for control.

However, we proposed above, to manage the limits of their span of control and attention, the chief(s) require the support of another capable guardian:

the risk owner. This actor takes closer ownership of the management of a risk or small number of risks which are manageable within the span of their own attention and control. As depicted at Figure 11.11, we propose that generally risk ownership is aligned to the responsibility for organisational capability, which in itself is delegated by the chief(s) to produce outputs and outcomes which contribute to the organisation's objectives.

The risk owner then owns a subset of the total permutations of the insider risk: those which impact on the capability(ies) and asset(s) that they have been delegated responsibility for by the chief(s). The conceptual model thus provides both a means for identifying the appropriate risk owners and a means of comprehending the risks to those assets (in a systematic way), along with the impact of controls on their ability to contribute to broader organisational objectives.

As we set out above, the model also provides a basis for mapping the relationships between risk owners, assets (and through assets the control environment which protects those assets), and control owners, effectively bridging the relationship between risk owner and control owner. In our view, this provides the basis for effective guardianship of the assets. This is because we have an identified role that owns the risk and is thus concerned with the effectiveness of all controls (control ownership), mitigating the risk that they own. We propose

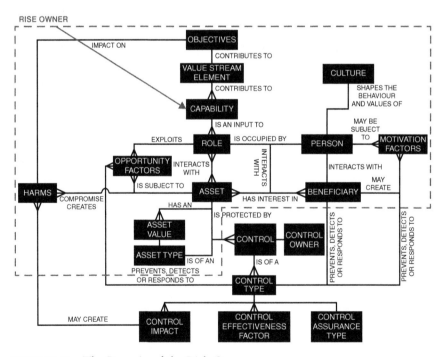

FIGURE 11.11 The Domain of the Risk Owner

that this constructive tension between risk ownership and control ownership will create the impetus for improvement in the control environment over time, in terms of both effort to create higher effectiveness and lower impact.

Control business case

As we set out throughout this body of work, the mitigation of insider risk requires the investment of resources. Such mitigation is not a cost-free exercise that can simply be absorbed into the organisation while simultaneously being effective. There appears to be a want of research into the mechanisms for sound decision-making around investment in mitigating insider threat and the inputs to those decisions.

In a general organisational context, decisions about the investment of resources to achieve an outcome are made through the mechanism of "business cases". A business case, in simple terms, is the collection of analysed information regarding the benefits of investing resources, the downsides and approach to effecting a decision made (including risks/uncertainty), and the costs involved in effecting the decision. Business case development has been subject to a body of research (see for example Marnewick & Einhorn, 2019). Decisions requiring business case analysis are underpinned by complexity, hence the need to analyse and assemble the information such that a busy executive can consume the information to make a defensible investment decision (whether ultimately correct or not).

The management of insider risk, as we've demonstrated, is a complex investment decision requiring the balancing of risk with the impact of control. There is no absolute measure of risk: only a relative measure of probabilities and impacts of risk on the business objectives. As a result, it is our view that the mechanism to improve decision-making about investment in mitigating risk is through a business case. It is our view that an information structure that does not capture the complexity of the risk landscape in detail; therefore, employing heuristic mechanisms to manage the complexity through often false generalisations or simplifications of information result in poor decision-making. Traditional two-dimensional risk tables are a good example of this issue. They capture basic information about risk and seek to encourage individuals to make uninformed determinations about the likelihood and consequences of insider risk. We argue that these models fail to provide the detail required for sound decision-making. By our definition, sound decision-making is that which invests the minimum resources to achieve the greatest mitigation while minimising the downside impacts.

Figure 11.2 (introduced in Chapter 2), proposes (amongst other issues) the following:

1 The highest risk is embezzlement: *but* the plan does not provide any information regarding which "roles" are capable of embezzlement.

Risk	Cause	Likelihood	Consequence	Rating	Current Controls	Treatment	Post Treatment Rating
Credit Card Fraud	Access to credit card	possible	Medium	Moderate	Card reconciliation Credit Card Training	Credit Card usage checks	Low
Unauthorised access to information	Password leaks Failure to secure documents	possible	Medium	Moderate	Access Control Safes Security Checks	Quarterly Security Sweep	Low
Embezzlement	Financial approval powers	possible	High	High	Financial Checks	Integrity Training	Low
Industrial espionage							

FIGURE 11.12 Example Excerpt Traditional Risk Spread Sheet

2 Integrity training will reduce the risk of embezzlement from high to low: *but* with no evidence or analysis in the risk plan regarding the effectiveness of the proposed control.
3 Credit card fraud is caused simply by access to a credit card: *but* the risk plan does not consider other factors such as the traceability of credit card transactions, which is a potential mitigation for risk.

These gaps in information could reasonably be expected to result in sub-optimal decision-making, including the following:

• Relying exclusively on the treatments in the treatment column to manage the risk, with little evidence they are effective.
• Over-investing in treatments across all roles in the organisation even though only a smaller sub-set is capable of the risk behaviour.
• Making assessments of the likelihood and consequence of the risk without a standard and repeatable process, creating a highly subjective-based approach to investment.

From our perspective, a business case–based approach to investment is a means of addressing the information gaps present in a more traditional risk assessment process. The business case itself is derived from information supplied from the conceptual model and comprised of several key areas of analysis as set out below.

Cost–Benefit Analysis

Cost–benefit analysis is a systematic means of cataloguing the benefits, both financial and non-financial, valuing in a common metric (e.g. dollars) with weightings and then determining the value of an investment relative to the status quo, by the net benefits (the benefits minus the costs) or benefit ratio (benefits divided by costs) (Boardman et al., 2006; Manning, 2014). This provides a decision-making tool to quantify in monetary terms the value of an investment to help allocate scarce resources more efficiently (Manning et al., 2016).

In the context of insider risk, cost–benefit analysis provides input to the business case for the investment in a control or set of controls, with two main applications:

1. Quantifying the value of a control or set of controls relative to the status quo (which effectively represents the acceptance of the level of risk).
2. Providing a basis for comparison between control options in terms of benefits/costs versus impacts.

These applications may be undertaken as simple calculations of the subtraction of costs from benefits or division of benefits by cost, thereby ignoring the inter-temporal elements of the investment decision; or through a net present value calculation. For those unfamiliar with the term, "net present value" simply refers to whether or not the investment (the control in our case) is profitable in the future (Manning, 2019).

To undertake a cost–benefit analysis in relation to the control environment, there are several elements of the insider risk which must be quantified:

- The anticipated cost of harm/consequences of a single incident of the insider risk under consideration.
- The anticipated frequency over a defined time period.
- The cost of the control including the cost of implementation and run costs.
- The anticipated control reduction in the harm/consequences (if less than total).
- The anticipated control impacts.

We will set out some considerations in relation to these elements below.

Cost of harm

As previously discussed, the harms which flow from insider threat are varied and depend significantly on the activities and objectives of the organisation. The primary harms to commercial organisations will be in terms of financial or revenue losses impacting on its commercial performance. As such, the harms can be quantified in financial terms. These would include the losses because of the incident itself but may include other flow on costs such as fines, compliance costs, and recovery costs.

The story for public sector and not-for-profit organisations is slightly different, insofar as their organisational objectives cannot be reduced so easily to quantified financial terms. In general, the purpose of these organisations is to produce some form of economic, social, or environmental benefit or in another form of words, to reduce an economic, social, or environmental harm. It is, therefore, important that these harms be quantified in these terms for such organisations.

To illustrate, we utilise some of our previous examples:

- For the border agency, the harms might be considered in terms of economic harms if drugs were to enter the domestic economy, which might be quantified in economic terms through hospitalisations, motor vehicle accidents, incidents of violence, hospitalisations from drug use, thereby providing a quantification of the harm if a shipment of drugs were allowed through border control.

- For a car licensing agency, the economic and social harms of unlicensed driving might be derived from hospitalisations, property damage, loss of life, providing a quantification of the harms of illicit grants of licenses.
- For our early environmental protection agency, the economic, social, and environmental costs of the grant of illicit logging licenses.
- For any of these organisations, the economic and/or social costs of leaks of commercially sensitive or personal information for the purposes of identity theft.

In relation to criminal activity, several models exist that attempt to provide indices and quantify the harms flowing from different crime typologies: for example the Cambridge Crime Harm Index (Institue of Criminology Sidgwick, 2023; Sherman et al., 2016). The approach of a crime harm index is novel in that rather than attempting to monetise all the benefits (both tangible and intangible) and costs of a crime prevention measure, it assesses different offences' harms: noting that "all crimes are not created equal in the harm they cause" (Institue of Criminology Sidgwick, 2023, p. 1). Therefore, simply counting the number of prevented or avoided crimes, irrespective of the crime type, is an insufficient basis for the allocation of prevention resources.

Linked with the above statement that societal harm caused by one crime is not comparable with that caused by another crime makes sense. However, subjectivity remains an issue with the crime harm index because recorded crimes are used to calculate harm. It is well known that the reporting and recording of crime vary by crime type. As such, crime harm indexes may be misleading. Further, sentencing guidelines, which form part of the metric in terms of weights attached to different crime types, are also subjective (albeit commonly accepted). In addition, judgements of crime seriousness are subject to change and often vary by jurisdiction (Teun van & Stijin, 2023).

In light of these limitations, however, crime harm indexes nonetheless retain value. From an insider risk perspective, such indexes might provide the framework for quantifying the harms flowing from corrupt policing, which effectively permits a level of predicate criminal activity to perpetuate. In addition, such indices generally provide guidance on the development of harm quantification models across many areas of public policy. With continual development the indices provide a promising framework.

In addition to the direct impacts of the insider threat, it may also be advantageous to consider secondary impacts and to include within the cost calculation those secondary impacts on the organisation. For instance, while the direct losses as a result of embezzlement will involve the value of those funds including their future interest or earning, assuming that the embezzlement involves the loss of brand reputation, this might result in quantifiable lost earnings because of a loss of competitiveness and market share.

Given it is likely that these costs will carry a degree of uncertainty, particularly if there is no reference data for similar losses within or outside the organisation, we propose that these costs be set out as a cost range and include confidence intervals. For example, regarding financial losses from embezzlement, the average losses quantified by the Association of Certified Fraud Examiners might provide a relatively high confidence around expected losses, whereas there are fewer – if any – studies on the environmental losses as a result of corrupt logging licenses, meaning that any attempts to quantify those losses would naturally involve a lower level of confidence. From a decision-making perspective, a loss range with confidence intervals provides a greater scope of inputs for the risk owner to make a decision on which controls are worthy of investment. Here we advise that the reader consider the use of a cost–benefit analysis tool, such as the Smart Cost Benefit Tool (SmartCBT) (e.g. Manning et al., 2024) as described in Manning et al. (2020). The SmartCBT was "developed to provide a straightforward but comprehensive format for assembling and analysing cost and benefit data of a program or intervention to provide a range of economic outputs (e.g. cost-feasibility, cost-effectiveness, cost-savings, cost-benefit analytics)".

Probability and frequency

As established earlier, risk management concerns itself with the "likelihood" and "consequence" or "impact" of uncertain events. We prefer the concept of "probability" insofar as it implies the ongoing pursuit of a level of statistical rigour to determine how "likely" an event will occur. In relation to the calculation of cost–benefit, we consider initially a frequentist model of probability in which probability is a factor of the frequency of an event within a timeframe. Under this conception over the "long-run" there are only two states of probability: an event is either capable of occurring or it isn't. What we are concerned with then is the period over which at least one incident will occur, involving the harm range set out above. This timeframe then becomes the baseline/consistent timeframe for the calculation of both costs and benefits.

While we use the word "frequentist" to describe probability, we do not intend to limit the means and methods of determining probability according to the particular circumstances and the data availability of the organisation in question. Bayesian or other actuarial methods for determining probability may be appropriate for an organisation where these methodologies are familiar, for example insider risk within the insurance sector, where risk quantification using actuarial methods is routine. However, equally it is not to limit more rudimentary methods of determining probability, which may in themselves be proportionate to the risk. For example, the frequency or annual volume of the transaction (decision asset) and a ratio of historical insider risk–exposed decisions might reasonably be used to determine the expected number of future affected decisions (this would be in the absence of new controls, since that is the subject of the cost–benefit assessment).

As we set out below, such rudimentary approaches to probability become less problematic when the cost–benefit calculation is not seen as purely point in time or static, but instead viewed as the subject of ongoing refinement on the basis of new information or data.

The calculation

We propose four forms of cost–benefit calculation, drawing on the elements above:

1. Simple net cost benefit (Ncb) for time t: the expected benefits (b) minus the anticipated costs (c); $Ncb_t = b_t - c_t$
2. Simple cost benefit ratio (cbR) for time t: the expected benefits (b) divided by the anticipated costs (c); $cbR_t = b_t/c_t$
3. Net present value: Present value of benefits (b_t) minus present value of costs (c_t), set out further below.
4. Capital efficiency ratio: Present value of benefits (b_t) divided by present value of costs (c_t), set out further below.

For the purposes of these calculations, we consider the following:

c_t = (for time t) total cost of control + cost of control impacts
   In this case, the cost of the control includes the cost of implementing the control and the cost of running the control in an ongoing sense. The cost of the control impacts is derived from the cost of the harms that the control produces as outlined above. For example, the impact of the control may be on productivity. The control cost would, therefore, be the harm impact of the anticipated loss of productivity within the business.

We can also consider within the costs the unmitigated harms which provide us with a residual economic harm (ch_t):

ch_t = (for time t) total cost of control + cost of control impacts + cost of unmitigated in respect of benefits:
b_t = (for time t) (total cost of harm – [% unmitigated harm × total cost of harm])

The total cost of harm considers primary and secondary costs of the insider incident, for example direct financial losses coupled with losses because of loss of market competitiveness. For the purposes of cost–benefit in the context of insider risk, these harms then become costs avoided because of successful controls. The calculation of benefits also considers the effectiveness of the control by subtracting the percentage of any unmitigated harm because of the control. For example, for a loss recovery control, the recoverable value of losses may only be a percentage of the total losses – let's say 85% of the total loss, in which case we would subtract 15% from the total costs avoided.

An example

Using our fictional Border agency, let us propose that 20 million people enter our hypothetical nation within a 12-month period. Based on the risk assessment, it would be reasonable to expect that up to 0.1% (or 20,000 per annum) of these border crossings may involve insiders facilitating border crossings for the purposes of drug importation with each being equivalent to 1 kilogram of opioids. Let's further propose, then, that the economic harm from a one kilogram of opioids is equivalent to around USD1 million.

As previously discussed, the low visibility and high authority opportunity factors may contribute to illicit border clearances and, therefore, the border agency is considering implementing a separation of duties control as a prevention measure. Implementing separation of duties involves recruiting a further 10 border control officers at a hiring cost of USD30,000 and USD70,000 for an ongoing salary. From a process perspective, the separation of duties results in an impact on productivity of 2 minutes per transaction. Let's propose that each minute is equivalent to USD100 in economic costs, because of aircraft being on the ground longer and flow on productivity costs to the economy.

In simple terms, then, the cost–benefit of this control is for 1 year assuming the control is 100% effective:

$$B_1 = (20,000 \times USD1,000,000) = USD20,000,000,000$$
$$C_1 = (\$70,000 \times 10 + USD30,000) + (20,000,000 \times 2 \times USD100)$$
$$= USD4,000,730,000$$

So, the simple net cost benefit over 1 year is as follows:

$$Ncb_1 = USD20,000,000,000 - USD4,000,730,000 = USD15,999,270,000$$

Simple cost–benefit ratio over 1 year is as follows:

$$cbR_1 = USD20,000,000,000/USD4,000,730,000 = 5.00$$

Let's continue by assuming that the separation of duties is not 100% effective and instead is only 80% effective. As such our calculations are as follows:

$$B_1 = (20,000 \times USD1,000,000) - (20,000 \times USD1,000,000 \times 20\%)$$
$$= USD16,000,000,000$$
$$C_1 = (USD70,000 \times 10 + USD30,000) + (20,000,000 \times 2 \times USD100)$$

Without considering the unmitigated harm the cost benefit is

Ncb_1 = USD16,000,000,000 – USD4,000,730,000 = 11,999,270,000
Ch_1 = (USD70,000 × 10 + USD30,000) + (20,000,000 × 2 × USD100) +
(20,000 × 0.2 × USD1,000,000) = USD8,000,730,000

So, the simple net cost benefit over 1 year at 80% effectiveness is (considering the unmitigated harm)

Ncb_1 (harms) = USD16,000,000,000 – USD8,000,730,000
= USD7,999,270,000

The simple cost–benefit ratio over 1 year is (considering the unmitigated harm)

cbR_1 (harms) = USD16,000,000,000/USD8,000,730,000 = 2.00

In both these scenarios, there remains a significant economic benefit to the implementation of the control despite the cost and productivity impact that a separation of duties would impose on the border clearance process.

Net present value

In insider threat scenarios involving impacts on present and future cash flows, net present value and capital efficiency ratio calculations are an effective means of determining the cost–benefit of controls while considering the time value of money to the organisation.

The net present value calculation is as follows:

$$NPV(i,N) = \sum_{t=0}^{N} \frac{B_t}{(1+i)^t} - \sum_{t=0}^{N} \frac{C_t}{(1+i)}$$

The capital efficiency ratio calculation is as follows:

$$CER(i,N) = \frac{\sum_{t=0}^{N} \frac{R_t}{(1+i)^t}}{\sum_{t=0}^{N} \frac{C_t}{(1+i)}}$$

For the purposes of these calculations, B_t and C_t are calculated as set out above. However, the time interval t would need to be the timeframe for the rate of preventable losses (for the benefits) based on the time interval at which the control becomes effective at preventing those losses. The discount rate i would depend on the relevant discount data for the organisation in question, but would likely consider inflation, investment rates of return, productivity inputs, and so forth.

An example where these calculations may be appropriate is in relation to the cash flow cost/losses of ratios of embezzlement to total revenues over time. These losses might be controlled through financial transaction anomaly detection controls, but these would not be fully effective for 12 months to 2 years while the data for detection matures and anomalies become more clearly delineated from legitimate transactions.

In this case, the return of the control will be in future dollars from up to 2 years away, and therefore not impacting on present losses. Another control may be capable of preventing the embezzlement losses in the short term and would have a higher net present value and capital efficiency ratio.

Continuous cost–benefit analysis

As is likely self-evident, the form of cost–benefit analysis we propose above relies on the availability and accuracy of structured data, which may not be immediately available when applying the model to an organisational context. The lack of data or inaccurate data would undermine the veracity of a cost–benefit analysis in respect of the implementation of new controls to mitigate insider risk.

It is our view, however, that the cost–benefit analysis should not be viewed as a static point-of-decision assessment. Instead, the analysis should be considered a continuous feature of a systemic approach to managing insider threat. This is particularly true of organisations where the inherent risk of insider activity is high, that is where there are high value assets to insiders and potential beneficiaries. Cost–benefit assessment should, in this case, be accompanied by an evaluation of the quality and completeness of the data utilised to make the assessment. And where there is expected value in enhancing the data, that new point of data should be collected to nuance and enhance the assessment.

Using our above example, the indexation of drug harm on the economy is a key element of the cost–benefit analysis for investing in a separation of duties for border officers. In practice, the development of such indices takes time and investment (Attewell & McFadden, 2008). However, given that one of the tasks of our fictitious border agency is to reduce the incidence of narcotics entering the country, then the development and refinement of such an index has value to the broader objectives of the business. It also has the additional benefit of assessing the risk of insider threat.

Other data points such as the expected rate of illicit clearance of drugs is specific to insider threat. This measure is a critical component to the business case for investment and equally requires investment to develop. It is our view that when the cost–benefit analysis is viewed as a continuous feature, the accumulation and correction of the data used to inform that assessment will yield a positive return overall. We base our view on the various studies of data valuation, in particular infonomics valuation models (Laney, 2023), which in part value data on its value to performance of economic systems. In respect of insider threat, it is our view that data is a critical input to the functioning of the system of risk management, particularly in complex organisational contexts. The alternative, as we've previously described, is ad hoc decision-making.

New data can only lead to four outcomes in respect of controls which have been previously considered:

1 The future assessment will confirm the positive return of an implemented control.
2 The future assessment will refute the return on investment of an implemented control. In this case, the control should be removed or replaced with an equivalent control with a positive return.
3 The future assessment will confirm a negative return for a previously considered control that was not implemented.
4 The future assessment will refute a negative return, and therefore the control should be implemented.

It is unlikely that any of these outcomes would be deleterious to an organisation and therefore the lack of current quality or complete data should not be a reason against the utilisation of cost–benefit analysis. There may, however, be utility in further research in the domain of data value in managing insider risk, particularly in the context of changing cyber-security and information management risks.

Control balancing and control configuration

The simple cost–benefit analysis provides the decision-maker with the assessment of the positive or negative return for the implementation of a single control. However, controls do not operate in isolation. Instead they are part of a broader control environment, which involves the interaction between different controls to achieve the necessary level of risk mitigation overall. As we discussed earlier, the primary mechanisms of control are prevention, detection, and response. These primary mechanisms interact with one another to mitigate risk in concert. For example, a risk event must be detected before a response can be derived and implemented. As a result, the creation of a response control in the absence of a precursor detection control will not create an effective control environment. Thus, decisions on investment by the chief(s) in the implementation of controls needs to consider the existing control environment and the alternative mechanisms for controlling the risk, while also considering the cost–benefit along with qualitative factors around effectiveness and impacts.

We propose then the twin concepts of *control balancing an–d control configuration*. In our semantics, *control balancing* refers to the decision-making process to determine where, in the control continuum of prevention, detection, and response to implement controls based upon their relative effectiveness and impact. *Control configuration* refers to the arrangement of the controls which have been staged. In effect, it is the description of the current or proposed placement of controls across the continuum of prevention, detection, and response. In this way, the act of control balancing creates different control configurations to protect different organisational assets. As we propose above, the conceptual model, when translated to data, is effectively a repository for the configurations of controls which protect different organisational assets from risk.

We use Figure 11.13 to illustrate, in simple terms, the configuration of multiple controls to protect an asset. In this example, the organisational asset is threatened by risk events A, B, and C. In the case of risk event A, control 3 is an effective prevention mechanism, which protects the asset from the effects of the risk. In the case of risk event B, none of the prevention controls mitigate the risk; however, control 5 effectively detects the risk, which enables control 7 to respond. These two controls work together to achieve the mitigation of risk: in the absence of detection by control 5 there would be no trigger for response for control 7, and vice versa; if control 7 were not implemented, then the detection by control 5 would not, on its own, manage the risk.

In respect of risk event C, none of the controls are effective in mitigating the risk and therefore to address the risk, new controls may need to be implemented if the risk has sufficient impact on the objectives of the organisation. On the face of it, if the asset were only threatened by risk events A, B, and C, then controls 2, 4, and 6 are superfluous given they have no effect on the risk. These are therefore sunken investment and will need enhancement to become effective controls or are controls which should be removed.

The control configuration, therefore, informs the decision-maker about the relationship between the controls and the risk and the controls amongst one another. This, then, becomes the basis for more nuanced decision-making in respect of the implementation of different control typologies across the continuum.

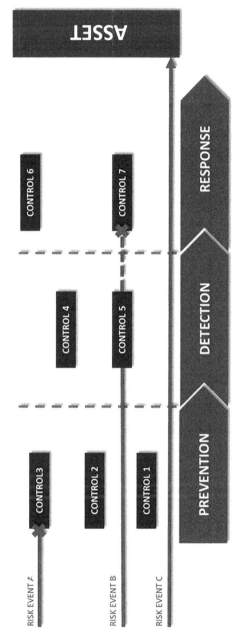

FIGURE 11.13   Control Orchestration

Continuing our example above:

We established that the simple net cost–benefit for the implementation of a separation of duties with 80% effectiveness is as follows:

$$Ncb_1 = USD16,000,000,000 - USD4,000,730,000 = USD11,999,270,000$$

$$Ncb_{1(harms)} = USD16,000,000,000 - USD8,000,730,000 = USD7,999,270,000$$

Let's then consider different control configurations to protect the same border clearance decision asset. Here, we assume that response controls investigation and post-entry seizure are capable of recovering 50% of drugs before they hit the market and impact the economy. These controls have no impact on the productivity of the clearance process, unlike the separation of duties. Investigations are, however, relatively expensive, with each simple investigation costing approximately USD80,000 and post-entry seizure activity around USD10,000 per seizure.

The triggering of the investigation control relies on an anomaly detection control, which is anticipated to be 90% accurate. The cost of this control is negligible.

$$B_1 = (20,000 \times USD1,000,000) \times 90\% \times 50\% = USD9,000,000,000$$

$$C_1 = ([USD80,000 + USD10,000] \times [20,000 \times 90\%]) = USD1,620,000,000$$

If we don't consider the unmitigated harms, then the simple cost benefit over 1 year is as follows:

$$Ncb_1 = USD7,380,000,000$$

However, if we include the unmitigated harms, we have

$$Ch_1 = ([USD80,000 + USD10,000] \times [20,000 \times 90\%]) + [(20,000 \times USD1,000,000) - \{(20,000 \times 1,000,000) \times 45\%\}] = USD1,620,000,000 + USD11,000,000,000 = USD12,620,000,000$$

The simple net cost–benefit over 1 year is as follows:

$$Ncb_1 = USD9,000,000,000 - USD12,620,000,000 = -USD3,620,000,000$$

Simple cost–benefit ratio over a year is as follows:

$$cbR_1 = USD9,000,000,000/USD12,620,000,000 = 0.71$$

If the chief(s) were deciding between these two potential configurations, these calculations, particularly when considering the unmitigated harm, demonstrate that even with the productivity loss, the separation of duties has a stronger business case. (Note: this is only true based on the assumptions we've made – in real scenarios the calculation may result in a different result.)

Let's consider, now, if these controls were implemented alongside one another. In this case we are no longer comparing the controls but determining the compounding effect of the control configuration. In this scenario, the separation of duties has already taken effect, leaving a residual 20% of illicit decisions which have not been prevented. Of those 20%, 90% are detected by anomaly detection controls, resulting in the investigation and seizure mitigating 50% of harms.

$$B_1 = (4,000 \times USD1,000,000) \times 90\% \times 50\% = USD1,800,000,000$$

$$C_1 = ([USD80,000 + USD10,000)] \times [4,000 \times 90\%]) = USD324,000,000$$

$$Ncb_1 = USD1,800,000,000 - USD324,000,000 = USD1,476,000,000$$

Given that we are not comparing between controls, the unmitigated harm is of less relevance to decision-making. This is because the return on the controls will be *in addition to*, rather than *instead of*.

The two controls have a compounding effect as follows:

$$Ncb_1 + Ncb_1 = USD11,999,270,000 + USD1,476,000,000$$
$$= USD13,475,270,000$$

In circumstances where risks cannot be mitigated entirely, it is those corresponding configurations that result in the greatest reduction of harm/loss that will make financial sense to implement.

As the example above illustrates, the balance of controls across the continuum of controls has both differential returns and impacts, and their effects may be compounding in mitigating the overall risk and consequences of those risks. The example also presents the decision-making inputs to control balancing based on cost benefit. However, purely quantitative cost–benefit data does not provide a complete account of the positive effects, effectiveness factors, or the impacts (as set out in Chapter 8) of a control such that a holistic decision can be made based on cost–benefit alone. For example, the culture and relationship impact of the implementation of certain controls cannot be readily reduced solely to quantitative benefits or losses.

Drawing on our border agency cost–benefit analysis above, on a whole-of-economy basis, the implementation of a separation of duties to mitigate the risk of illicit drug importation has a positive return on investment. However, in our example, the delay to airport processing results in costs to the air carriers because of longer wait times and airport costs. When deciding to implement this control then, the chief(s) need to be cognisant of these specific impacts, including the potential relationship impacts with the air carriers who may be a key stakeholder in the border control system. It may be that the non-financial impacts of the control outweigh the financial benefits. For example, the relationship impacts may be such that the agency loses the cooperation of the air carriers on other priorities which impact on the organisation's objectives, and these outweigh the benefits of managing the harms of the insider risk.

It is, therefore, important that the decision-maker consider both the quantitative costs and benefits and the qualitative effectiveness and impacts of controls when making a decision on balancing the controls. Appendix A sets out a structure of control typologies with impacts that can be considered as part of the decision-making in respect of implementing different typologies of controls.

Role of the steward: Cost–benefit and balancing

As the preceding sections illustrate, decision-making in respect of investment in controls is complex, involving numerous decision inputs: both quantitative and qualitative. In our view, the span of attention and technical knowledge required to undertake the calculations and development of business cases for investment in controls makes this a role best undertaken by a dedicated steward of the insider risk management system.

Controls in a changing context

Organisations exist within an environment of continuous change that impacts on the delivery of their objectives. The following apply here:

- Technology changes may create new means of delivering services to consumers or may create new forms of competitors for demand.
- Changes in supply and demand may call for venturing into new markets for profit.
- Legal and regulatory changes may modify the conditions in which business is delivered by both business and the public sector.
- Global economic and political changes may transform power dynamics between nations or create new sources of global political tension.

Organisations are also driven by internal change imperatives to improve and enhance efficiency and productivity, reduce cost, and improve effectiveness.

These changes equally impact on the insider risk environment, potentially exposing the organisation to new or changed risks.

Examples follow:

- Technology changes may provide insiders new opportunities to bypass controls or may provide new opportunities for technology-enabled controls.
- Entering new markets will involve new organisational assets, beneficiaries to those assets, business processes, roles, and opportunities.
- Changing political landscapes may provide new sources of politically based rationalisation.
- Changed economic conditions might create additional pressure on people within the organisation.

This in turn denotes that the control environment itself cannot remain static in the face of these changes and must instead be dynamic to respond to a changing environment. In our view, the approach to dealing with change should also be systemic in its approach.

We propose two forms of change that impact on the insider risk profile: *environmental change* and *organisational change*.

Environmental change

As outlined in Chapter 2, organisations are established as social constructs that interact with the environment external to themselves to create value: whether private interest value or public value. In our hypothetical border agency, the value it creates is the protection of economic, social, and environmental interests from harm by regulating the entry of people and products into the country. It interacts with international trade markets, the tourism industry, and offshore employment markets. It also has an enforcement role with respect to international criminal activity.

The external environment with which organisations interact is in constant flux. Aguilar (1967) developed PEST analysis as a means of structuring environment scanning as part of business strategy development and change. Aguilar's proposed technique remains relevant today and has been expanded to PESTEL or PESTLE, a mnemonic as described in the following:

- *Political*: concerning the way that government(s) intervene in the economy and society, and the changes that may occur in their policy frameworks: for example favouring pure liberalism or social investment.
- *Economic*: concerning the macro- and microeconomic conditions such as growth, inflation, exchange rates, interest rates, and market competition factors.

- *Social*: describing the social context in which organisations work, the cultural norms and expectations, social contract, and social trends and demand.
- *Technological*: concerning the technological changes, investment, and domains of research and development and pace of technological change.
- *Environmental*: concerning the effects of environmental change, climate, weather patterns, and ecological changes, such as soil, water, and air quality.
- *Legal*: concerning the legal and regulatory context in which organisations operate. From a private sector perspective this may place limits on their means of production while in a public sector setting organisations as the regulators and enforcers of those legal frameworks.

These elements are utilised to determine changes in the environment which may present market opportunities or threats to the organisation's objectives and means of delivering value through its value streams. In our conception, this is the domain of the chief(s) as part of their broader role in driving the objectives of the organisation and ensuring the organisation remains viable in the face of environmental changes. In a concrete sense, these changes may result in a need to change or create new capabilities of the organisation to meet the new exigencies from the environment.

In the context of insider threat, these environmental changes are of equal import to the change in the insider risk profile.

A few simple examples follow:

Technology change

Using our conceptual border agency example, let's assume that there is a technological boom in drone technology which revolutionises the movement of goods across borders, enabling ship-to-shore offloading of shipping containers while ships continue travelling at sea. These technological advances drastically improve productivity for shipping companies while reducing docking costs so ships only need to dock for refuelling.

The drones are operated by new companies established to provide this service to shipping companies. They establish new *droneports* for the landing, loading, and movement of containers, which are very different to traditional seaports.

To continue to meet its objectives to protect the economic, social, and environmental interests, the border agency now needs to establish capabilities to monitor the arrival of goods and undertake clearance at droneports. This involves new roles, new decision-types, and new sources of commercial data to the organisation, all which are potential targets for insider threat. Equally, the drone operators are potentially new beneficiaries to illicit clearance decisions, or the release of sensitive commercial information.

Political/social change

Geopolitical tensions emerge between nation A and nation B. The operations of a multinational company headquartered in nation B suddenly become politically and socially contentious, with the development of activist activity in nation A. Certain production activities are seen to support nation B. From an insider threat perspective, the politically contentious nature of those production activities creates a heightened risk of politically motivated rationalisation for insider activity.

Legal change

The government imposes new safety regulations for driverless vehicles which are regulated by the vehicle production regulator. The regulations require new quality assurance capabilities for vehicle manufacturers and for the regulator, including a new vehicle design clearance decision by the regulator. This decision becomes a valuable organisational asset to the driverless vehicle manufacturers.

These simple examples illustrate the effect of environmental change on the organisation, its means of delivering its objectives, and, from our perspective, the insider risk environment. To effectively manage insider risk, the effects of these changes need to be systematically assessed. The conceptual model that we have established provides the means of undertaking this assessment. It does this by providing a point of reference for examining the effect of PESTEL changes on each of the elements of the risk model and effectively re-assessing the risk as change is occurring or is predicted to occur. The following questions need addressing:

- Have changes in the political or social environment created new motivations for insider activity?
- Have economic changes created new market opportunities or competition that insiders could exploit? Or has it increased the harms in the event of insider activity (e.g. because losses will be higher than previously felt, or an asset at threat has a higher value than previously assessed)?
- Does technology change create new assets at risk or new opportunities for controls against insider threat?
- Do changes in the environment increase the harms of insider activity?
- Does the legal framework create new requirements that need to be complied with, and which could be undermined by deliberate or inadvertent insider activity?

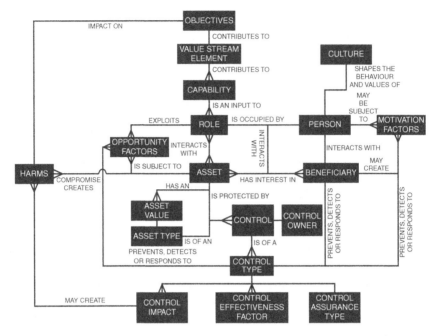

FIGURE 11.14 Insider Threat Management Model: Complete Conceptual Model

By linking together these elements of insider risk, as illustrated at Figure 11.4, we can more rapidly assess the flow on effect of these changes on the organisation and its risk exposure.

Organisational change

Environmental change precipitates organisational change for organisations to maintain their effectiveness in the face of environmental changes. Equally, organisations invest in continuous organisational enhancements to improve their productivity and efficiency at delivering their products and services and improving their overall effectiveness at delivering on their objectives. These changes may be incremental or transformational.

Modern organisations use a range of related disciplines, such as programme management, project management, and, as we outlined in previous chapters, business architecture to create a structured approach to managing business change. Importantly, each of these disciplines involves the governance throughout the lifecycle of a change (see Figure 11.15).

As we set out in Chapter 2, we have drawn on the business architecture disciplines when decomposing the elements of organisation (in particular BIZBOK®). It also provides a model to use a business architecture approach

FIGURE 11.15   Organisational Strategy Lifecycle

to describe the structured process for change. Initially, the requirement for change is driven by a need to modify the organisation's business strategy, often in the face of the environmental change pressures we've outlined above but also at a smaller level to improve the operation of some aspect of the business.

Once new strategies have been defined, the means of executing those strategies also need defining. This effectively means defining what "capabilities" are required to deliver on the new strategies or what changes need to be made to existing "capabilities". This requires assessing changes to the roles, business processes, information, and technology inputs to those capabilities. From an insider risk perspective, this provides the basis for re-assessing the risk using the same methodology we have proposed throughout this book, that is assessing the following:

- The value of any new or changed assets within those capabilities.
- The risk exposure of new or changed roles by evaluating any changes to the opportunity factors, or assessing the opportunities for new capabilities.
- New beneficiaries or changes in their capabilities, interaction, or intent as a result of changes to the organisational capability.
- New motivational factors.

Again, the conceptual model provides a point of reference for assessing these changes and for capturing proposed changes while respecting the relationships between the different risk objects described in the model.

Once the changes to the business architecture are understood, the initiative(s) required to deliver upon those changes are planned. This may include planning technology projects to update ICT software, human resource projects to change and recruit to roles, business analysis and business change projects, and procurement exercises to secure new equipment and tangible assets. In our view, it is at this stage that insider risk controls should be defined to protect the assets subject to change. Again we utilise the same methodology we have proposed for deciding upon the relative merits and balance of *preventative*, *detective*, and *responsive* controls, while equally considering the effectiveness requirements and impacts of those controls on the new business strategies and objectives.

The next stage is to effect the changes, often using sequential or iterative design and delivery methodologies. It is in this phase that we propose that the controls are implemented and embedded within the changes to the business. This ensures that assets are protected from the point of implementation rather than being left exposed until an insider risk event prompts the organisation to protect those assets.

Finally, once the change is embedded, the success of the new or changed strategies is measured to determine whether the change has made the expected improvements to the delivery on the organisations. Equally, the effectiveness of the insider risk controls on new business processes should be evaluated.

Tactical displacement

There is one other aspect of change which is worth further particularisation in the context of regulatory organisations: tactical displacement. As set out in Chapters 2 and 3, regulators are established to modify the behaviour of markets to protect economic, social, and environmental interests from externalities to that market behaviour. Market behaviour is managed through a set of risk controls (which are also preventative, detective, or responsive). For the purposes of differentiation, we can refer to these as "external controls" insofar as they are designed to modify the behaviour of the external market participants.

Using our conceptual border agency, the requirement to apply and meet certain conditions before importing goods along with the prohibition on importing certain goods acts to prevent the harm of those goods. The screening and clearance decisions also act as external controls to detect and prevent the entry of those goods at the border.

Regulatory organisations will also seek to enhance the effectiveness, efficiency, and productivity of these external controls. For example, this may require using new screening technology to enhance the accuracy in identify illicit and prohibited goods or modern data analytics techniques to promote the efficiency in profiling goods for inspection. The need for these improvements is driven by an ongoing intent by market players to remain non-compliant with the regulatory framework. In the case of the border agency, this would be continuing to import illicit goods.

The concept of tactical displacement (Figure 11.16), in this context, is that when those improvements are made, if the external controls are strengthened sufficiently, and the non-compliant intent (of the beneficiaries) remains, then it is plausible that the modus operandi of the beneficiary will shift towards utilising insiders to bypass the external controls (e.g. by illicitly clearing goods).

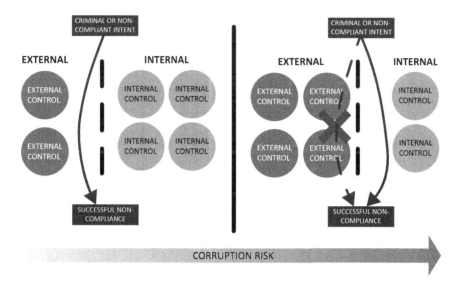

FIGURE 11.16   Tactical Displacement: Insider Threat

The upshot of this is that, in a regulatory context, when strengthening external controls, it is our view that this should also trigger the consideration of insider risk controls to guard against tactical displacement towards engaging insiders to perpetuate non-compliance with the regulatory regime.

The role of the steward: Change

Taking a systemic approach to managing insider risk should involve a systemic and reliable approach to dealing with changes that necessitate modifications or improvements to controls. We suggest this can be achieved by integrating insider risk assessment into enterprise change management processes as outlined below. This ensures that insider threat controls maintain pace with changes in the environment and changes that are made within the organisation, so that new risk exposures are not inadvertently introduced when making modifications to the business. It is a role for the steward to create this integration between change and insider risk management systems. It is also a role for the steward to provide assurance that risk has been adequately assessed and treated through each stage of the change lifecycle.

Governance of assurance and culture

In closing this chapter, we will briefly turn to the governance of the other two building blocks of a systemic approach to managing insider risk: assurance and culture (see Figure 11.17).

ORGANISATIONAL LEADERSHIP

INSIDER THREAT MANAGEMENT FUNCTION

ARTICULATE AND SUPPORT

The Threat Management Function supports the leadership to exercise their governance role through comprehensive analysis, structured decision information and articulating business cases for investment.

CHECK AND ADJUST

The Threat Management Function conducts and coordinates assurance activities for insider threat controls and provides support and recommendations to the organisational leadership to invest in adjusting and improving insider risk controls.

DISCUSS AND DESIGN

The Threat Management Function engages with business lines to define and embed insider threat controls. The Function orchestrates the alignment of controls across different lines of business.

INFORM

The Threat Management Function provides information and education to the organisation's staff to shape an integrity culture, inform them of their obligations and create resilience against attempts to corrupt them.

GOVERNANCE

CONTROL ASSURANCE

CONTROL DESIGN AND IMPLEMENTATION

CULTURE AND CAPABILITY

OVERSEE

The organisation's leadership oversee the overall system of insider threat management, providing focus, clear and evidence-based decision-making and investment mandates for the organisation, ensuring that insider risk is clearly on the organisational agenda.

SPONSOR

The organisation's leadership provides sponsorship and support to the programme of control assurance, ensuring it is targeted at the highest risks and that, where business cases for improvement are identified, they are thoroughly considered and invested in.

INVEST

The organisation's leadership invest time and resources into the controls identified through risk assessment process, based on their relative effectiveness and impact. Controls are thereby embedded within organisational practice.

MODEL

The organisation's leadership model and encourage integrity, insider threat vigilance and reward and recognise positive behaviour

FIGURE 11.17 Insider Risk Management Model: Assurance and Culture

Governance of assurance

As set out in Chapter 9, there are three lines of assurance:

- First line: Local management, supervision, and quality control.
- Second line: Independent quality checks and quality assurance (including a set of assurance typologies outlined in Chapter 9).
- Third Line: Internal audit.

Like all organisational activities, insider risk control assurance requires the investment of scarce resources to achieve the greatest reduction in risk. As a result, investment in assurance activities should be aligned to the relative risk associated with the different organisational assets, using the same relative risk assessment methodology we outlined above. In this way, the most valuable and at-risk assets are prioritised for assurance.

The role of the assurer

As set out in Chapter 9, there are a range of assurance typologies which are most appropriate for providing assurance over different controls. As a capable guardian of the system, it is the role of the assurer to hold the expertise over the most appropriate forms of assurance for different controls and to draw on the risk assessment to determine an annual plan of assurance to recommend to the chief(s).

Such a plan would set out the following:

- The assets subject to assurance activities and their relative risk.
- The types of assurance activities to be used.
- The cost of each activity and the total cost of executing the plan.

The plan would thereby enable the time- and attention-poor chief(s) to make informed decisions regarding the relative levels of investment in assurance across the organisation, while grounding these decisions on a real appreciation of the level of insider risk. While our focus is insider risk, in practice many organisations will already have in place assurance plans for broader assurance across other domains of risk, such as financial risk or safety risk. We are not proposing that a separate standalone plan need to be developed for insider risk. Instead, insider risk assurance activities could be incorporated into existing assurance plans.

Governance of culture

As discussed in Chapter 10, culture has a normalising role on behaviour, complementing the formal control environment to mitigate insider risk.

Applying the work of Johnson et al. (2008) to an insider threat context, we identified six elements (Figure 11.18) that illuminate the cultural paradigm of the organisation.

Research into fraud and financial management governance finds that the cultural structures are disproportionately set by the so-called *tone from the top* (D'Aquila & Bean, 2011; Rabasundram, 2015). This implies that the chief(s) have a special role in terms of determining the overall cultural norms for the organisation. These cultural norms will ultimately influence the behaviours that are exhibited by individuals, particularly in the absence of other forms of control. To be capable guardians of the insider risk management system, then, it is incumbent upon the chief(s) to be cognisant of the ethical culture of the organisation.

We propose that this can be achieved through the cultural analysis that we outline in Chapter 10, drawing on the Cultural Web. In our view it is the role of the steward of the system to undertake this analysis to support the time and attention poor chief(s). Such an analysis will isolate which elements of the organisational paradigm protect against insider threat, and which may promote a higher level of risk of unethical, reckless, or indifferent behaviour. It is then for the chief(s) to exhibit those cultural norms and to make decisions on the following:

- Promoting and communicating stories that showcase ethical behaviour, including determining who are the heroes and villains of those stories.
- Setting symbols that represent the ethical cultural norms of the organisation.
- Setting the power and incentive structures to support an ethical paradigm.

FIGURE 11.18   The Johnson and Scholes Cultural Web

- Setting the organisational structures and functions of the organisation, in particular the establishment of the insider threat management function and establishment of the role of steward (by whatever title it is given).
- Establishing and promoting the insider risk control environment.
- Promoting and exhibiting rituals and routines that are ethical and highlight the expectations around ethical behaviours.

Conclusion

Insider risk is defined by complexity, due to the sheer number of permutations of the interactions between the various drivers of risk. These include the assets at risk, the roles that interact with those assets, the opportunities that each of those roles may have to act unethically with respect to those assets, those who may benefit from unethical interactions, the motives, and cultural norms that generate unethical behaviour.

We find that traditional risk assessment practices ignore this complexity. Rather, they tend to focus on certain events or drivers and, in so doing, create an error-prone and ad hoc approach to managing risk. This results in poor investment decisions and continuing exposure, as evidenced by organisations that have put in place risk management systems and yet fall victim to uncontrolled insider risk events.

We have, therefore, attempted to develop a complete model of insider risk. The model standardises the language around the risk drivers, sets out the interactions between those drivers, and draws relationships between the drivers for insider risk and the controls that act as counter-measures against each of those drivers. In doing this, we hope to provide a more *systemic and structured approach* to investing scarce resources to where they are most needed and useful in managing the risks to the organisation. We equally recognise that insider risk control mechanisms may impact on other business objectives and therefore the controlling of insider risk needs to be balanced against those objectives. By providing analysis around the impacts of controls, we attempt to guide organisations on making those balancing decisions with an appreciation of the impacts of different control typologies.

Finally, drawing on routine activity theory, we recognise the role of the "capable guardian" to manage risk and attempt to define a system of typologies of "guardians" that play different roles within the insider risk management system, and as a collective, maximise the protection of organisations against insider risk within the scarce resources available to them.

In our view, this more complete examination of insider risk is capable of enhancing organisations' ability to manage risk and provide a framework for future research and the refinement of the concepts we introduce in this book.

Chapter key points

- Governance is the set of processes and practices of decision-making around the application of finite resources to meet objectives. In the context of insider threat governance, it is necessary to ensure those resources are directed to the highest areas of risk.
- We propose a system of seven "capable guardians" which form this system of governance. Each plays a distinct role in the system, which recognises different interests and expertise within a broader organisational context.
- A systemic risk assessment, based on our conceptual model, identifies the greatest areas of risk based on the complex interactions between risk drivers.
- Cost–benefit and impact analyses provide the evidence for robust investment decisions and the balancing of controls across the prevention, detection, and response continuum.
- The organisational environment is not static and, therefore, the insider risk control framework needs to be systematically reviewed and adjusted to meet new threats.
- The assurance system and cultural frameworks themselves require governance from the top, ensuring that these layers of the insider risk management system also have maximum effect on mitigating risk.

References

Aguilar, F. J. (1967). *Scanning the business environment*. Macmillan.

Association of Certified Fraud Examiners. (2022). *Occupational fraud 2022: A report to the nations*. https://legacy.acfe.com/report-to-the-nations/2022/

Attewell, R., & McFadden, M. (2008). Measuring the benefits of drug law enforcement: The development of the Australian Federal Police drug harm index. *Bulletin on Narcotics, 60*(1–2), 45–58.

Boardman, A. E., Greenberg, D. H., Vining, A. R., & Weimer, D. L. (2006). *Cost-benefit analysis: Concepts and practice* (3rd ed.). Pearson-Prentice Hall.

Braithwaite, J. (2002). Rewards and regulation. *Journal of Law and Society, 29*(1), 12–26.

Cohen, L., & Felson, M. (1979). Social change and crime rate trends: A routine activity approach. *American Sociological Review, 44*(4), 588–608.

D'Aquila, J., & Bean, D. (2011). Does a tone at the top that fosters ethical decisions impact financial reporting decisions: An experimental analysis. *International Business & Economics Research Journal, 2*(8), 41–54.

Geva, A. (2006). A typology of moral problems in business: A framework for ethical management. *Journal of Business Ethics, 69*(2), 133–147.

Graycar, A., & Prenzler, T. (2013). *Understanding and preventing corruption*. Palgrave Macmillan.

Guadalupe, M., Li, H., & Wulf, J. (2014). Who lives in the C-suite? Organizational structure and the division of labor in top management. *Management Science, 60*(4), 824–844.

Institue of Criminology Sidgwick. (2023). *The Cambridge crime harm index (CCHI)*. https://www.crim.cam.ac.uk/research/thecambridgecrimeharmindex#:~:text=

The%20Cambridge%20Crime%20Harm%20Index%20%28CCHI%29%20 is%20the,not%20just%20the%20number%20of%20officially%20recorded%20 crimes

International Organization for Standardization. (2018). *ISO 3100:2018 Risk management – guidelines*. International Organization for Standardization.

Johnson, G., Scholes, K., & Whittington, R. (2008). *Exploring corporate strategy: Text and cases*. Financial Times Prentice Hall.

Laney, D. (2023). *Why and how to measure the value of your information assets*. https://www.gartner.com/en/documents/3106719

Manning, M. (2008). *Economic evaluation of the effects of early childhood intervention programs on adolescent outcomes* [PhD, Griffith University].

Manning, M. (2014). Cost-benefit analysis. In G. Bruinsma & D. Weisburd (Eds.), *Encyclopedia of criminology and criminal justice* (pp. 641–651). Science+Business Media.

Manning, M. (2019). Economics. In R. Wortley, A. Sidebottom, N. Tilley, & G. Laycock (Eds.), *Routledge handbook of crime science*. Routledge.

Manning, M., Homel, R., & Smith, C. (2011). An economic method for formulating better policies for positive child development. *Australian Review of Public Affairs, 10*(1), 61–77.

Manning, M., Johnson, S., Tilley, N., Wong, G., & Vorsina, M. (2016). *Economic analysis and efficiency in policing, criminal justice and crime reduction: What works?* Palgrave.

Manning, M., Smith, C., & Homel, R. (2013). Valuing developmental crime prevention. *Criminology and Public Policy, 12*(3), 305–332.

Manning, M., Wong, G., & Vindanage, A. (2024). *Smart cost benefit tool*. https://manningcba.digital

Manning, M., Wong, T. W. G., Christen, P., Ranbaduge, T., & Vidanage, A. (2020). *Smart cost benefit tool*. https://dmm.anu.edu.au/SmartCBT/#

Marnewick, C., & Einhorn, F. (2019). The business case thrives on relevant information. *SA Journal of Information Management, 21*(1), 1–11.

Ocasio, W. (1997). Towards an attention-based view of the firm. *Strategic Management Journal, 18*, 187–206.

Rabasundram, G. (2015). Perceived "tone from the top" during a fraud risk assessment. *Procedia Economics and Finance, 28*(1), 102–106.

Rezzy, O. (2007). Sabanes-Oxley: Progressive punishment for regressive victiization. *Houston Law Review, 44*(1), 96–128.

Saaty, T. L. (1990). *Multicriteria decision making: The analytical hierarchy process*. RWS Publications.

Sherman, L., Neyroud, P., & Neyroud, E. (2016). The Cambridge crime harm index: Measuring total harm from crime based on sentencing guidelines. *Policing, 10*(3), 171–183.

Teun van, R., & Stijin, R. (2023). The adoption of a crime harm index: A scoping literature review. *Police Practice and Research, 24*(4), 423–445.

Urwick, L. (1956). The manager's span of control. *Harvard Business Review, 34*(3), 39–47.

Woodward, J. (1965). *Analysis of organizations, industrial organization: Theory and practice*. Oxford University Press.

APPENDIX A

Control typologies

This appendix identifies the typologies of controls which are structured against the risk factors established in Chapters 4–6. The table sets out the control group, control type, and the mechanism of the control as detailed in Chapter 7 along with a description of the control. The table also illustrates control effectiveness factors and impacts, as detailed in Chapter 8, and appropriate control testing methodologies as discussed in Chapter 9.

The table is intended to be comprehensive, but not exhaustive. New controls may be added under the same structured logic as new opportunities to control insider risk as they emerge.

Control Group	Control Type	Control Mechanism	Control	Control Description	Control Effectiveness Factors	Control Impact	Control Testing Methodologies
Prevention	Prevent Opportunity	Prevent Certainty	Daily Workforce Redeployment	Redeployment of staff to different roles within an operating environment to reduce the certainty of access to a decision, information, or asset.	– Diversity of roles and authority over assets – Roles that do not require specialist skills/knowledge	– Cost of maintaining a diverse workforce – System of rostering and deployment – Training in different roles	– Performance testing – Threshold pressure testing – Impact testing – Control vulnerability assessment
			Random Case Allocation	Allocation of cases and transactions on a random basis reducing the certainty that a particular case will be allocated to a particular officer.	– Uniform roles and skills for all cases	– Cost of case routing system and procedures	– Performance testing – Threshold pressure testing – Impact testing – Control vulnerability assessment
			Restriction on Self-Allocation	An officer cannot self-allocate decisions, thereby reducing certainty that they will have access to a particular case.	– Restriction enforced	N/A	– Performance testing – Threshold pressure testing – Impact testing – Control vulnerability assessment
			Staff: Workload Ratio Balancing	Rebalancing the ratio of personnel to workload/decision, to reduce the certainty that a particular randomly allocated decision will be made by a particular officer.	– Actual ratio required to reduce certainty	– Salary cost – Reduced efficiency – Increased cost per transaction	– Threshold pressure testing – Impact testing
			Reduced Workload Specialisation	Reduction in specialisation by particular team members, thereby reducing the certainty that a transaction will go to an officer.	– No specialisation/expertise required	– No point of escalation for more complex cases	– Performance testing – Impact testing
			Workload Centralisation	Centralisation of all transactions in a geographically distributed organisation where smaller offices would have greater certainty due to lower staff to workload ratios. Centralisation rebalances against the national personnel footprint, thereby reducing certainty.	– Centralised case management capability – Case routing capability	– Cost of centralisation – Reduced local experience/client knowledge	– Performance testing – Impact testing – Control vulnerability assessment
			Regional Case Routing	In a geographically distributed organisation, the routing of cases away from the receiving regional office: thereby, reducing the certainty of a case being received by an officer.	– Case routing capability – Ratio of staff in regional offices	– Productivity impact – Reduced local knowledge	– Performance testing – Impact testing – Control vulnerability assessment

(Continued)

Control Group	Control Type	Control Mechanism	Control	Control Description	Control Effectiveness Factors	Control Impact	Control Testing Methodologies
			Separation of Duties/Powers	A separation of duties between an assessor and decision-maker or initiator and acquitter, thereby reducing the individual authority that a person has over a decision, information, or a tangible/intangible asset.	– Relative seniority of the initiator (less senior) vs. the acquitter (more senior)	– Productivity or efficiency: more officers required for the same volume of activity or less activity for the same number of officers. – Potential cost impact for more officers	– Performance testing – Impact testing – Control vulnerability assessment – Threshold pressure testing
			Collective Case/Asset Management	Cases or assets are centrally managed by a team of people rather than individually managed from end to end by a single officer, thereby reducing individual authority over the decision or other asset.	– Central case management capability – Standard processes and training	– Potential productivity impact for more coordination of activity	– Performance testing – Impact testing – Control vulnerability assessment – Threshold pressure testing
	Prevent Authority		Delegation Limit	Limitation of the organisational level at which a decision can be made or other asset utilised, thereby reducing the number of persons with authority over the asset.	– Level to which asset can be delegated	– Cost for more senior officers to interact with asset	– Performance testing – Impact testing – Control vulnerability assessment – Threshold pressure testing
			Define Powers	Defining and limiting the powers of a role through policy, thereby limiting authority within defined parameters.	– Level to which powers can be defined – Level to which powers can be limited without impacting enterprise business	– Limitation on ability to respond to unforeseen circumstances	– Performance testing – Impact testing – Control vulnerability assessment
			Stakeholder Consultation Requirement	A requirement to consult with affected stakeholders prior to making a decision or taking an action, thereby limiting the authority over the decision.	– Interest and influence of the relevant stakeholders	– Cost for consultation	– Performance testing – Impact testing – Control vulnerability assessment

(Continued)

(Continued)

(Continued)

Control Group	Control Type	Control Mechanism	Control	Control Description	Control Effectiveness Factors	Control Impact	Control Testing Methodologies
		Prevent Low Visibility	Separation of Duties/ Powers	A separation of duties between an assessor and decision-maker or initiator and acquitter, thereby increasing the visibility that other people have over a decision, information, or a tangible/ intangible asset.	– Relative seniority of the initiator (less senior) vs. the acquitter (more senior)	– Productivity or efficiency: more officers required for the same volume of activity or less activity for the same number of officers. – Potential cost impact of more officers	– Performance testing – Impact testing – Control vulnerability assessment – Threshold pressure testing
			Active CCTV	Closed circuit television, which is actively monitored by operators in real time.	– Monitor: Operator ratio – Hours of operation – Blind spots – Operator working hours	– Cost of installation, operation and maintenance of CCTV infrastructure – Cost of active monitoring – Cultural impact of monitoring staff activities	– Performance testing – Impact testing – Control vulnerability assessment – Threshold pressure testing
			Open Plan Workspace	An open plan workspace where the activities of individual officers are visible to other officers within the space, thereby increasing the visibility to other staff of the activities of each individual.	– Blind spots – Ratio of staff to work points	– Productivity impact of open plan space	– Performance testing – Impact testing – Control vulnerability assessment – Threshold pressure testing
			Centralised Decision Queue	A centralised queue of decisions within a system which is visible to all operators, thereby increasing the visibility of each officer over the activities of the others.	– Central case management capability – Standard processes and training	– Cost to purchase/implement central capability	– Performance testing – Impact testing – Control vulnerability assessment
			Group Mailbox	A group mailbox used for correspondence between team members and clients/ stakeholders, thereby increasing the visibility of communication between team members and those stakeholders.	– Mandatory use of group mailbox	– Set up cost for mailbox	– Performance testing – Impact testing – Control vulnerability assessment
			Limit Personal Drive	Limitation on personal drive space, thereby limiting storage of files and information collected in the course of work activities in personal storage and increasing visibility of those files in central filing systems.	– Low level of private/personal data requiring separate storage – Central filing capability – Quality of filing structure and compliance	– Limit legitimate use of personal drive – Cultural impact	– Performance testing – Impact testing – Control vulnerability assessment

(Continued)

Control Group	Control Type	Control Mechanism	Control	Control Description	Control Effectiveness Factors	Control Impact	Control Testing Methodologies
			Information Publication Requirement	Mandatory publication of information related to the decision or asset, for example the reasons for decision or the interactions with the other asset, thereby increasing public visibility of the interaction with the asset.	– Low level of sensitivity/privacy relating to decision information	– Time/cost of publication	– Performance testing – Impact testing – Control vulnerability assessment
			Restriction on Out-of-Hours Work	Restrictions on working outside normal business hours when fewer officers are also working, thereby increasing visibility of activities during business hours.	– No need for flexibility in work hours (e.g. working across time zones).	– Reduction of work flexibility – Reduction of productive work hours – Cultural impact	– Performance testing – Impact testing – Control vulnerability assessment
			Collective Case/Asset Management	Cases or assets are centrally managed by a team of people rather than individually managed from end to end by a single officer, thereby increasing visibility over the decision or other asset.	– Central case management capability – Standard processes and training	– Potential productivity impact for more coordination of activity	– Performance testing – Impact testing – Control vulnerability assessment – Threshold pressure testing
			Floor Management	Operational area managed by mobile floor manager monitoring work activities and serving as a point of escalation, thereby increasing the visibility of work activities.	– Ratio of staff to floor manager – Size of operational space to be monitored	– Cost of floor manager – Floor management infrastructure	– Performance testing – Impact testing – Control vulnerability assessment – Threshold pressure testing
			Paired Work Arrangements	Work activities undertaken with a minimum of two people to provide oversight and support to one another.	– Availability of pairs	– Efficiency impact due to additional personnel required for paired activity – Productivity impact	– Performance testing – Impact testing – Control vulnerability assessment – Threshold pressure testing
			Peer Review	Mandatory peer review of decisions or actions for all or part of the decisions or actions, thereby increasing the visibility over those decisions or actions.	– Ratio of decisions subject to peer review	– Efficiency impact due to additional personnel required for peer review activity – Productivity impact	– Performance testing – Impact testing – Control vulnerability assessment – Threshold pressure testing

(Continued)

Control Group	Control Type	Control Mechanism	Control	Control Description	Control Effectiveness Factors	Control Impact	Control Testing Methodologies
			Audit	Mandatory audit of decisions or actions for all or part of the decisions or actions, thereby increasing the visibility over those decisions or actions.	– Ratio of decisions subject to audit	– Efficiency impact due to additional personnel required for audit activity – Productivity impact	– Performance testing – Impact testing – Control vulnerability assessment – Threshold pressure testing
			Restrict Personal Drive File Type	Restrictions on the types of files able to be stored on personal drive space: i.e. restricting business file types from personal storage, thereby increasing visibility of those files on shared filing systems.	– Low level of private/personal data requiring separate storage – Central filing capability – Quality of filing structure and compliance	– Limit legitimate use of personal drive – Cultural impact	– Performance testing – Impact testing – Control vulnerability assessment
Prevent Low Traceability			Complete Decision Recording	Mandatory recording of all elements of a decision including reasons and evidence supporting the decision, thereby increasing the traceability of the decision.	– Quality of data and evidence-recording capability – Data model – Metadata capability	– Time/cost of recordkeeping	– Performance testing – Impact testing – Control vulnerability assessment
			Access/Use Recording	Mandatory record of access and/or use of information or tangible/intangible asset, thereby increasing traceability of the access/use.	– Quality of data and evidence recording capability – Data model – Metadata capability	– Time/cost of recordkeeping	– Performance testing – Impact testing – Control vulnerability assessment
			Passive CCTV	Closed Circuit Television which is not actively monitored but which records enterprise business activity, thereby increasing traceability of the business activity recorded.	– Storage volume – Image quality – Storage timeframe – Blind spots	– Cost of installation, operation and maintenance of CCTV infrastructure – Cultural impact of monitoring staff activities	– Performance testing – Impact testing – Control vulnerability assessment – Threshold pressure testing
			Body-Worn Camera	Body-worn cameras which record enterprise business activity associated with a specific officer, thereby increasing traceability of their activities.	– Storage volume – Image quality – Storage timeframe – Ability to switch on/off camera	– Cost of purchase, operation, and maintenance of body camera infrastructure – Cultural Impact of monitoring staff activities	– Performance testing – Impact testing – Control vulnerability assessment – Threshold pressure testing

(Continued)

(Continued)

Control Group	Control Type	Control Mechanism	Control	Control Description	Control Effectiveness Factors	Control Impact	Control Testing Methodologies
			Event Recording	Mandatory recording of events impacting on a decision, information, or tangible/intangible asset, thereby increasing traceability of those events.	– Quality of data and evidence-recording capability – Data model – Metadata capability	– Time/cost of recordkeeping	– Performance testing – Impact testing – Control vulnerability assessment
			Record Quality Assurance	Mandatory assurance of the quality of recordkeeping, thereby improving the quality of records and enhancing traceability of business activity.	– Ratio of records subject to assurance	– Cost of assurance activities	– Performance testing – Impact testing – Control vulnerability assessment – Threshold pressure testing
			Daily Reconciliation	Daily reconciliation of decisions, information, or tangible/intangible assets, providing a daily record of activity thereby increasing traceability of those activities.	– Quality of data and evidence-recording capability – Data model – Metadata capability	– Cost of reconciliation activities	– Performance testing – Impact testing – Control vulnerability assessment
			Record of Destruction	Mandatory record of destruction of information or tangible/intangible asset, thereby increasing traceability of the asset.	– Quality of data and evidence-recording capability – Data model – Metadata capability	– Time/cost of recordkeeping	– Performance testing – Impact testing – Control vulnerability assessment
			Record of Modification	Mandatory record of modification of information or tangible/intangible asset, thereby increasing traceability of the asset.	– Quality of data and evidence recording capability – Data model – Metadata capability	– Time/cost of recordkeeping	– Performance testing – Impact testing – Control vulnerability assessment
			Record of Creation	Mandatory record of creation of information or tangible/intangible asset thereby increasing traceability of the asset.	– Quality of data and evidence-recording capability – Data model – Metadata capability	– Time/cost of recordkeeping	– Performance testing – Impact testing – Control vulnerability assessment
			Asset Location Record	Mandatory record of location of information or tangible/intangible asset thereby increasing traceability of the asset.	– Quality of data and evidence recording capability – Data model – Metadata capability	– Time/cost of recordkeeping	– Performance testing – Impact testing – Control vulnerability assessment

(Continued)

Control Group	Control Type	Control Mechanism	Control	Control Description	Control Effectiveness Factors	Control Impact	Control Testing Methodologies
			Locational/Movement Record	Mandatory record of movement of information or tangible/intangible asset, thereby increasing traceability of the asset.	– Quality of data and evidence-recording capability – Data model – Metadata capability	– Time/cost of recordkeeping	– Performance testing – Impact testing – Control vulnerability assessment
			Record Management	Capability to manage the organisation's records including creation, modification, utilisation, movement, and destruction thereby increasing traceability of those assets.	– Quality of data and evidence recording capability – Data model – Metadata capability	– Time/cost of recordkeeping	– Performance testing – Impact testing – Control vulnerability assessment
			Receipting	Mandatory process of receipting tangible/intangible assets received from third parties, thereby increasing traceability of those assets.	– Quality/reliability of receipting process – Quality of data and evidence-recording capability – Data model – Metadata capability	– Time/cost of recordkeeping	– Performance testing – Impact testing – Control vulnerability assessment
			Process Standardisation	Standardisation of business processes, thereby increasing the traceability of normal vs. abnormal processes.	– Level of standardisation available for process – Level of discretion/flexibility required	– Reduced flexibility of process/practice	– Performance testing – Impact testing – Control vulnerability assessment
			Asset Continuity Recording/Chain of Custody	Mandatory recording of chain of custody for information and/or tangible/intangible assets, thereby increasing the traceability of those assets.	– Quality of data and evidence-recording capability – Data model – Metadata capability	– Time/cost of recordkeeping	– Performance testing – Impact testing – Control vulnerability assessment

(Continued)

(Continued)

Control Group	Control Type	Control Mechanism	Control	Control Description	Control Effectiveness Factors	Control Impact	Control Testing Methodologies
		Prevent Access	Pass Access	Access to assets via an electronic pass, thereby reducing general access to the assets.	– Pass associated to individual – Photographic ID	– Cost of pass infrastructure – Cost of pass management capability – Restriction on movement	– Performance testing – Impact testing – Control vulnerability assessment
			Biometric Access	Access to assets via recorded biometric (face, fingerprint, retina, voice), thereby reducing general access to the assets.	– Quality of biometric recording process – Quality of biometric recognition accuracy	– Cost of biometric infrastructure – Cost of biometric management capability – Restriction on movement or ICT access	– Performance testing – Impact testing – Control vulnerability assessment – Threshold pressure testing
			Passcode Access	Access to assets via a passcode, thereby reducing general access to the assets.	– Passcode complexity rules – Passcode associated to individual	– Cost of passcode infrastructure – Cost of passcode management capability – Restriction on movement or ICT access	– Performance testing – Impact testing – Control vulnerability assessment
			Key Access	Access to assets via an electronic pass, thereby reducing general access to the assets.	– Individual key allocation – Key custody rules	– Cost of key infrastructure – Cost of key management capability – Restriction on movement	– Performance testing – Impact testing – Control vulnerability assessment
			Role-Based Access	Access to ICT systems based on the role rather than general access or access provided to individuals, thereby reducing access to those who have a need to interact with the asset.	– Maintenance of role records and access	– Cost of role-based security platform – Cost of role management capability – Restriction on ICT access	– Performance testing – Impact testing – Control vulnerability assessment
			Asset Compartmentalisation	Compartmentalisation of information and/or tangible/intangible assets, thereby reducing general access.	– Quality of compartmentalisation processes and restrictions – Quality of compartmentalisation decisions	– Reduction of shared organisational knowledge	– Performance testing – Impact testing – Control vulnerability assessment

(Continued)

Control Group	Control Type	Control Mechanism	Control	Control Description	Control Effectiveness Factors	Control Impact	Control Testing Methodologies
			Individual-Eased System Access	ICT system access provided on an individual, thereby reducing general access to the assets.	– Quality of access grant procedures – Quality of access maintenance procedures	– Cost of individual security management capability – Restriction on ICT access	– Performance testing – Impact testing – Control vulnerability assessment
			Access Maintenance	Capability to maintain access restrictions and authorisations, thereby reducing general access to assets.	– Quality of access grant procedures – Quality of access maintenance procedures	– Cost of access management capability	– Performance testing – Impact testing – Control vulnerability assessment
			Time-Based Access	Restriction of access to particular time periods: e.g. business hours, thereby reducing general access to assets.	– Quality of access grant procedures – Quality of access maintenance procedures	– Restriction on organisational flexibility outside of relevant time period.	– Performance testing – Impact testing – Control vulnerability assessment
			Access Can-cellation	Cancellation of access in the event of compromise of access capability, thereby reducing general access to organisational assets.	– Quality of compromise detection capability – Quality of access maintenance procedures	– Time/cost of cancellation procedures – Productivity impact of cancellation	– Performance testing – Impact testing – Control vulnerability assessment – Threshold pressure testing
			Guarding	Posting guards to monitor and restrict access to organisational assets, thereby restricting general access to those assets.	– Quality of guarding procedures – Blind spots	– Cost of maintaining guarding capability	– Performance testing – Impact testing – Control vulnerability assessment – Threshold pressure testing
			Electronic Funds Transfer	Restricting the transfer of value to electronic means, thereby reducing general access to assets of value.	– Quality of EFT security arrangements	– Cost of EFT platform – Restriction on payment methods	– Performance testing – Impact testing – Control vulnerability assessment
Prevent Motivation	Prevent Pressure		Conflict of Interest Policy	Established policy setting clear definitions and parameters in relation to the declaration and management of conflicts of interest, thereby reducing the potential for pressure on an individual.	– Quality of definitions and parameters – Compliance with policy	N/A	– Performance testing – Impact testing – Control vulnerability assessment
			Adversary Training	Training individuals to recognise the corrupting modus operandi of capable beneficiaries, thereby reducing their capability to apply pressure on officers of the organisation.	– Understanding/intelligence on modus operandi – Quality of training	– Cost of training and development	– Performance testing – Impact testing

(Continued)

Control Group	Control Type	Control Mechanism	Control	Control Description	Control Effectiveness Factors	Control Impact	Control Testing Methodologies
			Drug and Alcohol Policy	Established policy setting clear definitions and parameters in relation to drug and alcohol use, thereby reducing the potential for these to place pressure on an individual.	– Drug and alcohol testing – Strength of relationship between drug and alcohol use and insider risk	N/A	– Performance testing – Impact testing – Control vulnerability assessment
			Drug and Alcohol Testing	Testing of individuals for the presence of drugs and alcohol serving as a preventer and deterrent against use and, thereby, reducing the potential for these to place pressure on an individual.	– Accuracy of detection methods – Sample handling processes – Tamper proofing – Strength of relationship between drug and alcohol use and insider risk	– High cost of drug-testing capability	– Performance testing – Impact testing – Control vulnerability assessment – Threshold pressure testing
			Restrict Account Manager Decision-Making	Restrictions on account managers of beneficiaries to make decisions in relation to their cases, thereby reducing the potential for close relationships to create pressure on the individual.	– Quality of restriction procedures	– Reduced ability to use account knowledge for decision-making	– Performance testing – Impact testing
			Conflict of Interest Training	Training on the management of conflicts of interest in relation to decision-making or the utilisation of other organisational assets.	– Quality of training	– Cost of training and development	– Performance testing – Impact testing
			Pressure Due Diligence	Due diligence conducted over individuals to identify possible points of leverage which could be utilised by a beneficiary, such as financial pressures, gambling or drug addiction, or previous employment by commercial rivals, thereby preventing the entry into the organisation of persons with such vulnerabilities or enabling them to be managed.	– Quality, availability, and reliability of due diligence information – Quality of due diligence checks	– Cost of due diligence capability	– Performance testing – Impact testing – Control vulnerability assessment – Threshold pressure testing

(Continued)

Control Group	Control Type	Control Mechanism	Control	Control Description	Control Effectiveness Factors	Control Impact	Control Testing Methodologies
			Reasonable Performance Targets	Setting realistically achievable productivity and quality targets, thereby reducing pressure to "cut corners" to achieve targets.	– Quality of productivity measurements	– Impact on productivity/efficiency	– Performance testing – Impact testing – Control vulnerability assessment – Threshold pressure testing
			Reasonable Adjustment	Providing reasonable adjustments for individuals in relation to work patterns and requirements, thereby reducing pressure to "cut corners" to achieve targets.	– Quality of productivity measurements	– Impact on productivity/efficiency	– Performance testing – Impact testing
			Limit Decision-Maker Beneficiary Interaction	Restricting the interaction between beneficiaries and decision-makers through physical or procedural means, thereby reducing the potential for the relationship to create pressure.	– Quality of separation from beneficiaries	– Reduced ability to use knowledge of individual beneficiaries for decision-making	– Performance testing – Impact testing
			Employee Assistance Programme	Providing counselling and assistance to employees to resolve personal or professional challenges which may manifest as pressures.	– Quality, accessibility, and availability of support services	– Cost of employee assistance programme	– Performance testing – Impact testing
		Prevent Inducement	Adversary Training	Training individuals to recognise the corrupting modus operandi and inducements used by capable beneficiaries, thereby reducing the ability for those inducements to be successfully utilised.	– Understanding/intelligence on modus operandi – Quality of training	– Cost of training and development	– Performance testing – Impact testing
			Inducement Reporting	Providing a channel for reporting of inducements offered by beneficiaries, thereby reducing the successful inducement of officers within the organisation.	– Quality, accessibility, and availability of reporting channels	– Cost of reporting channel	– Performance testing – Impact testing

(Continued)

Control Group	Control Type	Control Mechanism	Control	Control Description	Control Effectiveness Factors	Control Impact	Control Testing Methodologies
			Inducement Support	Providing support and assistance to employees in the event they are subject to inducement, including negative inducement (such as threats).	– Quality, accessibility, and availability of support services	– Cost of support programme	– Performance testing – Impact testing
			Gift Policy	Established policy, setting clear definitions, and parameters in relation to the receipt and management of gifts, thereby reducing the potential for them to be used as inducements to act on behalf of a beneficiary.	– Quality of definitions and parameters – Compliance with policy	N/A	– Performance testing – Impact testing
			Minimise Aggregate Asset Value	Minimising the total value of assets held within the organisation: e.g. the amount of cash held at any one time, thereby minimising its ability to induce the behaviour of an actor.	– Ability to disaggregate assets/value – Control over asset value vs. market dictated value	– Impact of processes for disaggregation	– Performance testing – Impact testing
		Prevent Rationalisation	Insider Impact Case Studies	Publication of case studies setting out the impact of insider activities on the enterprise or other priorities, thereby preventing people from minimising and rationalising insider risk activity.	– Effectiveness detection capabilities – Quality of response capabilities	– Cultural impact – Stakeholder impact/ trust because of disclosed wrongdoing	– Performance testing – Impact testing
			Positive Culture Creation	Creation of a positive organisational culture thereby reducing a person's ability to rationalise wrongdoing against the organisation.	– Prevailing culture	N/A	– Performance testing – Impact testing
			Change Management	Formal procedures for change management to support organisational staff through changes to business strategy and practice, thereby reducing a person's ability to rationalise wrongdoing against the organisation.	– Quality of change management practices	– Cost of change management capability	– Performance testing – Impact testing

(Continued)

Control Group	Control Type	Control Mechanism	Control	Control Description	Control Effectiveness Factors	Control Impact	Control Testing Methodologies
		Prevent Interaction	Leadership	Positive leadership creating "sprit de corps" within an organisation, thereby reducing a person's ability to rationalise wrongdoing against the organisation.	– Quality of leadership capability – Organisational leadership culture	N/A	– Performance testing – Impact testing
			Employee Assistance Programme	Providing counselling and assistance to employees to resolve personal or professional challenges which may enable a person to rationalise wrongdoing against the organisation.	– Quality, accessibility, and availability of support services	– Cost of employee assistance programme	– Performance testing – Impact testing
			Public Awareness	Raising public awareness of the impact of insider threat thereby reducing a person's ability to rationalise wrongdoing against the organisation.	– Effectiveness Detection capabilities – Quality of response capabilities	– Cultural impact – Stakeholder impact/trust because of disclosed wrongdoing	– Performance testing – Impact testing
			Performance Management	Managing performance and underperformance of staff within the organisation, thereby reducing a person's ability to rationalise wrongdoing against the organisation as a result of poor performance management.	– Quality of performance management capability – Quality of supervisors' performance management	N/A	– Performance testing – Impact testing
Prevent Beneficiaries			Workforce Redeployment	Redeployment of staff to different roles within an operating environment to reduce the interaction between an officer and a beneficiary.	– Diversity of roles and authority over assets – Roles that do not require specialist skills/knowledge	– Cost of maintaining a diverse workforce – System of rostering and deployment – Training in different roles	– Performance testing – Impact testing – Control vulnerability assessment – Threshold pressure testing
			Beneficiary Due Diligence	Due diligence conducted over individuals to identify possible beneficiary relationships which might create insider risk, such as previous employment by commercial rivals, thereby preventing the entry into the organisation of persons with such vulnerabilities or enabling them to be managed.	– Quality, availability, and reliability of due diligence information – Quality of due diligence checks	– Cost of due diligence capability	– Performance testing – Impact testing – Control vulnerability assessment – Threshold pressure testing

(Continued)

Control Mechanism	Control Type	Control Group	Control	Control Description	Control Effectiveness Factors	Control Impact	Control Testing Methodologies
			Limit Decision-Maker Beneficiary interaction	Restricting the interaction between beneficiaries and decision-makers through physical or procedural means, thereby reducing the potential for the relationship to create insider risk.	– Quality of separation from beneficiaries	– Reduced ability to use knowledge of individual beneficiaries for decision-making	– Performance testing – Impact testing
			Restrict Account Manager Decision-Making	Restrictions on account managers of beneficiaries to make decisions in relation to their cases, thereby reducing the potential for close relationships to create insider risk.	– Quality of restriction procedures	– Reduced ability to use account knowledge for decision-making	– Performance testing – Impact testing
Detect Certainty	Detect Opportunity	Detection	Self-Allocation Flag	AICT system alert in the event an officer allocates a decision to themselves, thereby detecting an increase in certainty.	– Accuracy of alert	– Cost of implementing alert	– Performance Testing – Impact Testing – Control vulnerability assessment
			Self-Allocation Quality Assurance	Quality assurance of self-allocated decisions in the event these are allowed thereby detecting where self-allocation has been utilised to increase certainty.	– Quality of assurance procedures – Ratio of self-allocated decisions subject to assurance processes	– Cost of assurance activities	– Performance testing – Impact testing – Control vulnerability assessment – Threshold pressure testing
			Self-Allocation Anomaly Detection	Systemic identification of anomalies in respect of the self-allocation of decisions: for example in terms of volume compared to rest of population, thereby detecting an increase in certainty.	– Accuracy of anomaly: false positive/false negatives	– Cost of implementing anomaly algorithm	– Performance testing – Impact testing – Control vulnerability assessment – Threshold pressure testing
			Redeployment Exemption Request Anomaly detection	Systemic identification of anomalies in respect of the requests for exemptions to mandatory redeployment: e.g. in terms of volume compared to rest of population, thereby detecting an increase in certainty.	– Accuracy of anomaly: false positive/false negatives	– Cost of implementing anomaly algorithm	– Performance testing – Impact testing – Control vulnerability assessment – Threshold pressure testing

(Continued)

Control Group	Control Type	Control Mechanism	Control	Control Description	Control Effectiveness Factors	Control Impact	Control Testing Methodologies
			Regional Case Routing Anomaly Detection	Systemic identification of anomalies in respect of routing of cases regionally, for example volume of cases not referred, thereby detecting an increase in certainty.	– Accuracy of anomaly: false positive/false negatives	– Cost of implementing anomaly algorithm	– Performance testing – Impact testing – Control vulnerability assessment – Threshold pressure testing
			Shift/Roles Swapping Anomaly Detection	Systemic identification of anomalies in respect of swapping shifts or roles, for example in terms of volume compared to rest of population, thereby detecting an increase in certainty.	– Accuracy of anomaly: false positive/false negatives	– Cost of implementing anomaly algorithm	– Performance testing – Impact testing – Control vulnerability assessment – Threshold pressure testing
			Decision Delegation Anomaly Detection	Systemic identification of anomalies in respect of delegation or lack of delegation of business activities: e.g. in terms of volume compared to rest of population, thereby detecting an increase in certainty.	– Accuracy of anomaly: false positive/false negatives	– Cost of implementing anomaly algorithm	– Performance testing – Impact testing – Control vulnerability assessment – Threshold pressure testing
			Specialist Role Asset Interaction Review	Review of the interaction between small numbers of specialists and decisions, information or other assets to detect where their specialisation has been utilised to increase certainty.	– Quality of review procedures	– Cost of review activities	– Performance testing – Impact testing – Control vulnerability assessment – Threshold pressure testing
			Team Size Analysis	Analysis of team size relative to volume of assets, thereby detecting the level of certainty.	– Quality of review procedures	– Cost of review activities	– Performance testing – Impact testing

(Continued)

Control Group	Control Type	Control Mechanism	Control	Control Description	Control Effectiveness Factors	Control Impact	Control Testing Methodologies
		Detect Authority	Initiator/Approver Role Match Flag	AICT system alert in the event the initiator and approver of a decision is the same person, thereby detecting an increase in authority.	– Accuracy of alert	– Cost of implementing alert	– Performance testing – Impact testing – Control vulnerability assessment
			Delegation Anomaly Detection	Systemic identification of anomalies in respect of delegation or lack of delegation of business activities: e.g. in terms of volume compared to rest of population, thereby detecting an increase in certainty.	– Accuracy of anomaly: false positive/false negatives	– Cost of implementing anomaly algorithm	– Performance testing – Impact testing – Control vulnerability assessment – Threshold pressure testing
			Exceeding Authority Flag	AICT system alert in the event that a person exceeds their delegation in respect of a decision or action, thereby detecting an increase in authority.	– Accuracy of alert	– Cost of implementing alert	– Performance testing – Impact testing – Control vulnerability assessment – Threshold pressure testing
		Detect Low Visibility	Out-of-Hours Work Pattern Anomaly Identification	Systemic identification of anomalies in respect of out-of-hours work activity, for example in terms of volume compared to rest of population, thereby detecting a decrease in visibility.	– Accuracy of anomaly: false positive/false negatives	– Cost of implementing anomaly algorithm	– Performance testing – Impact testing – Control vulnerability assessment – Threshold pressure testing
			Review Systemic Blind Spot Activity	Systemic review of activity undertaking in CCTV and/or floor management contexts, thereby detecting a decrease in visibility.	– Quality of review procedures	– Cost of review activities	– Performance testing – Impact testing – Control vulnerability assessment – Threshold pressure testing
			Peer Review Anomaly Flag	AICT system alert in the event a decision is not subject to peer reviews in respect of a decision or action, thereby detecting a decrease in visibility.	– Accuracy of alert	– Cost of implementing alert	– Performance testing – Impact testing – Control vulnerability assessment – Threshold pressure testing

(Continued)

Control Group	Control Type	Control Mechanism	Control	Control Description	Control Effectiveness Factors	Control Impact	Control Testing Methodologies
			Peer Review Anomaly Identification	Systemic identification of anomalies in respect of peer review activity: e.g. in terms of matches between decision-maker and reviewer, thereby detecting a decrease in visibility.	– Accuracy of anomaly: false positive/false negatives	– Cost of implementing anomaly algorithm	– Performance testing – Impact testing – Control vulnerability assessment – Threshold pressure testing
			Pair Activity Anomaly Flag	AICT system alert in the event a person undertakes solo business activity which is subject to paired work arrangements in respect of a decision or action, thereby detecting a decrease in visibility.	– Accuracy of alert	– Cost of implementing alert	– Performance testing – Impact testing – Control vulnerability assessment – Threshold pressure testing
			Pair Activity Anomaly Identification	Systemic identification of anomalies in respect of paired activities: e.g. consistent matching of the same officers, thereby detecting a decrease in visibility.	– Accuracy of anomaly: false positive/false negatives	– Cost of implementing anomaly algorithm	– Performance testing – Impact testing – Control vulnerability assessment – Threshold pressure testing
Detect Low Traceability			Data/Record Quality Assurance	Quality assurance of record keeping of individual transactions to detect systemic decreases in traceability.	– Quality of assurance procedures – Ratio of files subject to assurance processes	– Cost of assurance activities	– Performance testing – Impact testing – Control vulnerability assessment – Threshold pressure testing
			Decision Evidence Quality Assurance	Quality assurance of record keeping of evidence supporting decisions to detect systemic decreases in traceability.	– Quality of assurance procedures – Ratio of files subject to assurance processes	– Cost of assurance activities	– Performance testing – Impact testing – Control vulnerability assessment – Threshold pressure testing
			Corrupted Record Identification	Systemic identification of corrupted records of decision or action records to detect systemic decreases in traceability.	– Accuracy of anomaly: false positive/false negatives – Relationship between corrupted records and insider risk	– Cost of implementing anomaly algorithm	– Performance testing – Impact testing – Control vulnerability assessment – Threshold pressure testing

(Continued)

Control Group	Control Type	Control Mechanism	Control	Control Description	Control Effectiveness Factors	Control Impact	Control Testing Methodologies
			Use of Personal Email Flag	AICT system alert in the event a person utilises personal email in relation to a business activity, thereby detecting a decrease in traceability.	– Accuracy of alert – Relationship between personal email use and insider risk	– Cost of implementing alert	– Performance testing – Impact testing – Control vulnerability assessment – Threshold pressure testing
			Audit Log Deletion Flag	AICT system alert in the event a person deletes the audit log in respect of decisions or actions, thereby detecting a decrease in traceability.	– Accuracy of alert – Relationship between audit log deletion and insider risk	– Cost of implementing alert	– Performance testing – Impact testing – Control vulnerability assessment – Threshold pressure testing
			Receipt Anomaly Identification	Systemic identification of anomalies in receipt records relative to the overall population of records to detect systemic decreases in traceability.	– Accuracy of anomaly – false positive/false negatives – Relationship between receipt anomalies and insider risk	– Cost of implementing anomaly algorithm	– Performance testing – Impact testing – Control vulnerability assessment – Threshold pressure testing
			Record Deletion Flag	AICT system alert in the event a person deletes a record which should not have been, thereby detecting a decrease in traceability.	– Accuracy of alert – Relationship between record deletion and insider risk	– Cost of implementing alert	– Performance testing – Impact testing – Control vulnerability assessment – Threshold pressure testing
			Record Deletion Anomaly Identification	Systemic identification of anomalies in deletion of records relative to the overall population of records to detect systemic decreases in traceability.	– Accuracy of anomaly: false positive/false negatives – Relationship between record deletion anomalies and insider risk	– Cost of implementing anomaly algorithm	– Performance testing – Impact testing – Control vulnerability assessment – Threshold pressure testing
			Record Modification Flag	AICT system alert in the event a person modifies a record which should not have been, thereby detecting a decrease in traceability.	– Accuracy of alert – Relationship between record modification and insider risk	– Cost of implementing alert	– Performance testing – Impact testing – Control vulnerability assessment – Threshold pressure testing
			Record Modification Anomaly Identification	Systemic identification of anomalies in modification of records relative to the overall population of records, to detect systemic decreases in traceability.	– Accuracy of anomaly – false positive/false negatives – Relationship between record modification anomalies and insider risk	– Cost of implementing anomaly algorithm	– Performance testing – Impact testing – Control vulnerability assessment – Threshold pressure testing
			CCTV/Body Cam Gap Identification	Systemic identification of gaps in CCTV or body cam footage, to detect systemic decreases in traceability.	– Relationship between footage gaps and insider risk	– Cost of gap identification capability	– Performance testing – Impact testing – Control vulnerability assessment – Threshold pressure testing

(Continued)

Control Group	Control Type	Control Mechanism	Control	Control Description	Control Effectiveness Factors	Control Impact	Control Testing Methodologies
		Detect Access	Tamper Proof Seals	Tamper-proof seals on doors, containers, packaging enabling the detection of access to an asset contained within.	– Quality of seal – Quality of procedures for sealing and recording sealing	– Cost of seals and sealing process	– Performance testing – Impact testing – Control vulnerability assessment
			On Leave Access Flag	AICT system alert in the event a person accesses an asset or location while they are on leave.	– Relationship between access while on leave and insider risk – Level of false positives/negatives	– Cost of implementing alert	– Performance testing – Impact testing – Control vulnerability assessment – Threshold pressure testing
			On Leave Access Identification	Systemic identification of anomalies in access to assets while on leave as compared to overall population.	– Relationship between access while on leave and insider risk – Level of false positives/negatives	– Cost of implementing anomaly algorithm	– Performance testing – Impact testing – Control vulnerability assessment – Threshold pressure testing
			Access Anomaly Identification	Systemic identification of anomalies in access to assets, including time, place, organisational structure, organisational level, and behaviour during access.	– Relationship between access anomalies and insider risk – Level of false positives/negatives	– Cost of implementing anomaly algorithm	– Performance testing – Impact testing – Control vulnerability assessment – Threshold pressure testing
			Key Stocktake	Stocktake of keys and key holders to detect people who should not have access and any missing keys.	– Key records	– Cost of stocktake activity	– Performance testing – Impact testing – Control vulnerability assessment
			Asset Stocktake	Stocktake of assets to detect missing, moved, or modified assets indicative of unauthorised access to those assets.	– Inventory of assets – Asset access records	– Cost of stocktake activity	– Performance testing – Impact testing – Control vulnerability assessment
			Passcode Access Compromise Identification	Systemic identification of compromised passcode indicating potential ability to access assets.	– Passcode reporting procedures – Passcode monitoring processes	– Cost of passcode monitoring	– Performance testing – Impact testing – Control vulnerability assessment
			Pass Movement Anomaly Identification	Systemic identification of anomalies in the movement of access passes, potentially indicating unauthorised access to assets.	– Relationship between anomalies and insider risk – Level of false positives/negatives	– Cost of implementing anomaly algorithm	– Performance testing – Impact testing – Control vulnerability assessment – Threshold pressure testing

(Continued)

(Continued)

Control Group	Control Type	Control Mechanism	Control	Control Description	Control Effectiveness Factors	Control Impact	Control Testing Methodologies
Detect Motivation	Detect Pressure		Drug and Alcohol Testing	Testing of individuals for the presence of drugs and alcohol detecting the potential pressure on the individual	– Accuracy of detection methods – Sample-handling processes – Tamper proofing – Strength of relationship between drug and alcohol use and insider risk	– High cost of drug testing capability – Cultural impact of invasion of privacy	– Performance testing – Impact testing – Control vulnerability assessment – Threshold pressure testing
			Financial Examination	Systemic examination and due diligence of personal financial status to detect potential financial pressures.	– Strength of relationship between financial pressure and insider risk	– Cost of financial due diligence – Cultural impact of invasion of privacy	– Performance testing – Impact testing – Control vulnerability assessment – Threshold pressure testing
			Suspicious Transaction Report	Systemic reporting by financial institutions of suspicious transactions by customers	– Legal framework for suspicious transactions reporting – Strength of relationship between suspicious transactions and insider risk	– Cost for capability to receive and analyse reports	– Performance testing – Impact testing – Control vulnerability assessment – Threshold pressure testing
			Controlled Operation	Controlled insider threat operation providing targeted employees with inducement to commit insider actions to detect pressure and general motivation for insider acts	– Legal and policy framework for controlled operations	– Cost for controlled operations capability and individual operations – Cultural impact of controlled operations on employees – Stakeholder impact	– Performance testing – Impact testing – Control vulnerability assessment – Threshold pressure testing
			Conflict of Interest Declaration	Declaration by employees of perceived or actual conflicts of interest thereby identifying potential pressure.	– Channels for declaration – Record of declaration – Analysis of declarations	– Cost for capability and channels to receive declarations	– Performance testing – Impact testing
			Conflict of Interest Check	Due diligence conducted over individuals to identify conflicts of interest enabling them to be managed.	– Quality, availability, and reliability of due diligence information – Quality of due diligence checks	– Cost of due diligence capability	– Performance testing – Impact testing – Control vulnerability assessment – Threshold pressure testing

(Continued)

(Continued)

Control Group	Control Type	Control Mechanism	Control	Control Description	Control Effectiveness Factors	Control Impact	Control Testing Methodologies
			Employment Screening Pattern Analysis	Pattern analysis of employment screening and due diligence results to identify patterns of failure to meet standards or in relation to investigated cases of insider activity.	– Quality, availability, and reliability of screening data – Quality, availability, and reliability of investigation information and data	– Cost of pattern analysis capability	– Performance testing – Impact testing – Control vulnerability assessment – Threshold pressure testing
			Beneficiary Email Match	Matching of private email correspondence by employees with known target beneficiaries	– Use of work email to communicate with beneficiaries	– Cost of matching capability – Cultural impact of staff email monitoring	– Performance testing – Impact testing – Control vulnerability assessment
			Secondary Employment Identification	Due diligence conducted over individuals to identify secondary employment which may represent a pressure.	– Strength of relationship between secondary employment and insider risk	– Cost of due diligence activity	– Performance testing – Impact testing – Control vulnerability assessment
			Contact Tracking	Tracking and surveillance of contact with potential or actual beneficiaries to identify potential pressure	– Tracking capability	– High cost of tracking and surveillance – Cultural impact of surveillance	– Performance testing – Impact testing – Control vulnerability assessment
			Interest Group Analysis	Due diligence conducted over an employee's membership of relevant interest groups which may create pressure to act against the enterprise's interests	– Strength of relationship between membership of interest group and insider risk	– Cost of due diligence activity	– Performance testing – Impact testing – Control vulnerability assessment
			Behaviour Change Analysis	Systemic analysis of behaviour change by individuals within the organisation as a means of identifying potential areas of high pressure.	– Strength of relationship between behaviour change and insider risk	– Cost of analytical activity	– Performance testing – Impact testing – Control vulnerability assessment
			Health and Wellbeing Analysis	Systemic analysis of health and wellbeing indicators such as unplanned absences and satisfaction survey results to identify areas in the organisation which may be subject to higher levels of pressure.	– Strength of relationship between health and wellbeing and insider risk	– Cost of analytical activity	– Performance testing – Impact Testing

(Continued)

(Continued)

Control Group	Control Type	Control Mechanism	Control	Control Description	Control Effectiveness Factors	Control Impact	Control Testing Methodologies
		Detect Inducement	Anomalous Funds Transfers	Identification of anomalous transactions at the individual or organisational level, which may be indicative of inducements paid to an individual.	– Level of false positives/negatives	– Cost of analytical activity	– Performance testing – Impact testing – Control vulnerability assessment
			Unexplained Wealth Identification	Systemic identification of unexplained wealth of individuals within the organisation to identify potential inducements.	– Level of false positives/negatives	– Cost of analytical activity	– Performance testing – Impact testing – Control vulnerability assessment
			Promotion Pattern Analysis	Systemic analysis of promotions within the organisation indicative of organisational advancement utilised as an inducement.	– Level of false positives/negatives	– Cost of analytical activity	– Performance testing – Impact testing – Control vulnerability assessment
			Blackmail/Threat Reporting	Reporting channel for threats or blackmail by a potential beneficiary to identify this as a form of inducement and modus operandi for that beneficiary.	– Availability and accessibility of reporting channel	– Cost of reporting channel	– Performance testing – Impact testing
			Behaviour Change Analysis	Systemic analysis of behaviour changes by individuals within the organisation as a means of identifying inducement.	– Strength of relationship between behaviour change and insider risk	– Cost of analytical activity	– Performance testing – Impact testing
		Detect Rationalisation	Staff Survey Analysis	Systemic analysis of staff satisfaction survey results, indicators to identify areas in the organisation which may be subject to higher levels of rationalisation.	– Strength of relationship between survey results and insider risk	– Cost of analytical activity	– Performance testing – Impact testing
			Underperformance Analysis	Systemic analysis of staff underperformance and performance management indicators to identify areas in the organisation which may be subject to higher levels of rationalisation.	– Strength of relationship between underperformance and performance management and insider risk	– Cost of analytical activity	– Performance testing – Impact testing

(Continued)

(Continued)

Control Group	Control Type	Control Mechanism	Control	Control Description	Control Effectiveness Factors	Control Impact	Control Testing Methodologies
	Detect Interaction		Employee Assistance Use Analysis	Systemic analysis of the use of employee assistance to identify areas in the organisation which may be subject to higher levels of rationalisation.	– Strength of relationship between use of employee assistance and insider risk	– Cost of analytical activity	– Performance testing – Impact testing
			Unplanned Absenteeism Analysis	Systemic analysis of unplanned absenteeism indicators to identify areas in the organisation which may be subject to higher levels of rationalisation.	– Strength of relationship between unplanned absenteeism and insider risk	– Cost of analytical activity	– Performance testing – Impact testing
			Attrition Analysis	Systemic analysis of staff attrition to identify areas in the organisation which may be subject to higher levels of rationalisation.	– Strength of relationship between staff attrition and insider risk	– Cost of analytical activity	– Performance testing – Impact testing
	Detect Beneficiaries		Beneficiary Email Match	Matching of private email correspondence by employees with known target beneficiaries.	– Use of work email to communicate with beneficiaries	– Cost of matching capability – Cultural impact of staff email monitoring	– Performance testing – Impact testing – Control vulnerability assessment
			Beneficiary Phone Number Match	Matching of private phone correspondence by employees with known target beneficiaries.	– Use of work phone to communicate with beneficiaries	– Cost of matching capability – Cultural impact of staff phone monitoring	– Performance testing – Impact testing – Control vulnerability assessment
			Beneficiary App Match	Matching of private communication application by employees with known target beneficiaries.	– Use of work ICT asset to communicate with beneficiaries	– Cost of matching capability – Cultural impact of staff communication monitoring	– Performance testing – Impact testing – Control vulnerability assessment

(Continued)

(Continued)

Control Group	Control Type	Control Mechanism	Control	Control Description	Control Effectiveness Factors	Control Impact	Control Testing Methodologies
Detect Incident	Detect Incident	Detect Incident	Modus Operandi Flag	An ICT system alert in the event of a pattern which matches a known modus operandi.	– Relies on modus operandi analysis response control; – Strength of relationship between modus operandi pattern and insider risk	– Cost of matching capability	– Performance testing; – Impact testing; – Control vulnerability assessment; – Threshold pressure testing
			Tip-Off/Disclosures	A channel for providing tip-off disclosures of suspected or actual insider risk behaviour.	– Quality, accessibility and availability of reporting channels; – Anonymity of reporting channel	– Cost of reporting channel	– Performance testing; – Impact testing
			Asset Stocktake	Stocktake of assets to detect missing, moved, or modified assets.	– Inventory of assets; – Asset access records	– Cost of stocktake activity	– Performance testing; – Impact testing; – Control vulnerability assessment
			Chain of Custody Acquittal	Acquittal of chain of custody to identify where the chain of custody has been broken.	– Chain of custody processes; – Chain of custody data	– Cost of acquittal process	– Performance testing; – Impact testing; – Control vulnerability assessment
			Financial Reconciliation	Financial reconciliation to identify financial losses within electronic and physical transactions.	– Accounting records and processes	– Cost of accounting and acquittal process	– Performance testing; – Impact testing; – Control vulnerability assessment
			X-ray Screening	X-ray screening of staff and assets to identify attempted theft or entry of prohibited or dangerous items.	– Accuracy of X-ray infrastructure and operators	– Cost of X-ray equipment and operators	– Performance testing; – Impact testing; – Control vulnerability assessment; – Threshold pressure testing
Response	Response	Resolution	Investigation	Capability to investigate perceived and actual insider incidents, either insourced or outsourced.	– Quality of investigative methodologies	– Cost of investigative capability or outsourced investigations	– Performance testing; – Impact testing
		Response	Prosecution	Capability to prosecute insider incidents.	– Quality of prosecutorial processes and practice	– Cost of prosecutorial capability and activities	– Performance testing; – Impact testing
			Law Enforcement Referral	Capability to refer insider risk matters to law enforcement organisations.	– Quality of referral processes and practice	– Cost of referral capability and activities	– Performance testing; – Impact testing

(Continued)

Control Group	Control Type	Control Mechanism	Control	Control Description	Control Effectiveness Factors	Control Impact	Control Testing Methodologies
		Harm Aversion	Penalty Application	Capability to apply penalties in the event of a substantiated insider incident, such as termination of employment, demotion, or jail.	– Robustness of penalty application if appealed – Specific and general deterrent impact of penalty	– Cost of application and defence of penalties	– Performance testing – Impact testing
			Information Recovery	Recovery of information which was lost or destroyed because of insider incident.	– Extent of recovery	– Cost of recovery capability and activities	– Performance testing – Impact testing
			Decision Reversal	Capability to reverse decisions made because of insider activity.	– Legal power to reverse decision – Quality of process of reversal	– Cost of reversal capability – Regulatory impact of reversal – Market impact of reversal	– Performance testing – Impact testing
			Asset Recovery	Recovery of tangible/intangible assets lost or destroyed because of insider incident.	– Extent of recovery	– Cost of recovery capability and activities	– Performance testing – Impact testing
			Cancel Decision	Capability to cancel a decision made because of insider activity before it takes effect.	– Legal power to cancel decision – Quality of process of cancellation	– Cost of cancellation capability – Regulatory impact of cancellation – Market impact of cancellation	– Performance testing – Impact testing
			Cancel Asset Transfer	Capability to cancel the transfer of a tangible/intangible asset made because of insider activity before it takes effect.	– Legal power to cancel transfer – Quality of process of cancellation	– Cost of cancellation capability – Regulatory impact of cancellation – Market impact of cancellation	– Performance testing – Impact testing
			Recover Information	Recovery of information before it is lost or destroyed because of insider incident.	– Extent of recovery	– Cost of recovery capability and activities	– Performance testing – Impact testing

(Continued)

(Continued)

Control Group	Control Type	Control Mechanism	Control	Control Description	Control Effectiveness Factors	Control Impact	Control Testing Methodologies
	Mitigation		Modus Operandi Analysis	Comprehensive analysis of insider activity modus operandi to understand and record it.	– Detail of analysis – Quality of investigation to identify modus operandi	– Cost of review activities	– Performance testing – Impact testing
			Control Effectiveness Assessment	Comprehensive analysis of control failures or gaps in the event of successful or unsuccessful insider activity to identify potential enhancements.	– Detail of analysis – Quality of investigation to identify control effectiveness or gaps	– Cost of review activities	– Performance testing – Impact testing
			Vulnerability Assessment	Comprehensive analysis of vulnerabilities/ opportunities to undertake insider activity to identify new or changed controls.	– Detail of analysis – Quality of investigation to identify vulnerabilities	– Cost of review activities	– Performance testing – Impact testing
			Control Strengthening	Systematic actions to strengthen controls in response to insider incidents, control effectiveness assessments and vulnerability assessments.	– Quality of implementation processes and practices	– Cost of implementation and change	– Performance testing – Impact testing

INDEX

Note: Page numbers in *italics* indicate a figure and page numbers in **bold** indicate a table on the corresponding page.